THE ECONOMIC LIFE OF NORTHERN INDIA

THE ECONOMIC LIFE OF NORTHERN INDIA

c. A.D. 700-1200

LALLANJI GOPAL

MOTILAL BANARSIDASS PUBLISHERS
PRIVATE LIMITED
DELHI

First Edition: 1965
Second Revised Edition: Delhi, 1989, 2013

ISBN: 81-208-0302-7

Also available at:
MOTILAL BANARSIDASS
Bungalow Road, Jawahar Nagar, Delhi 110 007
Chowk, Varanasi 221 001
Ashok Rajpath, Patna 800 004
24 Race Course Road, Bangalore 560 001
120 Royapettah High Road, Mylapore, Madras 600 004

PRINTED IN INDIA
BY JAINENDRA PRAKASH JAIN AT SHRI JAINENDRA PRESS, A-45 NARAINA INDUSTRIAL AREA, PHASE I, NEW DELHI 110028 AND PUBLISHED BY NARENDRA PRAKASH JAIN FOR MOTILAL BANARSIDASS PUBLISHERS PVT. LTD., BUNGALOW ROAD, JAWAHAR NAGAR, DELHI 110007.

to

Professor A. L. Basham

CONTENTS

ABBREVIATIONS

A.I.N.	*Ancient Indian Numismatics.* By D. R. Bhandarkar.
A.I.O.C.	*Proceedings and Transactions of All-India Oriental Conference.*
A.S.R.	*Archaeological Survey of India, Reports* by Sir A. Cunningham.
A.S.S.	Ānandāśrama Sanskrit Series.
B.E.F.E.O.	*Bulletin de l' École Francaise d' Extreme Orient*, Hanoi.
B.G.	*Bombay Gazetteer.*
B.I.	Bibliotheca Indica.
B.K.I.	*Bijdragen tot de taal—, land— en Volkenkunde van Nederlandsch-Indië, uitgegeven door het Koninklijk Instituut voor de Taal-, land en Volkenkunde van Nederlandsch Indië.*
B.S.	*Bṛhatsaṃhitā.*
C.C.I.M.	*Catalogue of the Coins in the Indian Museum, Calcutta.*
C.I.I.	*Corpus Inscriptionum Indicarum.*
C.M.I.	*Coins of Mediaeval India.* By A. Cunningham.
D.H.N.I.	*Dynastic History of Northern India.* By H. C. Ray.
E.I.	*Epigraphia Indica.*
H.R.S.	*Contributions to the History of Hindu Revenue System.* By U. N. Ghoshal.
I.A.	*Indian Antiquary.*
I.B.	*Inscriptions of Bengal.*
I.C.	*Indian Culture.*
I.H.Q.	*Indian Historical Quarterly.*
J.A.	*Journal Asiatique.*
J.A.H.R.S.	*Journal of the Andhra Historical Research Society.*
J.A.O.S.	*Journal of the American Oriental Society.*
J.A.S.B.	*Journal of the Asiatic Society of Bengal.*
J.B.B.R.A.S.	*Journal of the Bombay Branch of the Royal Asiatic Society.*
J.B.O.R.S.	*Journal of the Bihar and Orissa Research Society.*

J.D.L.	*Journal of the Department of Letters.*
J.E.S.H.O.	*Journal of Economic and Social History of the Orient.*
J.I.H.	*Journal of Indian History.*
J.M.B.R.A.S.	*Journal of the Malaya Branch of the Royal Asiatic Society.*
J.N.S.I.	*Journal of the Numismatic Society of India.*
J.O.I.	*Journal of the Oriental Institute.*
J.R.A.S.	*Journal of the Royal Asiatic Society of Great Britain and Ireland.*
J.R.G.S.	*Journal of the Royal Geographical Society of London.*
J.U.P.H.S.	*Journal of the U.P. Historical Society.*
K.S.S.	*Kathāsaritsāgara.*
M.A.S.B.	*Memoirs of the Asiatic Society of Bengal.*
Mbh.	*Mahābhārata.*
N.S.P.	Nirṇaya Sāgara Press
Num. Chron.	*Numismatic Chronicle.*
P.I.H.C.	*Proceedings of the Indian History Congress.*
Proc.Beng.A.S.	*Proceedings of the Asiatic Society of Bengal.*
Rāj.	*Rājataranginī.*
S.I.I.	*South Indian Inscriptions.*
S.I.S.	*Sino-Indian Studies.*
Yāj.	*Yājñavalkyasmṛti.*

FOREWORD

Socio-economic history represents a relatively recent development especially in the world of Indian historiography. It is noticeable, however, that in the post-Independence era increasing attention has been devoted in this direction. It would not be too much to connect this tendency with the current emphasis and preoccupation with the problems of socio-economic planning and growth. A study of the past inevitably sheds light on the present.

It was with this view of investigating the past to illumine the present and the future that a scheme of research on the social and economic history of ancient India was planned at the University of Allahabad many years ago and I had the privilege of helping several brilliant young scholars in producing a series of dissertations which also included Dr. Gopal's effort on the earlier economic development of ancient India. Seeking to continue his research, he later proceeded to England and the present work is the outcome of that effort. I welcome the present publication with particular happiness as it represents for me the beginning of a fulfilment of hope entertained for some time from one of my most brilliant pupils and colleagues at Allahabad.

Despite its increasing vogue significant socio-economic history is exceedingly difficult to write and remains a tricky business. Conceptual and methodological problems abound and are hardly susceptible of general and standardized answers. The researcher either tends to produce an inventory of well-known or little-known facts from documents or, if ambitious, tends to use a conceptual and interpretational framework derived from some standard work on western social history. It has, however, to be remembered that social being and consciousness, external relations and values, are inextricably mixed up and the genuine economic historian must be able to penetrate the hardened film of a long process of 'reification'—ancient and modern—to be able to communicate a socio-economic awareness without disturbing its inbuilt articulations so that it should scintillate with vital significance. This requires that serious attention be paid to the whole complex of terms and concepts embodied in the different *Śāstras* especially *Arthaśāstra* and *Dharmaśāstra*. It is only in the light of such a study of ideas that an adequate perspective can be provided for socio-economic history. I am glad that by his careful and patient analysis of terms and the immediately relevant ideas, Dr. Gopal has commendably helped the development of this kind of study.

Dr. Gopal's work is a mine of interesting and significant information covering a large range of literary and archaeological sources. At the same time it is neatly ordered and lucidly and concisely presented. Dr. Gopal has been able to illumine a comparatively little known period authoritatively and has sought to forge a link between the ancient and the mediaeval phases of India's history. His work throws particular light on the emergence of 'Feudalism' in Indian society. Any one going through it would feel that he has been a gainer.

Jaipur
The 11*th Feb.*, 1965.

G. C. Pande
Professor and Head of the Department of History & Indian Culture
&
Director,
School of Humanities,
University of Rajasthan

PREFACE TO THE SECOND EDITION

The present work, originally published in 1965, was well received and went out of print within a few years. The information collected and the views expressed have been given due consideration by subsequent writers. Though, on certain points, more details and references have been collected and some of the views have been debated and discussed, I find that the reconstruction offered by me requires only marginal adjustment in some cases and not a totally different reformulation. I have the satisfaction of provoking further researches on the early medieval economic life.

All these years I have been approached to bring out a new edition of the monograph. On account of my involvement with other problems I have been hesitant. Finally Shri N.P. Jain of Motilal Banarsidass has succeeded in circumventing my reservations. For historical reasons I have refrained from attempting a revision of the monograph; I have retained my original account. However, I have chosen to add two Appendices.

I take this opportunity to thank my friends who have advised me to reprint the work. I would gratefully welcome comments and suggestions for improvement which may help me bring out a revised account in due course of time.

May 13, 1989 LALLANJI GOPAL

PREFACE

The unique importance of the period under study consists in the fact that it links ancient to medieval India and sheds light on both by a sort of *dehalī-dīpaka-nyāya*[1]. It represents the culmination and degeneration of the classical traditions of ancient Indian culture and thus its study is important for determining the causes which sapped the vitality of Indians and rendered their resistance to the Muslim invaders surprisingly weak. On the other side, in order to have a proper understanding of the origins and true nature of the polity under the Turko-Afghan Sultāns one cannot ignore the institutions of the early medieval period. The Turko-Afghan rulers had as a matter of necessity to use much of the machinery of administration already in existence.

But the attention which this period has received from scholars of Indian history has not been proportionate to its importance. Like a man with two wives it has to face the scornful neglect of the historians alike of ancient and medieval periods of Indian history. Many historians of ancient India have not bothered to follow the course of events after the decline of the Guptas or in any case after the reign of Harṣa. On the other hand historians of medieval India have often concentrated on the period beginning with the establishment of the power of the Mamlūk Sultāns and have paid little attention to Sanskrit sources, which most of them were not competent to handle.

Ignorance as to the true historical details of the period explains the misconceptions which can be seen in earlier works on the period. Thus V. A. Smith described Harṣa as the last emperor in the history of ancient India, after whom it is only a confused story of "a medley of petty states, with ever-varying boundaries and engaged in unceasing internecine war"[2]. Such a view implies

1. The maxim that a lamp placed on the threshold illumines both the interior and the exterior of a house.
2. *Early History of India*, p. 370. See also ibid., pp. 371, 372.

an utter misunderstanding of the history of the early medieval period, the imperial ambitions of the important dynasties and, above all, the extent of the Pratihāra kingdom, which at its height covered a larger area than could possibly be claimed by an eulogist of Harṣa[1].

With a view to appraise correctly any aspect of social life we have to keep in mind the frame-work of the political history of the period. We can easily trace two dominant threads in the fabric of the political history. The period can be studied from the view-point either of the attempt of the native powers to achieve imperial glory, or of the gradual establishment of the political power of Islam. The death of Harṣa created a temporary vacuum on the political stage and there followed several attempts on the part of different kings and dynasties to establish their political supremacy. In the earlier part of the period Kanauj had come to acquire an imperial halo and was the most coveted prize for those participating in the contest for imperial supremacy. At the beginning of our period we find Yaśovarman ruling over Kanauj. With Lalitāditya Kashmir also entered into the arena of the politics of north India. Tibet also seems to have attempted to gain hegemony over some parts of north India. It is not unlikely that the activities of Kashmir and Tibet reflect the greater struggle for the control of the trade between the East and West fought on a larger scale in Central Asia[2].

But soon north Indian politics came to be dominated by the tripartite struggle for supremacy among the Rāṣṭrakūṭas, the Pālas and the Pratihāras. Though both the Pālas and the Pratihāras had alternate moments of rejoicing, the Pālas established their dominance over almost the whole of north India only under Dharmapāla and Devapāla. The Pratihāras no doubt achieved the zenith of their power during the reigns of Bhoja and Mahendrapāla, but they long enjoyed the position of the chief imperial power in north India. The struggle between the Pratihāras and the

1. R. C. Majumdar, "The Gurjara-Pratihāras" in *J. D. L.*, X, pp. 1-76 *The Age of Imperial Kanauj*, p. 39.
2. See infra pp. 106-7.

Pālas was intercepted by the occasional outburst of the military might of the Rāṣṭrakūṭas, whose armies at least on three occasions, under Dhruva, Govinda III and Indra III, overran northern India. But they do not seem to have attempted a serious and lasting occupation of the conquered areas, and were satisfied merely to force the defeated kings to accept their temporary subjugation. The attempted thrust of the Arabs of Sind towards Gujarat, the victories over the Arabs claimed for some of the Pratihāra kings, the feeling of animosity towards Islam which the Arab geographers ascribe to the Pratihāra kings and the sympathetic and patronising attitude of the Rāṣṭrakūṭa kings towards the Arabs make a good case for the view that the struggle in northern India may well be described as a quadrangular one. Obviously the desire for martial glory and imperial supremacy was the dominant motive force behind this struggle. But the participation of the Arabs would suggest that the concern for economic gains was also to some extent an important reason.

About the middle of the tenth century the Pratihāra empire disintegrated and gradually came to be confined to Kanauj and its neighbourhood. The history of the eleventh century is dominated by a number of states which had started their careers as the feudatories of the Pratihāras. These include the Cāhamānas in Rajasthan, the Caulukyas in Gujarat and the Paramāras in Malwa. Other important dynasties which participated in the imperial game were the Gāhaḍavālas, the Candellas and the Kalacuris. The history of the period is a record of continuous rivalry among these kingdoms, without any lasting success for any one of them. Besides these there were other smaller states. This political fragmentation sapped the vitality of the country and rendered it incapable of putting up an effective and combined resistance to the Muslim invaders.

The period under study can be described as forming the necessary background for the establishment of Muslim power in India. Here also we can point out several stages in this process. The Arabs conquered Sind in 712 A.D. but their attempts to occupy other interior areas were utterly unsuccessful. The Muslim state in Sind had a precarious existence, often threatened by the might of the Pratihāras. The Arab occupation was only an episode, of no importance to other parts of the country; for the narrative of the establishment of Muslim authority it is equally without much real value. The final conquest of northern India was effected by Muslim armies that came through the north-western frontiers. The period roughly before 1000 A.D. was one of successful resistance to Muslim invaders. The Muslims, however, never gave up the idea of extending their victorious arms to India. For over two hundred years they had continuously to hammer against the petty states of Kabul and Zabul, which offered stubborn and heroic resistance before they went down to the greatest military power of their times. The slow progress of the arms of Islam, which had brought under its mantle a considerable part of three continents, redounds to the credit of these two states. The next stage in this connection is marked by the date 997, when Mahmūd, son of Sabuktigīn, captured Ghazni and turned his attention to India. His conquests established Muslim power over Punjab, which thus served as the spring-board for the complete success of the Muslims. Even then the Muslims had to wait for some two hundred years until in 1193 A.D. Mu'izz-ud-dīn Ghūrī defeated Pṛthvīrāja Cāhamāna in the battle of Tarain. Now there was nothing to stop the onrush of the Muslims and the year 1206 witnessed the establishment of the Mamlūk dynasty.

× × × ×

There has been no serious attempt to delineate the economic life of northern India in the early medieval period. The over-emphasis by earlier Indologists on political and religious history had led to the neglect of social history in general and economic life in particular. Two early works on economic life in ancient India[1] do not pay much attention to the medieval period as they concentrate on the period upto the Guptas or Harṣa. In his work *A Study in the Economic Condition of Ancient India* Pran Nath lumps

1. N. S. Subba Rao, *Economic and Political Conditions in Ancient India*; S. K. Das, *Economic History of Ancient India.*

together evidence pertaining to different periods of Indian history. In continuation of his *Dynastic History of Northern India* H. C. Ray had proposed in 1931 to present an account of the economic life of northern India in the early medieval period. With his profound knowledge of the vast source material for the period he was eminently fitted to undertake such a study. It is regrettable that he was not able to do so after even more than thirty years. Some of the books on the early medieval period also discuss the economic life. By way of illustration we may mention the *History of Mediaeval Hindu India* by C. V. Vaidya. *The Age of Imperial Kanauj* and *The Struggle for Empire*, two volumes in the series *The History and Culture of the Indian People*, which cover the period we are investigating, have each a section on economic life. But as of necessity these accounts are brief and preclude a detailed and thorough analysis.

Of late there have been many good books on the history of individual dynasties and regions of northern India in our period. Some of these like the *History of Bengal* edited by R. C. Majumdar, the *Chaulukyas of Gujarat* by A. K. Majumdar and the *Early Chauhān Dynasties* by D. Sharma have attempted a detailed analysis of the economic conditions from their respective source material.

Recently B. P. Mazumdar has brought out his work on the *Socio-Economic History of Northern India* from 1030 to 1194 A.D. We could get Puspa Niyogi's *Contributions to the Economic History of Northern India from the tenth to the twelfth century A.D.* (Calcutta, 1962) only after a major part of our own work had been printed.

We may take a note of some monographs on specific topics connected with economic life. *Contributions to the History of the Hindu Revenue System* by U. N. Ghoshal is a good survey of the epigraphic evidence. *Sārthavāha* by Moti Chandra, which deals with trade activity in general in ancient times, surveys literary evidence, including foreign accounts, bearing on our period.

I take this opportunity to clarify a few points about this work. I have not discussed all the diverse aspects of economic life of the period, but have confined myself to those which have been neglected or not adequately dealt with in existing works. In the chapter on sea-trade, of necessity, I have had to discuss some points which do not appear to be directly concerned with northern India. There is no account of the sea-trade of the period emphasising Indian evidence and so I have attempted it, because the role of coastal regions of northern India cannot be appreciated unless one keeps in mind the overall picture.

As compared with the earlier periods of Indian history, our period is very rich in source material, both literary and epigraphic. We find valuable incidental references even in works which apparently have no connection with economic life.

It is not only in respect of volume but also of precision that the works of our period excel those of the earlier periods. No doubt we do not have a work of the nature and importance of the *Arthaśāstra* of Kauṭilya, but specialised works on several aspects of economic life are not wanting. On agricultural science we have valuable evidence in the *Kṛṣiparāśara* and the sayings circulating in the name of Khanā. There are several works dealing with elephants and horses[1] and many Tantric texts of the period deal with mineralogy and alchemy[2]. Likewise there are a few texts on jewels[3], and certain medical works[4] reveal considerable advance in the preparation of metallic compounds and the knowledge of vegetable and mineral substances. Certain works which are still to be published give interesting information on some of the crafts and industries of the period. Among these are the *Gandhasāra* of Gaṅgadhara and the *Gandhavāda*, two treatises on cosmetics and perfumery[5].

1. E. g., the *Mātaṅgalīlā* of Nārāyaṇa, the *Hastyāyurveda*, the *Aśvāyurveda* of Gaṇa, the *Aśvaśāstra* of Śālihotra, the *Aśvavaidyake* of Jayadatta and Dīpaṅkara, and the *Aśvacikitsā* of Nakula.
2. E. g., the *Rasaratnākara* of Nāgārjuna, the *Rasārṇava* and the *Rasaratnasamuccaya*. See P. C. Ray, *History of Chemistry*, pp. 128ff; B. K. Sarkar, *Positive Background*, pp. 70ff, 87-90.
3. E. g., the *Agastimata*, the *Ratnaparīkṣā* of Buddha Bhaṭṭa and the *Navaratnaparīkṣā* of Nārāyaṇa Paṇḍita.
4. E. g., the *Cikitsāsārasaṅgraha*, *Śabdacandrikā* and *Dravyaguṇasaṃgraha* of Cakrapāṇidatta and the *Śabdapradīpa*, *Vṛkṣāyurveda* and *Lohapaddhati* of Sureśvara.
5. P. K. Gode, *Studies in Indian Literary History*, Vol. III, pp. 1ff.

Sections on agriculture, botany, cattle-rearing and the making of various articles are to be found in the *Śārṅgadharapaddhati*, an anthology compiled by Śārṅgadhara in about 1363 A.D. The *Yuktikalpataru* ascribed to Bhoja and the *Mānasollāsa* by the Western Cālukya king Someśvara are in the nature of compendia of topics which are supposed to be of interest and advantage to a prince. These contain interesting and informative sections on jewels, furniture, cattle-rearing and horticulture. Similar sections were incorporated into the *Agni Purāṇa* and the *Garuḍa Purāṇa*.

For lack of space however we have not discussed in our present work the technological aspects of the economic life of the period under study[1].

For our purposes we have thoroughly analysed the epigraphic records of the period. Without entering into a discussion of the merits of the inscriptions as a source for the ancient history of India, we may say that the absence of any serious doubt about the reading, their contemporaneity and the certainty about their date make them the most reliable source of historical information for our period. Besides incidental references on many subjects, we find the inscriptions especially valuable for the agrarian system, the revenue system, the use of coins, guilds and economic occupations, and the movement of population.

The over-emphasis on the coins of the earlier periods has resulted in a sad neglect of those of early medieval times. These are yet to be properly catalogued, analysed and studied. It was in 1894 that Cunningham's *Coins of Mediaeval India* was published. Since then, except for a few short articles, there has been no systematic study of the coins of the period. The *Dravyaparīkṣā* of Ṭhakkura Pheru can serve as a valuable clue in analysing and identifying the coins of the period but a printed text is not available as yet and we had to depend on stray references to some of its contents made by the few scholars who have had an access to its single available manuscript.

---

1. See "Technique of agriculture in early medieval India" in the *University of Allahabad Studies*, Ancient History section, 1963-64, pp. 1-37.

Excavations at some of the sites in northern India provide significant material. But unfortunately the archaeologist does not pay much attention to the strata of this period, busy as he is in fixing the chronology for earlier levels. Excavations may yield valuable evidence for city economy in general, for those crafts and industries the products of which do not perish with time, and for the effects of wars and foreign invasions. It is hoped that in future the excavations at sites such as Kanauj and Banaras will take due notice of the remains belonging to the early medieval strata.

Our period is equally rich in foreign accounts. Among the Chinese sources the best known is the work of Chau Ju-kua, which preserves valuable information about the sea-trade in the period and the articles involved in this trade. The very nature of his work, however, rules out detailed references to different parts of northern India.

The Arab accounts are valuable for their evidence on the condition of trade, both overland and by sea, and give details about the economic life of different cities, ports and kingdoms. They help us in determining the important land-routes inside the country. The greatest of the Arab travellers, Al-Bīrūnī does not interest himself much in the economic life of the times. Much of his information on this subject is based on traditional accounts. He was too engrossed in the literature and culture of India to record the details of contemporary life from personal observation. But he describes the existing trade-routes in northern India. The Persian work *Ḥudūd al-'Ālam* is often neglected in a study of the early medieval period. For an economic study it is especially important. It refers to the products of the different cities, their importance as centres of trade and commerce, and also to the overland trade of India across the north-western frontiers. Some incidental information is also to be gathered from the Muslim accounts of the early Muslim conquests in northern India.

Among indigenous literary texts we would like to mention in the first instance the *Śukranīti* because it contains much refreshingly singular information on labour laws, revenue system, comparative value of metals and several economic occupations. Most scholars use this text for the early medieval period. We have definite indications to show that it is a nineteenth century composition and hence have not used it for our period[1].

The commentary by Medhātithi on the *Manusmṛti* is an important source for our period. By way of illustration, and sometimes in opposition to the laws of Manu, Medhātithi refers to the practices of his times. At places his commentary liberalises the injunctions in the original text. We have thoroughly studied the commentary and found much new and interesting information in it.

The *Kṛtyakalpataru* of Lakṣmīdhara, the minister for peace and war of king Govindacandra of the Gāhaḍavāla dynasty, is in the form of a digest. But we can easily deduce the views held by the author from the particular passages which he selects for emphasis from the earlier works and also from the short commentary which he adds at places.

Among other legal texts used by us we may mention the *Nītivākyāmṛta* of Somadeva and the *Rājanītiratnākara* of Caṇḍeśvara. We have also referred, for the sake of comparison, to some legal texts which are outside the chronological and geographical limits of our present study. By way of illustration we may mention the commentaries of Aparārka, Vijñāneśvara, Devaṇṇabhaṭa and Mādhavācārya (known as the *Parāśaramādhavīya*).

In recent decades Purāṇic studies have advanced considerably through the researches of Prof. R. C. Hazra. But still much remains to be done before we can safely use the material in the *Purāṇas*. There have been several accretions to the original *Purāṇas* with the result that the stratification of the Purāṇic texts is very difficult to determine. We have, therefore, chiefly used only two *Purāṇas*, the *Agni Purāṇa*, which is generally accepted as a text of the early medieval period, and the *Bṛhannāradīya Purāṇa*, which seems to refer to the Muslims.

1. *The Śukranīti—a nineteenth century text*" published in the *Bulletin of the School of Oriental and African Studies*, XXV, part 3.

The literary texts used by us are too many even to be enumerated. Interesting incidental references are to be found even in the least expected ones, e.g., the *Sāṅkhyatattvakaumudī* which is a philosophical text of the Sāṅkhya school of thought. We can, therefore, mention only a few of the most important works.

The *Rājataraṅgiṇī* of Kalhaṇa is a veritable mine of information not only for political history but also for social and cultural history in general. We have many valuable references to the economic life of Kashmir, to the crops, the irrigational devices, the life of villagers, the political and natural calamities affecting the fortunes of cultivators, the revenue system, the use of coins, the activities of merchants and bankers and the rise of a landed aristocracy. Other historical works of the period do not possess such a wide canvas for pictures from different fields of life and have not therefore proved so useful. More important among these are the *Dvyāśrayakāvya* of Hemacandra, the *Rāmacarita* of Sandhyākaranandin, the *Pṛthvīrājavijaya* of Jayānaka and the *Vikramāṅkadevacarita* of Bilhaṇa. The *Moharājaparājaya* of Yaśaḥpāla, though connected with a historical king, in the person of king Kumārapāla of the Caulukya dynasty, and with some of his administrative reforms, is an allegorical play. This text speaks of the opulence of the big merchants of Gujarat.

Two important prose romances of the period are the *Tilakamañjarī* of the Śvetāmbara Jain Dhanapāla, who wrote under the Paramāra king Muñja Vākpatirāja, and the *Udayasundarīkathā* (c. A.D. 1026-1059) of Soḍḍhala. Fashioned after the works of Bāṇa, these texts contain graphic descriptions, some of which are important for the study of the economic life. Of the two the *Tilakamañjarī* is more useful for our purposes. It has vivid descriptions of a habitation of cowherds and the stir caused in a village by an army on march. It graphically describes a naval expedition to Dvīpāntara and gives interesting information about Indian shipping and trade with south-east Asia.

Some of the stories in the narrative texts of our period give us some insight into the life of a cultivator, cowherd or a merchant.

Of these we have used the anonymous *Kathākoṣa* and the *Bṛhatkathākośa* of Hariṣeṇa. In using the *Kathāsaritsāgara* of Somadeva and the *Bṛhatkathāmañjarī* of Kṣemendra one can utilise only the incidental details and references. As these works are based on the *Bṛhatkathā* of Guṇāḍhya, any inference from material forming part of the original subject matter of the story will be applicable rather to earlier times than to ours.

The *Triṣaṣṭiśalākāpuruṣacarita* is a Jain text in the form of stories of 63 eminent persons in Jain history and tradition. Besides interesting incidental references on different aspects of economic life, it has a graphic account of a trade journey of a caravan. Jain works contain important references to economic life, especially those aspects which concern a merchant or trader. The Apabhraṃśa romance *Bhavisayattakahā* by the Digambara Jain Dhanapāla is the story of a merchant who rises to become the ruler of a kingdom. Here we find references not only to caravan journeys to other regions, but also to voyages to south-east Asian islands. The *Samarāiccakahā* of Haribhadra is an Apabhraṃśa text which describes the cycle of nine lives through which the hero Samarāditya passes, but also contains other stories to illustrate or corroborate certain points. Most of these stories, including the central tale, concern merchants, and hence contain interesting references to trade and commerce. The *Upamitibhavaprapañcākathā* of Siddharṣi is a Jain text in Sanskrit presented in the form of allegories. It is a very valuable text on a number of economic activities. We have made a thorough study of it and used its evidence suitably.

Many authentic historical details are preserved as traditions in Jain works such as the *Purātana-prabandha-saṅgraha* and Merutuṅga's *Prabandhacintāmaṇi.* Some of these traditional stories in the *Prabandhacintāmaṇi* concern merchants, villagers and craftsmen, and have interesting details about economic life. The Jain text *Kharataragacchabṛhadgurvāvali* is equally important for such a study and has greater historical authenticity, as it is in the nature of a record of contemporary events and was added to from time to time.

Among the literary compositions of our period in northern India we may refer to the works of Śrī-Harṣa, Rājaśekhara and Kṣemendra. Many works are ascribed to Kṣemendra, but the *Lokaprakāśa* and *Nītikalpataru* can only be used with reservations, because they have been elaborated in subsequent centuries. Kṣemendra specialises in presenting sharply outlined pictures of the important characters of his contemporary society from which we can learn much about merchant-bankers and petty local officers. His *Samayamātṛkā*, *Narmamālā*, *Darpadalana*, *Deśopadeśa* and *Kalāvilāsa* present such satirical cross-sections of society. In his *Sevyasevakopadeśa* he speaks of the relations between a master and his servant. The *Kuṭṭanīmata* of Dāmodara concerns courtesans but has interesting references to the life of a typical petty officer and the benefits of and difficulties involved in travelling.

The anthology, first published as the *Kavīndravacanasamuccaya* by F. W. Thomas but later shown by D. D. Kosambi to have really been the *Subhāṣitaratnakoṣa* of Vidyākara, has many characteristic descriptions of rural life. The *Dohākośa* of the Siddhas of later Buddhism is in Apabhraṃśa in Dohā verses. In it we find interesting casual references to the profession of a boatman, to cultivators, to poverty and to the use of cowries.

We have also analysed the lexica of the period for the terms connected with economic life. Of these the *Vaijayantī* of Yādava Prakāśa mentions the names of those foreign countries and islands which were known to its author. The names of certain commodities indicate the country from where India received them. The *Deśīnāmamālā* of Hemacandra gives *deśī* terms for several important things connected with economic life and thus clearly indicates that these really existed in the period and were in frequent use by the common man. Other lexica used by us are the *Abhidhānaratnamālā* of Halāyudha, the *Abhidhānacintāmaṇi* of Hemacandra and the *Nāmamālā*. The *Uktivyaktiprakaraṇa* of Dāmodara Paṇḍita illustrates its grammatical rules with sentences about things which were supposed to be well known to a young student. It has very interesting references about several aspects of economic life and we have for the first time used the text for a study such as this.

Likewise the *Prākṛta Vyākaraṇa* of Hemacandra has some useful casual references in its illustrations.

Among technical texts we may refer to the *Aparājitapṛcchā* of Bhuvanadeva and the *Samarāṅgaṇasūtradhāra* of Bhoja. In the latter text however the author seems to have given a free rein to his imagination, as would appear from the accounts for aeroplanes and machines guarding the gates of a fort. A mythical element is also found in the *Yuktikalpataru* of Bhoja, which otherwise has interesting details on polity, on making of furniture and other articles, and on industrial geography. The *Mānasollāsa* of the Western Cālukya king Someśvara is more balanced and authentic in its details. We have used this text even though it is not within the strict geographical limits of our study, because we do not envisage much radical difference in the basic facts of the economic life of the Cālukya kingdom and northern India.

We have for the first time emphasised the importance of mathematical texts for an economic study. These contain valuable material about the use of coins, prices, wages and other such aspects of economic life for which we do not find much help from other sources. No doubt such texts use figures to suit their calculations and sometimes imagine them, but it is obvious that in such cases the mathematician would not create absurd situations for the student. We have, therefore, used the *Gaṇitasārasaṅgraha* of Mahāvīrācārya and the *Līlāvatī* and *Bījagaṇita* of Bhāskarācārya.

The present work is my thesis which was approved for the degree of the Doctor of Philosophy of the University of London in 1962. Parts of Chapter I and IX have already appeared as articles in the *Journal of Economic and Social History of the Orient*, Vol. VI, part 3 and the *Journal of the Numismatic Society of India*, Vol. XXX.

I have great pleasure in acknowledging the help I have received in the preparation of the present work. I am indebted to the scholars whose works I have used and have acknowledged in suitable foot notes. I have received valuable guidance on a few chapters of my work from Dr. J. G. de Casparis who along with Prof. T. Burrow and Prof. E. H. Warmington formed the Board of Examiners at the University of London. Above all I record my deep gratitude to my revered teacher Prof. A. L. Basham, but for whose personal interest this work would never have been completed during my limited and busy stay in London. I do not have adequate words to express what I owe to my father Babu Hanuman Prasad and to my *sahadharmiṇī* Dr. Śrīmatī Krishna Kanti Gopal. I am grateful to Prof. A. K. Narain, Prof. G. R. Sharma, Prof. R. S. Sharma, Prof. H. L. Singh and Dr. J. W. Spellman for their kind interest in the publication of the present work. I offer my thanks to Prof. G. C. Pande for kindly wri ting a foreword to this book. I shall be failing in my duty if do not acknowledge my indebtedness to the British Council whose scholarship I enjoyed in 1960-61. The staff of the libraries of the School of Oriental and African Studies, Royal Asiatic Society, British Museum and India Office also extended me valuable help. Thanks are also due to my publishers, Motilal Banarsidass, and to Śrī Lakshmi Das, Manager, B.H.U. Press.

Varanasi
1-3-1965.

Lallanji Gopal

CHAPTER 1

OWNERSHIP OF LAND

On the vexed question of the ownership of land in ancient India there is a sharp division of opinion among scholars.[1] We have shown elsewhere[2] that even in ancient times there was no unanimity of opinion on this point. Those who advocated state ownership of land were in a minority, by no means insignificant, and the view of peasant-proprietorship was more favoured. For all practical purposes the peasant was the owner of the land. The king, as the sovereign lord of everything in his state, had some claim over the land and received from the peasant a revenue as the wages for the protection he afforded to the people; but all this did not amount to a proprietary right over the land.

Concept of ownership—

In the early medieval legal texts we find a definite notion of ownership. There was a discussion about the nature of ownership as to whether it is a separate category (*padārtha*) or a capacity.[3] Likewise there was a sharp difference of opinion about the question whether ownership is to be apprehended from *Śāstra* alone or is a matter of worldly usage. The first view is advocated by the *Smṛtisaṅgraha* and Dhāreśvara while the latter suggestion is supported by the *Mitākṣarā*, the *Vyavahāraprakāśa*, the *Vyavahāramayūkha*, the *Parāśara-mādhavīya* and the *Sarasvatīvilāsa*.[4]

The Mīmāṃsā view—

The treatment of the question in the texts of this period is mostly conditioned by the views of earlier authorities. We do not find any independent thinking on the subject; it is largely in the form of elaboration and interpretation of earlier texts. The

---

1 *J. E. S. H. O.*, IV, p. 240.

2 Ibid., pp. 257ff.

3 Kane, *History of Dharmaśāstra*, III. 547.

4 Ibid., 548—51.

Mīmāmsā view as originally stated by Jaimini[1] is that the earth equally belongs to all. Śabara-svāmin[2] in his commentary emphasises the distinction between the entire territory of the state and the private fields, the former being incapable of individual ownership and adds that by virtue of his protecting the crops that grow on the earth the king is entitled to a share of them as his remuneration but not to the lordship of the soil. These very points, the distinction of private and common property and the functional nature of sovereignty, were emphasised even by Mādhava[3] and Khaṇḍadeva,[4] two Mīmāṃsā commentators belonging respectively to the fourteenth and seventeenth centuries. But all this argumentation by Mīmāṃsā thinkers itself is a silent recognition that the claims of the state over the soil were increasing in actual practice. It is quite likely that the Mīmāṃsā view has to be traced to the protest recorded in the Brāhmaṇa literature[5] on the part of the Earth against its donation.[6] But it cannot be denied that there was a definite opinion among a section of the thinkers who denied the king the claim of ownership of the soil. And then the reputation of the Mīmāṃsā view as authoritative on legal and juristic issues would suggest that this was by no means a feeble opinion. We find that Medhātithi[7] discusses and explains the Mīmāṃsā standpoint on the question and by implication accepts its authoritative character. Even the seventeenth century text *Vyavahāramayūkha*[8] quotes Jaimini with approval and follows the discussion of the proprietary rights of a conqueror as found in Khaṇḍadeva, the Mīmāṃsā commentator. The Mīmāṃsā view has been dismissed in a recent study as only a wishful theory.[9] It is to be noted that in almost

---

1 *Mīmāṃsā-sūtra*, VI. 7.3.

2 *Mīmāṃsā-darśana*, VI. 7.3.

3 *Nyāyamālāvistara* (A.S.S.), p. 358.

4 *Bhaṭṭadīpikā* on *Pūrvamīmāṃsā-darśana* (Mysore), II, p. 317.

5 *Śatapatha Brāhmaṇa*, XIII. 7.1.15 ; *Aitareya Brāhmaṇa*, IV. 8.21.

6 Cf. S. K. Maity, *Economic life in the Gupta period*, p. 22.

7 On Manu, VIII. 99.

8 p. 91.

9 R. C. P. Singh, *Kingship in Northern India*, p. 339. Cf. S. K. Maity, Loc. cit.

all countries and all times we find the queer phenomenon that, whatever the juristic opinion about the ownership of land, the state does with the land what its needs dictate, though at times in order to satisfy the demands of democracy it advances compensation determined by the State itself.

Ownership in legal texts—

The legal texts of the period following earlier Smṛtis discuss legal questions concerning boundary disputes, dispossession and the alienation of land, including its lease, mortgage, sale and gift, thus by implication granting the rights which generally make ownership. The relative importance of possession and legitimate title, the two constituents of ownership, has been discussed at great length in the legal works.[1] Efforts were made by the commentaries and digests of our period[2] to reconcile the conflict in the opinion of the Smṛtis about the minimum period of adverse possession creating ownership. The impression which we gather from relevant references in the *Agni Purāṇa*[3] and the *Kṛtyakalpataru*[4] is that individuals possessed all the rights of granting or otherwise alienating their fields and could seek legal remedy against any encroachment or infringement of their right.

Medhātithi on ownership —

U. N. Ghoshal[5] has observed that Medhātithi makes two inconsistent statements about property, mentioning the king as the lord (*prabhu*) of the soil on one place and elsewhere stating that the field belongs to him who made it fit for cultivation by clearing it. R. C. P. Singh[6] points out that Medhātithi's views on Manu

1 *Mitākṣarā* on Yāj., II. 27; *Smṛticandrikā* (ed. Gharpure), II, pp. 70ff; *Vyavahāranirṇaya*, pp. 132, 73; *Sarasvatīvilāsa*, p. 124.

2 Cf. Kane, *History of Dharmaśāstra*, II, pp. 322ff.

3 LXX. 6; CLXXIII. 44; CCXI. 13—15, 33—37; CCLIII. 23, 52—3; CCLVII. 1ff.

4 *Dāna*, p. 191 for land-grants; *Vyavahāra*, p. 153 for sale deeds etc. of fields. *Gārhastha*, p. 182 explains *bhūmisvāmine* in Baudh., III. 2.1—15 as *bhūmirasyāstīti*.

5 *History of Indian Political Ideas*, p. 426.

6 Op. cit., pp. 338—40.

VIII. 39 and 99 appear to be contradictory; "one refers to the royal ownership while the other seems to maintain the communal ownership of land". He adds that if the communal ownership of land had been in Medhātithi's mind, he would surely have stated the fact more clearly and that we must look on his apparent support of communal ownership as pious theorising. He concludes that in practice Medhātithi admitted the king's ownership of the land.

We, however, feel that Medhātithi ascribed to individual ownership of land. This is clear from numerous passages in which he grants to an individual all the rights of ownership over a field.[1] In some of these he makes a clear reference to *kṣetra* or field being the agricultural land (*dhānyānāṃ bhavana-bhūmiḥ*).[2]

The statement of Medhātithi on Manu VIII. 39 is not his definite opinion on the legal question of the ownership of land. It is essentially of the nature of a general maxim which has been mentioned only as a second line of argument to justify the claims of the king to a share in the treasure-trove which actually the king receives on the grounds of the protection afforded by him. When Medhātithi speaks of the king as the master of the soil (*prabhur-asau bhūmeḥ*) and of the soil as belonging to him (*tadīyāyāśca bhuvaḥ*) he does not mean to lay down the legal status of the king as the owner of all cultivable land in the state but only points out the sovereignty of the king implying a general lordship of the king over all things in his kingdom.

It is in his commentary on Manu VIII. 99 that Medhātithi discusses the question of the ownership of land. Here he establishes individual ownership. R. C. P. Singh[3] interprets the commentary to indicate that Medhātithi refutes the individual ownership of land and establishes that land is common property. Discussing the statement of Manu that he who deposes falsely in regard to land kills all, Medhātithi poses the possible objection, based on the protest in the *Śatapatha Brāhmaṇa*[4] against land-grants, that the

1 On Manu, VIII. 144, 148, 151, 165; IX. 49, 55, 323.

2 Ibid., II. 246; XI. 162.

3 Op. cit., pp. 327—29.

4 XIII. 7.1.15.

earth is the common property of all men and kings are appointed only for taking care of it, and hence there cannot be any giving away or taking away of the whole of this earth or any disputes regarding its possession. Medhātithi replies that just as the entire earth is spoken of as *bhūmi* (land), so also are fields, villages, and platforms and over these latter, ownership is certainly possible; and the making over or taking away also of such ownership is directly perceptible; the taking away of this consists in asserting ownership in an improper manner and the mere dismantling of a house or the cutting of a tree or walking over another man's land or taking clay out of it does not constitute the act of taking away the land. Regarding the possible objection that the Mīmāṃsakas[1] declare land to be common to all, Medhātithi first quotes a verse of Kṛṣṇadvaipāyana (Vyāsa, the author of the *Mahābhārata*), referring to the gift of land, to indicate that the term land is found to be used in the sense also of parts of the earth, and then explains the assertion of land being common to all as referring to the entire globe, to roam about over which all men are equally entitled, and which therefore cannot be owned by anyone. He adds that in accordance with the Mīmāṃsā injunction villages and towns can be given away at the Viśvajit sacrifice. He concludes by quoting the lines "they present as sacrificial fee, the *bhūmi* with the exception of the platform (*sadaḥ*) and the wife's room (*patnīśālam*)" and observing that as this would not be applicable to the entire earth, the giving must refer to fields and such other parts of it only.

Peasant proprietorship in literary works—

Stray references in the literary works of the period also suggest individual ownership. Thus the *Deśopadeśa*[2] mentions the land of a miser along with his cash property, house and wife as objects which he hoards but are enjoyed by others. A verse in the *Subhāṣitaratnakoṣa*[3] which speaks of families (*kulas*) in a village oppressed by the feudal chief (*bhoga-pati*) as not willing to leave out of the consideration for the hereditary land (*nija-vaṃśa-bhūr-iti*) may be

1 Jaimini, VI. 3.3.

2 II. 6.

3 v. 1175.

construed to indicate that agricultural lands were owned by families. The *Mānasollāsa*[1] speaks of the stealing of a field along with that of a house, garments, grain, cash, etc. Elsewhere[2] it mentions gladiators called *bhūmyaṅka* who fought for houses, fields etc. and who acted as champions to decide boundary disputes.

Land-grants by private individuals—

Some inscriptions of our period which record cases of land-grants and land-sales by private individuals corroborate the testimony of the legal works. Thus a Bhubaneswar inscription[3] records that a certain lady named Maḍamadevī purchased in conjunction with a leading merchant (*sādhu-pradhāna*) from the hands of a *śreṣṭhin* a piece of land in Devadhara-grāma and granted it in favour of the god Kīrttivāseśvara or Śiva worshipped in the Liṅgarāja Temple. We have some other inscriptions from the Liṅgarāja Temple which prove the case. In one inscription a certain Bhāvasadāśiva-guru donates a piece of land purchased with the savings from his begging[4]. Another inscription would seem to have recorded the grant of sixty-five units of land in two villages made probably by a certain person belonging to the *kāyastha* community[5]. Another *kāyastha* is found donating five *vāṭikās* and five *mānas* of land.[6] Another private grant is about 2½ *vāṭikās* of land.[7] The *praśasti* of Baijnath from Kangra[8] records three land-grants by private individuals, one a field requiring one *vaha* (=four *droṇas*) of seed corn by an astrologer, another measuring half a plough by a certain brāhmaṇa and the third by a merchant. In an inscription from Sanderav

---

1 I, p. 4, v. 40.

2 II, p. 223, vv. 833—34.

3 *E. I.*, XXX. 160—61.

4 *I. C.*, III. 126.

5 Ibid., 124—25.

6 *I. H. Q.*, XXXI. 82—83.

7 *I. C.*, VI. 76. In another record the gift most probably made by two brāhmaṇas has been described as being of ten *pāṭikas-I. C.*, VI. 73. It is possible that the intended reading was *vāṭikās*.

8 *E. I.*, I. 104—7, vv. 32—34. See also *E. I.*, II. 116; XXIV. 329ff; XXX. 210.

(Jodhpur)[1] many cart-builders (*rathakāras*) residing at Sanderaka are said to have donated a plough (*hāela*) measure of land suitable for the cultivation of *yugaṃdharī* (millet) corn. An inscription from Dabok[2] records the grant of five fields and two shops, the fields being described as having been acquired by the donor himself, a certain physician, and at that time in the share of one of his sons.

Field owned by private individuals—

In some inscriptions lands owned by private individuals are mentioned in connection with the demarcation of the boundaries of the donated land[3]. Fields which were owned by cultivators themselves are generally described as *kauṭumba-kṣetras*.[4] Often the term *satka* is mentioned to convey the idea of ownership.[5] In this connection the testimony of some seventh century inscriptions of the Maitrakas is significant.[6] Besides the *brahmadeya* lands we have two distinct types of fields in these records. Some are described as being owned by a certain individual (*satka*) while others are mentioned as tilled by a certain individual (*prakṛṣṭa* or *kṛṣṭa*). It is clear that the basis of this difference in terminology was the claim to the ownership of land. This difference is to be noticed in the Ashrafpur plate of Devakhaḍga[7] which mentions a *pāṭaka* of land as enjoyed by Sarvāntara but cultivated by Śikhara and others.

Royal grants of villages and fields—

We have elsewhere[8] shown that the grant of a village did not amount to an assignment of the proprietary rights over the arable land in the village. This is supported by inscriptions which mention

---

1 *E. I.*, XI, p. 47.

2 *E. I.*, XX. 123—25.

3 *E. I.*, XX. 123—25; XXI. 172; XXXIII. 236—7.

4 *C. I. I.*, IV, no. 22, ll.20, 24; *E. I.*, XXII. 115—20; XXI. 183f; IV. 76—81.

5 *E. I.*, XXXIII. 236f; XXI. 172, 183f, 210f; IV. 76—81; XXII. 115—20; Gadre, *Inscriptions from Baroda*, I, pp. 16—24.

6 *E. I.*, XXII. 115—20; XXI. 183f; IV. 76—81.

7 *M. A. S. B.*, I. 88, 90.

8 *J. E. S. H. O.*, IV. 251ff.

the grant of a village together with a particular tract in it.[1] It seems that what was granted in the case of the village was the right to revenue, whereas in the case of a particular field it was the proprietary right over it. The king had the proprietary right only over certain fields and he could donate the ownership only of these cultivable lands. In the Dabok inscription[2] we see that in connection with the specification of the boundaries of the donated lands only some of the fields are described as king's fields (*rājakīyakṣetram*). It has to be noted that in the Jesar plates of Śīlāditya III,[3] slightly earlier than the period of our study, the grant consists of a reservoir of water (*vāpī*) extending over 25 *pādāvarttas* of land from the royal domain land (*rājakīya*), two pieces of land which belonged to extinct families of cultivators (*utsanna-kuṭumbika*) and which must have reverted to the king, and three pieces of land said to have been cultivated (*prakṛṣṭa* and not owned, *satka*) by a certain Kikaka. It is clear that the king could donate only those pieces of cultivable land which were in his direct ownership and not all the pieces owned by individuals. The necessity for the king to donate several pieces of land scattered over a large area and situated at a distance from one another[4] arose from this limitation to the proprietary rights of a king in the villages. This explanation has been controverted by R. C. P. Singh[5] on the ground that the donation of consolidated land would have meant dispossessing the earlier recipients of some of the religious grants. We fear the objection is not valid since in some at least of the inscriptions recording the donation of land in fragments the enumeration of boundaries does not mention *brahmadeya* lands but also some fields owned by private individuals and cultivators.[6]

1 *E. I.*, XIV. 184—87 (Part II, ll. 14—27).

2 *E. I.*, XX. 123—25.

3 *E. I.*, XXII. 115—20. In the Urlam (Ganjam) Plates of Hastivarman (*E. I.*, XVII. 332—33) the king is said to have purchased 2½ ploughs of land from the owner of an *agrahāra* land (*agrahārika*) in order to make a donation.

4 *E. I.*, XXIX. 1ff; XXII. 115—20; XXI. 183—4, 210—11; XI. 81—4; IV. 76—81; *I. A.*, XVII. 7ff; *I. B.*, III. 146ff; 165ff.

5 Op. cit., pp. 316—7.

6 *E. I.*, XXII. 115—20; XXI. 183—4; IV. 76—81.

Supporters of state ownership of land—

We get references to some thinkers advocating State ownership of land. Thus Bhaṭṭasvāmin, while commenting on a passage in the *Arthaśāstra*,[1] quotes a verse meaning that those who are well-versed in the sacred books declare the king to be the lord of land as well as water ; the householders have the right of ownership over all other things except these two. The *Mānasollāsa*[2] also appears to hold a similar view. It is to be noted that two verses of Kātyāyana,[3] often quoted to support the king's ownership of land,[4] are also quoted by Lakṣmīdhara, the Gāhaḍavāla minister, in his digest, the *Kṛtyakalpataru*.[5]

We have elsewhere[6] shown that in ancient times the king was said to have a general claim over everything in the state. In our period it appears that sometimes the peasant was viewed as having only a qualified ownership of the soil, the king being endowed with a superior claim to it. Thus the *Rājataraṅgiṇī*[7] speaks of king Śreṣṭhasena as the lord of those kings who are cultivators of the fields, that is the whole earth. Here king Śreṣṭhasena is said to have occupied the same position *vis-a-vis* the lesser kings, as does a king with the cultivators. The implication seems to be that the cultivators are the owners of their fields but the king has a superior title.

Royal claims over village land—

In any case it is clear from the land-grants of the period that the king had many claims over the village land and he transferred

1 II. 24; *J. B. O. R. S.*, XII, p. 138.

2 I, p. 61, v. 361.

3 16—17.

4 U. N. Ghoshal, *Indian Historiography and other essays*, p. 164.

5 *Rājadharma*, p. 90. Mitramiśra of a later date discusses the verses in a way which removes their ambiguity. *Vīramitrodaya*, *Rājanītiprakāśa* (Banaras), p. 271—*Rājā bhuvaḥ svāmī smṛtaḥ. Anyadravyasya bhūsambaṃdhidravyasya na svāmī. Anyathā bhūmisvāmyābhāve. Bhūtānām prāṇinām. Tannivāsitvāt bhūnivāsitvāt. Svāmitvam rājña iti śeṣaḥ. Ityataḥ tatkriyāb—aliṣaḍbhāgam prāpnuyāt.*

6 *J. E. S. H. O.*, IV. 257f.

7 III. 101—*Īśo nṛpāṇāṃ niḥśeṣa-kṣmā-kedāra-kuṭumbinām.*

these to the donees. These privileges would indicate that he claimed a theoretical ownership to the soil. Thus in the Pāla[1] records a village is said to be granted up to its boundaries, grass and pasture land (*sva-sīmā-tṛṇa-yūti-gocaraparyanta*), with its ground (*sa-tala*), with the space above the ground (*soddeśa*), with its mango and *mahuā* trees (*sāmra-madhūka*), with its water and dry land (*sa-jala-sthala*) and with its pits and saline spots (*sa-garttoṣara*). The grants of the Senas and the feudatory families[2] which arose in Bengal add to these the rights to the trees of *panāsa*, *gūvāka* and cocoanut (*nālikera*) and to salt (*sa-lavaṇa*). In a plate from Kelga (Sonepur[3]) the village is said to have been granted along with ivory, tiger's skin and various wild animals (*hastidanta-vyāghracarma-nānāvanacara-sameta*), with its water and dry land, with fish and tortoises (*sa-matsya-kacchapa*), with residences and plants (*sa-kheṭa-viṭapa*), with trenches and mounds (*sa-khallonnata*), with village habitations and forests (*sa-padrāraṇyaka*), with shrubs and creepers (*sa-gulma-latāka*), with mangoes, *mahuā*, tamarind, palmyra and various trees. The Irda grant of the Kamboja king Nayapāladeva[4] records that the village was donated together with homesteads and arable land, water-courses, pits and paths (*vāstu-kṣetra-jalādhāra--gartta-mārgga-samanvita*), with saline soil, land where sweepings are thrown and salt-mines (*soṣarāvaskara-sthāna-nivīta[5]-lavaṇākara*), adorned with groups of trees like mango and *mahuā* and along with the markets, bathing places and ferries (*sa-haṭṭa-ghaṭṭa-sa-tara*). In the records of the Kalacuris[6] the villages are granted together with pasture land for cows (*sa-gopracāra*), with its water and dry land, with mango and *mahuā* trees, with salt mines (*sa-lavaṇākara*), with its pits and saline spots,

1 E. g., *E. I.*, XV. 295—8. Cf. ibid., XXIX, p. 5, f.n. 3.

2 E. g., *E. I.*, XXXIII. 138—40; XXX. 262—3.

3 *E. I.*, XXVIII. 327—8.

4 *E. I.*, XXII. 154—7, vv. 18—21.

5 *Nivīta* in this context is difficult to explain. Derived from *ni* + √*vye* as an adjective it means "hung or adorned with". As a noun it means a veil, mantle or wrapper. See Monier-Williams, *Sanskrit-English Dictionary*, s. v., *nivye*. Probably the intended reading was *vivīta*.

6 *C. I. I.*, IV. 324—31; ibid., 645—52.

with the egress and ingress to it (*sa-nirgama-praveśa*), with fertile and marshy lands (*sa-jāṅgalānūpa*), with tree-groves, plant-gardens, grass and so forth (*vṛkṣārāmodbhid-odyānatṛṇādi sahita*) and with rivers and hills (*sa-nadīparvata*). In the Candella records we meet two enumerations of these privileges. Usually the village is granted along with its water and dry land, inanimate and animate objects (*sa-sthāvara-jaṅgama*),fenced by its own boundaries(*sva-sīmāvacchinna*), with what is under and above its soil (*sādha-ūrddha*), with its salt mines, stones, forests and trees and what is outside and inside (*sa-bāhyābhyantara*) and other things also (*apara vastu*).[1] The more detailed list of privileges mentions the grant of the village along with houses and fences (*sa-mandira-prākāra*), with the egress and ingress to it, with all articles of food (*sarvvāśana*),[2] sugarcane, safflower, cotton, *saṇa* (hemp), mango, *mahuā* and other trees, with forests, pits and hoards (*sa-vana-khani-nidhāna*), with the mines of iron and salt, and the place of the origin of leaves and others (*sa-loha-lavaṇa-tṛṇa-parṇṇādyākara*), with its ground (*tala*), reservoirs, rivers and hills, with its pits, squares (*catvara*), and saline soil, its wood (*kāṣṭha*), bricks and stones, its herds of cows (*sa-gokula*), its animals, beasts, birds and acquatic animals and all other things within its boundaries.[3] In the Paramāra records[4] the villages are granted along with the rows of trees (*sa-vṛkṣamālākula*), with houses, house-sites (*gṛha-sthāna*), granaries (*khala*), threshing-floor (*khala-sthāna*), pits (*tala-bhedyā* ?), cow-sheds (*go-vāṭikā*), temples, gardens, tanks, step-wells (*vāpī*), wells, etc. In the grants of the Pratihāras[5] and the Gāhaḍavālas[6] also we find that the privileges transferred to the donees were similiar in nature. Scholars do not agree on the extent to which these rights were actually exercised by the

1 E. *I.*, XX. 135—6.

2 According to Monier-Williams, *Sanskrit-English Dictionary āśana* is *Terminalia Tomentosa.*

3 E. *I.*, XXXII. 121—3. Often the two lists are mentioned together- E. *I.*, XX. 129—31.

4 E. *I.*, XXXII. 148-56.

5 E. *I.*, XVIII. 322—4; XXX. 148—50.

6 E. *I.*, XXXIII. 178—80.

king.[1] What, in any case, is obvious is the fact that the king was making a public claim of these rights, which may be interpreted as a general indication of the increasing claim of the king over the land.

In the *Rājataraṅgiṇī*[2] king Jayāpīḍa is said to have gone, in his persistent greed, so far in cruelty that for three years he took the whole harvest, including the cultivator's share. This was no doubt an unusual action, rightly censured by Kalhaṇa, but we have to note the suggestion that sometimes kings viewed themselves as owners of the entire arable land in the state and hence as entitled to the whole or a major portion of the crop. In two inscriptions[3] of the reign of the Caulukya king Bhīmadeva I we find that the fields donated are described as being owned (*satka*) by private individuals. There can be many possible explanations of the owners losing their rights over the plots.[4] As rightly pointed out by the learned editor of one of these inscriptions,[5] the grants being made on religious occasions, the king, anxious to do a work of piety, might well have commandeered the fields in return for compensation. But it looks rather strange that, unlike other similar cases,[6] the two grants are totally silent about the way in which the owners came to lose their rights, whether by escheat or by sale. If the individuals said to have been owners of the fields were occupying the fields at the time of the grant, this may indicate that sometimes in practice also the ownership of the individuals was viewed as a qualified one when compared with the over-riding rights of the king.

Rights of feudatories—

In our period we witness the emergence of the feudal chief as a third claimant to the ownership of soil. The feudatories

1 A. S. Altekar, *State and Government in ancient India*, p. 211; C. V. Vaidya, *History of Mediaeval Hindu India*, II. 460—61; A. K. Majumdar, *Chaulukyas of Gujarat*, p. 248.

2 IV. 628.

3 *E. I.*, XXXIII. 236—7; XXI. 172.

4 Cf. *E. I.*, XXXIII. 235.

5 Ibid.

6 E. g., Jesar Plates of Śīlāditya III—*E. I.*, XXII. 115—20 and the Urlam Plates of Hastivarman—*E. I.*, XVII. 332—3.

and feudal chiefs had a restricted title. The *Mitākṣarā*[1] observes that the privilege of making a gift of land belonged only to the king and not to the fief-holder. We have some references to indicate that the suzerain ruler had the right to grant land which was directly held by his vassals. Thus, a feudatory ruler Gaṅgadeva made a land-grant as desired by his suzerain king Jayavarman of the Paramāra dynasty.[2] Likewise Naravarman, another Paramāra emperor, donated lands in a village under his feudatory Rājyadeva.[3] Though theoretically the feudatory rulers were not entitled to make land-grants, we find that in reality they did donate lands.[4] We can classify such charters into many kinds according to the degree of dependence or independence of the feudatory rulers. In some cases the grant is said to have been made at a request of a certain feudatory. When the feudatory was of no great importance the record would not make even this reference, but would simply introduce the name of the feudatory.[5] In the Gāhaḍavāla empire we find the land-grant of a *rāṇaka* being announced by the heir apparent (*mahārājaputra*) Govindacandra on behalf of the emperor.[6] Sometimes the imperial permission was granted through an officer. Thus, we see that the land-grant of the feudatory ruler Avanivarman II was approved by Dhiika, the *tantrapāla* (most likely an officer like the resident political agent) of Mahendrapāla, the Pratihāra emperor.[7] In the Partabgarh inscription we find that the Cāhamāna *mahāsāmanta* Indrarāja had to request Mādhava, the provincial governor at Ujjain, for the grant of a village.[8] If, however, the feudatory had sufficient power and

1 On Yāj., I. 318—*Anena bhūpatereva bhūmidāne nibandhadāne vādhikāro na bhogapateriti darśitam.*

2 *E. I.*, IX. 120ff.

3 *E. I.*, XX, no. 11. Cf. *E. I.*, I. 89 for an instance from Gujarat.

4 *E. I.*, XXXIII, p. 50; IX. 174ff; XXI. 32ff: *I. A.*, XVIII. 80ff; XVII. 227ff.

5 Ibid., pp. 51—53.

6 *I. A.*, XVIII, pp. 14—19. Cf. *E. I.*, XX, no. 11 for Paramāra king Naravarman notifying two land-grants made by a provincial governor and his wife. See also *E. I.*, XXIX. 48ff.

7 *E. I.*, IX, pp. 6ff.

8 *E. I.*, XIV. 184—7 (Part II, ll.14–27). Cf. *E. I.*, XXXII. 139ff.

importance he issued his land charters without reference to his overlord's permission.[1] With a further growth in power the feudatory ruler must have asserted his claim to the soil and insisted on putting his sign-manual on grants concerning his territory though made by the overlord himself. There is one instance where the feudatory got another set of plates issued with his name also on it, as the original plates issued by his overlord did not contain his sign.[2]

Land assignments to officers—

The feudal elements must have gained in importance in the period, with the growing tendency to remunerate the officers in the form of assignments of land. It would appear from the combined testimony of Hsüan Tsang[3] and Bāṇa[4] that in the time of Harṣa the state officers were paid mostly in the form of land-grants. But it is only from the ninth century that we get epigraphic references to land-grants made to officers, and these increase in number from the eleventh century.[5] The rights of these officers however appear to have been of a restricted nature. Thus in an inscription of the Cāhamānas of Sambhar we have a reference to the religious grant of a village of his fief made by a *duḥsādhya* but with the permission of his master.[6] According to a copper

---

1 *Proceedings of All India Oriental Conference*, I. 325f; *I. A.*, XVIII. 84f; *E. I.*, XXVIII. 201, 266, 332; XXX. 139. Cf. *I. A.*, XVIII. 80ff; *E. I.*, XIX. 69ff.

2 *J. B. B. R. A. S.*, XXVI. 258.

3 Watters, I, p. 176.

4 *Harṣacarita* (ed. J. Vidyasagara), p. 93.

5 *J.E.S.H.O.*, IV. 99f. We have to notice three types of assignments to state officers. Cases where officers are said to have received villages from the king would not, strictly speaking, come under the category of assignments in lieu of their salaries. As has been made clear in some of these cases the villages were granted by the king who was pleased with the officer for some valuable service. Cf. *I.A.*, XXI. 170-71. There are also references to state officers possessing and granting villages which were most likely by way of their remuneration. We have indications to suggest that sometimes the officers were assigned a share in the revenue from the village.

6 *E.I.*, II, no. 8

plate dated 1260 A.D.[1] king Jayavarman II caused a certain *pratihāra* (head of the palace-guard) to donate a village to three brāhmaṇas. This officer appears to have been enjoying the village as his assignment because it is he who is said to have performed the religious ceremonies connected with the grant, but he had to do it with the permission of his master who signed it and made it a royal charter. The Bargaon plate[2] records the grant of a village by king Vajrahasta III but an endorsement at the end makes it clear that the grant was actually made by an officer of the king out of his own fief. It would appear that the grant of the officer had to be issued in the name of the king.[3] Another similar case seems to have been preserved in the Mehar plate, which records a grant of land by king Dāmodara but introduces Gaṅgādharadeva, the officer in charge of the royal elephant force, who is mentioned after the reference to the king. An inscription of Mahendrapāla II[4] which records the grant of a village by the emperor in the possession of *talavarggika* Hariṣaḍa indicates that the officer had been given the village but had only a limited right in the sense that the king could give it to another. A more abiding claim of these officers is suggested by the inscription in which king Vākpatirāja is said to have re-granted to a goddess a village when requested to do so by the wife of the *mahāsādhanika* Mahāika[5] who obviously had received it as an assignment. A regent of five districts under king Vajrahasta of the Gaṅga dynasty is found giving a village to the bridegroom on the occasion of the marriage of his daughter.[6] In the *Rājataraṅgiṇī*[7] Suyya, the engineer, is said to have granted a village to the brāhmaṇas. King Avantivarman is said to have divided his kingdom among his relatives and officers, most likely in the form of estates and fiefs.[8] A story

1 *E.I.*, IX, no 13 (B).

2 *E.I.*, XXIX, pp. 48 ff.

3 *E.I.*, XXVII. 182 ff.

4 *E.I.*, XIV. 182-84 (part I, ll.1-14).

5 *I.A.*, XIV. 160

6 *E.I.*, III, no. 31.

7 V. 120.

8 Ibid., V. 121

in the *Bṛhatkathākośa*[1] would indicate that the service tenure villages were not necessarily always permanent grants. We read that a *sahasrabhaṭa* warrior had been granted a number of villages as his tenure but after his death his fief was not inherited by his son but by another man who was skilled in the use of javelin and spear and was appointed as *sahasrabhaṭa* warrior. The *Udayasundarīkathā*[2] refers to a *kāyastha* officer enjoying a tenure which was permanent and hereditary. Significantly enough Lakṣmīdhara explains *deśapati* as "soldiers etc",[3] suggesting thereby that the usual mode of remunerating warriors was through land assignments which carried with them some abiding claims of ownership. Thus service and rulership would appear to have been often associated together in the early medieval period. Such close political and administrative control over a limited area would often tend to help the emergence of rights of ownership.

Landed aristocracy—

Even more significant than this was the emergence of a class of landed aristocracy as an intermediary enjoying the revenues of one or more villages. We have already referred to the practice of villages being granted to vassals and officials as a mark of the favour of the king. Religious grants to individuals and institutions alike must have gone a long way to create a class of landlords. We find that individuals sometimes acquired the status of village lords, and that this right could be transferred and bought and sold like any other commodity. In the Madras Museum Plates of the time of king Narendradhavala[4] we find that a certain Seḍā purchased a village as a *kraya-śāsana* (land sold by a deed of purchase) and some years later re-sold it as a *kraya-śāsana* to three persons. An inscription from Kaman (Bharatpur) refers to a village owned by a certain man named Untaṭa.[5] In an inscription from Hazaribagh roughly assigned to the seventh

1 p. 59

2 p. 152-*Pūrvapuruṣakramāgatāyā dhruvavṛtteḥ prabhuḥ.*

3 *Kṛtyakalpataru, Brahmacāri*, p. 251-*deśapatiḥ sainikādiḥ.*

4 *E.I.*, XXVIII. 49-50.

5 *E.I.*, XXIV. 336, ll.19-21.

or eighth century we find that with the consent of the king three brothers were accepted by the people of three villages as their rulers.[1] It can very well be imagined that these local chiefs and village lords would have converted their power of administration and right to revenue into claims of rulership and ownership. The weakening of the central authority in general must have favoured such a development.

Feudal chief's title to ownership—

We have certain references which indicate that the feudal chief claimed some form of ownership over the land. Hemacandra[2] speaks of the feudal assignment which had to be protected against encroachment by neighbouring chiefs as the ancestral property or land. The growth in the claims of the feudal chief naturally weakened those of the cultivators. It is not without significance that in a village owned by a certain individual a brāhmaṇa is mentioned as cultivating a field measuring three ploughs, but soon it was given to a ploughman (*hālika*) and then before long it was donated as a religious gift.[3] In the Rajor inscription the feudatory chief Mathanadeva grants a village and in enumerating the rights and privileges transferred to the donee describes it as accompanied with all the neighbouring fields cultivated by the Gurjjaras.[4] There is a suggestion in a verse in the *Śārṅgadhara-paddhati*[5] that generally the cultivators did not own the land and the acquisition of the proprietary right to their fields was a distinct rise in their status. It is not unlikely that the growing restrictions on the claims of the peasant to his field, as implied in the emergence of feudal chiefs and village lords, was at the back of the explanations given in the legal texts of the period that ownership does not comprise only what one can dispose of at one's will but what is

1 *E.I.*, II, p. 343.

2 *Prākṛit Vyākaraṇa*, IV. 395, v. 6-*Puttem̥ jāeṃ kavaṇu guṇu avaguṇu kavaṇu mueṇa. Jā bappī kī bhuṃhaḍī campijjaï avareṇa.*

3 E.I., XXIV. 336, ll.10-21.

4 E.I., III. 266-67.

5 v. 2508-*Niyoginaḥ kṣatriyasya durgā cenmastake viśet. Padapratiṣṭhāvaśyaṃ syādbhūmilābhaḥ kuṭumbinaḥ.*

capable in appropriate circumstances of being disposed of as one likes.[1] We have already pointed out that these texts attach importance to the discussion about ownership as being a separate category or capacity.[2]

Quasi-manorial rights—

There is no indication that in ancient India cultivators were tied to the soil like the European serfs. They enjoyed the freedom to migrate to another state if they were oppressed.[3] This right is implied in the texts of the early medieval period. Thus, the *Bṛhannāradīya Purāṇa*[4] says that when much afflicted by the sufferings caused by famine and taxation people feel distressed and migrate to countries rich in wheat and barley. A verse in the *Subhāṣitaratnakoṣa* of Vidyākara[5] speaks of men in a village leaving it when oppressed by the feudal chief. In the entire range of Sanskrit literature the only reference suggesting some form of manorial right which we have been able to trace is in the *Upamitibhavaprapañcākathā* of Siddharṣi.[6] In a city described as the fief (*bhukti*) of a certain king Karmma-pariṇāma the entire population is said to have been thrown into cells and kept huddled together for a long time.[7] Another king named Sadāgama from time to time liberated some of these people and settled them in another city which could not be approached by Karmma-pariṇāma. In this way the popu-

1 *Madanaratna* q. by Kane, *History of Dharmaśāstra*, III. 555. Cf. Jīmūtavāhana, Nīlakaṇṭha and Mitramiśra q. by U.N. Ghoshal, *Agrarian System in Ancient India*. pp. 85f. Also *Vyavasthācandrikā* (ed. S. C. Sircar), I (i), cl. 51 and *Smṛticandrikā*, I, cl. 25.

2 See supra p. 1.

3 *Mahābhārata*, XII. 89.24

4 XXXVIII.87

5 v. 1175. The position seems to have hardly changed even in the time of Bābar who observes that "in Hindustan hamlets and villages, towns indeed, are depopulated and set up in a moment! If the people of a large town, one inhabited for years even, flee from it, they do it in such a way that not a sign or trace of them remains in a day or a day and a half"—*The Bābur-nāma* tr. A. S. Beveridge, II, p. 488.

6 pp. 176-78.

7 *Apavarakeṣu nikṣipya sampiṇḍitāḥ sakala-kālaṃ dhāryante.*

lation under king Karmma-pariṇāma would have thinned, but his sister brought people from another city to take the places of those whom Sadāgama had liberated.

Epigraphic references—

In the early medieval period, however, we find signs of serfdom and of manorial villages in some parts of northern India.[1] The earliest known reference is in the Nirmand (Kangra) copper plate inscription of *mahāsāmanta mahārāja* Samudrasena[2] which can be assigned roughly to the seventh century A.D. Samudrasena grants to a body of brāhmaṇas a village together with its inhabitants (*sa-prativāsi-jana-sametam*).

A stray plate from Nanana (Marwar),[3] belonging to the twelfth century, records certain persons being granted or permanently allotted to the god Tripuruṣa. It is clear from the plate that these people were not slaves but independent persons including cultivators, songstresses and musicians. Section I records that a flute player (*vāṃśika*) named Lhauḍiyāka was allotted to the

1 U. N. Ghoshal, *Contributions to the History of the Hindu Revenue System* and *The Agrarian System in Ancient India,* does not take any notice of this question. B. P. Mazumdar, *Socio-Economic History of Northern India* (1030-1194 A.D.), is also silent about it. The recent standard works on the early medieval period (R. C. Majumdar and A. D. Pusalker Ed., *The Age of Imperial Kanauj* and *The Struggle for Empire*) including studies of dynasties and regions in the period also neglect this problem. D. D. Kosambi, *An Introduction to the Study of Indian History*, p. 298 gives a few references. It is, however, to be noted that the Neulpur (Cuttack) grant of king Śubhākara (*E.I.*, XV. 1 ff, 363) which may be assigned to the latter half of the eighth century does not refer to the "giving" of village workmen. Probably Kosambi bases his view on the expression *sarva-satvānāñca* occurring in line 9. But the context leaves no doubt whatsoever that the inhabitants were not granted and that the inscription refers to the grant as having been for the increase of the merit of all created being along with that of the donor and that of his parents. R. S. Sharma, *J.I.H.*, XXXIX. 310 notices the prevalence of the practice of granting villages along with the inhabitants in Orissa and in the Candella kingdom.

2 J. F. Fleet, *C.I.I.*, III, no. 80, 1.10.

3 *E.I.*, XXXIII. 244 ff.

deity. In section II we read of two persons named Śilapati and Śrīpāla, who were probably engaged in working the *araghaṭṭa* (Persian wheel) at Devananditagrāma, being allotted to the same god along with several other persons who probably lived in the locality where the temple stood. These were six songstresses, a *suravāla* (a type of singer), a *paṇavika* (drum-player), a *doyaraka* (another class of singer) a *mṛdaṅga*-player and a flute-player. All these are named individually. Section VI records that *mahārājādhirāja* Ratnapāla (of the Cāhamāna family of Nadol) gave away a certain Noriyāka together with his family. In section VII *mahārājaputra-kumāra* Sāhaṇapāla is said to have granted to the temple in V.S. 1192 (A.D. 1135) two agriculturist householders (*kuṭumbikas*) formerly living at the village of Naṃdāṇā, together with their sons and grandsons so long as they lived.[1] Section VIII records that *mahārāja* Ālhaṇadeva granted in V.S. 1205 (A.D. 1148) two agriculturist householders (*kuṭuṃ=kuṭumbikas*) who were formerly living in the village of Naṃdāṇā and also certain brothers whose names cannot be made out, and who, as the word is in the plural, must have been more than two in number.

A Caulukya grant dated A.D. 1207 from Timaṇa (Bhaunagar)[2] records that the Mehara king Jagamalla established two *liṅgas* and consecrated to them 55 *pāthas*[3] of cultivated and fallow land in a certain village, also giving 55 *pāthas* of land in another village. For his spiritual merit the donor is said to have given three men to be cultivators of the land granted by himself.[4] Their names are recorded as Saüṃsariyaü, the son of a certain husbandman (*kuṭuṃvika*), *pañcakula* Cāṇḍapa, and Cāiyā, the son of a Kolika.

From a number of inscriptions from Orissa[5] we learn that the king claimed some sort of ownership over men of certain

---

1 D. Sharma, *Early Chauhan Dynasties* p. 299 notices only this part of the grant. See also *ibid.*, Appendix G (iii), l. 20.

2 *I.A.*, XI. 337 f.

3 According to H. H. Wilson, *Glossary of Judicial and Revenue Terms*, s. v., *pātha*, one *pātha*=240 sq. ft.

4 *Ete trayo janāḥ pradattāḥ kuṭuṃvikatvena.*

5 For the grants of the kings of the Bhauma-Kara dynasty, founded in the middle of the eighth century A.D., see Terundia (Puri) plate of

occupations and crafts and would often transfer his right over them.[1] In these records the stock list of the rights accompanying the grant includes those over weavers (*tantravāya* or *tantuvāya*), milkmen (*gokuṭa* or *gokūṭa*),[2] distillers (*śauṇḍhika* or *śauṇḍika*)[3] and other subjects (*prakṛtika*).[4] That it was not

Śubhākara II-*E.I.*, XXVIII. 215 f; Hindol plate of Śubhākaradeva III (year 103)—B. Misra, *Orissa under the Bhauma kings*, p. 15, ll. 18f; Dhenkanal plate of Tribhuvanamahādevī I (year 110)—*J.B.O.R.S.*, II. 421 ff. l. 28; Talcher plate of Śubhākaradeva IV (year 141)—B. Misra, loc. cit., p. 36, l. 37 (here the expression is abridged as *sa-śauṇḍikādiprakṛtikaḥ*); Talcher plate of Śivakaradeva (year 149)—B. Misra, loc. cit., p. 44, l. 24; also ibid., p. 51; Santigrama (Cuttack) grant of Daṇḍimahādevī—*E.I.*, XXIX. 87 ff; Ganjam grant of Daṇḍīmahādevī—*E.I.*, VI. 141 f; Ganjam grant of Daṇḍimahādevī (year 180)—*E.I.*, VI. 137 ff; Kumurang (Puri) plate of Daṇḍīmahādevī (year 187)—B. Misra, loc, cit., p. 63, l. 31; Taltali (Cuttack) plate of Dharmma-mahādevī—*I.H.Q.*, XXI. 219, l. 32. The grants made by the feudatories of the Bhauma-Karas also contain this expression. For the Bhañjas see Adilpur (Mayurbhanj) plate of Narendrabhañjadeva—*E.I.*, XXV. 159 f, ll. 17 f. For the Śūlkis see the Dhenkanal grants of Jayastambhadeva—*J.B.O.R.S.*, II. 413 ff, l. 20; II. 406 ff, l. 13.

1 B. Misra, loc. cit., pp. 30, 95 takes these expressions to refer to additional taxes from the weavers, cowherds, distillers of spirituous liquors and all other tenants. He adds that the agricultural people who formed the majority of the population of a village are not mentioned because the gift of the village implied the bestowal of the right to enjoy the land taxes. The grant of the village did not expressly imply the taxes levied from weavers etc. and hence the rights to these taxes have been specifically mentioned. But *uparikara* is not used as a general term to cover the items that follow it. *Uparikara*, in other grants of ancient India also, appears as a specific item of revenue. The Orissa grants do not employ any term standing for the taxes from the professions mentioned in them; they clearly refer to the grant of persons following these professions.

2 B. Misra, loc. cit., p. 95 suggests that the Oriya word *gauḍa* has been Sanskritised. R. S. Sharma, *J.I.H.*, XXXIX. 310 emends it as *gokula*.

3 The Dhenkanal grant of Jayastambha (*J.B.O.R.S.*, II. 406 ff, l. 13) has *kaivarta* (boatman) in place of *śauṇḍika*.

4 *Prakṛti* at times is found used in the narrow sense of men belonging to crafts and occupations formed into guilds. See *Abhidhānacintāmaṇi* of Hemacandra (in the *Abhidhānasaṅgraha*, Vol. II, N.S.P., III, v. 714—*Prakṛtayaḥ paurāṇāṃ śreṇayo'pi ca*.

a theoretical claim but had practical application would follow from set II of the Kendupatna plates (Śaka 1217 = A.D. 1295) of Narasiṃha II.[1] This records that king Narasiṃha donated to Bhīmadeva-śarman several plots measuring 100 *vāṭikās* of land and as a part of this donation (*etacchāsanasyāṅgatayā*) granted as servants and subjects permanently attached (*parajāḥ*) seven men named in the record—a maker of conchshell bangles (*śaṅkhakāra*), a merchant (*śreṣṭhin*), a goldsmith (*suvarṇṇakāra*), an oilman (*tailika*), a milkman (*gopāla*), a potter (*kuṃbhakāra*) and another oilman (*teli*). The Dibbida (Vizagapatam) plates of Arjuna of the Matsya family (A.D. 1269) record the grant of a village which included a grant of the village artisans, the carpenter, goldsmith, barber, blacksmith, potter and sesamum-grinder.[2] In the Kharepatan (Ratnagiri) plates (Śaka 930 = A.D. 1008)[3] Raṭṭarāja records that he assigned to his teacher families of female attendants (*dārikā-kuṭumbāni*), a family of oilmen, a family of gardeners, a family of potters and a family of washermen.

The Bhatera (Sylhet) inscription (A.D. 1049)[4] states that Govinda-Keśavadeva donated to the god Śiva 375 *halas* of land with 296 houses in various villages and also gave many attendant subjects who belonged to ordinary social groups and lived on the donated land (*nānāparijanāṃstasmin janajātīnanekaśaḥ*). That the grant really carried with it a legal claim over the people inhabiting the houses and lands donated should be clear from the fact that the inscription devotes considerable space (lines 29 to 51) to enumerating the different plots of land and houses in different villages. The inscription mentions the individual occupants of the houses by name ; in some cases they are said to have been craftsmen, including, cowherds, a bell-metal worker, a barber, a washerman, a boatman and an ivory-worker.

1 *E.I.*, XXVIII. 190-91.

2 *E.I.*, V. 110-12, v. 22—*Takṣaka-suvarṇṇakāraśca kṣaurikaḥ karmmakārukah. Kulālastilahaṃttā ca pradattā grāmakārukāḥ.*

3 *E.I.*, III. 297-302.

4 *E.I.*, XIX. 279-86. In the Tezpur grant (*J.A.S.B.*, IX, 1840, pp. 766 ff, v. 24) king Vanamāla is said to have made to the temple of Hāṭakeśvara Śiva a gift consisting of villages, men, prostitutes and elephants.

Prajā or parijana —

In the above-mentioned inscriptions the people who are attached to a deity as a religious grant are either agriculturist householders or men belonging to occupations which had a low social status. The term *prajā* or *parijana*[1] employed for them is used in modern times in a sense which has to be distinguished from servants and slaves alike and stands for men of certain occupations who are in a way permanently associated with the chief of the village as his attendants.[2] As against these there are a few inscriptions in some parts of northern India which indicate that kings claimed some sort of ownership over the inhabitants of villages in their jurisdiction. Thus, in Assam we find that Vallabhadeva (A.D. 1184-85) granted seven villages to an almshouse[3] and the list of rights accompanying the grant includes that over the people living in them (*sajanān*). He also gave five persons, whose names are recorded, as assistants (*sahāyāḥ*), together with their wives and children (*putra-dāra-samanvitāḥ*). In the Madanpur (Dacca) plate of Śrīcandra,[4] who ruled in Bengal towards the close of the tenth and the beginning of the eleventh century A.D., the land is granted along with the people (*sa-prajā*). A plate in

---

1 It is sometimes pronounced *parjā*, or corruptly, *purjah*. It means progeny, offspring, subjects, people, tenants and dependants. In Cooch Behar it stands for a cultivator-at-will, who gets half the produce of the land, but is removable at the pleasure of the proprietor, to whom he is usually in debt for advances, and is more like a serf than a free agent. In Cuttack the term is applied to low castes, such as the barber, washerman, fisherman, weaver, leather-worker, and toddy tapper, who would formerly sometimes sell themselves and their families into slavery until they repaid the purchase-money. The children born during this period became the property of the purchaser, and with their parents, might be bought, sold, or let out for hire. They lived apart from their masters. They did not forfeit their caste or forego their occupations, and retained a title to their hereditary possessions—H. H. Wilson, *Glossary of judicial and revenue terms*, s. v., *prajā*.

2 Cf. *Kṛtyakalpataru* of Lakṣmīdhara, *Vyavahārakāṇḍa*, p. 56—*tad-adhīna-kuṭumbinyah* is explained as *gopāla-śauṇḍikādi-striyah*.

3 *E.I.*, V. 183 ff, vv. 17, 22.

4 *E.I.*, XXVIII. 56-58 dated in the year 44 of his reign.

the India Office,[1] on palaeographic considerations assigned to the eleventh or twelfth century, records that a certain king Vijayarājadeva[2] granted to some people the cultivated lands, wells, houses and *kuṭumbikas* in the estate (*paribhoga*) of Kesarikoṭṭa which were not enjoyed by Mūladeva,[3] and a village along with its bipeds (*dvipada*), quadrupeds (*catuṣ-pada*), fields and the *kuṭumbikas*.[4] The Candella grants are more clear in this respect. The donated villages are described as carrying with them the right over the artisans, cultivators and merchants living in them.[5]

Status of the prajās—

As regards the status of the men said to have been attached to the donee as a religious grant it is clear that they were not slaves but independent persons. They have also to be distinguished alike from serfs, if serfdom is conceived as a perpetual adherence to the soil of an estate owned by a lord. If performance of services for other persons is taken as the essence of the status of a serf,[6] the men of our inscriptions may be described as serfs but only in a restricted sense. The comparison is probably closer with the villeins of the European manorial system which is associated with dependence of a population on a ruler consisting not in ownership extending over persons nor in contractual arrangements, but in various forms and degrees of subjection, chiefly regulated by custom.[7]

---

1 *E.I.*, III. 313 f.

2 There is nothing to connect him with any of the known dynasties of the period. It is even difficult to be certain about the region in which he ruled.

3 Most likely the name of a certain deity in a temple who possessed a major portion of the land in Kesarikoṭṭa or else a feudatory chief.

4 The editor of the plate translates *kuṭumbika* as a house-slave, but we prefer the more usual explanation of an agriculturist householder.

5 Plates of Madanavarman dated A.D. 1136—*E.I.*, XXXII. 121-23, ll. 29-34—*sa-kāru-karṣaka-vaṇig-vāstavyam*. See R. S. Sharma, *J.I.H.*, XXXIX. 310. The Charkhari plate of Paramardin (*E.I.*, XX, p. 131, l. 19) has *sa-kārukapiṅkavaṅgi-vāstavyaṃ*. The mistakes in the expression were not realised earlier and hence scholars had difficulty in explaining it—*J.U.P.H.S.*, XXIII. 240, f. n. 33.

6 *Encyclopedia Britanica*, s. v., *serf*.

7 Ibid., s. v., *manor*. In medieval England we find that the two standard

We find it difficult to determine the precise status of the men of our grants. The records are totally silent about their obligations and the claims of the ruler. In one respect, however, their position seems to have been worse than the legal status of a villein or even a serf. Even if unfree a villein was not exposed to the arbitrary will of his lord ; he was not a slave and was not bought and sold apart from his holding. The serf was also not given over to his lord to be owned as a thing or an animal. The records which speak of the men being granted or attached to the donee as living on the land granted contemplate a position similar to that of the manorial system. But in some of the donations of the stray plate from Nanana and set II of the Kendupatna plates of Narasiṃha II the men so attached are described as belonging to villages other than that granted. This would mean that in these cases the rulers transferred their rights over the subjects and attendants even without actually disposing of the land on which they dwelt, and in doing so could compel a man to move from one village to another.[1]

In medieval English society we find that there was a large and growing class of tenants who did not render any services, or did only insignificant services.[2] The *Rājataraṅgiṇī* and some of the inscriptions of the early medieval period show that the obligation

---

tests to determine the status of a villein were—uncertainty of services and the payment of merchet, though in practice the proof of villeinage was a very intricate matter, and one on which there was often much room for doubt—A. Lane Poole, *Obligations of Society in the XII and XIII centuries*, p. 14. But we have no means to find out if any such tests were applied in India. The essence of villeinage was labour service ; the villein must work for his lord for so many days in the week in addition to boon works, special tasks, precaria, at certain seasons of the year—A. Lane Poole, loc. cit., p. 15. We may say that the Indian epigraphic references in the early medieval period also imply such obligations.

1 Even in England many aspects of medieval serfdom were very like slavery. In theory, at least, a lord could do what he pleased with his villein except kill or mutilate him and there are occasional records which show that a lord could sell his villein to another—A. Lane Poole, op. cit., p. 14.

2 Ibid., p. 24.

to do forced labour was not always performed but was sometimes commuted by some payment in cash or kind. These inscriptions[1] describe the grant as accompanied by the right of *utpadyamāna-viṣṭi*. It refers to the dues paid by the villagers in place of the forced labour they had to perform for the state. In Kashmir the system of forced labour appears as *rūḍhabhārodhi*. The *Rājataraṅgiṇī* suggests that it was not always necessarily the actual carriage of loads but might be commuted by some payment in cash or kind. King Śaṅkaravarman is said to have introduced this system of forced labour. He fined the villagers failing to carry loads for one year, at the value of the load calculated according to the highest prices in the regions concerned.[2] In the reign of Harṣa (A.D. 1089-1101) a certain temple was plundered, hence the members of the *purohita* corporation requested him to be exempted from *rūḍhabhārodhi* (forced labour).[3] This reference also favours the suggestion that the forced labour was often commuted for payment in cash or kind.

In England we find that many a villein gained his liberty by escaping to a town where, if he remained unclaimed for a year and a day, he became free. A villein obtained his freedom also by entering the orders of the church. But the surest methods of obtaining manumission were by charter or by purchase, the money for which was provided by a third party, as the villein's property was in theory his lord's. Sometimes freedom was granted in return for services rendered, for example going on crusade in place of his lord. The enfranchisement of a serf was a solemn and a public act. The investiture with the arms of a freeman, the spear and lance, was part of the formal ceremony of manumission.[4] We have no records to determine if there were in early medieval India also set rules for manumission or any formal ceremonies connected with it. We can, therefore, only conjecture the possibilities. It is obvious that a runaway villein if not recovered was in practice free. Like-

1 *E.I.*, IX, no. 1 (B).

2 *Rājataraṅgiṇī*, V. 172 ff.

3 Ibid., VII. 1088; also ibid., VIII. 2513.

4 A. Lane Poole, Op. cit., pp. 28-34.

wise a master, if pleased with his villein, often might have freed him from his obligations. As we know that slaves in India could be emancipated if their purchase money was paid,[1] we can postulate a similar rule in the case of the Indian counterparts of villeins. We have some references to suggest that in India certain formalities were observed in connection with the manumission of a slave.[2] Similar formal ceremonies were probably performed at the time when a "villein" obtained his freedom.

Origin of the system —

Such a quasi-manorial system must have evolved as a response to the narrowing horizon of economic wants and political requirements. The decline in the volume of trade activity and the political insecurity resulted in giving an agricultural basis to the social and political life. The weakening of the central authority naturally resulted in the increase in the power of local chiefs and lords. The strengthened political power of local chiefs in certain areas was bound in the course of time to lead to the establishment of such manorial rights.[3]

There were certain tendencies in earlier times which helped the emergence of a tenure resembling the manorial system. Even in the early legal texts we find that the king is given the power to exact forced or unpaid labour from artisans and labourers.[4] An early epigraphic testimony to the existence of *viṣṭi* is to be seen in the Junagadh inscription (A.D. 150) of Rudradāman.[5] In the *Arthaśāstra*[6] forced labour seems to have been a regular thing, which the state utilized to its best advantage, recording the labour rendered by each citizen. We get an idea of the nature of the work included

1 *Artha*, III. 13; Nārada, V. 29-38.

2 *Nāyādhammakahā* I, p. 21; *Vyavahārabhāṣya*, 6. 208.

3 R. S. Sharma, *J.I.H.*, XXX. 310 suggests that "in Orissa it may have been found necessary on account of the scarcity of working population for running rural economy".

4 Gautama, X. 31-32; Manu, VII. 138; *Viṣṇu Dharmasūtra*, III. 32; *Agnipurāṇa*, CCXXIII. 33; *Śaṅkhalikhita* q. in *Vivādaratnākara* of Caṇḍeśvara, p. 662.

5 D. C. Sircar, *Select Inscriptions*. p. 372.

6 II. 35.

under *viṣṭi* from the *Kāmasūtra* (c.4th-5th century)[1] which speaks of peasant women as being compelled to perform for the village headman unpaid work of various kinds, such as filling up his granaries, taking things into or out of his house, clearing or decorating his residence, working in his fields, and spinning yarn of cotton, wool, flax or hemp for his clothes. The obligation of the peasant to cultivate the state land in the form of *viṣṭi* is referred to in the commentary on the *Mahābhārata*.[2] In the hands of local chiefs or donees, who were in a position to exploit the rural resources fully, the right to forced labour could be put to an effective use. The long list of rights accompanying the grants of the early medieval period indicates that, as opposed to earlier times when only revenues were given, now actual proprietary rights were transferred. The enumeration of these concessions, which often include rights over land, water, trees, forests and other similar things, suggests that properties which were customarily under the undefined enjoyment of villagers were increasingly being brought under the personal possession of donees.

The subjection of the people to the village chief may be traced back to the rights of the donee and the obligations of the residents in the village granted as they appear even in the earlier land-grants. In these records the villagers are required, besides paying their dues in cash and kind, to listen to the orders of the donee and to carry them out,[3] to perform personal services to him[4] and to convey his messages.[5]

Another earlier tendency which favoured the emergence of manorial tenure was the practice of letting out land to cultivators who received half the produce. Some early records would suggest that such men tilling land for half the crops were sometimes closely associated with the land granted and the grant was accom-

---

1 V. 5. 5.

2 XII. 140. 21—*Yah kīnāśah śataṃ nivartanāni bhūmeḥ karṣati tena viṣṭirūpeṇa rājakīyam api nivartana-daśakaṃ karṣaṇīyam svīyavad rakṣaṇīyaṃ ca.*

3 *E.I.*, II, no. 30; IX, nos. 21, 39; XXIII, nos. 3, 9; *C.I.I.*, III, nos. 25, 26, 40.

4 *E.I.*, XXVIII, no. 2.

5 *E.I.*, XII, no. 17.

panied with a provision for these cultivators also. Thus, the plates of the Śāiaṅkāyana Vijaya Devavarman (c. 320 A.D.),[1] which record a grant of twenty *nivartanas* of land, mention along with it that a house-site was granted to cultivators who wórked for half the crops (*addhiya-manussāṇaṃ*). Likewise the Hirahadagalli plates of the Pallava king Śivaskandavarman (latter half of the third century A.D.)[2] also provide for such cultivators called here *addhikā*. The land-grants often mention that the donees had the right to cultivate the land or get it cultivated. This right of subinfeudation implied that of ejecting an actual tiller of the soil, which in some cases must have reduced the peasants to the status of tenants-at-will.

It would appear that even by the fifth century there had come to emerge some form of manorial tenure in connection with the estates of religious establishments.[3] Fa-hsien (c. 405-411 A.D.)[4] says that, after the Nirvāṇa of the Buddha, the kings, elders and lay Buddhists built monasteries for the monks and provided them with houses, gardens and fields, with husbandmen and cattle to cultivate them. The history of feudalism in north India indicates that secular land-grants to officers and vassals probably took the religious grants as their prototypes.[5] We may suggest a parallel development from religious examples in the case of manorial rights of secular chiefs of villages.

1 *E.I.*, IX, no. 7

2 D. C. Sircar, *Select Inscriptions*, p. 440.

3 The land-grants to temples and monasteries are sometimes specifically said to have been made to meet the expenses of presenting unguents, flowers, fragrant materials, lamps, music and offerings to the deity, repairing the temple, maintaining the priests and feeding the poor, the sick, the old and ascetics—*E.I.*, XII, no. 7 ; VI, no. 29 ; XVII, p. 110 ; XXVIII, no. 3 ; XXI, no. 43 ; *C.I.I.*, III, no. 25. Generally the expenses on these items were met out of the revenues from the land-grant. It is, however, not unlikely that in some cases the villagers were either individually required to provide for a specific item, or paid their share of all these items. Some of these services probably helped in the crystallisation of manorial obligations.

4 *Chinese Literature*, 1956, no. 3, p. 153.

5 *J.E.S.H.O.*, IV. 103.

Prevalence of the system —

The villeins formed the largest group in the structure of society in medieval England, representing in association with the smaller peasantry approximately 70 per cent of the population.[1] After the Norman conquest, economic and humanitarian motives, both the convenience of the masters and the preaching of the Church, worked for the abolition of slavery in the proper sense of the term. The emancipation of a large number of slaves affected the social position of the class into which these were thrust and tended to drag down the villeins, who now became the lowest class, on the downward path to serfdom.[2] But in India we do not find such a situation. There always existed a class of slaves and land less labourers below the peasants. In England the sharp distinction between freeman and villein begins to emerge in the twelfth century with the growth of royal writs and possessory assizes. The king did not wish to interfere with the private jurisdiction which a lord had over his villeins and so it became necessary to decide who could and who could not get the protection of his rights and property in the king's court[3]. But we do not find in early medieval India any practical need or juristic keenness to determine the status of peasants. Here the class of slaves existed as distinct from all other social groups[4].

It is to be remembered that this type of tenure was not found alike in all parts of northern India. On the contrary it seems to have prevailed only in certain scattered areas, chiefly in Rajasthan, Orissa and Assam. Usually peasants and other villagers were free and masters of their own persons. The reason why the manorial system did not become widespread in India was that there was not a

1 A. Lane Poole, Op. cit, p. 12.

2 Ibid., pp. 12 f.

3 Ibid., p. 13.

4 It is, however, likely that the transformation of the śūdras into cultivators from the Gupta period onwards (R. S. Sharma, *Position of Śūdras in ancient India*) gradually brought about the depression of the earlier economically and socially backward peasants to a status resembling that of villeins.

total collapse of imperial machinery and commercial intercourse. We know that several empires rose in different parts of the land and generally managed to preserve the administrative machinery in some form or other. Moreover, commercial intercourse between different parts of India, though it slackened and lessened, was still considerable in volume. Thus, there was not any great need for building up a new social and political system in the form of manors. It is to be noted that the epigraphic records which testify to manorial tendencies belong chiefly to regions which represented backwaters in the economy of north India.

CHAPTER II

REVENUE SYSTEM

Bhāgabhogakarahiraṇya—

In the land-grants of the period *bhāgabhogakarahiraṇya*, sometimes with a little variation, appears almost universally to denote the taxes and dues which the king received from a village. Generally it is included in the list of dues which the cultivators are directed to pay to the donee, but in some cases it is mentioned along with the rights and privileges, including dues, which accompanied the grant of the village.

Bhāgabhogakara—

Out of this the part *bhāgabhogakara* has been variously interpreted. Kielhorn[1] translates it as share of the produce. U.N. Ghoshal[2] also takes it as one single expression and identifies it with the usual grain-share of the king, called *bhāga* in the *Arthaśāstra* and *bali* in the Smṛtis. Fleet[3] interprets *bhāgabhoga* to mean enjoyment of taxes. A. S. Altekar[4] splits the expression into two, *bhāgakara* being the land-tax and *bhogakara* representing petty taxes in kind paid to the king every day but in practice usually assigned to local officers. Generally however *bhāga*, *bhoga* and *kara* are taken to refer to three different taxes[5].

But the fundamental mistake in these views is that they do not recognise the possibility of regional differences in the meanings of the revenue terms and try to impose a uniform interpretation. Moreover, we have to recognise the possibility of change

1 *E. I.*, VII, p. 160.
2 *H. R. S.*, p. 214.
3 *C. I. I.*, III, p. 254, f.n. 4.
4 *Rāshṭrakūṭas and their times*, pp. 214—16.
5 Tripathi, *History of Kanauj*, p. 348; R. K. Dikshit, *J.U.P.H.S.*, XXIII, p. 243; Vogel, *Antiquities of the Chamba State*, pp. 167—69; R. D. Banerji, *E.I.*, XV, no. 23; D. C. Sircar, *E.I.*, XXIX, p. 5, f.n. 3; S. K. Maity, *Economic Life in the Gupta period*, pp. 57—60.

in the import of some of these terms in course of time. We have a valuable contemporary reference to this possibility in the commentary of Medhātithi[1] who observes that the various kinds of royal dues are known by several names in several countries.

In any case it is clear that *bhāgabhogakara* denoted the most common and important due or dues which the king realised from a village. It is to be noted that in the twenty-one copper plate grants of the Gāhaḍavāla dynasty from Kamauli *bhāgabhogakara* alone is mentioned in all the grants while it is the only tax mentioned in the plate of Govindacandra dated A.D. 1120[2]

In some grants of the Pālas[3] *kara* is found in place of the more usual *bhāgabhogakara*. If *bhāgabhogakara* is used as contrasted with *hiranya* which generally follows the former, *bhāgabhogakara* may be taken to refer to the revenue generally paid in kind, irrespective of whether it refers to two different taxes or a single specific tax[4]. Two land-grants of the feudatories of Mahendrapāla from Kathiawar bring out the opposition between the two terms by mentioning them separately and not as a compound[5]. In the grants of some feudatory families from Bengal the usual expression is *samastarājabhogakara* in place of *bhāgabhogakara*[6]. This would also support the suggestion that, irrespective of the precise significance of its component parts, the expression *bhāgabhogakara* was often used to refer in a general way to the revenue paid in kind.

Bhāgabhoga—

Sometimes we find the expression *bhāgabhoga* being used in place of *bhāgabhogakara*[7]. In some inscriptions the peasants are ordered to bring to the donee *bhāgabhogakara* whereas the grant of

1 On Manu, VIII. 307—*baliprabhṛtīni rājagrāhyakaranāmāni deśabhede sūpamāṇavakavatprasiddhāni.*

2 *E.I.*, IV, no. 11.

3 *E.I.*, XVIII. 304—7; *I.A.*, XXI. 256.

4 Cf. R. Niyogi, *History of the Gāhaḍavāla Dynasty*, p. 168.

5 *E.I.*, IX, no. 1 (A and B). Cf. Prince of Wales Museum plates of Govindarāja, *E.I.*, XXVI. 252—5—*sahiraṇyādānaḥ sabhogabhāgaḥ.*

6 *E.I.*, XXXIII. 138—40; XXX. 257—9, 262—3.

7 *C.I.I.*, IV, pp. 252—63.

the village is described as accompanied by the right to *bhāgabhoga*[1]. It would follow from this that *bhāgabhoga* stood for the revenue paid in kind. In some inscriptions only *bhāgabhoga* is mentioned as the dues to be paid by the villagers to the donee[2].

Some grants from the region of Gujarat have the form *bhogabhāga* in place of *bhāgabhoga*[3]. Fleet[4] takes *bhāgabhoga* and *bhogabhāga* alike as one expression meaning respectively 'enjoyment of shares' and 'share of the enjoyment'. It may be conceded that in some of the references, at least where the rights and privileges accompanying the village granted are enumerated, the expressions have the meaning suggested by Fleet. But the meaning at least of *bhāgabhoga* would not suit cases where it is mentioned along with other specific dues and objects which the villagers are ordered to bring to the donee. The expressions may be taken to refer in general to the revenues paid in kind. Significantly we find two Rāṣṭrakūṭa grants from Gujarat using *bhogabhāga* and *dhānyāya* as if they were interchangable[5].

Sometimes *bhāgabhoga* or *bhogabhāga* is mentioned along with *dhānya*[6]. U. N. Ghoshal[7] explains these cases by interpreting *dhānya* as a fixed contribution in kind as distinguished from the contribution consisting of a share of the produce. But the possibility cannot be ruled out that in order to make their list of privileges and rights as exhaustive as possible these plates incorporate terms which had almost identical import but were used in different regions and contexts.

---

1 Mahudi and Betma Plates of Paramāra Bhoja—*E.I.*, XXXIII. 217ff; XVIII. 322—4; Mandhatạ Plates of Devapāla—*E.I.*, IX. 108—13. Also *E.I.*, VII, no. 9 for a Kalacuri grant.

2 Kuretha grant of Pratihāra Malayavarman—*E.I.*, XXX. 148—50; Charkhari Plates of Candella Vīravarmadeva and Hammīravarmadeva—*E.I.*, XX. 133f, 135f.

3 *E.I.*, XXVI. 252—55, I, no. 8; VII, no. 6 for grants of the Rāṣṭrakūṭa family; *J. N. Banerjea Volume*, pp. 96ff for the grant of an Arab feudatory and *I.A.*, XII. 193—4 for the grant of a Cāpa feudatory.

4 *C.I.I.*, III, p. 120, f.n. 1.

5 *E.I.*, I, no. 8; VII, no. 6.

6 *J. N. Banerjea Volume*, pp. 96ff; *C.I.I.*, III, no. 39.

7 *H.R.S.*, pp. 218f.

There are indications to suggest that the expressions *bhāgabhogakara* or *bhāgabhoga* did not always indicate a single fiscal expression, and that their component parts stood for different taxes. In some records we find *kara* mentioned before *bhāgabhoga*[1] while in others it appears after *bhāgabhoga* but with the intervention of some other terms[2]. In a land-grant of the feudatory chief Mathanadeva *bhāga* and *bhoga* are mentioned separately as two distinct items of revenue[3].

Bhāga—

Bhāga has been generally explained by scholars as the king's customary share of the produce[4]. This is supported by Kṣīrasvāmin[5] who quotes the *Arthaśāstra* text defining *bhāga* as one-sixth and the like payable to the king. Bhaṭṭasvāmin[6] also explains *ṣaḍbhāga* in the general sense of royal share (*rājabhāga*) and adds that it includes by implication other rates such as one-third and one-fourth prevailing in different tracts.

Bhoga—

R. S. Tripathi[7] had conjectured that *bhoga* referred to the rights that the landlord enjoyed when the land was left fallow or to the use of waste and taking of grass etc. from the field, when the cultivator's crops had been removed. R. K. Dikshit[8] and A. K. Majumdar[9] have explained *bhoga* in terms of eight *bhogas* of the records. South Indian inscriptions often describe villages and lands granted as accompanied by the *aṣṭabhogas* which they themselves sometimes define as consisting of the following eight privileges

1 Ratnagiri plates of Somavaṃśī Karṇa—*E.I.*, XXXIII. 266—68.

2 Charkhari plates of Candella Paramardin—*E.I.*, XX. 129—31—*bhāgabhogapaśuhiraṇyakaraśulkādi.*

3 *E.I.*, III, no. 36.

4 U. N. Ghoshal, *H.R.S.*, p. 290 ; D. C. Sircar, *Select Inscriptions*, p. 372, f.n. 7.

5 On *Amara*, II. 8.28.

6 On *Artha*, II. 15 ; *J.B.O.R.S.*, XI, pt. III, p. 83.

7 *I.H.Q.*, IX. 128.

8 *J.U.P.H.S.*, XXIII. 243.

9 *Chaulukyas of Gujarat*, p. 248.

fixed by usage : (a) *nidhi* (treasure-trove), (b) *nikṣepa* (under-ground deposits), (c) *jala* (water-reservoirs), (d) *pāṣāṇa* (stones, mines, quarries), (e) *akṣiṇī* (actual privileges or present profit), (f) *āgāmī* (future profits), (g) *siddha* or *siddhāya* (land already brought under cultivation) and (h) *sādhya* (waste land that may in future be brought under cultivation)[1]. Eight would appear to have been the conventional number of these privileges. In the Kalegaon plates of Yādava Mahādeva[2] eleven types of enjoyment have been enumerated, besides others implied by the expression *ityādi* (etc.), and still they are called *aṣṭabhogas*. Again, this grant mentions only four of the enjoyments, *nidhi*, *nikṣepa*, *jala* and *pāṣāṇa*, from the traditional list. These enjoyments are in the nature of privileges and rights and do not fit in with most of the grants in northern India, where the villagers are ordered to bring (*samupanī*) *bhoga* along with other dues and objects to the donee. We feel that the original suggestion of Bühler[3] that *bhoga* means the periodical supplies of fruits, fire-wood, flower and the like which the villagers had to furnish to the king is a better explanation of the term. This interpretation is supported by Manu[4] and the commentators Medhātithi and Kullūka[5].

We can illustrate the wide divergence in the interpretations of the term *kara* by noting the explanations given by the commentators of Manu and the modern translators of the *Arthaśāstra*[6]. We feel that the term had many uses and their difference should be noticed in individual cases.

There are many references where *kara* has been used in the most general sense of tax[7]. The meaning of *bhāgabhogakara* suggested by U.N. Ghoshal and A. S. Altekar is based on this

1 *E.I.*, III. 123, 245 ; XIII. 34, f.n. 1 ; XV. 22 ; I.400 ; XXXII. 42 ; *I.A.*, XIX. 244.

2 *E.I.*, XXXII. 42.

3 *E.I.*, I. 75. f.n.

4 VII. 118.

5 On Manu, VIII. 307.

6 S. K. Maity, *Economic Life in the Gupta period*, pp. 59f.

7 Cf. Medhātithi on Manu, VIII. 307—*baliprabhṛtīni rājagrāhyakaranāmāni.*

use of the term. R. K. Dikshit[1] takes *kara* as meaning local taxes, but this is not supported by any independent evidence.

Shamasastry translated *kara* at one place in the *Arthaśāstra*[2] as meaning taxes or subsidies paid by vassal kings and others. This is supported by references in inscriptions and literary works to *kara* or tribute being paid by kings or chiefs to their overlord. Thus, the *Rājataraṅgiṇī* employs the word in the sense of tribute at many places.[3]

But obviously this meaning would not suit the land-grants, where the villagers are ordered to bring *kara* along with other dues to the donee. We have pointed out earlier that in some of the grants of the Pālas *kara* has been used in place of *bhāgabhogakara* and, contrasted with *hiraṇya*, would seem to stand for the revenue paid in kind. In the dictionaries of the period *kara*, as also *bali* and *bhāga(-dheya)* appear as the common designations of the land-tax[4]. In the commentaries of our period we find the term being used as the annual land-tax or as a periodical tax levied primarily upon agricultural land over and above the king's normal grain-share often fixed and calculated in the form of cash payment and sometimes as a property-tax, but in most cases associated with villages. Medhātithi[5] paraphrases it as the receipts of commodities (*dravyādānam*). But Kullūka explains it as the tax payable by villagers and townsmen either monthly or in Bhādrapada and Pauṣa. Rāghavānanda restricts it to a monthly payment by villagers. The *Abhidhānarājendra* quotes a text describing villages as liable to the *kara*, from which the towns were immune[6]. Bhaṭṭa-

1 *J.U.P.H.S.*, XXIII. 243.

2 Tr. p. 58.

3 VII. 265—67, 991; VIII. 1970. Cf. Allahabad Pillar Inscription, l.22—*sarvva-kara-dānājñākaraṇa-praṇāmāgamana* etc.

4 *Vaijayantī*, p. 107, l.89; *Abhidhānaratnamālā*, v. 433.

5 On Manu, VIII.307. Rāmacandra explains it as dues paid at military stations—*gulmadāyādikam*. S. K. Maity, *Economic Life in the Gupta period*, p. 59 translates it to mean contribution in the form of grass, wood, etc.

6 s.v., *gāmāgāra*.

svāmin[1] in his commentary on the *Arthaśāstra* defines the term as the annual tax paid during the month of Bhādrapada, Vasanta and the like. Abhayatilaka Gaṇi[2] explains *kara* as the share due to the king by one who has used the royal land for cultivation and grazing, it being payable during the harvesting season in corn. The *Kṛtyakalpataru*[3] describes *kara* as the receipt of fixed money from artisans and cultivators. Sarvajñanārāyaṇa also takes it to mean a fixed payment on land to be made in cash (*bhūminiyataṃ deyaṃ hiraṇyam*). The *Arthaśāstra* text quoted by Kṣīrasvāmin[4] explains it as a charge upon all movable and immovable articles. Haribhadra Sūri in his commentary on the *Kalpasūtra*[5] interprets it as a property tax when describing it as the amount payable every year to the king on every cow and the like.

We find it difficult to choose between these explanations. In any case the appearance of *kara* in the land-grants along with *bhāga* would suggest that here it is not to be translated as the usual land revenue. It might have been a periodical tax over and above the grain-share and was often realised from village people as a fixed amount calculated on the basis of property like land and cows. As has been pointed out[6] the Junagadh rock inscription of Rudradāman[7] also suggests that *kara* was not a part of the regular land-tax but a special oppressive tax like *viṣṭi* (forced labour) and *praṇaya* (emergency tax or benevolence).

Hiraṇya—

Hiraṇya also appears almost universally in the land-grants of the period. It occurs in the legal texts as well. Various interpretations of it have been offered. Often it is translated literally

1 On *Artha*, II. 15 ; *J.B.O.R.S.*, XI, part III, pp. 83—84.

2 *Dvyāśraya Kāvya*, III. 18.

3 *Gṛhastha*, p. 255—*'Karaḥ' kārukṛṣīvalebhyo niyatadhanādānam.*

4 On *Amara*, II. 8.28.

5 p. 253 q. by Pran Nath, *Economic Conditions*, p. 59, f.n. 3—*Karo gavādīn prati prativarṣaṃ rājagrāhyaṃ dravyaṃ.*

6 S. K. Maity, *Economic Life in the Gupta period*, p. 60.

7 *E.I.*, VIII, p. 44.

as gold[1]. Some other suggestions are tax in money[2], payment in money[3] and tax in cash[4]. N. C. Bandyopadhyaya[5] explains it as a tax on the hoard or capital or on the annual income. Beni Prasad[6] interprets it as the right of the state to the gold and probably other mines as well. U. N. Ghoshal[7] proposes to take it as a tax in cash levied upon certain special kinds of crops as distinguished from the tax in kind which was charged upon the ordinary crops, and this view has been generally accepted[8].

Here also we feel that the attempt to seek a uniform meaning for the term in all references, literary and epigraphic alike, creates confusion. Thus the explanation suggested by Ghoshal ill suits the use of the term in the legal works which speak of the king as receiving specific shares of *hiraṇya* along with those of other commodities[9]. Here *hiraṇya* would not be a tax but should be translated as 'gold', which in practice might have meant capital in the form of cash. We would not favour the meaning of 'hoard' or 'mine' for *hiraṇya* as the legal texts discuss the question of king's share in these two separately elsewhere. *Hiraṇya* could not be a tax on gold mines because though the term is found in the inscriptions from almost all parts of northern India we do not think so much gold could have been produced everywhere as to form a regular source of revenue.

In the land-grants where *hiraṇya* has been contrasted with *dhānya* it may mean cash. Likewise where it is used as opposed to *bhāgabhogakara* it is best explained as dues paid in cash. We would suggest that it refers to lump assessment in cash upon villages as distinguished from the king's grain-share assessed

1 Bühler, Jolly, Shamasastry, Meyer, Fleet, R. D. Banerji, D. R. Bhandarkar and N. G. Majumdar referred to by U. N. Ghoshal, *H.R.S.*, p. 60, f.n. 5.

2 Senart, *E.I.*, VII. 61f.

3 Kielhorn, *E.I.*, VII. 160.

4 Vogel, *Antiquities of the Chamba State*, pp. 167—69.

5 *Kauṭilya*, I, pp. 139f.

6 *State in Ancient India*, p. 302.

7 *Hindu Revenue System*, p. 62.

8 D. C. Sircar, *Select Inscriptions*, p. 372, f.n. 7.

9 Gautama, X. 25; Viṣṇu, III. 25; Manu, VII. 130—32; *Agni Purāṇa*, CCXXIII. 27—29.

upon the individual cultivators. As has been rightly noticed by U. N. Ghoshal[1] in some of the Pāla grants *piṇḍaka* has been used in place of *hiraṇya*. *Piṇḍaka* would appear to have been the same as *piṇḍakara* of the *Arthaśāstra*[2] which has been explained by Bhaṭṭasvāmin as comprising taxes levied upon whole villages. The prevalence of this practice is testified to by some inscriptions of Bengal which mention the annual revenue calculated in cash for fields and villages. D. C. Sircar[3] convincingly explains the letters *sāṃ hi* used in this context as being abbreviations of the expression *sāmvatsarika hiraṇya*. The practice would appear to have been known to Sarvajñanārāyaṇa, the commentator of Manu[4], who explains *kara* as the fixed cash to be paid on land (*bhūminiyataṃ deyaṃ hiraṇyam*). In the Mallasarul (Burdwan) grant[5], a little earlier than our period, the list of officers includes *hiraṇya-sāmudāyika* who collected the dues called *hiraṇya*. The suggestion of U. N. Ghoshal that certain crops were taxed in cash appears to be unlikely because in that case we have to postulate separate administrative machinery for realising the revenue from ordinary crops and from crops which were difficult to divide in shares. There is however no such difficulty if we accept the explanation suggested here. The parallel case of officers known as *āgrahārika* who supervised *agrahāra* villages would go to support our suggestion that *hiraṇyasāmudāyika* was the officer who collected the lump revenue in cash from villages so assessed.

Udraṅga and uparikara—

In the grants of the Gupta and post-Gupta periods the terms *udraṅga* and *uparikara* are of frequent occurrence. In our period we find them mostly confined to western India[6]. These two

1 *H.R.S.*, pp. 244f.

2 II. 15.

3 *E.I.*, XXX, p. 55.

4 VIII. 307.

5 *E.I.*, XXIII. 159ff.

6 *J.B.B.R.A.S.*, XX, no. 9; *I.A.*, XIV, pp. 196ff; Chinchani Plates of the Arab feudatory Sugatipa—*J. N. Banerjea Volume*, pp. 96ff; feudatories of the Pratihāra king Mahendrapāla—*E.I.*, IX, no. 1 (A and B); Hansot Plates of Bhartṛvaḍḍha III—*E.I.*, XII. 197.

fiscal terms generally appear together, thereby creating the impression that they have been used antithetically. But there are instances where these terms have been used separately. Thus in a grant of the Pratihāra chief Mathanadeva[1] and in some of the grants of the Rāṣṭrakūṭas[2] we find only *udraṅga*, whereas the grants of the Pālas[3] and the Paramāras[4] mention only *uparikara*.

Despite desparate attempts[5] to explain these terms there has been no satisfactory suggestion hitherto. U. N. Ghoshal[6] interprets *udraṅga* as the tax levied on permanent tenants and *uparikara* as the tax on temporary cultivators. We have elsewhere suggested that *udraṅga* and *uparikara* may be equated with *kḷipta* and *upakḷipta* of other records[7]. *Kḷipta* is known to have been used in the *Arthaśāstra*[8] in the sense of a fixed tax. *Upakḷipta* may therefore mean an extra cess on the cultivators over and above the fixed revenue of the state[9]. A. S. Altekar[10] equates *udraṅga* and

---

1 *E.I.*, III, no. 36.

2 *E.I.*, I, no. 8 ; VII, no. 6.

3 U. N. Ghoshal, *H.R.S.*, p. 243.

4 Ibid., p. 260. Also Mandhata Plates of Devapāla—*E.I.*, IX. 108 –13 ; Ratnagiri Plates of Somavaṃśī Karṇa—*E.I.*, XXXIII. 266—68.

5 S. K. Maity, *Economic Life in the Gupta period* p. 62 suggests either that *udraṅga* may be the same as *draṅga* and is a sort of police tax levied on the district, for the maintenance of the local police station or that it is connected with *udaka* and to be interpreted as a water-tax. But these attempts based on the slender similarity in sound do not carry us far. A still better suggestion of the same type would be to equate it with *utsaṅga* in the *Arthaśāstra*, II. 15 which has been defined by Bhaṭṭasvāmin as what is paid by the inhabitants of the city and country-part on the occasion of some festive event such as the birth of a prince.

6 pp. 210f. D. C. Sircar, *Select Inscriptions*, p. 371, f.n. 5 explains *udraṅga* in this fashion but differs as regards *uparikara*. Fleet (*C.I.I.*, III, p. 98, f.n. 1), Hoernle (*J.A.S.B.*, LXVI, pp. 128f) and B. K. Barua (*Cultural History of Assam*, I, pp. 81f) explain *uparikara* as a tax on cultivators who have no proprietary rights in the soil.

7 *J.I.H.*, XXXVIII. 587—88.

8 II. 6.

9 In the *Kṛtyakalpataru*, *Vyavahāra*, pp. 535f *upakḷipta* has been explained as objects which have been made fit for being consumed ("*upakḷiptāni*" *upayoga-yogyatām nītāni*). It may therefore refer to *bhoga* of other grants

uparikara respectively with *bhāgakara* and *bhogakara* into which he splits the expression *bhāgabhogakara*. V. V. Mirashi[1] holds that *udraṅga* and *uparikara* correspond both to *kḷipta* and *upakḷipta* and to *bhāga* and *bhoga*.

Though *udraṅga* and *uparikara* are generally not used with *bhāga* and *bhoga* there are some cases where they are so used. This weakens the suggestion that the two pairs of terms are synonymous. We may, however, suggest that these antithetical groups of *udraṅga* and *uparikara*, *bhāga* and *bhoga* and *dhānya* and *hiraṇya* were overlapping in their import and referred to the land revenue and allied state income from slightly different standpoints. The composer of the grants, in order to convey the idea of the full rights of the owners, sometimes used these terms together.

However, the possibility cannot be ruled out that *udraṅga* and *uparikara* refer to two specific additional state impositions whose nature cannot now be determined[2]. Thus we see that the Mallasarul grant referred to earlier[3] includes in its list an officer called *audraṅgika*, who must have been charged with the realisation of this impost. The formation of the term *uparikara* would in any case indicate that it was an extra tax charged over and above the land revenue (*upari* means upon, extra or super). The oppressive character of this impost is testified to by certain inscriptions of our period from Assam[4]. Thus, the grants of

---

which is generally explained as the periodical supply of flowers, fruits, vegetable, grass etc.

10 *Rāshṭrakūṭas and their times*, pp. 214f. D. Sharma, *Early Chauhān Dynasties*, p. 211 holds that *bhoga* and *udraṅga* are synonymous, but not *bhoga* and *uparikara* as both are used together in a record. However, the contention that *udraṅga* and *bhāga* are never used together in inscriptions is not justified. See *C.I.I.*, III, no. 39 ; *J. N. Banerjea Volume*, pp. 96—109 ; *E.I.*, IX, no. 1 (A and B).

1 *C.I.I.*, IV, p. cxli.

2 It has been suggested that these refer to two kinds of very common additional impositions on the excess income of the people, to be paid in cash or kind—*P.I.H.C.*, XIX. 93. But unfortunately the summary is silent about the grounds for this view.

3 *E.I.*, XXIII. 159ff.

4 U. N. Ghoshal, *H.R.S.*, p. 248

Ratnapāla and Indrapāla include *uparikara* tax among the oppressions from which the land is exempted, while in a grant of Balavarman the officer charged with the *uparikara* tax is mentioned in the list of oppressors who were not to enter the land granted[1].

Daśāparādha—

Another fiscal term which is very common in the grants of our period is *daśāparādha* sometimes mentioned as *daśāparādha-daṇḍa*[2], *daṇḍadaśāparādha*[3] and *daśāpacāra*[4].

U. N. Ghoshal[5] explains the term as the right of a donee to be exempted at least in part from the ordinary penalties for the commission of some traditional offences by the villagers. The suggestion would not be applicable to all land-grants but only to those of the Senas[6] and some other kings in Bengal[7] in which the form of the expression is *sahyadaśāparādha* (with toleration for ten offences). From the commentary of Haribhadra Sūri on the *Kalpasūtra*[8] we learn of the exemption granted from the complete or partial payment of fines for offences.

We have seen elsewhere that in general the term is to be explained as meaning the right to the fine realised for ten offences committed by the villagers[9]. It is interesting to note that U. N. Ghoshal[10] himself admits that the phrase undoubtedly stands for

1 L. D. Barnett treats *uparikara* as analogous to the Tamil *melvaram* (the crown's share of produce) as *mel*=Skt. *upari*—*J.R.A.S.*, 1931, p. 165. V. V. Mirashi, *C.I.I.*, IV, p. cxli makes it an additional tax which may have included the miscellaneous taxes in kind paid by traders and artisans.

2 *E.I.*, II. 359–61 grant of Govindacandra.

3 *E.I.*, IX, no. 1 (A and B) grant of feudatories of Madanapāla.

4 *E.I.*, XV. 295—8—grant of Vigrahapāla III.

5 *H.R.S.*, pp. 219f.

6 Ibid., p. 264.

7 *E.I.*, XXX. 262—63.

8 p. 253 q. by Pran Nath, *Economic Conditions*, p. 59, f.n. 3—*Adaṃḍa kodaṃḍimaṃ = Daṇḍo yathāparādha-rājagrāhyam dhanaṃ, kudaṇḍo mahatyaparādhe alpaṃ rājagrāhyaṃ dhanaṃ tābhyāṃ rahitām.*

9 *J.I.H.*, XXXVIII, pp. 589f.

10 Loc. cit., p. 220.

a kind of income accruing to the king from the villages, since it is included along with the contributions in grain and in domestic animals in a list of the king's receipts (*utpatti*) in the Cambay grant of the Rāṣṭrakūṭa Govinda IV[1]. Its position in the grant, its form as *sadaśāparādha* and not as *adaśāparādha* and the fact of its being granted even to institutions like temples[2] and not merely to individuals suggest that it does not refer to an immunity from the fines to certain offences but to a positive right in the form of income from the fines imposed on villagers for committing any of the ten offences. As rightly pointed out by P. V. Kane[3] no king would ever think of exempting donees in pious grants or the villages in those grants from the results of such grave offences as the murder of a woman, adultery, theft and abortion.

Similar rights of income in the shape of receipts from fines are granted to the donees in the land-grants of the Candellas[4], the Kalacuris[5] and the Rāṣṭrakūṭas[6]. The Bombay Secretariat grant of Caulukya king Ajayapāla[7] has a more graphic expression meaning the receipts from the fines for offences (*daṇḍa-doṣa-prāptādāya*). In the fragmentary grant of Govinda IV from Ujjain[8] we have a very clear reference to the fines inflicted on the commission of ten offences being granted along with other incomes. From the *Lekhapaddhati*[9] we learn that in farming out a village the overlord reserved for himself the income from five specified offences. The term *daśāparādha* would refer to the transfer to the donee of similar rights to receive fines from certain offences.

B. C. Mazumdar[10] holds that the term implies the donee's right of jurisdiction over the offences committed. In all these

1 *E.I.*, VII, p. 36.
2 *C.I.I.*, III, no. 46.
3 *History of Dharmaśāstra*, III. 264—66.
4 *I.A.*, XVI, p. 201.
5 *E.I.*, II, no. 23—*daṇḍadāyakarotpatti.*
6 *I.A.*, XIX, p. 165.
7 *I.A.*, XVIII. 80.
8 *E.I.*, XXIII. 106—8—*sa-vṛkṣamālāku(laṃ) sa-dhānyahiraṇyadeyaṃ daṇḍadoṣanda(=da)śāparādhaṃ samasto(tpa)ttiśulkotpattisahitaṃ.*
9 pp. 12, 16 (for the specification of the fines).
10 *J.B.O.R.S.*, 1916, p. 53, f.n.

grants the villagers residing in the village granted are asked by the king to obey the orders (*ājñā-śravaṇa*) of the donee. But this cannot be construed to refer to the orders passed in dealing with suits. At most it stands for occasional services rendered to the donee. We know that the Indian legal tradition did not grant *śreṇī* and *gaṇa* tribunals jurisdiction to sit in judgment over cases of violent crime (*sāhasa*)[1]. It would be quite opposed to this tradition if we postulate that any private individual was given such a right. The inscriptions of the Pālas[2] and a grant of Lalitāsuradeva from Kumaon[3] mention an officer called *daśāparādhika*. It may be suggested that this officer was authorised to deal with cases falling under *daśāparādha* and the donee was entitled only to the fines imposed for the commission of the ten offences.

There has been some speculation about the ten offences coming under the term. Būhler[4] had conjectured that the ten faults refer to the ten actions about land possible under the *sīmāvivāda prakaraṇa*. But the use of the term *aparādha* refers to offences of a more serious nature. Fleet[5] took the term to refer to a classification in the *Dharmasindhusāra*[6] of Kāśīnāthopādhyāya and *Aṣṭāṅgahṛdaya*[7] of Vāgbhaṭa of three specified sins of the body, three of the mind, and four of speech. But, as has been rightly pointed out[8], it is highly improbable that the offences of the mind are made the subject of legal punishment.

Jolly[9] enumerated the ten crimes after Nārada[10], who gives them as disobedience to the king's order, murder of a woman, intermixture of the castes, adultery, theft, pregnancy from one not the husband, abuse and defamation, obscenity, assault, and abortion.

1 P. V. Kane, *History of Dharmaśāstra*, III. 264—66.
2 E. g., *E.I.*, XVII, p. 321 ; *I.A.*, XV, p. 306.
3 *I.A.*, XXV, p. 18.
4 *I.A.*, V, p. 115, f.n. 3.
5 *C.I.I.*, III, p. 189, f.n. 4.
6 II. 19ff.
7 *Sūtrasthāna*, ch. 1, vv. 21f (Bombay, 1880, p. 38).
8 Beni Prasad, *State in Ancient India*, p. 303.
9 *Hindu Law and Customs*, pp. 268, 70.
10 I. 11ff.

The list with some differences is also attributed to Saṃvarta[1]. The *Śukranīti*[2] also mentions the ten offences in the form given by Nārada.

But Hiralal[3] identified the ten *aparādhas* of the inscriptions with ten sins enumerated in another passage of the *Śukranīti*[4]. But this is not sound because the second list is of moral sins, several of which are obviously outside the reach of the law, whereas the first list which is also found in Nārada enumerates ten *aparādhas* or offences which were met with fine.

Beni Prasad[5] is in favour of interpreting *daśāparādha* in the sense of judicial fines in general. This suggestion would seem to be likely because, as we have seen, in the land-grants of some of the dynasties we have reference to the right to the receipts from fines in general in place of those from ten offences. Then the list of the ten offences practically covers all important crimes. But the very fact that *daśāparādha* and not some term covering fines in general has been mentioned would suggest that the right was restricted only to ten specified offences.

Taxes in the Gāhaḍavāla kingdom— Pravaṇikara—

In the land-grants of the Gāhaḍavāla kings we find long lists of fiscal terms, some of which do not appear elsewhere and have baffling forms difficult to explain. Of these *pravaṇikara* would appear to have been a very common and important item of revenue being mentioned in nineteen out of the twenty-one grants of the dynasty recovered from Kamauli[6]. Outside the Gāhaḍavāla empire the expression occurs only in a grant of a Somavaṃśī king of Trikaliṅga.[7] However, the grants of the Kalacuris of Tripuri[8]

1 q. by *Smṛticandrikā*, II, p. 28.
2 IV. 5. 161—64.
3 *E.I.*, IX, p. 47, f.n. 1.
4 III. 6.
5 *State in Ancient India*, p. 303.
6 *E.I.*, IV, no. 11.
7 *E.I.*, XI, no. 14.
8 *C.I.I.*, IV, pp. 324—31, 645—52.

sometimes mention *pravaṇi* as one of the items of state income transferred to the donee.

R. S. Tripathi[1] suggests that *pravaṇikara* was either a tax on turnpikes, intended to preserve the peace of the village by discouraging the advent of large numbers of visitors or a tax for the upkeep of the road. This is a possible interpretation, as *pravaṇa* means road-crossing (*catuṣpatha*). But we have to account for the substitution of *i* for *a* in *pravaṇa*.

R. Niyogi[2] has suggested that it was the tax paid for the services of the state guides posted in every village, whose duty probably was to escort and guide the merchants from the interior of the country to the highway crossing leading to the next village or town. This interpretation is far-fetched and such a tax would not appear to have been so important as would follow from its frequent occurrence in the land-grants.

U. N. Ghoshal[3] suggests it to be a tax on *pravaṇis* whom he describes as some class of merchants. Leumann[4] takes *pravaṇi* to mean a retail dealer or perhaps a second hand dealer. Mirashi[5] suggests that it means a banker (*śreṣṭhin*). In the Rajor inscription of Mathanadeva[6] *pravaṇi* follows *vaṇik* (merchant) in the list of villagers addressed. We would favour the suggestion made by U. N. Ghoshal[7] that *pravaṇikara* was analogous to the toll or *śulka* of the technical literature and inscriptions. The prominence of *pravaṇikara* in the list of incomes granted in the Gāhaḍavāla and Kalacuri records also supports the suggestion. In both cases *pravaṇikara* or *pravaṇi* is mentioned at the top of the list second only to *bhāgabhogakara* or *bhāgakara*. We have seen that

1 *History of Kanauj*, p. 348. See also R. Niyogi, *History of the Gāhaḍavāla Dynasty*, p. 176.

2 R. Niyogi, Loc. cit., p. 176.

3 *H.R.S.*, p. 263.

4 *E.I.*, III, Additions and Corrections, p. viii.

5 *C.I.I.*, IV. 324—31.

6 *E.I.*, III. 266—67.

7 *H.R.S.*, p. 263.

in the Gāhaḍavāla records from Kamauli[1] *pravaṇikara* occurs more frequently than the other minor taxes and is second only to *bhāga-bhogakara*. In the grant of a Somavaṃśī king referred to above *pravaṇikara* is one of the two taxes mentioned, the other being *kṣetrakara*. The interpretation of *pravaṇikara* as toll (*śulka*) would be further supported by the fact that none of these inscriptions having *pravaṇikara* or *pravaṇi* mentions *śulka*, which is prominently mentioned in other records as an important and common source of state income.

Turuṣkadaṇḍa—

The term *turuṣkadaṇḍa* is found exclusively in the land-grants of the Gāhaḍavāla dynasty. It was levied by Candradeva, the first real founder of the dynasty; it appears in the first land-grant of the family dated A.D. 1090 and continues to appear in the records of Madanacandra, Govindacandra and Vijayacandra. But it is not to be found in the grants of Jayaccandra and his son Hariścandra, suggesting thereby that it was abolished by Jayaccandra[2].

An early suggestion[3] to interpret *turuṣkadaṇḍa* as a tax on aromatic reeds finds no support among modern scholars. The existing theories have been elaborately discussed by R. Niyogi[4].

Some scholars[5] hold that this tax was realised to make annual payments of tribute to the Sultān of Ghazni and that to enforce the regular payment of this tribute the Muslims from time to time led expeditions against northern India. But there is no definite proof to establish the domination of the Ghaznavides over the Gāhaḍavālas in any period of their history. The identification of Cānd Rāi, who helped Mahmūd, with Candradeva is doubtful. In any case the records of the Gāhaḍavālas show that from A.D. 1091 onwards Candradeva was an independent ruler. The continuance of the tax in later reigns when the dynasty had reached

1 *E.I.*, XI, no. 14.
2 R. Niyogi, Op. cit., pp. 177—78.
3 *J.A.S.B.*, LVI, p. 113.
4 Op. cit., pp. 176—81.
5 C. V. Vaidya, *History of Medieval Hindu India*, III, p. 211; D. C. Ganguly in *Struggle for Empire*, p. 51.

glorious heights would ill suit the suggestion that it was reminiscent of their earlier subordinate status. In the Muslim accounts Ala-ud-daulah is said to have defeated but released on payment of a large sum of money Malhi, king of Kanauj, who is identified with Madanacandra. But a parallel victory over the Turks has been claimed by Govindacandra in the reign of his father Madanacandra. Not only Govindacandra but also his son Vijayacandra claim to have repulsed the attacks of the Muslims. As has been pointed out, "even the Turki claim does not go so far as payment of tributes regularly at stated intervals by the Gāhaḍavālas. Had a tax been levied specifically to pay the tribute to the Turks, why should there be fresh attacks again and again?'[1]

Following V. A. Smith[2] scholars generally interpret the term to mean the tax levied to meet the cost of resisting the Turkish invaders[3]. Altekar[4] refers to a similar tax levied by the Coḷa king Vīrarājendra to finance his war against the Cāḷukyas of Veṅgi. R. Niyogi[5] demonstrates how this interpretation suits the known history of this tax. It is argued that after the establishment of the strong Cāhamāna power between the Gāhaḍavāla and Turk dominions and in view of the increasing weakness of the later Yāminī Sultāns Jayaccandra thought that the Turuṣka menace was over and abolished the tax, for which he found no justification.

But this suggestion does not explain the absence of the tax in the records of the closing years of the reign of Jayaccandra and also the reign of his son Hariścandra. In this period the Turuṣka menace was really overwhelming the empire and the revival of the old tax had every justification. Another objection would be that

1 B. P. Mazumdar, *Socio-Economic History*, p. 127, f.n.

2 *Early History of India* (4th ed.), p. 400, f.n.

3 U. N. Ghoshal, *H.R.S.*, p. 263; A. S. Altekar, *State and Government*, p. 277; K. V. R. Aiyangar, *Kṛtyakalpataru*, *Rājadharma*, Introduction, p. 53, f.n. 1; R. Niyogi, Op. cit., pp. 180—81.

4 Loc. cit. Following S. Levi, U. N. Ghoshal, loc. cit., p. 233 proposes a similar interpretation for *mallakara* mentioned in the records of the Licchavi kings.

5 Loc. cit.

if the tax was meant to raise funds to fight the menace of the Turks there was not much propriety in granting it to a brāhmaṇa[1]. The donor king could very well have transferred other state dues to the donee and retained the *turuṣkadaṇḍa* for himself. We know from records of some such dues or state receipts which the king did not grant to the donee as they were meant to fulfil certain specific tasks like the one contemplated for the *turuṣkadaṇḍa*[2].

We would suggest that the term stood for a tax collected from the Turuṣka settlers in the kingdom. This explanation was originally offered by Sten Konow[3] and has received occasional support from scholars[4].

The initial objection raised against the view is that *daṇḍa* or fine is a penal measure and cannot technically be described as a tax[5]. But we do have some references where *daṇḍa* has been used in the general sense of a tax. R. Niyogi herself quotes a Yādava inscription[6] in which *daṇḍa* means a contribution which is not a penalty. Likewise we have *suvarṇṇadaṇḍa*, *ahidaṇḍa* and *vartmadaṇḍa* in the Kelga Plates of Someśvaradeva[7] and *hastidaṇḍa*, *baladaṇḍa* and *bandhadaṇḍa* in the Ratnagiri Plates of Somavaṃśī Karṇa[8]. In the *Rājanītiratnākara*[9] *daṇḍa* has been used in connection with the dues and tributes which a feudatory pays to

1 This objection is all the more applicable against the first theory discussed above which seeks to explain the term as tribute collected for the Sultān of Ghazni.

2 *Coravarjjam, cauravarjjam* or *coradrohakavarjjam*. See *J.I.H.*, XXXVIII. 590f. See D. Sharmā, *Early Chauhān Dynasties*, p. 187, II, for an epigraphic reference that *balādhipābhāvya* was not transferred to the grantee by the original donor of a village.

3 *E.I.*, IX, p. 321.

4 B. P. Mazumdar, *Socio-Economic History*, p. 126.

5 R. Niyogi, Op. cit., p. 179.

6 *I.A.*, XIV, p. 318—*vasati-daṇḍa-prayāṇa-daṇḍau.*

7 *E.I.*, XXVIII. 324—6.

8 *E.I.*, XXXIII. 266—8.

9 p. 4—*Adhīśvaro dvividhaḥ śauryyādakarah samrādanugrahādakaraḥ. Ādyaḥ svecchayaiva daṇḍādi dadāti. Dvitīyopyanugrahāt.* Cf. *Triṣaṣṭiśalākāpurusacarita*, IV. 24—*diśodaṇḍaḥ*.

his overlord. In the commentary of Medhātithi[1] the term *daṇḍa* at one place is explained as intended to include taxes (*kara*), tolls (*śulka*) and the like.

The geographical references in the land-grants indicate that the *turuṣkadaṇḍa* was collected from all parts of the Gāhaḍavāla dominion[2]. It has therefore been argued that if the term is to be explained as a fine collected from the Turuṣka prisoners, we have to make the unlikely presumption that in many villages even in the remote parts of the Gāhaḍavāla dominion Turuṣka prisoners were billetted in considerable numbers[3]. But the objection is not much to the point There is no need to restrict the scope of the tax to prisoners only. It was realised from Turuṣkas in general. As regards the geographical distribution of the Turuṣka population it may be said that the fiscal terms are in the form of set formulae of the important sources of state income and it does not necessarily mean that all these taxes were equally important for each village granted. Moreover, as we have seen[4], there are many indications that Muslim population in the Gāhaḍavāla kingdom was by no means insignificant. Besides this Muslim merchants were also frequenting northern India.

Sten Konow[5] had described *turuṣkadaṇḍa* as a Hindu Jizya. Scholars find it difficult to reconcile this description of the tax with the Indian tradition of extreme tolerance of other religions[6]. There is however nothing improbable about such a punitive tax. Several inscriptions from southern India, of which the earliest is the grant of Siṃhavarman Pallava (c. A.D. 450) and the latest the Guḍihalli inscription dated 1346[7], mention the Ājīvika tax along with other

1 On Manu, IX. 323—*Daṇḍagrahaṇaṃ karaśulkādīnāmapi pradarśanārthaṃ vyācakṣate.*

2 R. Niyogi, Op. cit., p. 177.

3 Ibid., p. 179.

4 See infra Chapter VI

5 Op. cit.

6 R. Niyogi, Op. cit., p. 179.

7 A. L. Basham, *History and Doctrines of the Ājīvikas*, pp. 187—90.

general taxes which accompanied the grant of a village and which was a special tax on the Ājīvika laymen, the Ājīvikas appearing to have been held in general disfavour[1]. In two of these inscriptions[2] the Ājīvika poll-tax is referred to in close association with the tax on the Uvaccas. Significantly enough the term Uvaccas is sometimes used in Tamil for Muslim settlers, and Hultzsch interpreted it in this sense[3].

We however feel that the motive was not religious antagonism alone but mostly economic considerations. We have elsewhere[4] suggested that the Pratihāra kings imposed checks and restrictions to discourage the influx of Muslim merchants. It is quite possible that the Gāhaḍavālas followed this policy but did not impose a total ban on them and imposed a tax on them which must have provided a valuable source of income.

The last objection that has been raised against this interpretation of the term is that it does not explain the discontinuance of the tax from the beginning of the reign of Jayaccandra[5]. We may suggest that it was to appease the Turks that Jayaccandra and his son abolished this tax.

Kumaragadiāṇaka—

Recently there have been some attempts to explain the fiscal term which appears in the Gāhaḍavāla grants as *kumaragadiāṇaka* or with slight variations in spelling as *kumaragadiaṇaka*, *kumaragadiyaṇaka* or *kumāragadiaṇaka*[6]. Thus, B. P. Mazumdar[7] suggests that it was a tax in gold coins known as *kumāragadyāna*. But there is no other indication of the existence of coins of this name.

---

1 Ibid., pp. 191f.

2 Tiruvorriyur inscription (dated 1223) of the reign of Rājarāja III—A. L. Basham, loc. cit., p. 188, no. 6—*Ācuvikaḷ-pērāṟ-kācu* and *Uvaccarpēṟāṟ-kuṭi-k-kācum*; Padavedu inscription dated 1259—A. L. Basham, loc. cit., p. 189, no. 10—*Uvaccaṉ-per-k-kaṭamai* and *Ācuvikāṉ-per-k-kaṭamai*.

3 *S.I.I.*, I, p. 82, n. 4.

4 See infra Chapter VI.

5 R. Niyogi, Op. cit., p. 180.

6 Ibid., p. 183.

7 *Socio-Economic History*, p. 237.

On the basis of a south Indian inscription, which speaks of land under the *kumari* cultivation by the hill tribes[1], R. Niyogi[2] suggests that it was the tax imposed on land under *kumri* cultivation carried on in some places in the hill areas and the forest tracts in the Gāhaḍavāla kingdom, and that the Gāhaḍavālas adopted this tax from south India, where the cultivators were required to pay an amount equal to one *gadyāṇaka* for some specified measure, and even retained the south Indian coin name *gadyāṇaka*. But the references to this tax indicate that it was one of the important items of state income, in any case not so insignificant as is implied by the interpretation proposed above. It does not appear that *kumari* or *kumri* cultivation was so widely resorted to in the Gāhaḍavāla kingdom as to become a common tax. Further, it is to be noted that the form of the first part of the expression is *kumara* and in some cases *kumāra*. *Kumāra* means a prince and *kumara* represents the intermediate stage in the transformation of *kumāra* into *kumvara* or *kuṁara*.

In the stray plate from Nanana (Marwar)[3] belonging to the twelfth century we have an interesting reference to a due which has been called both *kumaradroṇa* and *kumāradroṇa*. This plate would suggest that the dues realised for the *kumāra* or prince were not confined, as is generally supposed, to the Gāhaḍavāla empire but were found elsewhere with only this difference that whereas in other states they were generally determined in kind, the Gāhaḍavālas collected them in cash. This plate helps us in determining the nature of the due. It records that out of the *kumaradroṇas* of wheat realised from the water-machine (*araghaṭṭa*) at a certain village five *droṇas* were allotted to a certain temple-dancer (*mehari*). It would appear that the tax had a more regular character than is implied when it is explained as a present or *nazrānā* of a *gadyāṇaka* on the birth of a prince[4]. U. N. Ghoshal[5] suggests that it was a

1 *E.C.*, X, pp. 86ff.

2 Op. cit., p. 183. It has been claimed that the *Yuktikalpataru* (p. 6) explains the *kumari* or *kumri* cultivation as shifty (*sic*) cultivation. But we fear that the reference given contains no such information.

3 *E.I.*, XXXIII.244-45 (ll.2-8, 10-16).

4 V. V. Mirashi in *J.N.S.I.*, VII. 29.

5 H.R.S., p. 294.

tax on behalf of the royal princes at the rate of so much per *gadyāṇaka*. But the analogy of the *kumaradroṇas* in the stray plate would indicate that *gadyāṇaka* like *droṇas* stood for the actual tax realised. In this plate the tax on behalf of the *kumāra* realised from the water-machine would seem to have been more than five *droṇas*. The tax of the Gāhaḍavāla grants may be suggested to have been one *gadyāṇaka* per family annually. Though *kumāra* means prince[1] it is not unlikely that the tax was by way of present to members of the royal family in general.

Kūṭaka—

Kūṭaka also appears only in the land-grants of the Gāhaḍavālas. B. P. Mazumdar[2] explains it as a tax on each *kūṭaka* weight of a commodity. But we find the suggestion of R. Niyogi[3] to be better. If the reading *kuṭaka* found in some records is to be accepted then it refers to a tax on houses, since according to the dictionaries *kuṭa* means a house. But the more usual spelling is *kūṭaka*[4] and it may be taken to stand for a plough-tax because *kūṭa* means a plough and *kūṭaka* a ploughshare. In the *Maināmati* songs a plough-tax is mentioned as only a pice and a half per plough a month[5]. The earliest epigraphic reference to a plough-tax (*halikākara*) is found in the grants of the Uccakalpas[6].

Jalakara—

Jalakara[7] has been mentioned in a few inscriptions of the Gāhaḍavālas beginning with the Gagaha inscription of Govinda-

1 The editor of the plate from Nanana had taken *kumara* as the name of the lessee of the *araghaṭṭa* who used to pay the annual rent for it in wheat—*E.I.*, XXXIII.241.

2 *Socio-Economic History*, p. 233. U.N. Ghoshal, *H.R.S.*, p. 294 leaves the term unexplained.

3 Op. cit., p. 183.

4 In the Allahabad Museum Plate of Govindacandra (*E.I.*, XXXIII. 178-80) *kūḍī* is obviously a mistake for *kūṭaka*.

5 T. C. Dasgupta, *Aspects of Bengali Society*, p. 268.

6 U. N. Ghoshal, *H.R.S.*, p. 213. Cf. *sahala* in the Rithapur plates of Bhavattavarman—*E.I.*, XIX.102f.

7 There is no justification for the emendation *jātakara* proposed by Kielhorn, *E.I.*, IV. 117-20.

candra dated A.D. 1142[1]. On the basis of the expression *samatsyā-kara* included in the list of rights accompanying the grant R. Niyogi[2] says that fish was a source of revenue in this period and hence takes *jalakara* as a tax on the produce of water, fish for example. But we would prefer the more obvious interpretation of the term as irrigation cess. We may point out that *sajala* also appears in the list of rights transferred to the donee and hence water was also a source of revenue.

Gokara—

Gokara is also mentioned in those among the Gāhaḍavāla grants which refer to *jalakara*[3]. There have been several speculations about the precise nature of this tax on cows. Generally on the analogy of the tax called *naḷḷa* or good cows in south Indian inscriptions[4] it is taken to be a tax on the breeding of cows[5]. The *Arthaśāstra*[6] recommends such a tax during a financial crisis. On the basis of the reference to taxes on the sale and tending of cattle in the *Arthaśāstra*[7], R. Niyogi[8] has suggested the possibility of *gokara* being a tax on the sale of cows in the villages. The alternative interpretation offered by R. S. Tripathi[9] is that it was the charge covering grazing rights. B. P. Mazumdar[10], relying on a *Śukranīti*[11] passage which forbids the king from collecting taxes on the milk of cows and rice for family consumption, describes *gokara* as a tax on the milk of cows. It is very difficult to choose between these suggestions. We must also consider the possibility that *gokara* was a general cattle-tax like the *paśu* of the Candella inscription. The legal works postulate a tax on cattle at the rate of 1/5[12].

---

1 R. Niyogi, Op. cit., p. 173.
2 Ibid., pp. 173f.
3 R. Niyogi, Op. cit., p. 173.
4 Gupta, *Land System*, p. 363.
5 R. S. Tripathi in *I.H.Q.*, IX.129.
6 V.2.
7 II. 29-30.
8 Op. cit., p. 174.
9 *I.H.Q.*, IX. 129.
10 *Socio-Economic History*, p. 237.
11 IV. 2. 127.
12 U.N. Ghoshal, *H.R.S.*, pp. 60f.

Valadī—

The Rohan grant of Govindacandra dated A.D. 1108[1] refers to a tax named *valadī* . B. P. Mazumdar[2] takes it to mean a tax for recruitment of the army. But the form of the term is not *valādi* but *valadī*. *Balada* in Hindi is derived from Sanskrit *vardda* and means a bullock[3]. The *Uktivyaktiprakaraṇa*[4] of Dāmodara Paṇḍita, associated with the Gāhaḍavāla court, uses *valada* as meaning a bullock. Now, there can be many possible explanations of the word as a fiscal term. R. Niyogi[5] suggests it to be a tax on the breeding of bulls like the *naḷḷeruḍu* (good bull) of south Indian inscriptions[6]. It is also likely that it has been used in place of the *gokara* of other grants. B. N. S. Yadav[7] takes it as a special tax on plough-bullocks. Another possibility is to interpret it in line with *āpāramparabalīvaddagabaṇam* of the grant of Pallava Śiva-skandavarman[8] as the right to have from the villagers bullocks in relays for transport.

Lavaṇakara—

Lavaṇakara, mentioned only in the Machlishahr grant of Hariścandra dated A.D. 1195[9], may be explained as the tax on the private manufacture of salt which from the list of rights transferred to the donee in the Gāhaḍavāla grants is known to have been a state monopoly[10].

---

1 *I.A.*, XVIII.17.

2 *Socio-Economic History*, p. 235. U. N. Ghoshal, *H.R.S.*, p.299 leaves it unexplained.

3 *Bhāṣā Śabda Koṣa* ed. Ramāśaṅkara Śukla 'Rasāla', s. v. *balada*. See also *Saṃkṣipta Hindī Śabda Sāgara* ed. Rāmacaṃdra Varmā, s.v., *balada*.

4 p. 40, l.6-*rāḍa valada joḍa* (=*raḍḍo balīvarddān joḍayati*). Cf. *Dohākośa*, p. 361 (XVI.4).

5 Op. cit., p. 183.

6 Gupta, *Land System*, p. 333.

7 *Some Aspects of Society in Northern India in the 12th century* A.D. (Thesis approved for the D.Phil. degree of the University of Allahabad), p. 291, f.n.1.

8 *Select Inscriptions*, pp. 437ff.

9 E.I.. X. 95.

10 Cf. *sa-loha-lavaṇākaraḥ*.

Parṇakara—

Parṇakara also appears only in the above-mentioned Mach'i-shahr grant. It may be taken to refer to the tax on the collection of grass and wood. But *parṇa* meaning leaves is not a happy term for grass and wood. We wonder if it could have been a tax on betel leaves.

Daśabandha—

Daśabandha is mentioned in two Gāhaḍavāla inscriptions[1]. In Manu[2] the term is used for a fine on witnesses, of loans of money, who do not appear. In the *Arthaśāstra*[3] it means the share of one-tenth of the produce given by a landlord to a cultivator or labourer. K. A. N. Sastri[4] prefers to interpret this term as it appears in the inscriptions of south India to refer to the ear-marking for a specified public purpose of one-tenth of a given source of revenue[5]. In the Gāhaḍavāla grants the term appears to have been used as a tax of one-tenth of the income. This would be supported by the Cāhamāna inscription from Nadol dated 1143[6] which records that a certain *rāṇaka* exempted the dancing girls of a temple from paying *daśabandha*. It is interesting to note that the *Lekhapaddhati*[7] records the sale of a horse in which the *daśabandha* to be paid actually amounts to one-tenth of the price.

Akṣapaṭalaprastha, pratīhāraprastha and viśatiaṭhūprastha—

The Basahi plate of *mahārājaputra* Govindacandra[8] mentions three fiscal terms *akṣapaṭalaprastha*, *pratīhāraprastha* and *viśatia-ṭhūprastha*. U. N. Ghoshal[9] took these terms as referring to

1 Basahi grant of A.D. 1103—*I.A.*, XIV. 103; Kamauli (Banaras) grant of A.D. 1104—*E.I.*, II.260. R. Niyogi, Op. cit., p. 170 does not take any notice of the second reference.

2 VIII.107.

3 (Tr.) p.200.

4 In Yazdani, *Early History of the Deccan*, p. 414. Cf. Gupta, *Land System*, p. 222.

5 *I.A.*, XXX, p. 267, f.n.2.

6 *D.H.N.I.*, II. 1113.

7 p. 13.

8 *I.A.*, XIV. 103.

9 *H.R.S.*, p. 296.

contributions of so much per *prastha* payable by the villagers on account of the officers concerned. B. P. Mazumdar[1] explains *viśatiaṭhūprastha* as a tax on each *prasthaka* weight of commodity and *pratīhāraprasthaka* as a tax collected on some commodities by the *pratīhāra.* But the similarity in the form of the three expressions would suggest that they have a similar meaning and we would agree with U. N. Ghoshal that these refer to the contributions made to these three officers. This is clear from the form *akṣapaṭalādāya* which we find in another grant of *mahārājaputra* Govindacandra dated 1109[2]. *Akṣapaṭala* and *pratīhāra* refer respectively to the officer in charge of records and accounts and the doorkeeper or the head of the palace guards. It is difficult to determine the officer denoted by the term *viśatiaṭhū.* It has been suggested[3] that he may be the officer in charge of the revenue collection of 28 villages and that the expression *viṃśaticchavatha* found in another grant of *mahārājaputra* Govindacandra dated 1105[4] may be a variation of *viśatiaṭhūprastha.* As regards the actual contribution made to these three officers we would differ from U. N. Ghoshal and take it to be one *prastha* of the produce from every household.

Varavajha—

The Basahi plate of *mahārājaputra* Govindacandra[5] also mentions *varavajha* as a tax but we cannot make out anything about its nature.

Viṣayadāna—

Viṣayadāna is found only in the Candravati inscription of Candradeva[6]. It may be interpreted as some kind of a district tax[7], probably paid in connection with a *pattalā*[8].

Tarādāya and svanaukābhāṭaka—

1 *Socio-Economic History*, p. 233.

2 *I.A.*, XVIII. 17.

3 *J.E.S.H.O.*, IV, pp. 86f.

4 *E.I.*, II. 360.

5 *I.A.*, XIV. 103.

6 *E.I.*, IX. 302.

7 R. S. Tripathi, *History of Kanauj*, p. 349.

8 R. Niyogi, Op. cit., p. 183.

Two other taxes which are also mentioned only in the Candravati inscription are *tarādāya* and *svanaukābhāṭaka*. The first refers to ferry dues and the second to the rent paid by fishermen and others for the private use of the royal boats[1]. It is significant that the *pattalā* granted in this inscription was bounded by rivers on its three sides[2].

Yamalikāmbali—

In some of the grants of Jayaccandra[3] we find a tax called *yamalikāmbali* or *yavalikāmbali*[4] which is difficult to explain. It has been pointed out by B. N. S. Yadav[5] that *yamalikā* means a sort of singer and *ambali* a tax on the analogy of the term *uṇbali* or *umbaḷi* which is used in the Cālukyan inscriptions as a tax surrendered by the state in favour of some person or institution[6]. Thus *yamalikāmbali* may have been a tax levied on a particular type of singer minstrel.

Dagapasadīdīrghagovica—

The Machlishahr grant of Hariścandra[7] has a fiscal expression *dagapasadīdīrghagovica* of which it is difficult to make any sense. We wonder if it had anything to do with the branding of cattle.

Ākara—

The Basahi grant of *mahārājaputra* Govindacandra[8] mentions *ākara* also as a tax. It refers to the tax on the output of mines which were allowed to be worked by private individuals.

Nidhinikṣepa—

In the Kamauli inscription dated A.D. 1172[9] *nidhinikṣepa* is mentioned along with other taxes and dues. It has been

1 Cf. *Artha*, II. 28

2 R. Niyogi, Op. cit., pp. 186f.

3 Ibid., p. 184.

4 U. N. Ghoshal, *H.R.S.*, p. 300. In the Lucknow Museum Plate (*E.I.*, XXIV. 293-5) the form is *yamalikāmbali*.

5 Op. cit., p. 290, f.n. 3.

6 *I.H.Q.*, XX. 287.

7 *E.I.*, X. 100.

8 *I.A.*, XIV. 101-4.

9 *E.I.*, IV. 124.

explained as a tax on the property held in trust[1]. But generally the term is included in the list of the rights and privileges transferred to the donee and its inclusion among the dues is only a mistake.

Vāhyāvāhyaṃtarasiddhi—

Likewise the Rahan grant[2] has *vāhyāvāhyaṃtarasiddhi* in its list of taxes. But the expression mostly occurs in connection with the boundaries of the village granted and is intended to convey an idea of the fullness of the rights of the donee[3]. It apparently refers to the right of the king to treasure-trove (*nidhi*) and unclaimed deposits (*nikṣepa*).

Taxes in Bengal:— *Cauroddharaṇa*—

In the land-grants of the Pālas and other contemporary dynasties[4] besides the usual land revenue we have references to *uparikara* (extra cess), *daśāparādha* (fines realised from villagers for committing the ten offences) and *cauroddharaṇa*. *Cauroddharaṇa* has been variously interpreted as the right of extirpation of robbers,[5] the special privilege of apprehension of thieves[6], police protection[7] and things recovered from thieves[8]. But in explaining the term we have to emphasise two points, firstly the form (*sa-cauroddharaṇa*) and position of the term in the records indicate that it refers to an item of income to the king, and secondly in some inscriptions of Assam[9] *cauroddharaṇa* is included in the list of oppressions from which the donee is exempted. Thus, we find that U.N. Ghoshal's[10]

1 R. Niyogi, Op. cit., pp. 171f.

2 *I.A.*, XVIII. 17.

3 R. Niyogi, Op. cit., p. 188 splits the first part of the expression into *vāhyāvānyaṃ* and *tara*. But the land-grants from other parts of India also indicate that it is not to be thus split up but rather has to be corrected as *vāhyābhyaṃtara*.

4 U. N. Ghoshal, *H.R.S.*, pp. 243-46.

5 R. D. Banerji in *E.I.*, XIV, no. 23.

6 Vogel, *Antiquities of the Chamba State*, p. 129.

7 N. G. Majumdar, *Inscriptions of Bengal*, III, p. 8

8 D. C. Sircar in *E.I.*, XXIX, p. 5, f.n.3.

9 *E.I.*, XXX. 205-9; XXXII. 288-92; U.N. Ghoshal, *H.R.S.*, p. 248.

10 *I.H.Q.*, V. 277-9.

suggestion that it was a tax imposed upon villagers for protection against thieves is the best. Choudhury[1] proposes to interpret the term as the money and food to be given to the police officers who might enter the land in connection with the apprehension of thieves. But there would not be much propriety in transferring these provisions to the donee and hence we support the explanation offered by Ghoshal.

Besides these taxes we can infer the existence in the Pāla kingdom of two more, customs and tolls (*śulka*) and ferry dues (*tara*) from the reference to the officials *śaulkika* and *tarika* in the Pāla grants[2]. A grant of the Sena dynasty[3] refers to the income derived from betel-leaf plantations (*barajas*) and the price of betel-nuts[4].

Taxes in Orissa :—

In some of the land-grants from Orissa we find fiscal terms which are not found elsewhere[5]. It has been suggested[6] that *hastidaṇḍa* is a tax on the maintenance of elephants, *varabalīvardda*[7] is the tax on superior bulls, *hala-daṇḍa* is the tax on ploughs, *padātijīvya* is subsistence for the infantry, *vandāpanā* is tribute to the king, *vijaya-vandāpanā* is the tribute paid after the king obtained a victory and *ahi-daṇḍa* is a tax on snake-charmers. We may suggest that of the unexplained terms in these inscriptions *suvarṇṇadaṇḍa* is a tax either on goldsmiths or on gold-washing, *vartma-daṇḍa* is a road-cess, *viṣayālī* is a district tax and *khaṇḍapālīya* is a tax for the chief of the administrative division called *khaṇḍa*. There still remain some terms for which we fail to offer any explanation, *ciṭṭola*, *andhāruā*, *pratyandhāruā*, *adattā*, *antarāvaḍḍi*, *āturāvaḍḍi*, *rintakāvaḍḍi*,

1 *History of the Civilization of Assam*, p. 297.

2 *E.I.*, XVIII.304-7; XV. 295-8.

3 *I.B.*, III, no. XV.

4 U. N. Ghoshal, *Hindu Revenue System*, pp. 266f.

5 *E.I.*, XXXIII. 266-8; XXVIII. 324-6.

6 *E.I.*, XXXIII. 264.

7 In the Kelga Plates (*E.I.*, XXVIII.324-6) the reading *carabalīvarda* if not a mistake for *vara-balīvarda* would imply two distinct taxes on the use of pasture and the possession of superior bulls.

vasāvakī, bandhadaṇḍa, tṛṇodakaśāsanārddhika[1], *ārthāruā, pratyarthāruā* and *gogauḍa.*

Taxes in the Candella kingdom :—

The detailed specimens of Candella land-grants[2] mention along with the usual *bhāgabhogakara* and *hiraṇya, paśu* and *śulka* also as the dues which the villagers were required to pay to the donee. *Śulka* stands for tolls and *paśu* may be explained, as has been done by R K. Dikshit[3], as either a tax on cattle or the right to commandeer the people's bullocks etc., for state service. In some of these Candella records the feudatories (*rāja*), royal officials (*rājapuruṣa*), forest officials (*āṭavika*) and *cāṭas* are required to transfer their perquisites (*ābhāvya*) as gifts to donees, which indicates that they had originally been assigned certain rights in the villages[4]. Some Candella grants[5] include the receipts from fines (*daṇḍādāya*) also in the list of revenues assigned to the donee.

Taxes in the Kalacuri kingdom :—

The land-grants of the Kalacuris also contain terms which in some cases cannot be satisfactorily explained.[6] *Pravaṇi* may be equated with *pravaṇikara* of the Gāhaḍavāla records but *vāḍa* is difficult to explain. Hiralal[7] takes *pravaṇivāḍa* as a single expression meaning the dues for occupying camping grounds but gives no arguments in favour of this interpretation. We would prefer to treat *pravaṇi* and *vāḍa* as two distinct terms, as in some grants *pravaṇi* appears by itself and *vāḍa* follows after three more terms[8]. We can offer no satisfactory interpretation of

1 It may refer to the dues paid to the state for the land granted as a *karaśāsana*.

2 *E.I.*, XXXII. 121-23; XX. 129-31; XVI. 12-14.

3 *J.U.P.H.S.*, XXIII. 243.

4 It has been suggested by R. S. Sharma, *J.E.S.H.O.*, IV. 80f that this development began in the later half of the 12th century under Paramardi. But the expression *rājarājapuruṣāṭavikacāṭādibhiḥ svaṃ svamābhāvyam parihart tavyam* appears also in the plates of king Madanavarman dated 1136 A.D.—*E.I.*, XXXII, 121-23.

5 *I.A.*, XVI. 201ff.

6 *C.I.I.*, IV. 324-31, 645-52; *E.I.*, XXI, no. 15.

7 *E.I.*, XXI, p. 93.

8 *C.I.I.*, IV. 645-52.

vāḍa. *Carī* may be taken to be the tax on grazing cattle. *Rasavatī* has been explained as the liquor tax[1] or the dues for extracting toddy[2].

Hiralal[3] explains *kāmata* and *viseṇimādāya*[4] to mean respectively "a rigid form of home-farm" and the dues for crossing rivers. By the first explanation he presumably means the delegation of the right to collect taxes. We see no reason why *kāmata* should mean this. His interpretation of the second, for which he gives no basis, does not convince us, and we prefer to take these terms as unexplained.

Paṭṭakilādāya may easily be taken to stand for the tax payable by the villagers to the village headman (*paṭṭakila*). *Duṣṭasādhyādāya*[5] also appears as *dussādhyādāya*. Hiralal explains it as a tax for "mending the incorrigibles" by which we assume he means the reform of hardened criminals. Mirashi takes it to be a tax for *dussādhyas* whom he explains as criminals and other suspects living within the limits of the village. But it has not been noted that in these Kalacuri records themselves *duṣṭasādhya* appears as the designation of an officer who seems to have been in charge of criminal administration. *Duṣṭasādhyādāya* may therefore be explained as the dues realised for paying this officer. *Ardhapuruṣārikādāya* is difficult to explain. It may refer to the dues collected for the officer designated *ardhapuruṣārikā* but we cannot suggest any explanation of this title.

Viṣayikādāya may be explained as the district dues. *Ghaṭṭādāya* refers to dues paid at the fords. In place of the term *daṇḍa* of these grants, we find the compound *daṇḍādāyakarotpatti* in other records of the same dynasty[6] which has to be translated to mean the income from taxes and the receipts from fines.

---

1 Ibid.

2 *E.I.*, XXI, p. 93.

3 Ibid

4 Mirashi translates it as the cess on *viseṇimā*. On the analogy of the expressions which follow it may be suggested that it was the tax for an officer designated *viseṇimā*, but the meaning of this term is quite unknown.

5 It has been left unexplained by U. N. Ghoshal, *H.R.S.*, p. 254, f.n.2.

6 *E.I.*, II, no. 23.

Mārgaṇaka—

Mārgaṇaka of these records is to be found elsewhere also. A. K. Majumdar[1] proposes without extending any reasons in his support to take it to mean the forced labour which Manu[2] permitted the king to exact from mechanics, artisans and śūdras one day in each month. In a grant of the Somavaṃśī king Karṇa[3] *mārggaṇī* seems to have been used in the general sense of petty dues. But *mārgaṇaka* in these records is used as the name of a specific tax. *Mārggaṇa* means a request and hence the term may refer to a benevolence[4]. It was possibly an emergency tax in the form of theoretically voluntary gifts.

Taxes in the Paramāra kingdom :—

A Paramāra grant from Mandhata[5] belonging to the last quarter of the thirteenth century, besides mentioning the usual dues *hiraṇya*, *bhāgabhoga*, *uparikara* and *daṇḍa*, refers to certain taxes which were probably paid in kind. These are : *śākamuṣṭi* (handfuls of vegetables), *tailapalikā* (small measures of oil) and *kumbhapūraka* (vesselfuls most probably of grain).

Ākāśotpatti and pātāla—

These terms are followed by *ākāśotpatti* and *pātāla*. U. N. Ghoshal[6] notes *ākāśotpatti* in a few land-grants of the feudatories of the Cedi and Candella kings and relying on its literal meaning "the produce of the sky" identifies it with the *bhūtavāta* of the older inscriptions. But the form of the term to be equated with *ākāśotpatti* would have been *vātabhūta* and not *bhūtavāta*. In the Kuretha (Gwalior) grant of the Pratihāra king Malayavarman[7] the village granted was accompanied with the produce of the sky and the under-world (*ākāśapātālotpattisahitaṃ*). This would suggest that all these expressions are to be equated with *ākāśapā-*

1 *Chaulukyas of Gujarat*, p. 250.

2 VII. 138.

3 *E.I.*, XXXIII. 266-68.

4 U. N. Ghoshal, *H.R.S.*, p. 237.

5 *E.I.*, XXXII. 148-56.

6 *H.R.S.*, pp. 254f.

7 *E.I.*, XXX. 148-50.

tāla which is mentioned in some Gāhaḍavāla records[1] not in connection with the enumeration of dues and income but with the rights and privileges transferred to the donee. *Ākāśa* may be taken to refer to what is acquired only accidentally and *pātāla* to what is inside the earth.[2] But it is to be noted that in some of the records having these expressions we have a separate reference to *nidhi* and *nikṣepa* and mines[3]. We would suggest that these expressions have been mentioned only to convey the sense of the fullness of the rights of the donees over the land or village granted.

Kalyāṇadhana—

Kalyāṇadhana which also appears in some of the grants of the feudatories of the Cedi and Candella kings has been left unexplained by U.N. Ghoshal[4]. We may suggest that it stands for the dues collected on auspicious occasions.

Taxes in the Cāhamāna kingdom :—

D. Sharma[5] has collected the fiscal terms occurring in the records of the Cāhamāna empire. *Talārābhāvya*[6], *selahathābhāvya* and *balādhipābhāvya* refer to the share respectively of officers called *talāra*, *selahatha* (*śalyahasta*) and *balādhipa* in the revenue collected at the custom's house. *Dāna* is used in the sense of customs tax. *Ādāna* may be the full form of *dāna* or is a general term for dues. *Lāga* is generally contrasted with *bhāga* and may refer to imposts. In the Nadlai inscription of Rājyapāla[7] *ātmapāilā* refers to the *pāilā* measure of articles for the *bhoktā* or *jagirdar* who appears as the donor of the grant. *Halusadi* is a tax calculated per plough.

1 R. Niyogi, Op. cit., p. 188.

2 We wonder if these terms were put to cover the existing superstitions which viewed certain objects as not produced on the earth but falling from the sky or the nether world.

3 *E.I.*, XXXII. 148-56; R. Niyogi, Op. cit., p. 188.

4 *H.R.S.*, pp. 254f.

5 *Early Chauhān Dynasties*, pp. 207-11.

6 (*Bhavnagar*) *Prakrit and Sanskrit Inscriptions*, p. 158 translates it as "revenue of a *talāra* area".

7 *E.I.*, XI, p. 37.

Daśabandha, as we have seen[1], is a tax amounting to one-tenth of the income. *Rājakīyabhoga* stands for the shorter and more common term, *bhoga*. Besides these we find references to *udraṅga*, *uparikara* and *daṇḍa* also.

Taxes in the Pratihāra kingdom :—

In the Rajor grant of the Pratihāra chief Mathanadeva[2] we have, besides *udraṅga*, *bhoga*, *bhāga*, *daṇḍadaśāparādha* and *dāna*, many new taxes. *Mayūṭa* is difficult to explain. U. N. Ghoshal[3] suggests that it is probably a contribution of the type of *bhoga*.

Khalabhikṣā appears elsewhere also[4], sometimes as *khalaka*.[5] Literally it means begging at a threshing-floor[6], and has been taken to stand for the demand for a portion of the crop, over and above the usual grain-share that was collected from the grain heaped upon the threshing-floor[7]. The Karitalai inscription of Lakṣmaṇarāja II[8] records the donation of four *khalabhikṣās*. It may be suggested that the state probably enjoyed the monopoly of threshing-floors to which the cultivators had to bring their corn for threshing, and that the term *khalabhikṣā* refers to a tax in kind which was paid to the state when the corn was threshed.

U.N. Ghoshal[9] proposes to treat *prasthaka* as the contribution at a specific rate for every *prastha* measure of liquid. But we suggest, on the analogy of *akṣapaṭalaprastha* and similar other terms in the Gāhaḍavāla records, that it refers to a contribution at the rate of a *prastha* from every household. We have explained

1 See supra p. 57.

2 *E.I.*, III. 266-7.

3 *H.R.S.*, p. 237.

4 *E.I.*, XXV. 280f.

5 *I.A.*, XVIII. 114, l.55.

6 The *Deśīnāmamālā*, VII. 89 explains *vippayaṃ* as *khalabhikṣā* which suggests that the literal meaning of the term *khalabhikṣā* was its original use and it was on the analogy of the alms given on the threshing—floor that the due was called.

7 U. N. Ghoshal, Op. cit., p. 237.

8 *E.I.*, II. 174ff.

9 Loc. cit.

mārgganaka elsewhere[1]. A. S. Altekar[2] suggests that *skandhaka* refers to the liability of labourers to carry the luggage of the touring officers upon their shoulders. But as it is mentioned under the dues received by the king (*pratyādāya*) we feel that U. N. Ghoshal's[3] suggestion that it is a contribution at specific rate for every shoulder-load of articles is a better one.

Aputtrikādhana which means the property of one who in the absence of sons has not appointed his daughter to raise male issue for himself has justly been interpreted as the right of the king to the property of a person dying sonless.[4] U. N. Ghoshal[5] does not say anything about the term *naṣṭibharaṭa.* We wonder if it refers to something like a death duty which the widow, with no son to inherit the property, paid before being awarded the necessary permission to own the property[6].

A land-grant of Mahendrapāla from Malwa[7] mentions besides the usual royal dues *skandhaka* and *mārgganaka.* Two land-grants of the feudatories of Mahendrapāla from Kathiawar[8] include the term *collaka* in their list of royal dues. We may interpret the term in the light of the Rajor inscription[9] which mentions the toll of 50 leaves on every *collikā* (probably a measure of load) brought from outside. *Collaka* may therefore be taken as the contribution of one *collaka* of certain commodities.

Utpadyamānaviṣṭi—

One of these inscriptions from Kathiawar describes the grant as accompanied with the right of *utpadyamānaviṣṭi*[10]. U.N. Ghoshal[11]

1 See supra p. 64.
2 *State and Government in Ancient India*, p. 281, f.n.5.
3 *H.R.S.*, p. 237.
4 Ibid.
5 Ibid.
6 The *Mitākṣarā* on Yāj., II. 135-36 gives a sonless widow the right to succeed on the sole condition of her chastity
7 *E.I.*, XIV, no. 13 (Part II).
8 *E.I.* IX, no. 1 (A and B).
9 *E.I.*, III. 266-67.
10 *E.I.*, IX, no. 1 (B).
11 *H.R.S.*, p. 238.

translates it as the forced labour as it falls due. Mirashi[1] takes it to mean "forced labour arising therefrom" (i.e., from the transfer of the land to the donee). R. S. Sharma[2] has suggested that the expression refers to the right to impose forced labour as occasion might arise, which suggests that the donees could determine these occasions at their discretion. This may be supported on the ground that, though according to the legal texts the amount of forced labour which a king could exact was fixed, the actual practice in the days before the abolition of *zamindari* was that the landlord could demand it as and when he needed it.

But we must note that the expression appears in the list of taxes transferred to the donee, often specifically implied in the form of the expression as *utpadyamānaviṣṭipratyāya*. Thus D. C. Sircar[3] seems to be nearer to the form of the expression when he translates it as the tax payable in lieu of free labour. We would substitute 'free' by 'forced' and suggest that it refers to the dues paid by the villagers in place of the forced labour they had to perform for the state. In Kashmir the system of forced labour appears as *rūḍhabhāroḍhi*. The *Rājataraṅgiṇī* suggests that it was not always necessarily the actual carriage of loads but may be commuted by some payment in cash or kind. King Śaṅkaravarman is said to have introduced this system of forced labour. He fined the villagers failing to carry loads for one year, at the value of the load calculated according to the highest prices in the regions concerned[4]. In the reign of Harṣa a certain temple was plundered, hence the members of the *purohita* corporation requested him for being exempted from *rūḍhabhāroḍhi* (forced labour)[5]. This reference also favours the suggestion that the forced labour was often commuted in the form of cash or kind payment.

Taxes in the Caulukya kingdom :—

In the grants of the Caulukyas of Gujarat we have besides

1 *C.I.I.*, IV, p. 89.
2 *J.E.S.H.O.*, I. 319.
3 *E.I.*, XXXII. 48.
4 *Rāj.*, V. 172ff.
5 *Rāj.*, VII. 1088. Also ibid., VIII. 2513.

the usual terms *dānībhāga* or *dānībhogabhāga*, *navanidhāna* and *abhinavamārggaṇaka*[1]. U. N. Ghoshal[2] explains *dānībhāga* as the periodical supplies of fruits, firewood and the like by the villagers. But in the *Lekhapaddhati*[3], *dānī* has been used as meaning land-tax and we think the Caulukya records employ the term in the same sense. U. N. Ghoshal[4] explains *navanidhāna* as a kind of cess upon agricultural land imposed for the first time at the date of the grant, but observes in the case of *abhinavamārggaṇaka* that the original imposition of this kind had become permanent, and that an additional levy was made at this time. D. Sharma[5] on the basis of the Bamnera grant of Kelhaṇadeva[6] suggests that *nidhāna* refers to articles such as treasure-trove. In the Rajor inscription[7] also *nidhi* and *nidhāna* have been used together. *Navanidhāna* appears not only in epigraphic records but also in the *Lekhapaddhati*[8]. It is likely that *nava* stands for 'nine' and not 'new' on the analogy of the common fiscal term *aṣṭabhoga*[9].

Bhūtavātapratyāya—

In the inscriptions of the Gujarat branch of the Rāṣṭrakūṭas *bhūtavātapratyāya* is mentioned as one of the items of income. U. N. Ghoshal[10] could not find the precise meaning of the term and only translated it literally as the revenue derived from the elements and the winds. S. K. Maity[11] has suggested to take the term as denoting two different kinds of cess for the maintenance of rites respectively for the winds (*vāta*) and for the spirits (*bhūta*). The explanation is quite likely for the form *bhūtavāta* which no doubt is the most usual one.

1 U.N. Ghoshal, *H.R.S.*, p. 256.
2 Ibid.
3 pp. 7, 16, 18f.
4 Loc. cit., pp. 256, 295.
5 *Early Chauhān Dynasties*, p. 210.
6 *E.I.*, XIII. 210
7 *E.I.*, III, no. 36.
8 p. 6.
9 U. N. Ghoshal, *H.R.S.*, p. 240.
10 Ibid., pp. 215, 217.
11 *Economic Life in the Gupta period*, p. 63.

But we have to note the forms *sambhṛtopāttapratyāya* and *bhūto-pāttapratyāya* found in some records. These favour the suggestion of A. S. Altekar[1] that the expression stands for a tax on what has been produced in the village (*bhūta*) and what has been imported (*upātta*). This suggestion receives support from the Siroda (Goa) Plates of Devarāja[2] which use words which make the meaning of the expressions in question clear. It speaks of the grant being accompanied by the income accruing from the output of the village and also the income realised from things brought (*parivṛttena cānītena yanniṣpadyate*). It is quite likely that *avāta* or *vāta* was the Sanskritised form of the Prakrit equivalent for *upātta*. We have elsewhere pointed out[3] that in the Khoh Plates of Jayanātha[4] and Śarvanātha[5] *āvātāya* and *śulka* have been used as if they were interchangeable. So we can treat Altekar's suggestion as the best explanation in the present state of our knowledge.

---

1 *Rāshṭrakūṭas and their times*, pp. 228ff.
2 *E.I.*, XXIV. 145.
3 *J.I.H.*, XXXVIII. 589.
4 *C.I.I.*, III, no. 27
5 Ibid., no. 31.

CHAPTER III

SLAVERY

In respect of the position of slaves the early medieval period has to be regarded as an age of decline. We find a definite deterioration in the standard of values, a worsening of the plight of the slaves and an increase in the number of slaves. The legal works of the period, concerned mainly with the explanation of the earlier texts, do not reflect the real condition of the age and an exclusive reliance on them may give a wrong impression about slavery in the period[1].

Increase in the number of slaves—

The frequent feudal wars and raids must have resulted in the enslavement of the people of the country defeated or attacked. The practice of enslaving prisoners no doubt goes back to an early period[2], but in our period the attacks by feudal chiefs on neighbouring areas were often motivated by the desire not for territorial gain but for loot, even in the form of slaves. Medhātithi observes that 'the captive of war' mentioned by Manu (VIII. 415) does not refer to the kṣatriya made captive in war but to the slave who after the defeat of his owner is brought over and enslaved by the captor. It may follow from this that a war brought to the victor not only slaves previously owned by the vanquished but also captives. It appears that in some cases the feudal raids were accompanied by the abduction or enslavement of the people in the country attacked. The girls said in the documents of the *Lekhapaddhati*[3] to have been brought from raids on other countries and sold into slavery most likely belonged to this category. The very fact that out of the four documents on slavery the *Lekhapaddhati* devotes two to this type indicates how widely prevalent

1 Cf. G. H. Ojha, *Madhyakālīna Bhāratīya Saṃskṛti*, pp. 48-50.

2 *Mbh.*, IV. 33.59-60 ; III. 256. 11 ; *Jātakas*, III. 147 ; IV. 220 ; V.497 ; VI. 220.

3 pp. 44f.

it was. In one document a certain *rāṇā śrī* Pratāpasiṃha is said to have brought the girl in question from an attack made on a foreign state[1]. In the second document a certain *rājaputra* is said to have captured the girl when fighting in the service of *mahāmaṇḍaleśvara rāṇaka śrī* Vīradhavaladeva in his attack on Mahārāṣṭra[2]. It would appear that on the second occasion very many people were sold into slavery. The document does not record proper names of the buyers and sellers but uses the expression 'so and so' implying that several general drafts were made so that the names of the buyers and sellers could be entered when the sale was finalised.

The deterioration in the general economic condition of the masses was another factor responsible for the increase in the number of slaves. Indebtedness often led people to sell themselves as slaves. Thus, Medhātithi[3], concerned at the practice, probably quite prevalent in his time in some places, of the debtor being made to repay the debt by selling himself, observes that it is an instance of local and king-made laws which are contrary to the *Smṛtis* and therefore are not to be obeyed. One of the documents in the *Lekhapaddhati* concerns a destitute girl selling herself as a slave[4]. Here also we do not have pesonal names of the slave and the purchaser suggesting its very frequent use. During famines, which were not rare in the period, people accepted slavery to maintain their lives. Besides natural calamities, feudal plundering would also have reduced people to dire straits. The depredations of the Muslims would have further contributed to the economic exhaustion of the masses. All these factors working for the increase in the number of the slaves appear to have been recognised in a *Lekhapaddhati* document which describes how as a result of a Muslim invasion and plunder a famine visited a village and it was abandoned; a girl unable to support herself from begging had to request people to accept her as a slave[5].

1 p. 44.

2 pp. 44f.

3 On Manu, VIII.46.

4 p. 47.

5 pp. 45-47.

Trade in slaves—

A regular trade in slaves seems to have existed in this period. We often read in the stories of villages of robbers, who used to capture people and sell them into slavery. The forest tribes are often described as indulging in such activities[1]. In the *Upamitibhavaprapañcākathā* we have an interesting reference to robbers feeding a man so that he might be sold for a handsome price.[2] It would appear from the stories of the period that there was a regular export of slaves to Persia[3]. The *Prabandhacintāmaṇi* states that Tejapāla, the minister of Vīradhavala, earned merit by banning the abduction of men by seamen[4]. We can legitimately doubt the complete success of this measure, but what is significant is the suggestion that the number of slaves exported from Gujarat had been such as to create a serious problem for the sincere Jain minister. Significantly enough in the above-mentioned story in the *Upamitibhavaprapañcākathā*[5] also the robbers happily think of the high price that their slave would fetch in a foreign country (*parakūle*). A document in the *Lekhapaddhati*[6] also refers to slaves being shipped to overseas and sold or exchanged for other commodities. It would appear that even some kings participated in the slave trade. Thus, according to the *Rājataraṅgiṇī*[7] king Vajrāditya of Kashmir sold many men as slaves to the *Mlecchas*.

The institution of slavery was by now thoroughly conventionalised. This is suggested by the fact that we have set forms for recording the sale of slaves in the *Lekhapaddhati*. As we shall see later[8], these forms detail the duties of a slave girl even when she was meant to serve rather as a concubine than as a menial.

---

1 E. g., *Samurāiccakahā*, II, pp. 91f.

2 pp. 404-5.

3 Cf. *Kathākoṣa*, p. 157; *Samarāiccakahā*, p. 342.

4 p. 99, l. 20.

5 pp. 404f.

6 p. 47.

7 IV. 39.

8 See infra p. 80.

But in spite of the growth in the volume of slave trade we do not find any reference to regular slave-markets. In one of the documents in the *Lekhapaddhati*[1] we find the girl being made to stand at the *catuṣpatha*[2] and then sold. In another document also when the girl is said to have asked a man to keep her as a slave he accepted her request at the *catuṣpatha*[3]. Thus, it seems likely that the *catuṣpatha* served as the regular place for the sale of slaves, and was chosen so that the sale might be made known to everybody in the city.

Decline in human values—

The most remarkable change in the period would appear to have been a definite decline in human values. From the *Lekhapaddhati*[4] we learn of a *rājaputra* girl falling at the feet of a merchant and begging to be kept as a slave. It is stated that at the *catuṣpatha* of the city and with the knowledge of the people of all the four castes he accepted her as a slave girl. This clearly indicates a change for the worse when compared with the humane attitude of Kauṭilya[5] who declared that an *Ārya* was not to be reduced to slavery. The case recorded is also in violent opposition to the earlier rule in the *Smṛti* texts which disallows a man reducing to slavery people belonging to castes higher than his own[6]. This decline is noticed also in regard to the duties performed by slaves. As we shall see, according to the *Lekhapaddhati* a slave girl was required to throw away night soil[7]. Earlier rules as found in the *Arthaśāstra*[8] lay down that causing a slave to remove dead bodies, ordure, urine or leavings of food, hurting or abusing him and employing a female to attend on the master while he was bathing naked involved the forfeiture of the price paid for the slave.

---

1 p. 44.

2 A place where four roads meet and hence the central most area of the city.

3 pp. 45-7.

4 Ibid.

5 *Artha*, III. 13.

6 Yāj, II. 183 ; Nārada, V. 39 ; Kātyāyana, 716 ; Viṣṇu q. in *Parāśaramādhavīya*, p. 154.

7 p. 44.

8 III. 13.

Treatment meted out to a slave—

The condition of a slave was bad. As in earlier periods the expression 'son or daughter of a slave girl' is used to imply utter contempt[1]. People in general do not seem to have felt any sympathy for the miseries of a slave. In the *Dhūrtaviṭasaṃvāda*[2] we have a sarcastic reference to the fake weeping of a slave girl which is born out of nothingness and is difficult to cure. The usual picture of a slave girl was of drooping limbs fatigued with doing all the work[3]. From the *Lekhapaddhati*[4] too we learn that a slave was expected "to work hard, zealously and tirelessly by day and night, in rains, heat and cold without caring for hunger or thirst". Torture and beating were the usual fate of a slave. The *Triṣaṣṭiśalākāpuruṣacarita*[5], referring to the normal treatment of slaves, says that they are beaten like mules, bear very heavy loads, endure thirst etc. In the *Lekhapaddhati*[6] the owner of a slave girl is empowered, in the case of her running away, stealing or spreading any rumour about him, to knock her down, drag her by her hair, bind her, beat her, and set her again to work as a slave. In one document we read that if she did not obey his orders the owner could kick her and beat her with sticks even to the extent of killing her without incurring any guilt[7]. We can imagine the cruel beatings which the slave received from the fact that these documents contain a clause to the effect that if after being beaten a slave girl commits suicide by jumping into a well she will be reborn as a she-ass, bitch or a *cāṇḍālī*, and the owner will be absolved of guilt merely by bathing in the Gaṅgā[8]. It would appear from one document that beating was not the only reason for the slaves committing suicide. Their general condition was so bad as to give frequent occasions for their attempting suicide[9].

1 *Karpūramañjarī*, pp. 22, 31, 156; *Samayamātṛkā*, VIII. 18.
2 *Caturbhāṇī*, II, p. 2.
3 *Kavīndravacanasamuccaya*, v. 505.
4 pp. 45-47.
5 I, p. 56.
6 pp. 44-47.
7 pp. 45-47.
8 pp. 44-45.
9 pp. 45-47.

It is really significant that the *Lekhapaddhati*, though detailing the duties of a slave and the powers of the owner, makes no pro vision to safeguard the rights or needs of a slave. The documents require the slave girl to serve the owner till her death. In one case the purchaser is called *janma-grāhaka* thereby referring to his rights over the life of the slave[1]. There is nothing in the documents to suggest that the slave could ever or in any manner regain his freedom. On the other hand we have a definite statement that no relation of the slave girl could possibly interrupt her work as a slave by reclaiming her[2].

The legal works of the period make it quite clear that a slave was entitled to nothing but bare maintenance[3]. Medhātithi[4] also implies that a slave is merely to be fed and clothed. A *Lekhapaddhati* document stipulates that a slave girl is to be paid by her owner according to his capacity only with food, clothing and foot-wear and adds that she will want nothing more[5]. From another document we learn that the highest which a slave faithful to his duties could expect was to receive, without having to ask for it, food, clothing and the like according to the customs, country and times and also the capacity of the owner[6].

The sons of slave girls would appear to have been a burden on society, wasting their energies in unsocial activities. Thus, it appears from Haribhadra's commentary on the *Daśavaikālika-sūtra*[7] that a slave girl's son often had only a thread-bare garment and was a rogue who would for the sake of stakes in gambling burgle a house, kill the residents by kicking them, and then visit a prostitute and drink wine and eat fish.

All this makes dismal reading and indicates what a wretched life a slave had to lead. Rāhula Sāṃkṛtyāyana[8] goes to the extent

1 p. 47.
2 pp. 44-45.
3 Cf. *Vyavahāramayūkha*, p. 114.
4 On Manu, IX. 143.
5 pp. 45-7.
6 p. 44.
7 p. 54.
8 *Hindī Kāvya Dhārā*, Introduction, pp. 17f.

of suggesting that slaves in the period were treated as sub-human beings. But such a view arises from a lop-sided emphasis on the dark aspects of the picture. The slave was after all a part of the household and it is easy to imagine that the constant association could not but have created in the more humane owner some consideration. Actually the condition of a slave largely depended upon the master. From the Tilotha image inscription[1] we know of five female slaves who accompanied their master *nāyaka* Pratāpadhavala on a pilgrimage. The fact that the master had the names of the female slaves recorded at the foot of the image indicates that they were not regarded as nonentities or sub-human beings, but received kind consideration.

It is also to be realised that idealist thinkers who felt genuine sympathy with the miserable condition of the slaves were not wanting. Thus, we find Medhātithi trying to minimise the rigours of the rules in Manu by offering a liberal interpretation. In commenting upon the statement that the wife, the son and the slave have no property and whatever they acquire is the property of him to whom they belong, Medhātithi[2] takes cognisance of the fact that, as a matter of fact, slaves also have proprietary rights over their property, and observes that what is meant by the text is only that the slave and others are dependent and subservient and without the master's sanction cannot employ their wealth as they choose. Likewise he explains Manu's[3] precept that an erring slave, wife or son should be beaten with a rope or a split bamboo, as enjoining a method of correcting them and not as ordering an actual beating in every case. He adds that verbal chastisement should be applied to correct them, beating being resorted to only when the fault is serious. The *Mānasollāsa*[4] includes slaves under the head of servants (*bhṛtya*) and observes that one who aims at his good in this life and the next should protect, feed and nourish his servants and also bestow gifts and honours on them.

1 *E.I.*, XX. 249.

2 On Manu, VIII.416.

3 VIII. 299.

4 I, p. 28, vv. 303—4.

Work done by slaves—

There is nothing to show that slaves were exclusively used for economic enterprises or that the economic life of the times depended upon them. It appears that the slaves were essentially domestic servants and had to perform diverse household tasks including those in the fields. This is clear from the fact that the lexicons do not maintain any difference between a slave and a servant[1]. Bhaṭṭotpala[2] also explains *dāsa* (slave) as meaning *karmakāra* (labourer). We have already mentioned how the *Mānasollāsa*[3] includes wage-earners, slaves, labourers and others under the general name of servants (*bhṛtya*). Even in Medhātithi[4] we read that the bath-attendant, the toilet-man (*prasādhaka*), the cook and so forth who are employed for performing definite tasks are *dāsas*. This is however not to imply that there was no difference between a servant and a slave. Medhātithi[5] recognises the difference between serving (*paricaryā*) and slavery (*dāsyam*) and observes that slavery consists in doing base (*nikṛṣṭa*) work and in not objecting to going anywhere while serving may consist in shampooing the body, guarding the family or property and so forth. Aparārka[6] and Devaṇṇabhaṭa[7] quote Kātyāyana, who makes a clear distinction between a slave and a hired servant.

The duties of a slave girl as enumerated in the *Triṣaṣṭiśalākāpuruṣacarita*[8] included threshing, grinding, carrying water, sweeping the house, smearing the house with cow-dung and the like. In the *Lekhapaddhati* we get detailed enumerations of the tasks done by a slave girl. Thus she had to cut (vegetables), pulverise (the spices), smear the floor (with cow-dung), sweep, bring fuel and

---

1 Cf. *Vaijayantī*, p. 136, ll.3-5 ; ibid., p. 175, l.51 ; *Abhidhānaratnamālā*, vv. 365, 492.

2 On *Bṛhatsaṃhitā*, CIII.41.

3 I, p. 28, vv. 303—4.

4 On Manu, IX. 143.

5 On Manu, VIII.415

6 p. 788.

7 *Smṛticandrikā*, II. 197.

8 III. p. 248.

water, throw away night soil (of the master's family)[1], milk the cow, the buffalow and the goat, churn the curd and carry whey to the field and threshing-floor and do field-work such as bringing fodder and weeding and cutting grass[2]. In the second document, cooking is added to the list and the duties connected with the threshing-floor are mentioned along with those of the field[3]. The new duties found in a third document are ploughing, washing the hands and feet (of the master), cleaning the gutters (*khāla*) and reservoirs of water (*kuṇḍika*), tending the cattle and going to far and near places[4]. In these documents we find work connected with cultivation and cattle-rearing included in the list of the duties of a slave girl. But there is no indication of her being employed exclusively in these tasks, or of these economic activities being performed on any remarkable scale by slaves. All these duties form the necessary functions of a household in a predominantly agricultural society. But in at least one of the documents there is a provision that on the orders of her owner the slave girl should perform all these tasks in another house or family[5]. This may suggest that some slave-owners at times made their slaves serve elsewhere, in some cases possibly to earn money. But it does not seem likely from the reference that there was any noticeable economic use or exploitation of the slaves in such a manner.

Slave girls have been used as concubines since very early times[6]. In our period this practice would appear to have been quite common. Thus, according to the commentator Maheśvara the practice of keeping female slaves mentioned in the *Dāyabhāga*[7] refers to women kept for enjoyment. Medhātithi[8] also speaks of slave girls who are kept for pleasure and receive food and clothing.

1 It may incidentally be pointed out that there was no feeling of ritual impurity to these slaves throwing away night soil as may be gathered from their being employed for cooking.

2 p. 44.

3 pp. 44-5.

4 p. 47.

5 Ibid.

6 *Artha*, III. 13; Kātyāyana, 728; *Jātakas*, I. 225, 451f; III. 409, 444; VI. 110, 117, 285.

7 p. 149.

8 On Manu, IX. 143.

The *Mitākṣarā*[1] also explains slave girls of the *avaruddhā* and *bhujiṣyā* types in terms of their use for sexual enjoyment. From the *Lekhapaddhati* also we can demonstrate that slave girls were often kept rather for sexual pleasure than for their utility as maid servants. The list of duties has to be included in a conventional form of slave-deed. But it would appear that the slaves had not necessarily to perform these duties. The documents often emphasise the form, complexion and young age of the slave girls. Thus we find reference to their being of white complexion, sixteen years old and with pleasing and auspicious limbs[2]. In one document the slave girl is described as having black eyes, a sharp nose, and long hair, being neither too high nor too short and with all her limbs in proper form[3].

Influence of the Muslims—

Finally we may note the influence of the Muslims on the condition of slavery in India. We have already seen how the Muslim invasions often created famine conditions which forced people to accept slavery. It has also to be noted that the Muslim invaders often reduced the defeated and captured people to slavery. Thus we have the testimony of Al-'Utbī that after Maḥmūd's victory over Nidar Bhim, slaves were so plentiful that they became very cheap[4]. As a result of the Muslim victory in Gujarat in 1197 more than twenty thousand slaves are said to have fallen into the hands of the victors[5]. Likewise we learn of fifty thousand men coming under the collar of slavery after the capture of the fort of Kalinjar[6]. But in the long run Muslim influence would have been for the betterment of the conditions of slave. Islam with its ideal of universal brotherhood does not attach much stigma to slaves. On the other hand we definitely see that it was a matter of honour to be the slave of an important man. We can see the working of the Islamic attitude in the fact that some of the slaves in Muslim states rose to the highest posts including even kingship.

---

1 On Yāj., II. 290.
2 pp. 44-45.
3 p. 47.
4 Elliot and Dowson, II. 39.
5 Ibid., 230.
6 Ibid., 231.

CHAPTER IV

GUILDS

Decline in the importance of guilds—

In the early medieval period the guilds, which had played an important role in the industrial organisation of the early centuries of the Christian era, were no longer very effective. The bonds which united the craftsmen or artisans of any particular industry in any area appear to have slackened. The guilds would seem in general not to be in a position to wield effective control over their members. This becomes clear from Medhātithi[1] who distinguishes between *śreṇī* and *gaṇa* and observes that though the members of the former follow the same profession they can act singly also, whereas the *gaṇas* always act collectively.

We have seen elsewhere[2] that, unlike earlier times, we do not find many references in this period to guilds receiving permanent endowments and paying periodical interest on them. It may be inferred that the guilds did not seem to the people of those times to be lasting bodies. It is also likely that their prestige and prosperity had also suffered much as a result of weak organisation.

We are not sure what led to this change in the position of the guilds. However, the instability and chaos resulting from feudal wars, which did not encourage craftsmen to settle down or to form lasting groups, must have been one of the important reasons for this. Moreover the guilds had to face strong competitors in the form of temples who could obviously be regarded as safer bodies for the purposes of managing permanent deposits. The vicissitudes of trade probably served as a contributory factor. Thus in a slightly earlier period the changes in the fortunes of the trade with Rome vitally affected the guild of silk-weavers in Gujarat who had to move away into the interior of the country[3]. The

1 On Manu, VIII. 2.

2 See infra Chapter VIII—Credit and banking.

3 S. K. Maity, *Economic Life in the Gupta period*, p. 138.

growth of feudalism with its emphasis on a rural and self-sufficient economy can also be expected to have had an adverse impact upon the fortunes of the guilds.

It appears from Medhātithi[1] that there was a tendency in the period for the members of the guilds to refer their disputes to the king. The guilds did not like this because, as Medhātithi says, it gave the king's officers an opportunity to interfere in their work. It would follow from Medhātithi that the hold of the guilds over their members was becoming loose and they could not effectively carry out their decisions against members. Medhātithi adds that hence they always take from the parties concerned sureties against their deviating from the decision arrived at, before they proceed to investigate a dispute, the understanding with the surety being that if the party deviates from the decision arrived at by the guild, he shall pay a stipulated fine, or he should compel him to abide by it.

Guilds as occupational sub-castes—

The guilds by this period appear to have become mostly fossilised into occupational sub-castes which no doubt retained some form of corporate life with some social control over the members. Economic co-operation, which in the earlier period had brought the guilds money, power and prestige, was in most cases negligible. This is clearly recognised by some texts of the period which frankly explain *śreṇīs* in terms of caste. The *Mitākṣarā*[2] still clinging to the occupational origin of a *śreṇī* explains it as a group of people of different castes, who subsist by the occupation of one caste like the *beḍābukas* (horse-dealers), *tāmbūlikas* (betel-sellers), *kuvindas* (weavers) and *carmakāras* (shoe-makers). The *Smṛticandrikā*[3] and the *Vīramitrodaya*[4] clearly admit the change and explain *śreṇī* as meaning the eighteen low castes such as the *rajaka* (washerman). The transformation of guilds into sub-castes

1 On Manu, VIII. 2.

2 On Yāj., II. 30

3 III (*Vyavahārakāṇḍa*), part 1, p.40.

4 *Vyavahāra*, p. 12.

appears to have gone much ahead even by the time of Bhaṭṭotpala[1] who, ignoring the professional basis of the guilds, explains them simply as the corporation of many people belonging to the same caste. The *Vaijayantī*[2] also takes *śreṇī* as the term for a body of people belonging to the same caste and profession. In the *Kānhaḍadeprabandha*[3] we have a reference to eighteen *varṇas,* besides the four high castes, which establishes clearly the transformation of guilds into sub-castes.

In the *Abhidhānacintāmaṇi*[4] *śreṇī* and *prakṛti* appear as synonymous terms. This usage receives support from the fact that Pitāmaha[5], as quoted by the legal works of the period, gives the number of the *prakṛtis* as eighteen, which we know is also the traditional number of *śreṇīs* in the Buddhist and Jain texts. References to eighteen *prakṛtis* are found in the inscriptions of the period also[6]. It has to be noted that Pitāmaha describes the *prakṛtis* as outside the pale of the four *varṇas* and *āśramas.* This may account for the low position of the guilds in this period. The guilds were assigned a social status equal to that of the low castes and sometimes even to that of the outcastes. Thus we find that the *Kathākośaprakaraṇa*[7] of Jineśvara Sūri mentions the members of *śreṇīs* such as the goldsmith, potter, blacksmith and the washerman and other craftsmen and artisans (*śilpa-karma-kara-samudāya*) as forming the *adhama* (degraded) class of society. It was the association with the low castes and groups that brought down the guilds in general to a low rung of the social ladder. It should be noticed that in the Jain list[8] some of the guilds are those of aboriginal people

---

1 On *Bṛhatsaṃhitā*, XXXIV. 19—*Bahūnāṃ samānajātīyānaṃ saṅghaḥ śreṇī.*

2 p. 237, 1.179—*Sajātiśilpasaṃhatyāmaṣaṇḍaḥ śreṇiḥ.*

3 I. 238 q. by D. Sharma, *Early Chauhān Dynasties*, p. 252.

4 III, v. 714—*Prakṛtayaḥ paurāṇāṃ śreṇayo'pi ca.*

5 *Smṛticandrikā*, II, p. 29; *Parāśaramādhavīya*, III, p. 46. See also *Sarasvatīvilāsa*, p. 74.

6 *E.I.*, II, p. 220; *Proc. Beng. A. S.*, 1877, p. 73; Vogel, *Antiquities of Chamba State*, pp. 162 (1.11), 166 (1.10), 193 (1.15). See also *Skandapurāṇa* q. by D. Sharma, loc. cit.

7 Introduction, pp. 116f.

8 *Jambūdīpa*, 43, p. 193.

and some are of base occupations, especially from the point of view of the *ahiṃsā* ideal. The text itself indicates this when it divides the eighteen guilds into two groups, the *nāruā* (*nārukāḥ*) being touchables and the *kāruā* (*kārukāḥ*) untouchables. But the fact of the guilds being bracketed with the low sub-castes or groups could not by itself have been sufficient to bring them down in social ranking. It is obvious that there had already appeared a corresponding decline in their economic position.

Local character of the guilds—

It appears that the guilds had only a local character concerned only with the men of a certain profession in a particular area. They do not seem to have had any organisational connection with their counterparts elsewhere. It can be demonstrated from Medhātithi that the industrial or occupational guilds did not cover wide areas. Thus he defines *śreṇī* as a body of traders and others who follow the same profession[1] and illustrates by mentioning tradesmen, artisans, money-lenders, coach-drivers and so forth[2]. Elsewhere he defines *saṅgha* as a community of persons following the same pursuit, though belonging to different castes and regions (*deśa*), and by way of illustration mentions the *saṅghas* of mendicants, of *vaṇiks* (merchants) and of those versed in the four Vedas[3]. It is significant that artisans or other professions are not mentioned in connection with the *saṅghas* suggesting thereby that associations of these people covering several districts were not fashionable in the time of Medhātithi. In the *Triṣaṣṭiśalākāpuruṣacaritra*[4] we read of *śreṇīs* and *praśreṇīs*. But *praśreṇīs* should not be taken to stand for the branches of a central guild distributed in the constituent districts. They may refer to the sub-groups into which any particular guild or occupation was divided on the basis of division of labour. In the Gwalior inscription[5] are recorded two perpetual endowments made respectively by the members of

1 On Manu, VIII. 2.

2 Ibid. 41.

3 Ibid. 219.

4 I, p. 258.

5 *E.I.*, I. 159f, ll. 11-20.

the guild of oil-millers headed by their chiefs (*mahattakas*) whose names are given and who dwelt in Śrīsarveśvarapura and the members of the guild of gardeners with their seven chiefs (*maharas*) who dwelt on the top of Śrī-Gopagiri. The use of the singular number indicates that in both the cases there was only one guild of the occupations in the localities mentioned. It is likely that the persons named as chiefs occupied an important place in their guilds through their being better off than others. However the possibility cannot be ruled out that there were sub-groups like the *praśreṇīs* of the Jain text in different wards of the city and the chiefs were their heads. From epigraphic references also it appears that the guilds of any one area regulated their affairs without any reference to their counterparts in other districts or to any central body, if it existed at all[1]. The expression *Vārendraka-śilpi-goṣṭhī-cūḍāmaṇi* used for *rāṇaka* Śūlapāṇi in the Deopara inscription[2] has often been taken to mean that he was the head of the guild of the artisans of Varendra (North Bengal)[3]. We very much doubt if there was one such guild for all the artisans in Varendra. The use of the term *cūḍāmaṇi* (crest-jewel) and not the specific name of the office indicates that it was only a stylistic way of expressing his artistic excellence. Thus the term *goṣṭhī* here does not stand in the technical sense of a guild or corporate body but refers to assemblage or collection.

Chief of the guild—

It appears that by this period the importance of the chief of the guild within the organisation had increased. The tendency seems to have started earlier[4], as is suggested by an inscription of A.D. 465[5] which mentions one Jīvanta as heading the oilmen's guild at Indor. Aparārka[6] utilises Bṛhaspati to establish the power of the head of a guild to reprimand, condemn and even

1 Cf. B. N. Puri, *History of the Gurjara-Pratihāras*, p. 129.

2 *E.I.*, I. 307ff, v. 36.

3 B. P. Mazumdar, *Socio-Economic History*, p. 211.

4 *J.E.S.H.O.*, II. 283.

5 *C.I.I.*, III, no. 16.

6 p. 794.

excommunicate wrong-doers. In the inscriptions of our period we often find references to heads of guilds. Thus the Karitalai inscription mentions the chief (*pradhāna*) of the *vāgūlikas* (traders in betel-leaves)[1]. In the Jhalarapatan inscription of 1086 A.D. we have reference to a *tailika-paṭṭakila* or the head of a guild of oilmen[2]. A *tailikarāja* (chief of the guild of oilmen) is mentioned in an inscription from Shergadh[3]. In the Gwalior inscription[4] we meet many chiefs of the oil-millers (*tailika-mahattakas*). We likewise find references to the chiefs of the gardeners (*mālika-mahara*)[5], of the distillers of liquor (*kallapāla-mahattaka*)[6] and of the betel-sellers (*tāmbolika-mahara*)[7]. It appears that the chief could accept any endowment and in fulfilling it could impose a cess on the members of the guild[8]. We also find that in one case a temple built by the chief of a guild received endowments from the members of his profession[9]. The accentuated importance of the heads of guilds is reflected in the *Smṛticandrikā*[10] which discusses in detail the situation when the *samūhas* find themselves incapable of stopping the insolence of their *mukhyas* (chiefs). In such cases the king was required to interfere and to set the chief on the proper path. If the *mukhya* was still recalcitrant he was to be fined on a graduated scale according to the extent of his solvency, sometimes even suffering the confiscation of all his property, and in extreme cases he was to be banished from the kingdom by the king, who alone was competent to inflict such punishments. The text however adds that if the *samūha* is at all competent to do so, it alone shall exercise this authority to punish the chief.

1 *C.I.I.*, IV, no. 42, ll. 33-34.
2 *J.A.S.B.*, 1914, pp. 241-43.
3 *E.I.*, XXIII. 138.
4 *E.I.*, I. 159ff.
5 Ibid., l.17
6 Ibid., p. 175, l.26.
7 Ibid., p. 174, ll.8-10.
8 Ibid.
9 B.N. Puri, *History of the Gurjara-Pratihāras*, pp. 131f.
10 III, pp. 53 0f.

Organisation of the guilds—

As we have seen, Medhātithi[1] implies a closer bond of union among certain professions than those ordinarily covered by the term guild. For these closely-knit associations he employs the term *gaṇa* and says that they always function collectively (*gaṇa-śaścāriṇaḥ* or *sambhūyakāriṇaḥ*). The examples of such bodies cited by Medhātithi are masons (*gṛhaprāsādādikarāḥ*) and temple-priests. He says that the *gaṇas* of these people investigate the disputes arising among themselves and appoint committees to enforce their decisions. Elsewhere Medhātithi[2] observes that among architects, masons, carpenters and the like who work jointly, their several shares according to the agreement of the group (*sva-samaya-prasiddho yāvān-aṃśaḥ*) shall be allotted on the principle that the man who does the most laborious and difficult parts of the work receives more, and he who does the easier receives less.

The details of the working of the guilds in the legal works of the period do not show any improvement upon the rules in the Smṛtis. Thus the *Smṛticandrikā* says that because of differences of opinion among their members, who are unlimited in number, the *samūhas* are incapable of deciding unanimously and should therefore appoint boards of two, three or five superintendents (*kāryacintakas*). It requires the members to obey not only the superintendents but also those who, though not belonging to the group, advise for its good. It also gives the *samūhas* power to punish members who are hostile to the advisers, deny a speaker his opportunity, make an unreasonable speech, betray secrets, create dissensions, or are guilty of similar offences[3]. We have already seen how, according to Medhātithi, the guilds were keen to protect themselves from frequent interference by the king's officers[4].

The legal works of the period also refer to the power of the guilds to frame rules to regulate their activities. Thus the

1 On Manu, VIII. 2.

2 Ibid. 211.

3 III, pp. 526f.

4 On Manu, VIII. 2.

Smṛticandrikā[1] shows that the guilds might decree that a certain commodity was not to be sold on a particular day, or that it was to be sold by a particular guild alone. From inscriptions we know that the guilds could impose on their members periodical cesses, sometimes in consideration of an amount paid to or deposited with them[2].

It would appear that even in this period some of the guilds still had their armed forces. In support of this we have not only the inclusion of guild troops in the traditional six kinds of troops[3] but also the clear testimony of the *Mānasollāsa*[4] which distinctly describes *śreṇībala* as the troop of those who are connected through caste and profession (*janma-karma*) and who have entered into a compact (*niścitaṃ samayaiḥ*).

Occupations organised into guilds—

The number eighteen for the guilds is found in the *Triṣaṣṭiśalākāpuruṣacarita*[5] but for specific names we have to rely on the *Jambūdvīpaprajñapti*[6]. The text mentions guilds of *kuṃbhāras* (potters), *paṭṭaillas*[7] (weavers), *suvaṇṇakāras* (goldsmiths), *sūvakāras* (cooks), *gandhavvas* (musicians), *kāsavaggas* (barbers), *mālākāras* (garland-makers or gardeners), *kacchakaras* (rope-makers), *taṃbolias* (betel-sellers), *cammayarus* (leather-workers), *jantapīlagas*[8] (oil-pressers), *gañchias*[9], *chimpāyas* (cloth-printers), *kaṃsakāras* (braziers), *sīvagas* (tailors), *guāras* (? *gopāla*, cow-herds), *bhillas*[10] and *dhīvaras*

1 III, part 1, p. 66.

2 *E.I.*, XXIV. 333-36. See ibid., p. 333.

3 *Agnipurāṇa*, CCXLII.1-2.

4 I, p. 79, v. 558.

5 I. 258; III. 316. See also *Padmānandamahākāvya*, XVI. 193.

6 43, p. 193.

7 A. K. Majumdar, *Chaulukyas of Gujarat*, pp. 264ff leaves the expression unexplained. Johnson, *Triṣaṣṭiśalākā*, I, pp. 258f, f. n. 315 suggests head of a village. We feel that it is a mistake for Skt. *paṭṭakāra*.

8 A. K. Majumdar, loc. cit., translates it as presser of sugarcane. Johnson, loc. cit., has presser of grain.

9 The *Deśīnāmamālā*, II. 84 takes it to mean *varuḍa* a low-caste man.

10 The *bhillas* were the aborigines inhabiting forests and often robbing travellers and caravans and indulged in slave-trade. They had a close group life with a chief exercising the highest power, which probably explains their inclusion in this list.

(fishermen). Al-Bīrūnī[1] mentions fowlers, shoe-makers, jugglers, basket and shield-makers, sailors, fishermen, hunters of wild animals and birds and weavers as the eight classes of people who formed guilds. It is to be noted that he does not refer to guilds of craftsmen but confines himself to those who are generally regarded as the *antyajas*. The legal works of the period mention some names in discussing guilds. Thus Medhātithi[2] mentions artisans, tradesmen, moneylenders and coach-drivers. The *Mitākṣarā*[3] refers to the horse-dealers (*beḍābukas*), weavers, shoe-makers and betel-sellers. The *Smṛticandrikā*[4] mentions only weavers. Guilds referred to in the inscriptions include those of oilmen (*tailika*)[5], betelsellers (*tāmbolika*)[6], distllers of liquor (*kallapāla*)[7], gardeners (*mālika*)[8] and elephant-drivers (*mahāmātra*)[9].

Apprentice—

We know from earlier Smṛtis that the new member of a guild learned his craft or trade from an elder member whom he served as an apprentice. It appears from the *Kṛtyakalpataru*[10] that this form of carrying down the knowledge of the craft in the guilds was still alive in this peiod. The text however aimed at making the rules of apprenticeship more humane. Thus it tried to curb the power of the master to punish the apprentice. It explains the power of the master to order the *vadha* of the apprentice if the latter is wicked as meaning only beating him with a bamboo-stick and adds that it merely empowers the master to inflict some corporeal punishment.

———

1 I. 101.
2 On Manu, VIII. 41.
3 On Yāj., II. 30.
4 II, p. 223.
5 *E.I.*, I. 159f, 1.16. Also ibid.XXIII. 138.
6 *E.I.*, I. 175, 1.26. Also *C.I.I.*IV, no. 42, 1.34.
7 *E.I.*, I. 174, ll. 8-10. Also *C.I.*, IV, no. 42, 1.33.
8 *E.I.*, I. 159f, 1.19; XXIV. 331.
9 *C.I.I.*, IV, no. 120, ll.4ff.
10 *Vyavahārakāṇḍa*, p. 384.

CHAPTER V

INLAND TRADE

Inter-state trade—

Inter-state trade continued in our period. This is obvious from the fact that many important items of daily use like spices, luxury goods, metals and salt which were used in all parts of India came from different regions. We need not list literary or epigraphic references to prove that commodities of one part were being consumed in other parts.

Medhātithi makes a reference to the vaiśyas as carrying on inter-state trade. He is not satisfied merely with referring to the travels for trade on land and water as one of the functions of a vaiśya but specifically refers also to his importing useful goods from other states into the kingdom in which he lives[1]. He advises that a vaiśya should know the states where large supplies of *vrīhi* are available, the time when barley is profuse, the custom of the states, the nature of the people, the advantages and disadvantages relating to the different states[2] and also the languages of Mālava, Magadha, Draviḍa and other countries, i.e., in such a country this word is employed to denote this thing[3]

We have many references to indicate that traders of one part of India visited other parts. Thus we read in the *Samarāiccakahā* that a merchant named Dharaṇa belonging to the city called Mākandi goes to Acalapura, sells his goods by taking certain portion of profit and spending some time in purchase and sale finally returns with merchandise fit for trade at Mākandi[4]. The *Kathāsaritsāgara*[5] refers to the son of a merchant who was ordered by his

---

1 On Manu, I. 90, 31.

2 Ibid., IX. 331.

3 Ibid., IX. 332.

4 VI, p. 16.

5 p. 85.

father to go to another country where he had some business interests. Another story in the same text speaks of a merchant of Pāṭaliputra going to Valabhī on business[1]. The *Kuvalayamālākathā* refers to merchants of the different regions of north and south meeting together[2]. An inscription from Ahar (Udaipur) dated A. D. 953[3] mentions merchants from Karṇāṭa, Madhyadeśa, Lāṭa and Ṭakka (the region between the upper waters of the Chenab and the Ravi)[4] coming to the place and agreeing to pay a levy on their articles of sale. A similar agreement arrived at by horse dealers from different parts is recorded in the Pehoa (Karnal) inscription dated A. D. 882-83[5].

Cultural contacts between regions—

The commercial contact between the different regions is to be studied in the background of the cultural intercourse between them. The frequent religious journeys to the places of pilgrimage (*tīrthas*) scattered throughout the country must have kept alive the contacts between the different parts[6]. Educational centres in one part of the country attracted students from all corners of the country. We can form some idea of the number of students coming to Kashmir from Bengal from the fact that Kṣemendra in presenting the typical characters in the Kashmirian society devotes the sixth chapter of his *Deśopadeśa* to the evil manners and the vulgar attitude of the students from Gauḍa studying in Kashmir. It would appear that people frequently visited other parts of the country. Thus according to the *Rājataraṅgiṇī*[7] for the residence of the people from Madhyadeśa, Lāṭa and Saurāṣṭra a *maṭha* was constructed by queen Diddā. In our support we may refer to an inscription from Elleswaram (Nalgonda, Andhra) in florid Nāgarī characters of about the tenth century which mentions a *rājaputra* from Varendri-viṣaya

1 p. 130.

2 *Apabhraṃśa-kāvyatrayī* (G.O.S.), Introduction, p. 91.

3 *Prācīnalekhamālā*, Vol. II, p. 24.

4 *D.H.N.I.*, I, p. 119.

5 *E.I.*, I. 186.

6 *Indian Archaeology*, 1957 58, p. 55.

7 VI. 300.

(north Bengal)[1]. It is well known that saint Nimbārka, a south Indian, went to the birth place of Śrī Kṛṣṇa and for long years resided there. The educative and cultural values of travelling have been emphatically brought out by the *Kuṭṭanīmata*[2] which says that those who have not travelled, and are ignorant of the manners, customs and character of alien peoples, and have thus not learned to pay respect to the respectable, are like bulls without horns. From the land-grants we find that pious and learned families of the brāhmaṇas travelled far and wide, and receiving donations at the hands of a patronising king settled in distant lands. Thus we find many brāhmaṇa families migrating from Madhyadeśa to Bengal, Malwa, Dakṣiṇa Kośala, Orissa and many other countries. Even in the far south in the Pāṇḍya kingdom there was a large settelment of brāhmaṇas from Magadha[3]. Many brāhmaṇa families from Bengal are known to have settled in Orissa, Mālava and the Deccan[4]. In the land-grants of Bengal we have references to the settlements in Bengal of brāhmaṇas coming from Lāṭa, Madhyadeśa and many other places[5]. The career of Bilhaṇa illustrates how scholars and poets in the period covered long distances in search of patronage. From Kashmir he went to Mathurā and then passing through Kannauj and Prayāga reached Banaras. Staying at the court of the Kalacuri king Karṇa for some years he went to Dhārā, Anahilavāḍa and Somanātha. From the port of Berāvala he sailed for Hoṇāvara near Gokarṇa. Travelling towards south he went upto Rāmeśvaram. Finally he moved north and for many years enjoyed the patronage of the Western Cālukya king Vikramāditya. The speed with which ideas travelled from one part of the country to another indicates the close contacts between them. Thus the commentary of Aparārka, though written in southern India, seems to have become popular in Kashmir within a few years of its com-

---

1 *Indian Archaeology*, 1955-56, p. 30.

2 v. 211.

3 *I.A.*, 1893, p. 74.

4 *History of Bengal*, I, pp, 581f.

5 Ibid., p. 579, f.n. 1. Also D. C. Ganguly, *History of the Paramāra Dynasty*, p. 240 ; Barua, *Cultural History of Assam*, p. 109.

position[1]. The Gāhaḍavāla dynasty is known to have maintained close relations with southern India which are reflected in the names of some of the revenue items appearing in the land-grants[2]. We learn that king Harṣa introduced in Kashmir some of the dresses, ornaments and coin-types of southern India[3].

Caravan trade—

The merchants who participated in the inter-state trade generally travelled in groups. Viśvarūpa[4] explains *naigama* (corporation of the merchants) as a group of caravan traders and others[5]. Aparārka explains the term to mean traders of different castes who travel together for the purposes of carrying out trade with other countries. In the popular stories of the period we often read of a merchant and caravan leader, approaching the king of another state and offering valuable presents in order to secure his permission to do business[6]. The *Tilakamañjarī*[7] in speaking of the outskirts of a city mentions the caravans as camping there. The caravans were regarded as a safe protection against the robbers infesting the highways. A verse in the *Suvṛttatilaka*[8] says that in pride of power a man in the company of his caravan paces across the extremely dreadful wilderness made all the more terrible by pitiless robbers.

From the *Bhavisayattakahā*[9] we learn that the big merchants before proceeding on their caravan journey used to proclaim their intention to the other merchants in the city and invite them to join them by offering a number of facilities. In the *Samarāiccakahā*[10] the leader of the caravan tells the travellers, when they had collected, the advantages of the route he proposes to take and gives them many pieces of advice for their guidance. The *Triṣaṣṭiśalākā*-

1 Kane, *History of Dharmaśāstra*, II. 333f.

2 *Kumāragadīāṇaka* and *yamalikāmbali*.

3 *Rāj*., VII. 921-26.

4 On Yāj., II. 192—*sārthavāhādisamūho naigamaḥ*.

5 p. 796—*saha deśāntaravāṇijyārthaṃ ye nānājātīyā adhigacchanti te naigamāḥ*.

6 *Bṛhatkathākośa*, LV. 200ff.

7 p. 117.

8 p. 11 (II. 29).

9 pp. 16f.

10 pp. 476f.

puruṣacarita[1] gives a vivid description of the journey by the caravan under the leadership of a wealthy merchant Dhana in the city Kṣitipratiṣṭhita. Planning to go with much merchandise to another city he proclaimed with the beat of drums throughout the city his proposed journey and invited others to go with him. He offered to give merchandise to those without it, conveyance to those who had no conveyances, companions to the friendless, and provisions to those lacking in provisions and to protect his weak followers from robbers and from attacks by wild animals on the way and to cherish them like relatives[2]. At an auspicious moment propitious rites were performed by highborn women and the merchant ascended his chariot and went outside the city. All the people who were going to Vasantapura came there at the sound of the drum of departure. Then the caravan set out with horses, camels, carts and oxen. Dhana went at the head of the caravan and a friend of his, Maṇibhadra, brought up the rear. They advanced unhindered, attended by multitudes of horsemen at their sides. The merchandise, difficult to carry, was carried by camels, buffaloes, fine oxen, mules and donkeys. The mules had sacks on their sides. The merchants were sitting in carts which looked like moving houses. The huge-bodied and high-shouldered buffaloes were carrying water. The camels were carrying large loads. Surrounded on all sides by armed guards, the caravan advanced safely along the road; robbers, fearing its might, stayed at a distance from the caravan. Dhana was equally eager for the poor man's obtaining and the rich man's enjoying and led them all as befits a true leader.

In the summer season members of the caravan stopped at every tree near a pond and took rest and drank water. The travellers alleviated the fatigue caused by the scorching heat of summer by fans made of leaves. We read of the presence of matrons also in the caravan.

In rains as a result of the impassability of the road from the water, thorns, and mud, two miles seemed like eight hundred.

---

1 Vol. I, pp. 7ff.

2 It was not out of economic considerations that he offered such generous terms. The explanation is to be sought probably in the Jain piety.

Travellers advanced very slowly, and were covered with new mud up to the knees "as if they had put on boots". The carts mired everywhere in the terrible mud on the road. The camels led by ropes by their riders who had dismounted, slipped at every step and fell on the road. When the merchant Dhana noticed the impassability of the road, he stopped and made a camp at that very place in the forest. To pass the season thatched huts were made. In course of time provisions of food were exhausted and everyone got very worried.

But one morning Dhana found that the roads had become easily passable with their mud dried up by the sun's rays. Thinking that it was time for departure the merchant had the departure drum sounded. At the sound of the drum the caravan set out. Dhana himself set out only after providing for the protection of the caravan by guards in front, at the rear, and at the sides. After crossing the great forest the caravan travelling without hindrance arrived at Vasantapura. In a short time Dhana sold his merchandise and took exchange goods. Thereafter he returned to his own city Kṣitipratiṣṭhita.

Transport and conveyance—

In this description we have noticed a reference to the beasts of burden. Medhātithi[1] makes a clear reference to the carts (*gantrī*) and describes them as drawn by bullocks, mules, buffaloes and other animals and adds that these same animals also when ridden upon may be taken as denoting conveyances. The *Bṛhannāradīya Purāṇa*[2] mentions as a peculiar custom of its time the prohibition of a householder's riding camels or cars drawn by them. This probably reflects the opinion prevailing in the eastern regions of northern India about the use of camels which probably had not become very popular outside the desert areas.

It would appear that providing for transport and conveyance was a very lucrative business in this period. In the *Upamiti-bhavaprapañcākathā*[3] the list of trades and professions which were

1 On Manu, VIII. 290.
2 XXIV. 26.
3 pp. 867-68.

supposed to yield the highest income makes a prominent reference to sending caravans of large carts and providing of herds of big camels and mules. The *Līlāvatī*[1] poses a mathematical problem to calculate the cart-hire for transporting logs of wood of given dimensions over a specified distance.

The rules for hiring a conveyance or a labourer to transport merchandise which appear in earlier legal texts[2] would seem to have held ground in our period also. The commentaries do not have much new legislation on the point and are concerned only with clarifying the existing rules. But by way of elucidation they add more details. Thus Medhātithi[3] says that a merchant borrowing wheeled conveyance but not actually proceeding on his journey is not to pay the entire amount of interest stipulated; when the oxen go a long distance, it involves much labour on their part, so that it is right that the reward of their owner should be commensurate with that labour; but when they have returned sooner than stipulated, it is open to the owner to make further profit on them by hiring them out afresh. The same rule applies to the cases like those where a man takes bullocks for a month but returns them earlier.

Roads—

In the dictionaries of the period we have many terms for a carriage street, a small street, a high street and a high road[4]. The *Deśīnāmamālā* gives many terms which it explains as *rathyā*[5] (a carriage street) or *laghurathyā*[6] (a small carriage street) but we cannot find out if there was any minute technical difference in the meaning of these. It is significant that the *Abhidhānaratnamālā*[7] mentions the terms in connection with a city. The *Samarāṅgaṇasūtradhāra*[8]

1 p. 35 (no. 84).

2 Nārada, VI. 7-9; Yāj. II. 197.

3 On Manu, VIII. 156.

4 *Vaijayantī*, p. 160, ll. 31-33; *Abhidhānaratnamālā*, v. 289.

5 III. 31; IV. 8; VI. 39; VII. 55; VIII. 6; I. 145.

6 III. 31.

7 v. 289.

8 I, p. 39, vv. 6-14.

also speaks of many kinds of roads in its chapter on the lay-out of a city. No doubt the villages did not have well-planned streets like those in a city. But it would appear that they were often connected with the high roads. In many land-grants highways are mentioned in connection with the enumeration of the boundaries of the donated land[1].

The important roads seem to have been well demarcated with mile-stones. In giving the details of the important trade routes the Arab accounts mention the exact distance between any two places. It would be reasonable to suppose that these accounts were based on the actual distances as recorded on the mile-stones erected by the state.

Difficulties and discomforts of road-journey—

But the condition of the roads would appear to have been far from satisfactory. We have already seen in the passage from the *Triṣaṣṭiśalākāpuruṣacarita* that during the rains the roads were often impassable. In the *Sandeśarāsaka*[2] it is said that in the rainy season the travellers with shoes in hand waded through the waters, waves roared in rivers rendered uncrossable and travellers had to halt midway, using boats if business still forced them to travel. The roads do not appear to have been well maintained. We often read of the rugged character of the road[3]. The uneven nature of the roads was a general complaint which deterred people from undertaking a journey[4]. The number of well maintained and regular roads would not seem to have been very large. Medhātithi[5] speaks of an army on march cutting down the trees, bushes and creepers obstructing the path, and levelling the undulations of the ground, preparing fords in rivers and steps to cross ravines, destroying the wild animals besetting the path, winning over the path-finders to its side, and getting together supplies of

1 *I.B.*, III. 158ff ; *Kāmarūpaśāsanāvalī*, p. 180.

2 vv. 141-42.

3 *Dohākośa*, p. 311 (XIV. 20).

4 *Upamitibhavaprapañcākathā*, p. 863—*viṣamā mārgāḥ*.

5 On Manu, VII. 185.

food and fodder etc. In the *Triṣaṣṭiśalākāpuruṣacarita*[1] also it is said in connection with the march of an army that ten thousand men, carrying axes and pickaxes, cut the tree etc. from their road and made the ground level.

The *Kuṭṭanīmata*[2] gives a very dismal picture of the difficulties which a traveller might face. At the fall of day he drags himself to some village, his body covered with rags, his strength exhausted by the long march, all grey with a layer of dust, and asks for shelter in very humble words. He is greeted with rebukes and harsh words and if he is fortunate enough to get a seat in the corner of an old hut the neighbouring housewives flock to express their apprehension of his being a thief. Having thus visited a hundred houses and suffered the tortures of privation, the unfortunate traveller will soon come down to begging by the roadside a meagre handful of rice or beans, of peas or lentils. The text discourages travelling, extols the joy of remaining in one's own house, and adds that a traveller's food depends upon the caprice of others; the earth is his bed, the temple his home and a broken brick is his pillow. This account applies only to the poor traveller and intentionally exaggerates the horrors of travelling with a view to discouraging a man from undertaking it.

Facilities for travellers—

We have references to public supplies of water on the roadside[3]. The *Tilakamañjarī*[4] describes a water reservoir for the use of travellers on the outskirts of a city. Its banks were surrounded by circular white-washed cloister (*varaṇḍikā*), it was made of compact piles of bricks and had rows of stairs going down into water. In the *Samayamātṛkā*[5] we read of a woman who kept an inn (*pānthāvasatha-pālikā*). There were small shops of general merchants who used to supply the travellers and caravan-men with

1 IV, p. 325.
2 vv. 218-29.
3 *Kavikaṇṭhābharaṇa*, V, p. 22; *Deśīnāmamālā*, VIII. 21.
4 p. 117.
5 II. 3.

provisions for their journeys. The mathematical texts[1] give mathematical problems in which a traveller asks a shop-keeper to hurry and supply him with provisions for a certain amount of money. As in earlier texts providing facilities and comforts for travellers is mentioned in the texts of this period as an act of merit. In the *Kṛtyakalpataru* water-giving and building water-sheds is mentioned under miscellaneous gifts[2]. Hemādri[3] and later writers devote a separate section to the merit of providing wells and water-sheds in desert places and roads and giving a pot filled with cool water to a traveller. This aspect of charitable work was noticed by Abū Zaid Hasan[4] who says that one part of the devotion of the Indians consists in building inns upon the highways for the accommodation of travellers, where they also set up dealers, of whom the passengers may purchase what they want. Tejapāla, the minister of Vīradhavala, is said to have constructed many water-sheds[5]. In the *Bṛhatkathāślokasaṅgraha*[6] we have a reference to a charitable house where travellers were shaved, attended to and massaged. From the *Prabandhacintāmaṇi*[7] it would follow that conscientious kings maintained charitable houses (*sattrāgāra*) where travellers coming from other parts were given food, hot water and oil to wash their feet to remove fatigue and a room to pass the night. In the *Tilakamañjarī*[8] the king is found making the officers in-charge resume providing food, drink, beds and medicine to the poor, orphans, travellers and caravan-men in the charitable houses which had been reported as closed down.

In some of the land-grants of our period[9] the list of officers addressed includes *gamāgamika* who probably not only kept

1 *Bījagaṇita*, p. 255 ; *Līlāvatī*, pp. 39f, no. 97.

2 *Dāna*, pp. 257a, 261, 263.

3 *Caturvargacintāmaṇi*, *Dānakhaṇḍa*, pp. 421ff.

4 *Ancient Accounts of India and China*, pp. 87f.

5 *Prabandhacintāmaṇi*, p. 99, l.29.

6 XVIII. 355-56.

7 p. 106, ll. 4-7.

8 p. 66.

9 *C.I.I.*, IV, nos. 7, 25, 26.

a watch on persons coming into or going out of the village but also looked to their comforts.

River-traffic—

In the plains of northern India rivers were often a better and safer means of travelling and of transporting merchandise than roads. The *Caryāpadas*[1] often illustrate their philosophy with the help of similes drawn from the life of a boatman, the construction of the boats and the actual method of plying boats. It would appear from the *Uktivyaktiprakaraṇa*[2] that river traffic was very common in eastern U.P. and the boatmen had gained an intimate knowledge of the course of the rivers and their depth at different places. In the *Rājataraṅgiṇī*[3] we find many references to river journeys. Some of the rivers in Assam also seem to have been used for transport and travelling[4].

Ferry dues seem to have been an important source of state income. Officers in charge of ferries are often mentioned in the records of our period[5]. The fiscal expression *svanaukābhāṭaka* appearing in one of the Gāhaḍavāla records[6] would suggest that the state had its own boats which could be used by private persons and boatmen by paying the necessary fare. The state would seem to have kept strict control over the ferries. In the *Prabandhacintāmaṇi*[7] we read that when once Bhoja fell seriously ill, the officers, who did not want the news to spread, controlled the roads leading to the fords and completely stopped the coming of the people from other states.

Bridges—

It is however to be noticed that though bridges seem to have been constructed in the hilly areas of Assam and Kashmir,

1 *Bauddha Gān O' Dohā*, vv. 13, 38, 49. See also *Caryāgītikoṣa*, Introduction, p. 21.

2 p. 46, l. 11 ; p. 39, l. 7.

3 V. 84 ; VII. 347, 714 , 1628.

4 P. C. Choudhury, *History of Civilization of Assam*, p. 379.

5 *Tarika* and *tarapati*.

6 Candravati grant of Candradeva dated A. D. 1093—*E.I.*, XIV. 193-96.

7 p. 51, ll. 13-15.

they were not much in use in the plains. In the *Rājataraṅgiṇī*[1] there is a reference to the making of boat-bridges over the river Vitastā as early as the reign of Pravarasena II (6th century A. D.). In later times also we read of the erection of boat-bridges. Thus Sujji is said to have constructed a boat-bridge over the river Gambhīrā which was of great advantage to him in the battle of Gambhīrā[2]. From the Muslim accounts we learn that there were in Assam stone bridges over the rivers and the soldiers of Assam defeated the attack of Bakhtyār Khaljī by destroying one of these[3]. But in the plains bridges do not seem to have been much in use. In the literary references we find no instance when people are said to have crossed a river by a bridge. The commentary of Medhātithi supplies us with negative evidence on this point. Thus in describing the march of an army it speaks of cutting the trees, thickets and creepers obstructing the path, levelling the ground and preparing fords in rivers and ravines, but is silent about the construction or repair of bridges[4]. Likewise Medhātithi explains *saṃkrama* (crossing) in Manu not as a bridge but as a contrivance by which people enter the water to bathe[5]. The commentary on the *Rāmacarita*[6] speaks of Rāmapāla, when he went out to crush the Kaivarta rebellion as crossing the Gaṅgā on a bridge of boats.

Insecurity on the highways—

The volume of trade in our period seems to have gone down as a result of the insecurity of the highways. The absence of a strong central power led to the growth of feudal anarchy and the increase in the power of unsocial elements. This state of affairs would appear to have begun in the period of political disintegration following the disappearance of the Guptas from the scene. It is significant that Fa-hsien was never troubled by robbers in his

1 III.354.
2 VIII. 1502.
3 Raverty, *Tabaqāt-i-Nāsirī*, pp. 569f.
4 On Manu, VII. 185.
5 IX. 285—*Saṃkramaḥ. Yena saṃkrāmanti mārgeṇāvataranti jalopasparśādinā nimittena.*
6 II. 10—*Gaṅgāyāṃ taraṇi sambhavena naukāmelakena.*

journey through India, but Hsüan Tsang was twice molested by them[1]. In the *Sandeśarāsaka*[2] a traveller describes the night journey as troublesome because the road is difficult and is full of perils. We have seen above in the *Triṣaṣṭiśalākāpuruṣacarita* passage that the caravans often stood in danger from the robbers on the highways and it was only the armed guard that kept the robbers away. The *Upamitibhavaprapañcākathā* refers to the general fear the merchants had for robbers[3]. It was not unusual for a caravan to be looted by the robbers infesting a forest. In the popular stories of the period we often read of the merchants and their caravans being attacked by forest tribes or robber chiefs[4]. In one of his songs Bhūsuku tells that when after crossing the Padmā canal he reached East Bengal the dacoits took away whatever he had in his boat[5]. The *Rājataraṅgiṇī*[6] speaks of a powerful robber chief and his gang near Gayā who had become a scourge to wayfarers.

Feudal chiefs and their wars—

It would appear that the merchants feared not only the gangs of professional robbers but also petty feudal chiefs who, taking advantage of the existing political chaos and the weakness of the central authority, found robbery highly profitable. Medhātithi interprets the injunction in Manu[7] to consider the welfare (*yogakṣema*) of the merchants in imposing taxes on them to refer to the apprehension of or freedom from robbery from both king and robbers while the merchants are passing through a forest. From the Muslim accounts we learn that it was a problem for the early Muslim rulers to deal effectively with petty feudal chiefs who molested and plundered traders on the highways[8]. We can

1 *The Life*, pp. 60f, 73f, 86, 198ff. See also I-tsing, pp. xxxi-xxxiii.

2 v. 117—*maggu duggamu sabhaü.*

3 p. 863.

4 *Upamiti*, pp. 633f; *Kathākoṣa*, p. 207.

5 *Bauddha Gān O' Dohā*, v. 49.

6 VII. 1009.

7 VII. 127—"*Yogakṣemam*" *araṇye kāntāre vā gacchato rājabhayaṃ caurabhayaṃ niścauratā vetyādi.*

8 Elliot and Dowson, II, p. 380 for the *Tabaqāt-i-Nāsirī*. See also Habib, Introduction (pp. 73f) to Elliot and Dowson, Vol. II. Cf. Vidyāpati's *Kīrtilatā* (Ed. B.R. Saksena), II :p. 16—*Ṭhākura ṭhaka bhaë.*

fairly assume that these chiefs had started looting and robbing even earlier when the absence of a central power strong enough to curb them helped the feudal tendencies to gain momentum. Significantly enough the *Vastupālacarita*[1] mentions a feudal chief (*maṇḍalīka*) named Ghūghula who used to plunder the caravans of merchants. The career of Lakṣmaṇa, the founder of the Cāhamāna dynasty of Nadol, would suggest that the feudal chiefs of the period often indulged in such activities. As convincingly suggested by D. Sharma[2] the traditions recorded in the *Purātanaprabandha-saṅgraha* and Nainsī's *Khyāt* indicate that Lakṣmaṇa robbed some caravan of all its horses and that his looting expedition extended to the confines of Mewar and Gujarat.

The political vicissitudes of the time and the frequent feudal raids and internecine wars must also have hampered trade by adding to the insecurity and disturbances created by other factors. Medhātithi[3] speaks of the merchants who prepare to go on a trading journey to a distant city but are unable to do so, being forced back by difficulties in the form, among other things of political upheavals and disturbances (*rāṣṭropaplava*). An important argument which a mother puts forward to dissuade her son from going out with a caravan to trade is the danger of war[4]. The *Prabandhacintāmaṇi*[5] speaks of travelling becoming difficult due to the political insecurity and turmoil about the year A.D. 1219.

In some of the commentaries of our period we find an ignorance about the use of the term *sārtha* for a caravan in the original text. Thus the *Parāśaramādhavīya*[6] explains it as the assemblage of people collected on the occasion of village festivities and mentions the village headman as an illustration of its chief. The *Vyavahāra-*

1 p. 100.

2 *Early Chauhān Dynasties*, pp. 121f.

3 On Manu, VIII. 156.

4 *Bhavisayattakahā*, p. 17—*Vihi paḍikūlu amha paḍisakkai. Atthaham cheū karibi ko sakkai.*

5 p. 100, ll. 8f—*Rājyavikalatāyāṃ tīrthamārgāṇāṃ vaiṣamyam.*

6 III, p. 25—*Sārthino grāmayātrādau milito janasaṅghaḥ. Mukhyā grāmaṇyādayaḥ.*

prakāśa[1] agrees with this and explains *sārthavāha* as the chief of the assemblage of people collected on the occasion of village festivities and religious ceremonies. Likewise Bhaṭṭotpala[2] explains *sārtha* as a group of people and calls its chief *arthapati*. We may suggest that this confusion about the real import of the term was really due to the fact that caravan journeys had ceased to be made as frequently as in earlier periods.

---

1 p. 9—*Sārtho grāmadevayātrādau milito janasaṅghaḥ tanmukhyāḥ sārthavāhādayaḥ*.

2 On *B. S.*, LXXXV. 11—*Sārthe pradhānaṃ—sārhe janasamūhe pradhānam-arthapatim*.

CHAPTER VI

FOREIGN TRADE—(A) LAND ROUTE.

Political background—

The Himalayan ranges in the north-west of India have through their passes provided a convenient passage not only to invading hordes from outside but also to daring merchants on both sides. The overland route connected India on the one hand with China and on the other with Persia, Arabia and Asia Minor. The trade across these overland routes has been vitally affected by the policies of the state and the political stability in the areas concerned. Under the Kuṣāṇas this trade was in a flourishing condition. The growth of the Hūṇa power had a serious impact upon the trade activity. We find the Hūṇas spreading over the entire western half of the overland route passing through Central Asia.

Appearance of Islam—

But it would appear that trade between Europe and the Orient continued even during these times of turmoil. The appearance of Islam seriously diminished the volume of European commerce. The two religions across the Mediterranean being unfriendly, the free flow of commerce between the areas on its two sides was severely affected[1].

The Arabs created difficulties for this trade in the early years of the expansion of Islam. We have the testimony of I-tsing[2] who speaks of the Ta-shī as interfering with travel on the road to Kapiśa. We may connect their expansion towards Central Asia with their desire to control the overland trade between the east and the west. The Arabs made repeated attempts to advance towards India though it was only in 712 that they succeeded in occupying Sind and Multan. They only gained control of the route passing through north-western India in about 1022 A.D.

1 H. Pirenne, *Economic and Social History of Medieval Europe*, pp. 1-3.

2 Chavannes, *Religieux eminents*, 25.

Quadrangular struggle—Tibetan expansion—

In the first half of the seventh century the Chinese empire had carried its influence to the borders of Persia[1]. From the Chinese sources we learn that the period roughly from 650 to 750 witnessed a quadrangular struggle between the Turks, the Tibetans, the Arabs and the Chinese for the occupation of Central Asia[2]. The period is characterised by a considerable expansion of Tibetan arms. The Tibetans were troublesome neighbours for the Chinese. They established their hegemony over Central Asia, especially the regions in the north-east and south-east and appear to have expanded their influence southwards to Bengal. It is not without significance that Al Iṣtakhrī and Ibn Haukal call the Bay of Bengal the Tibetan Sea[3].

Role of Kashmir—

The Indian states especially those in the north felt the impact of this struggle[4]. It has been suggested that Kashmir was a subordinate ally of the Chinese in the seventh century and it was Chinese aid in men and money which led to the spectacular rise of Kashmir in the period. Kashmir fought against the Arabs, Tukhāras and Daradas and blocked the route to Tibet. We may add that the policy of Karkoṭa Kashmir of aggrandisement in the north Indian plains may also be attributed in the same manner to a desire to bring to an end the expansion of Tibetan arms in Bengal.

Rivalry between Tibet and China—

The Chinese seem to have been much concerned with the threat from Tibet and were earnestly trying to enlist the sympathies of Indian powers on their side. The Chinese sources represent the Pallavas as begging Chinese aid against the Arabs and the Tibetans[5]. We may legitimately suspect the correctness of this.

---

1 Yule, *Cathay*, I, 98ff.

2 Tsui Chi, *A Short history of Chinese civilization*, p. 144.

3 Reinaud, *Aboulfeda*, I, p. ccclviii.

4 *I.H.Q.*, XXX. 89-92.

5 K. A. N. Sastri, *Foreign Notices*, p. 16.

It is clear that the southern Indian state had not much to fear from these powers and it was the Chinese emperor who had sought the help of the Pallavas. We learn from the Chinese sources that the Chinese emperor in 787 applied to the Uighurs, the princes of India and the Caliph of Baghdad for alliances against the Tibetans[1].

It is fair to expect that the Tibetans must have decreased the volume of trade flowing between India and China. It is probably to this that the Chinese narratives refer when they observe that towards 758-60 China having lost the country of Holong (according to Yule Khulum in the valley of the Oxus) the kings of India ceased to send homage[2]. From the accounts of Abū Zaid we get a hint of commercial rivalry between Tibet and China. He observes that the musk of Tibet is far preferable to that of China[3].

Central Asian route—

Abū Zaid indicates that by his time the Central Asian route had once again come into use. He describes the route between Transoxiana and China but at the same time notes that it is a two months journey through impracticable deserts and through a country covered with sand, where no water is to be found. Daring traders could be found who with a vessel full of musk on their backs travelled on foot from Samarkand to Khanfu (Canton), but their number was hardly worth taking note[4]. Ma Tuan-lin and the *Sung-shï* speak of the journey in the east of Fu-lin starting from western Ta-shī to Yū-tin (Khotan), Hui-ho, Ch'ing-t'ang and then finally to China[5]. The *Sung-shī* further refers to a priest of the Wëi-chou returning to China from the Western Regions with a foreign priest and presenting to the Emperor letters from the Prince of Northern India, and also from the Prince of the Diamond Throne (Vajrāsana, Bodhgaya) of Nālandā[6]. Some of the Buddhist monks travelling between India and China in the

1 Ibid., p. 17.

2 *Cathay*, I. 72.

3 *Ancient Accounts of India and China*, p. 76.

4 Ibid., pp. 75-76.

5 F. Hirth, *China and the Roman Orient*, pp. 62, 88f.

6 Chau Ju-kua, p. 114, ll. 23ff.

tenth century used the route from Kashmir, Peshawar, Khulum, Khotan, Kucha, Karashahr, I Chau (Kamul), Sha Chau and Kan Chau and knew the route connecting Udyāna, Gandhāra, Nagarahāra, Lamghan, Ghazni and Persia[1].

Larger use of sea-route—

We can demonstrate with the help of Chinese accounts how the Central Asian route was gradually being replaced by the sea-route[2]. Thus the *Sui-shu* at one place speaks of the kingdom of Ts'au or Ki-pin (Kabul) as having *an-si-hiang*, *ts'ing-mu* (putchuck) and other aromatic substances and in another context mentions *an-si-hiang* among the products of K'iu-tzï (Kuchar, Chinese Turkestan). The *Pön-ts'au-kang-mu* gives *kü-pei-lo* as the foreign name of *an-si-hiang* which is thus *khādira* (catechu) or *kundura* (Indian frankincense). It would follow from this that China received *an-si-hiang* from India through the overland route connecting Ki-pin and Kuchar. The *Yu-yang-tsa-tsu* in stating that *an-si-hiang* tree comes from Po-ssï (Persia) was obviously implying the existence of the route across Central Asia. Significantly enough Chau Ju-kua is silent about *an-si-hiang* which suggests that it did not reach China in his time. The *Pön-ts'au* would suggest that the transit across Central Asia was replaced by one across the seas by way of Indonesia. It says that formerly *an-si-hiang* came from Persia but now Annan, San-fo-ts'i (Palembang, E. Sumatra) and all foreign countries have it.

China's disinterest in the Central Asian route—

The decline of the trade-route across Central Asia was to a great extent due to the loss of Chinese interest in it. This disinterest may have been due in part to their inability to control the Central Asian states. But even as early as the second half of the seventh century the sea-route between India and China was more in use than the overland route. Thus, out of the sixty Chinese pilgrims to India mentioned by I-tsing thirty-seven are found to

1 *Cathay*, I. 72-73.

2 Chau Ju-kua, pp. 201-2, f.n.

have gone by sea[1]. We have seen elsewhere the gradually increasing emphasis on sea-trade in the policy of China[2]. Kia Tan as quoted by Chau Ju-kua[3] explaining the preference for the sea-route says "As Ta-mo (Dharma)[4] came sailing across the sea to P'an-yū (Canton), we may fairly ask whether the sea journey is not more expeditious than the long overland one". The religious sanction was merely an excuse to cover China's inability to participate in the overland trade.

Routes through Assam, Burma and Sikkim—

It would appear that chaotic conditions on the route across north-western India and Central Asia led merchants to seek and develop possibilities in other directions. From very early times we have references to routes connecting India and China through the hills of Assam and Burma and through Sikkim, the Chumb valley and Tibet. The report submitted by the Chinese ambassadoı Chang-kien would indicate that even about 126 B.C. a trade route connected southern China across upper Burma ultimately with Bactria[5]. From I-tsing we learn that in the third and fourth centuries some twenty Chinese priests came to India from Szuchuan through upper Burma[6]. The embassy to China sent by a king of the Kapili valley, referred to in the *Shung-shu* (A.D. 420-479)[7], most likely used the route across upper Burma. From Hsüan-Tsang[8] also it appears that Kāmarūpa had contacts with China. In the early medieval period the route across upper Burma came in for greater use. The itinerary of Kia Tan (A.D. 785-805) gives a very detailed account of the land route from Tonkin to Kāmarūpa, implying a regular use of it. The route passed through Yunnansen, Yunnan-fou and Talifou ; going westwards it crossed the Salween

1 Chavannes, *Mem. sur les Religieux eminents*, passim.

2 See infra ch. VII—Foreign trade—the Sea route.

3 p. 97.

4 This is Bodhidharma, by now a legendary figure in China.

5 See P. C. Bagchi, *India and China*, pp. 7f, 16f.

6 P. C. Choudhury, *History of Civilization of Assam*, p. 381.

7 *J.R.A.S.*, 1910, pp. 1187f.

8 *Si-yu-ki*, II, pp. 195-98. See also P. C. Bagchi, *India and China*, pp. 200f.

at Young-chang and then led to Chou-ko-leang to the east of Momein between Shiveli and the Salween. From Chou-ko-leang the main route passing through Si-li (halfway between Ta-gaung and Mandalay), Toumin (Pagan), Prome and the Arakan mountains reached Kāmarūpa. The minor route going to the west of Chou-ko-leang reached Teng Ch'ong (Momein) and then passing through Li-Shouei (on the Irrawaddy near Bhāmo) and crossing the river Māgaung finally reached Kāmarūpa through the town of Nagansi[1]. In the tenth century some three hundred missionaries from China on their journey to India used this route through Yunnan[2]. Chau Ju-kua speaks of tradition saying that north of Kiau-chī (Tongking) one comes to Ta-li (Yün-nan), and west of Ta-li one comes to Wang-shö-ch'öng (Magadha) in less than forty days journey. He quotes Kia Tan to show that there was an overland route from Annam to T'ien-chu (India)[3]. It is clear from all these references that there was a change between the time of Kia Tan and that of Chau Ju-kua and the land route had fallen into disfavour in comparison with the sea-route. However even as late as the sixteenth century the route continued to be in use. An Indian Buddhist monk named Buddhagupta belonging to the sixteenth century refers in his biography to the well-known land route connecting Kāmarūpa and Burma and is said to have himself used this route in travelling from Gauhati to Pagan[4].

Route through Tibet—

Another overland route passed through Bihar to Tibet and on to China[5]. The route between Magadha and Tibet must have

---

1 P. C. Bagchi, *India and China*, pp. 18f.

2 R. C. Majumdar, *Hindu Colonies in the Far East*, pp. 226f.

3 p. 97.

4 *I.H.Q.*, VII. 683-701.

5 It has been suggested that in the time of the *Periplus* and Ptolemy a route connected Assam with Bactria through Bhutan and Kabul—Choudhury, *History of the Civilization of the people of Assam*, pp. 383f. But the geographical obstacles on the suggested route make it highly impracticable for even the most daring mountaineer. It is obvious that to get from Assam to Bactria one would go by way of the Gaṅgā.

had greater use during the period of Tibetan expansion. The frequent journeys of Buddhist monks between Magadha and Tibet must have heightened the importance of the route[1]. The commercial intercourse between India and Tibet and China along the routes passing through Nepal radically influenced the economy of Nepal in our period. As pointed out by S. Levi[2] at the time when the *History of the T'ang* (A.D. 618-905) was compiled, merchants were numerous and cultivators rare in Nepal. The epigraphic records of earlier times reflect a rural community, but the growth of commercial activity through Nepal resulted in the growth of commerce and city life and the development of manual arts and industries. From the *Tabaqāt-i-Nāsirī*[3] we learn that Bengal received large number of horses which merchants brought through this route. Between Kāmarūpa and Tibet it speaks of thirty-five mountain passes through which horses were brought to Lakhnauti in Bengal. A town variously named as Karam-bain, Laram-bain or Karambatan and situated somewhere at the foot of the Himalayas[4] was the centre of the trade in horses carried along the route from Tibet. All the saddle horses which Lakhnauti received are said to have been brought from that place. The *Tabaqāt-i-Nāsirī* says that every morning about fifteen hundred horses were sold in the market of that city.

It was the lucrative trade passing through Tibet and Assam to China that led Mongols and also Indian kings to make efforts to dominate these routes. The possibilities of the trade impelled them to undertake daring expeditions along these difficult routes. Thus we read of a Mongol invasion of Bengal in 1244 "by way of Cathay Tibet". Bakhtyār Khaljī also advanced along the Assam valley. Malik Yuzbek undertook a similar enterprise in 1256-7. Muhammad Tughluq also sent an expedition against China but with no more success than the earlier expeditions referred to above[5].

1 *History of Bengal*, I, p. 663.

2 *Le Nepal*, II, p. 185.

3 Elliot and Dowson, II, pp. 311f.

4 Not as yet satisfactorily identified.

5 Yule, *Cathay*, I, pp. 78f.

Indian merchants on the north-western route—

We have evidence to suggest that Indian merchants actively participated in the trade along north-western India. It appears that though the Indians did not venture much into Central Asia they visited Iran going right up to the Oxus valley. Indian learning is found penetrating right up to Baghdad, sometimes through Iran and sometimes directly. The occupation of Sind by the Arabs brought India and the Muslim world closer to one another. During the reigns of Al-Manṣūr (754-775) and Harun Al-Rashīd (786-809) there was much direct intercourse with India. Under Harun Al-Rashīd the contact between the two regions became closer still through the active promotion by the ministers of the Barmak family. Standard Sanskrit works on medicine, mathematics, astrology, astronomy and philosophy were translated into Arabic and Indian specialists on these subjects were invited to Baghdad[1].

It is but natural to suppose that trade must have followed in the wake of the cultural contact. Ibn Khordādbah gives a detailed account of a road to eastern countries from Karkūz in Persia to Nārmasīrā on the boundary between Persia and Sind and connected with Debal[2]. For going to Sind, Al-Bīrūnī mentions the route from the country of Nīmroz or Sijistan and for India from Kabul, and adds that this is not the only possible road[3]. The people living between Multan and Mansura had camels which were much sought after in Khurāsān and other parts of Persia[4]. According to Al-Mas'ūdī, Multan was the place where the caravans for Khurāsān assembled[5]. Al-Idrīsī speaks of cotton cloths made at Kabul being exported to China, Khurāsān and Sind[6]. In the narratives of Chau Ju-kua we read of Tién-chu (India) trading

1 See the *Age of Imperial Kanauj*, pp. 448-452.

2 Elliot and Dowson, I. 14.

3 I. 198.

4 Ibn Haukal—Elliot and Dowson, I. 38 ; Al-Idrīsī—Elliot and Dowson, I. 83.

5 Elliot and Dowson, I. 21.

6 Ibid, 92.

yearly with Ta-ts'in and Fu-nan[1] most likely through the land route across north-western India. From Muhammad 'Aufī we learn of a Hindu merchant named Wasa Abhir from Nahrwala who had trade agents at Ghazni. His property at Ghazni was valued at ten lacs of rupees which suggests his flourishing trade. It is recorded that after his defeat at the hands of the Gujarat army, Mu'izz-ud-dīn bin Sam was advised to confiscate the property of Wasa Abhir[2]. Mu'izz-ud-dīn is said to have turned down the advice on grounds of justice. It may be suggested that Indian merchants at Ghazni must have acquired such influence and yielded such huge dues that the state did not dare to stop this channel of income for all times.

Imports through the north-western route—

It would appear that a considerable number of horses imported into India came along the overland route. Among the lists of horses in Sanskrit works we find names of breeds from countries naturally connected by the land-route. Thus, Bāhlika, Kāmboja and Turuṣka are mentioned by the *Upamitibhavaprapañcākathā* as the best[3]. The *Abhidhānaratnamālā* mentions horses from Persia, Vanāyu, Kāmboja, Bāhlika, Sindhu and the land bordering on the Sindhu as good ones[4]. From the *Vaijayantī* it follows that Bāhlika (Balkh) was sending not only its horses[5] but also saffron and asafoetida[6]. The same text suggests that the Ramaṭhas (living between Ghazni and Wakhan) were also known for their asafoetida[7]. The synonym *kāpiśāyana* for wine[8] suggests that wine from Kapiśā also came to India along the north-western route[9].

---

1 p. 111.
2 Elliot and Dowson, II. 200f.
3 p. 474.
4 (Aufrecht) II. 284.
5 p. 111, l. 189.
6 p. 252, l. 51.
7 p. 133, l. 262.
8 (Aufrecht) II. 174.
9 *Bhandarkar's List*, no. 170.

Contacts with countries to the north-west of India—

The frequent journeys of merchants and scholars gave Indians a good knowledge of these regions. Thus the composer of a Paramāra panegyric describing the conquests of the Paramāra king Lakṣmadeva after the fashion of the *digvijaya* of Raghu in the *Raghuvaṃśa* rightly substitutes Turuṣkas for Hūṇas on the banks of the Vaṃkṣu. The Kāmbojas, Turuṣkas and the Cīnas were no less known than the Indian provinces of Trigarta, Gauḍa, Aṅga and Vaṅga[1]. In several texts of the period we find long lists of peoples living on the north-west of India. Thus, the *Vaijayantī*[2] mentions the Cīnas or Kharaṃbharas, the Gāṃdhāras or Dihaṇḍas (Rawalpindi and Peshawar), the Yavanas or Huruṣkaras (a mistake for Turuṣkas), the Laṃpākas or Muruṇḍas (Laghman in Afghanistan), the Tokṣāras or Yugālikas (Tukharistan of the Arabs), the Ṭarkas or Bālhīkas (Balkh), the Vāhīkas or Vāhlikas (in Punjab), the Kāśmīras or Kīras, the Turuṣkas or the Śākhis (probably for the Ṣāhis) and the Sindhas or the Dāradas (Daratpuri in northern Kashmir). We find similar lists in the *Kāvyamīmāṃsā*[3], *Abhidhānacintāmaṇi*[4] and *Trikāṇḍaśeṣa*[5].

The list of peoples found in the *Mārkaṇḍeya*, *Vāyu*, *Brahmāṇḍa*, *Matsya* and *Vāmana Purāṇas* and also given by Al-Bīrūnī reveals a knowledge of areas across the north-western boundaries of India. We read of the Vāhlīkas (Balkh, northern Afghanistan), Kālatoyakas (Kalat, Baluchistan), Pahlavas (Pahlavis or Persians), Carmakhaṇḍikas (Samarkand), Gandhāras (Rawalpindi and Peshawar), Yavanas (Indo-Greeks in north-western India)[6], Pāradās (Parthians in Khorasan), Hārahūṇakas or Hārahūras (probably Hūṇas in

---

1 Cf. *Samayamātṛkā*, II. 104.

2 p. 37, ll. 46-47, 50-54. The list is corrupt at places.

3 pp. 94, 51, 98.

4 pp. 382, 383.

5 p. 31.

6 There were surely no Greeks in the region at this time. The term is just a conventional survival from an earlier age. The occurrence of Yavanas shows that the *Purāṇas* just knew vaguely of the existence of these countries and sometimes their knowledge was centuries out of date.

Herat), Ramaṭhas (between Ghazni and Wakhan), Ruddhakaṭakas (Rudok, Tibet), Daśamānakas (Dasht valley, Kalat), Kāmbojas (near Badakhshan beyond the Hindu Kush), Daradas (Daratpuri in northern Kashmir) Cīnas, Tuṣāras or Tukhāras (Tukharistan of the Arabs), Prasthalas or Puṣkalas (Prang-Charsadda-Mir Ziyarat region Peshawar), Lampākas (Laghman, Afghanistan), Āvaganas (Afghans), Cūlikas (Sogdians to the north of the Oxus), Jāguḍas (southern Afghanistan), Aurasas (Urasa, Hazara), Ānibhadras (?), Kirātas (?), Tomaras (?) and Haṃsamārgas (Humza, N.W. Kashmir)[1]. The condensed list as found in the *Viṣṇu*, *Kūrma* and *Brahmāṇḍa Purāṇas* adds the Pārasīkas (Persians) to this list[2]. The knowledge of the Purāṇic writers about the area is further evinced by the fact that they know not only the names of the rivers Sītā (Syr Darya or Jaxartes) and Cakṣu (Vakṣu, Vaṃkṣu, Oxus or Amu Darya)[3] but also enumerate the names of the countries through which they flow[4].

In the lists in the *Vaijayantī* and the *Purāṇas* alike Cīna has been mentioned along with the areas across the north-western frontiers of India[5], thus giving evidence that Indians travelled to China across these regions[6]. That the Cīna of these texts was the famous country of China and not some area inhabited by a Tibeto-Chinese people[7] is clear from the fact that the *Vaijayantī*[8] speaking about the *pāṣaṇḍas* (heretical sects) which seek emancipation (*mokṣāvalaṃbinaḥ*)[9] and have their distinct signs (*bāhyaliṅginaḥ*) says that in the court of the emperor of China (*Cīneśasamsadi*) there

---

1 D.C. Sircar, *Studies in the Geography of Ancient and Medieval India*, pp. 23-26.

2 Ibid., p. 38.

3 Ibid., p. 58.

4 Ibid., p. 60.

5 Ibid., p. 61.

6 We have seen (supra pp. 108-9) that contact with China was commoner by sea in the middle ages. Perhaps the reference to China as a north-western country is based on earlier information, from sources of earlier centuries before the sea-route was developed.

7 D.C. Sircar, *Studies in Geography*, p. 25.

8 p. 103, ll.479f. Also *Nāmamālikā*, p. 27, ll.424f.

9 Obviously a reference to the *nirvāṇa* ideal of the Buddhists.

are three hundred and sixty sub-sects distinguished by their peculiar garments, ways of living and doctrines (*veṣājīvakṛtāntādyaiḥ*). If we read the passage in association with the fact that in the Purāṇic literature of the period *pāṣaṇḍa* is often used exclusively for the Buddhists[1] we can see in the passage a clear reference to China.

Role of Muslim merchants—

We find that gradually the Indian merchants were losing to the Muslims a considerable part of not only the foreign trade but also the domestic commerce incidental to it. We have evidence to show that Muslim traders were coming to India and sometimes penetrated far into the interior. We have the explicit testimony of the *Kāmil-ut-Tawārīkh* of Ibn Asir that there were Mussalmāns in the country of Banaras from the days of Mahmūd bin Sabuktigīn[2]. From Muhammad' Aufī we learn that Bahrām Gūr of Iran clothing himself in the garb of a merchant came to Hindustan[3]. It is also significant that when Bakhtyār Khaljī appeared before the city of Nadiyā with only eighteen horsemen people thought that he was a trader in horses[4]. It is clear from this reference that the visit of Muslim merchants to Nadiyā must have been quite frequent so as not to create any apprehension in the local population. Traditions recorded by Tārānātha mention settlements of Turks in the Antarvedī or Gaṅgā-Yamunā doab[5]. From the same source we learn that during the time of Lavasena and his successors and prior to the invasion of Odantapurī and Vikramaśilā the number of Turks had increased[6]. According to the *Samayamātṛkā* the Muslims singing songs in the bazars was a usual feature of a city night[7]. Moreover, it was obviously in the wake of the merchants

1 R. C. Hazra, *Studies in the Upapurāṇas*, I, Index, s. v., *pāṣaṇḍa*, especially pp. 143, 147, 278, 326.

2 Elliot and Dowson, II. 251.

3 Ibid., II. 159.

4 Ibid., II. 308-9.

5 *I.A.*, IV. 366.

6 *I.H.Q.*, XXII. 240. Cf. traditions about Turkish settlers at Maner (Patna)—*A.I.O.C.*, VI, pp. 123ff.

7 III. 26—*caranti mlecchagāyanāḥ*,

that Sufi saints came to India. In the eleventh and the twelfth centuries we find them at Bahraich, Ajmer, Jarua (Hajipur) and Netrokona (Mymensingh)[1]. It has been rightly suggested that the far-flung campaigns of Sultān Maḥmūd would have been impossible without an accurate knowledge of trade-routes and local resources of India, which he probably obtained from Muslim merchants[2]. Several Arab narratives contain accounts of the land-routes in India with minute details of the distance between the cities and of their products. It is clear that they were compiled from the information supplied by Muslim merchants who had visited these regions and were meant to serve as guides for those who were to go there in future. That these routes were being used by Muslim merchants receives the remarkably clear testimony of Al-Bīrūnī who in describing the route across the Himalayas in the north observes that Rājāwarī was the farthest place to which Muslim merchants traded, and beyond which they never passed[3].

Policy of the Pratihāras and the Gāhaḍavālas—

The Arab writers unanimously accuse the Pratihāra kings of being unfriendly towards the Arabs and Islam[4]. Political antagonism with the Arab state could not have been sufficient to deserve such strong opinions. Other Indian states on the north-west who opposed the Muslim armies tooth and nail have not received such a censure. It may be that the Pratihāras realised the economic menace in the form of Muslim merchants flooding India. In the interests of the indigenous merchants they discouraged the influx of Muslim merchants and probably imposed checks and restrictions in furtherance of their policy. That the Pratihāra administration was highly efficient has been admitted by the Arab writers themselves[5]. It is likely that the strict attitude of the

1 *I.C.*, I. 205ff; Titus, *Indian Islam*, p. 43.

2 M. Habib in his Introduction (p. 46) to Elliot and Dowson, II.

3 I. 207-8.

4 Sulaimān in Elliot and Dowson, I. 4; Al-Mas'ūdī in ibid., I. 21.

5 Sulaimān says "There is no country in India more safe from robbers"—Elliot and Dowson, I.4.

Pratihāra officers in the matter of Muslim merchants was the reason for the displeasure of Arab writers. It is to be noted that these Arab accounts were written by merchants themselves, or in any case for the guidance of the merchants. If, as has sometimes been done[1], we interpret the term *turuṣkadaṇḍa* appearing in the land-grants of the Gāhaḍavālas, who succeeded to the central portion of the Pratihāras, to mean an impost upon the Muslim settlers in the Gāhaḍavāla kingdom we may say that the Gāhaḍavālas followed the policy of the Pratihāras. For many reasons the Gāhaḍavālas did not impose a total ban on the coming of the Muslim traders but imposed a tax on them which must have provided a valuable source of income.

Prof. Habib on decline in Indian participation in overland trade—

Prof. M. Habib[2] has suggested that the new Indian custom that the Hindus should not travel overland into countries where the *muñja* grass does not grow and the black gazelles do not graze practically handed over all foreign commerce to outsiders, along with the domestic commerce incidental to it. Obviously he is basing his view on the testimony of Al-Bīrūnī[3]. But as Al-Bīrūnī himself clearly states this restriction was for the brāhmaṇas only. Again, when Al-Bīrūnī observes that people say that a brāhmaṇa is not allowed to stay in a country of the above description he is referring to a theoretical restriction in the legal texts about whose practical implementation he himself appears to have had no idea. It has also to be noted that this was not a custom new to the period. We can trace it back in any case to the time of the *Manusmṛti*[4]. We must confess that in the present state of our knowledge we cannot lay hands on any specific reason for the objection to crossing the borders of Āryāvarta. It may, however, be suggested that the prevailing political chaos had something to do with it.

---

1 See supra pp.50-52.

2 Introduction (p. 46) to Elliot and Dowson, II.

3 II. 134f.

4 II. 23—*Kṛṣṇasārastu carati mṛgo yatra svabhāvataḥ. Sa jñeyo yajñiyo deśo mlecchadeśastvataḥ paraḥ.*

CHAPTER VII

FOREIGN TRADE (B) SEA ROUTE

International background of the trade—

The history of India's sea-trade in the early medieval period has to be studied in a wider context. It is only a link in the trade activities throughout the Indian Ocean and the Pacific Ocean in which many nations from Africa to China were participating.

Before our period of study this oceanic trade was shared by the Persians, Indians, Indonesians and Ceylonese. Gradually, however, the share of he Persians was increasing. But with the coming of Islam on the scene we find the Arabs replacing the Persians. At first the Arabs interested themselves in sea raids[1], but the conquest of Sind, soon after A.D. 710, gave them an opening towards the east[2]. The year 758 is remarkable in this history. The number of the Arabs (Ta-shih) and the Persians (Po-sse)[3] had

1 Hourani, *Arab seafaring*, pp. 53-55.

2 Ibid., p. 63.

3 Hadi Hasan and following him Hourani and others refer all accounts of Po-sse to Persia. Sinologists however headed by T. Kumazo, B. Laufer and G. E. Gerini hold that there existed another country and people of the same name, and always written in a like manner, the location of which is referred to the Southern Ocean, and which must have belonged to the Malayan group. A third group of scholars including R. Braddell, K. Yamada and Gibson-Hill admit Po-sse to be a transcription of Parsa or Persia, but believes that Chinese authors sometimes mistook the provenance of commodities which they ascribed to that country. P. Wheatley holds that the name, though applied by the Chinese originally to Persia, became increasingly associated with products which found their way to China along the Southern Sea route, so that by T'ang and Sung times the old association of the name with the Middle Eastern country had been forgotten and it came to stand as a collective name for the countries of the South Seas and the Indian Ocean, with the exception of India and later on seems gradually to have become identified with an unspecified realm in that part of the world—*J.M.B.R.A.S.*, XXXII, Pt. 2 (1959), pp. 14f.

grown so large that they could sack and burn the city of Canton[1]. But this is the last occasion when the Po-sse are mentioned in Chinese accounts. Instead we find the Ta-shih as the most important foreign community.

It was the simultaneous existence of the Umayyad caliphs in the western world and of the T'ang dynasty in China which fostered this trade[2]. Its growing importance explains the rather fuller accounts of southern Asia in the Chinese annals of the sixth and seventh centuries. The earliest Chinese testimony for this trade comes from the eighth century. It was in 607 that the Chinese emperor sent a mission by sea to open commercial relations with Chi-tu (Siam). The nascent Chinese seamanship regarded even this an unusually daring voyage[3]. However, the itineraries compiled by Kia Tan between 785 and 805 indicate that the Chinese had no first hand information of the sea-route between Canton and the Persian Gulf, especially to the west of Quilon[4]. The Chinese were slow to participate actively in this lucrative sea-trade. The Arab geographers, no doubt, refer to the presence of ships of China (*marākib al-Ṣīn*) and Chinese ships (*sufun Sīnīyaḥ*) even up to Aden. But these refer to the ships in the China trade, which, even if constructed in China, were not owned and navigated by the Chinese. The Chinese were ignorant even of the names of Aden and Siraf down to the close of the twelfth century[5].

The sack of Canton directed trade to Tongking for some time; but Canton was re-opened in 792. The flourishing trade in the period is reflected in the extensive contemporary literature on navigation[6]. The period witnessed the growth of Ts'üan-chou, near Amoy, as another entrepot of the sea-trade[7]. However the

1 Hasan, *Persian Navigation*, p. 99.

2 Hourani, Op. cit., pp. 61-62.

3 Chau Ju-kua, pp. 7-8.

4 Ibid., pp. 9-10.

5 Cf. Hourani, Op. cit., pp. 75-76 for the passage of Al-Mas'ūdī. See also Chau Ju-kua, p. 15, f.n. 3; *Cathay and the Way Thither*, I, p. 87.

6 Hourani, Op. cit., pp. 65-66.

7 Chau Ju-kua, pp. 17-18.

Arab sources, though indicating a knowledge of Korea and Japan, do not suggest that the Arab traders visited them[1]. The climax appears to have been reached when the political disturbances in China in 878 brought the sea-trade to an abrupt end. Abū Zaid tries to account for the interruption of the trade with China and refers to the oppression of the merchants and sailors and to the political disunity of the Chinese empire[2]. It must, however, be remembered that the decline of the T'ang dynasty was accompanied by a parallel dismemberment of the Abbasid empire[3].

The centre of trade now shifted to the port of Kedah on the west coast of the Malaya peninsula to which came ships both from China and the Arabic world. The importance of the Indonesian empire in this trade is testified to by Arab narratives of the tenth century[4].

It would however appear that towards the close of the tenth century Canton and Ts'üan-chóu had revived. The trade was becoming important to the Chinese state which converted it into a monopoly and sent trade missions abroad, offering special privileges to the foreign traders coming to China. All this effort resulted in a phenomenal increase in the volume of trade which is also reflected in the measures the government took to regulate and control it[5]. However, even in the twelfth century we find that the Chinese were content to leave the actual trade in the seas to Arab and other foreign traders[6]. Later the Southern Sung Dynasty made Hangchow, one of the important centres of navigation, its capital, and this indicated its sea-minded policy[7]. Chinese maritime enterprise appears to have reached a high peak controlling the sea-routes to the south-east and India[8]. Under Kublai Khan the Chinese participation in the sea-trade received a further fillip

1 Ibid., p. 168, f.n. 1; p. 172, f.n. 1.
2 *Ancient Accounts of India and China*, pp. 40ff.
3 Hourani, Op. cit., pp. 77-78.
4 R. C. Majumdar, *Suvarṇadvīpa*, II. 30.
5 Chau Ju-kua, pp. 18-20.
6 Ibid., p. 22.
7 J. J. L. Duyvendak, *China's Discovery of Africa*, p. 15.
8 K. S. Latourette, *The Chinese*, p. 237.

by his active encouragement. The Arab monopoly of the trade in the south seas must have received a set back from the expansion of the Chinese traders. It is not without significance that the Arab geographical literature after the tenth century is not so abundant as in the earlier period ; without any newness in its treatment it merely repeats the existing information[1]. The process must have been gradual indeed, but by the time of Ibn Batūta the Chinese appear to have established themselves strongly in the sea-route up to Calicut and other Malabar ports[2].

Countries participating in the trade : *Arabia*—

Thus we see that the role of India in the sea-trade of the period was conditioned by the existence and gradual progress of rivals in different areas and periods. To start with the Arabs were the foremost maritime power, pushing the limits of their economic influence slowly and gradually towards the east. By the middle of the ninth century they had established themselves as the master partner in this trade and we find that even in subsequent centuries, when powerful contenders had arisen, the Arabs did retain a considerable part of this trade in all the areas. However, from the tenth century they had to yield a part of the monopoly, especially to the west of the Indonesian countries, to the ports of Sumatra, Java and Malaya. From the twelfth century they had to face a strong rival in the Chinese who eventually succeeded in establishing their commercial hegemony right up to the Malabar ports.

Much of the credit for this remarkable expansion of Arab enterprise has to be ascribed to the flood of force released by the new religion of Islam[3]. The prestige of a merchant in Islam may be connected with the fact that Muhammad himself was a merchant in his early life[4]. The Arabs, owing to the geographical conditions of the country and its situation, have, from very early times, enjoyed a prominent part of the sea-trade between the east and

---

1 Hourani, Op. cit., p. 83.

2 Ibid.

3 Ibid p. 53.

4 K.A.N. Sastri, *Foreign Notices*, p. 20.

the west[1]. Moreover, the development would not appear to have been altogether new in the sense that Islam, by assimilating the Persians, was actually stepping into the shoes of the Persian seamen who in those times had succeeded in carving out a high position for themselves in the field of maritime trade[2]. The political unity of western Asia resulting from the expansion of Islam and the Arabs, which brought the Persian Gulf and the Red Sea under one power, an ideal which had been the despair of all the earlier empires in the area, had also an important influence on the expansion of Arab maritime enterprise[3]. By uniting western Asia and Egypt they were able to control all the sea-routes going towards India and other eastern countries and achieved what even the Achaemenids could not. Though precise details are lacking, it is also likely that the period saw some improvements in the construction of Arab ships[4]. In one Chinese account we have a reference to foreign ships "so high out of water that ladders several tens of feet in length had to be used to get aboard"[5]. From the prominence of the Arabs as the foreign traders coming to China we can, with fair plausibility, utilise the reference for the Arab ships of the period.

Ceylon—

However, according to the Chinese testimony even in the middle of the T'ang period, the largest foreign ships were those of the Ceylonese people[6]. Ceylon had another basic advantage. The position of monsoon made direct communications between Ceylon and the Malaya straits possible from a very early time. Even in the time of Fa hsien one had to come from Tāmralipti to Ceylon in order to sail for Sumatra[7]. This continued to be the case even when I-tsing visited India[8]. Cosmas testifies to the

1 Chau Ju-kua, p. 4.

2 Hourani, Op. cit., pp. 65-66.

3 Ibid., p. 53.

4 Moti Chandra, *Sārthavāha*, p. 202.

5 Chau Ju-kua, p. 9.

6 *J.M.B.R.A.S.*, XXXI, Part 2, p. 106.

7 (Legge) p. 100.

8 pp. xxv, xxxiv.

central position of Ceylon in the transit trade between the east and the west[1]. A story in the Jain text *Samarāiccakahā* also records that from Śrīpura in Suvarṇabhūmi vessels sailed for Sīhaladvīpa daily[2].

China—

The Chinese, who appear to have been the last to enter the arena, gradually outdid all other competitors in the field. The Chinese ships were decidedly better, bigger and safer than the others. It was, therefore, quite natural that people preferred to sail in Chinese ships. The Chinese ships were broad and almost square, and had a narrow keel. Their masts numbered between four and six and had sometimes as many as twelve sails. The ships are said to have had four decks and were divided into water-tight compartments. Besides 600 men as passengers the ships had 400 armed men to fight against pirates[3]. Moreover, the Chinese ships appear to have had larger and better rigged sails than those of the Arabs[4]. Towards the close of the eleventh century the Chinese are found using the mariner's compass, though, to start with, the sailors still mostly relied on winds, sun and stars to guide the course of their ships[5]. During the course of centuries the Chinese improved and expanded their knowledge of overseas countries, gradually progressing towards the west[6]. Moreover the Chinese empire also actively encouraged and promoted Chinese maritime enterprise. The start made by the Southern Sung Dynasty was followed up with remarkable results by Kublai Khan.

Indonesia—

Indonesia enjoyed a natural advantage from its central position. Contacts with different foreigners were probably utilised in improv-

1 *Christian Topography*, p. 365.

2 pp. 327-28.

3 J.J.L. Duyvendak, *China's Discovery of Africa*, p. 18; H.A.R. Gibb *Ibn Batūta*, p. 235.

4 J. Poujade, *La Route des Indes et ses Navires*, p. 162.

5 Chau Ju-kua, pp. 20, 34.

6 Ibid., Introduction.

ing the art of shipping. We get the impression from a story in the *Kathākoṣa*[1] that the interests of the Indonesian shipping were actively watched and protected by the state. In this story Sundara the king of Suvarṇadvīpa on hearing of the ships of Nāgadatta having fallen into the hollow of a snake-circled mountain sends a sailor to help them. Even if the story narrated by Abū Zaid about the Mahārāja of Zābaj (Java) attacking the kingdom of Kumar (Khmer) be of a doubtful historicity it does indicate the high prestige enjoyed by Java in the estimation of the people in that period[2].

Disadvantages of Indian traders : Technique of shipping and navigation—

It would appear, on the other hand, that "Indian techniques of ship construction and navigation had by this time fallen behind those of the Arabs and Chinese"[3]. The relative insignificance of Indian shipping explains the absence of any reference to it in the Chinese and Arab accounts[4]. There are indications to suggest that the Indian ships were smaller than those of China. Thus for example the *Ling-wa-Tai-ta* (A.D. 1178) observes that the Chinese traders with big ships who wish to go to the country of the Arabs, must tranship at Ku-lin (Quilon) to smaller boats before proceeding further[5]. Moreover, we have the clear testimony of Marco Polo[6] who describes the ships of Manzi, or S. China, as larger than those of India.

1 (Tawney) pp. 28-29.

2 Elliot and Dowson, I. 8f.

3 A.L. Basham, *Arts and Letters*, XXIII, p. 69.

4 The suggestion that the Arabs and Chinese might have regarded Indian shipping and Sumatran and Javanese shipping as the same, as they viewed Sumatra and Java as parts of India (Moti Chandra, Op. cit., p. 207), is not strong. Both these sources refer to India and Sumatra and Java separately and in the same context. Though they felt that Sumatra and Java were for all purposes a continuation of India they realised their separate existence. Moreover these sources are found referring not only to the different parts of India but also of Sumatra and Java. If there is any validity in the suggestion the use of the term Indian in place of Sumatran and Javan shipping would have been more appropriate.

5 Chau Ju-kua, p. 91, f.n. 17.

6 Yule, II, p. 391, n; A.L. Basham, Loc. cit., p. 69.

Speed of Indian ships—

Again, the Indian ships lagged behind the Chinese and Arab ones in the matter of speed. Thus Chau Ju-kua states that from San-fo-ts'i (Palembang, E. Sumatra) Nan-p'i (Malabar) is a little more than a month's voyage[1]. Elsewhere he says that it takes a Ts'üan-chòu ship a month to reach Ku-lin (Quilon) from Lan-li (extreme N. W. coast of Sumatra)[2]. Likewise the *Akhbār* of Sulaimān gives one month as the time taken to reach Kalah Bār (Kedah) from Kūlam Mali (Quilon)[3]. It is therefore significant in this connection to find the *Samarāiccakahā* stating that the ship sailing from Tāmralipti reached Suvarṇabhūmi in two months[4]. Even if we make due allowance for the great exaggeration in all that has come down to us concerning the embassy to China sent by the king of Chu-lién (Cola)[5], we can have an idea of the slow speed of Indian ships from the fact that the journey took the mission 1150 days[6] out of which it was under sail for only 247 days. From Chau Ju-kua[7] it would appear that the Ta-shih (Arabs) took some hundred days to reach their own country from Ts'üan-chóu. The *Akhbār* of Sulaimān seems to corroborate it when it gives 120 days as the time for the voyage from Masqat to Canton[8].

Political factors—

Another reason for the declining condition of Indian shipping might have been the apathy and inability of the Indian states to protect its interests. In the earlier period we find the state actively participating in the sea-trade. The *Arthaśāstra*[9] mentions state owned vessels which were lent out to merchants and were used for carrying passengers and merchandise. A remarkable confirmation

1 p. 87.
2 Ibid., p. 89.
3 Hourani, *Arab seafaring*, p. 75.
4 p. 327.
5 Chau Ju-kua, p. 101, n. 11.
6 Ibid., p. 99, n. 3.
7 Ibid., p. 114.
8 Hourani, Op. cit., p. 75.
9 II. 28.

of this is to be found in Megasthenes[1], who records that the Indian ship-builders were salaried public servants and that ships built in the royal yards were hired to voyagers and merchants. A *Jātaka*[2] story also refers to sailors as being in the king's service. The *Periplus*[3] speaks of native fishermen in the king's service, stationed at the entrances of the western ports in well-manned large boats going up the coast as far as Syrastrene, from which they pilot vessels to Barygaza. These men in the pilot service of the state are referred to as *sāgara-paloganānaṃ* in a Kanheri inscription[4]. The Sātavāhana policy of actively promoting and regulating shipping is reflected in the ship coins of Śrī Yajña Śātakarṇi[5]. This policy was followed by the Pallavas and Kuruṃvara kings some of whose coins resemble these Sātavāhana coins[6]. This aspect of Indian polity continued to be important even up to the early years of the seventh century when Bhāskaravarman, the king of Assam, is found owning 30,000 ships[7].

Piratical activities of Kings—

In the period under study it would appear that the coastal powers often resorted to piracy. Owing to the growth of feudalism the states were generally small in size and power and thus might have found active promotion of shipping beyond their means. Piracy would have appeared more lucrative than actual participation in sea-trade, especially in view of the meagre resources of the state. The growing maritime power of the Arabs also probably led these states to realise the futility of competing with them. Even about 636 the governor of Al-Baḥrayan had raided Thana near Bombay and also the Bay of Daybul at the mouth of the

1 McCrindle, *Ancient India as described in Classical literature*, p. 53.

2 No. 539.

3 44.

4 *P.I.H.C.*, 1960, pp. 55-57.

5 Rapson, *Coins of the Andhra dynasty*, pp. 22f; *J.N.S.I.*, III, pp. 43-45. Cf. the title *trisamudrādhipati* in the *Harṣacarita*, p. 224 and Cape Andrai Satimoundon in Ptolemy, VII. 4.3.

6 Elliot, *Coins of Southern India*, p. 35, Plate I. 38.

7 *The Life*, pp. 171f; Watters, I. 348. The number seems to be exaggerated.

Indus[1]. The conquest of Sind also indicated the maritime superiority of the Arabs. This became more apparent when Muhammad Ghūrī scored a decisive victory in his naval war with the Jats[2].

In the *Daśakumāracarita*[3] we have a definite reference to a piratical expedition undertaken by the prince of Tāmralipti, who with a fleet consisting of one large vessel and several smaller boats swarmed round a Yavana ship. In the *Prabandhacintāmaṇi*[4] we read of the three princes of king Yogarāja looting near the port of Someśvara a ship belonging to another country. Significantly enough king Yogarāja in this connection refers to the bad name which some of his predecessor kings had earned and observes that kings of other countries brand the state of Gurjara as that of robbers. A strikingly close parallel is to be found in the Motupalli Pillar Inscription[5] in which the Kākatīya king Gaṇapatideva claims that former kings forcibly took away the wares of ships voyaging from one country to another which were wrecked, driven ashore or forced to touch at a place that was not meant as a port of call, owing to unfavourable winds. Ibn Batūta[6] also testifies to the royal support for piratical activities[7].

1 *Islamic Culture*, XX, p. 55.

2 Elliot and Dowson, II. 478.

3 (Tr. Ryder) p. 164.

4 p. 14.

5 *E.I.*, XII, p. 195.

6 (Tr. H.A.R. Gibb) pp. 233, 254.

7 In this context it may be suggested that at times the unnecessarily stringent rules and practices of the custom officers, which were vexatious to foreigners, were labelled as piracy. Cf. A. K. Majumdar, *Chaulukyas of Gujarat*, p. 479, f.n. 56. From the *Mānasollāsa* (II, p. 62, vv. 374-76) it appears that the coastal states had adopted some kind of a licence system and enforced it strictly. The boats of sailors residing in the country had to pay one-tenth of their cargo as duty on returning to the harbour; whereas in case of foreign boats driven to the harbour by an unfavourable wind the king was to confiscate all the merchandise or to allow the merchant to keep a little. Thus confiscation of unlicensed ships was quite within the laws of the Indian states. In the Motupalli Pillar Inscription (loc. cit.) also the ships which are said to have been

(Continued on p. 129)

Increase in piracy—

In this period piracy would appear to have increased. No doubt references to piracy are found from early times. But whereas previously it was confined to small areas, it had now become quite widespread. A number of sources clearly indicate that great pirate ships called *bīra* were molesting sailors and merchants from the Gulf of Cutch to the coasts of Ceylon, the mouth of the Tigris and the southern part of the Red Sea and occasionally also to Zanzibar[1]. The dangerous activities of the pirates are found not only near the Andamans[2] but also in Indonesian waters[3].

In the *Prabandhacintāmaṇi*[4] we have a reference to merchants out of fear for the pirates (*jalacora*) hiding gold slabs in sacks of *manjiṣṭhā* (Indian madder). In the graphic description in the *Upamitibhavaprapañcākathā*[5] of preparations being made before the ship set sail we have a definite reference that war preparations, obviously for protecting the ship from the pirates, were made.

Piracy must have deterred Indian merchants from resorting to frequent voyages to distant areas. We have a significant reference in the *Bodhisattvāvadānakalpalatā*[6] that some traders vexed by the piracy committed by the Nāgas, most probably the inhabitants of Andaman and Nicobar, were contemplating to leave trade for some

---

confiscated would appear to have been those without licence. This receives support from the fact that the inscription records that as opposed to the existing practice king Gaṇapatideva issued a charter of security (*abhaya-śāsana*) and fixed the customs to be paid. It is to be noted that in the *Prabandhacintāmaṇi* (p. 14) also the sons of king Yogarāja are said to have looted the ship of another king which driven by storms, had come to the port of Someśvara and was passing through their country, clearly without previous permission.

1 Al Bīrūnī, I. 208 ; Marco Polo (Yule), II. 389 ; Ibn Batūta, *Voyages* (ed. C. Defremery and B. R. Sangiunetti), IV. 59f ; G. P. Badger, *A History of the Imams and Sayyids of Oman*, pp. 12-13.

2 Cf. *Bodhisattvāvadānakalpalatā* of Kṣemendra, pp. 113f.

3 Chau Ju-kua, pp. 84, 85.

4 p. 70, ll.2ff.

5 pp. 870-72—*vidhīyate raṇasāmagrī.*

6 pp. 113-14.

other occupation. This may reflect the prevailing attitude of the sea-traders of India in that age.

The Indian merchants do not appear to have done much by way of providing for the safety of their ships. It is not without significance that whereas references for the Arab[1] and Chinese[2] ships being manned with soldiers are forthcoming, we have not much to suggest this for their Indian counterparts[3].

It is difficult to account for this apathy on the part of Indian traders. It might have been due to the essentially peaceful nature and upbringing of a vaiśya. Significantly enough we do not have many references to the interest of a vaiśya in military pursuits and warlike activities. We cannot say how far Jainism was the underlying reason for this. It may, however, be noticed from the early Buddhist literature and inscriptions that in earlier times Buddhism was quite popular among merchants. The early medieval period was apparently one of decline for Buddhism. Instead we find Jainism flourishing among the merchants near the coast. In some of the Jain stories of the period we find enterprising young merchants being discouraged from resorting to sea-trade[4]. We do not know how much of this attitude was due to the Jain faith.

Taboo against sea-voyages—

However, it has to be noted that there had grown in this period a definite taboo against sea-voyages in the orthodox Brahmaṇical group. Thus, the *Bṛhannāradīya* includes the undertaking of sea-voyage (*samudra-yātrā-svīkārah*) in its list of practices which, being unfavourable for the attainment of heaven and disliked by the people, have been forbidden for the Kali age[5]. Underlying this restriction must have been the feeling that on a ship one cannot observe his religious rites and rituals in all their meticulous details, especially as regards ceremonial purity. After the advent of

1 Ibn Batūta (H.A.R. Gibb), p. 230.

2 Ibn Batūta, *Voyages*, III. 88-91.

3 Contra see *Upamitibhavaprapañcākathā*, pp. 870-72.

4 Cf. *Upamitibhavaprapañcākathā*, p. 867.

5 XXII. 12-16. See Kane, *History of Dharmaśāstra*, III, p. 928 for other references.

Muslims the need for such restrictions would have been felt all the more. It has been suggested that the intensification of religious prejudices was the expression of the decay of Indian maritime activity due to practical and economic reasons[1]. P. V. Kane[2] interprets the relevant passages to show that the prohibition against sea-voyage affected only brāhmaṇas and even then they did not apparently become altogether unfit to be associated with. But what cannot be denied is that there was a definite disparagement of sea-voyages especially for merchants[3].

Decline in Indian shipping—

That there had been a definite decline in the shipping activity of the Indians is undoubted. At any rate it had ceased to be of much significance to some of the thinkers of northern India such as Medhātithi and Lakṣmīdhara, who were undoubtedly not associated with coastal areas. Manu[4] had laid down that the interest to be paid is to be fixed by persons expert in sea-voyages and those capable of calculating the profits in connection with a particular place and time. Commenting on this, Medhātithi observes that the sea-voyage has been mentioned only by way of illustrating a journey; the sense is that whatever interest is fixed by traders, who know all about journeying by land and water, it should be determined as the exact amount to be paid. Lakṣmīdhara also explains the expression 'experts in sea-voyages' to refer by implication to the merchants in general[5].

Trade with China—

The journeys of the Buddhists between China and India provide a convenient background for the understanding of the commercial intercourse between the two countries. The eighth century witnessed the close of the most brisk period of Sino-Indian intercourse. Relations were revived under the Sung dynasty to

1 A.L. Basham, *Arts and Letters*, XXIII, p. 69.

2 Op. cit., p. 934.

3 Cf. *Vyavahāramayūkha* referred to in Kane, Op. cit., p. 936.

4 VIII. 157.

5 *Kṛtyakalpataru*, *Vyavahāra*, p. 284.

such an extent that the Chinese chronicles themselves hold the number of Indian monks in the Chinese court towards the close of the tenth and the beginning of the eleventh century as the highest in Chinese history. But soon the climax would appear to have been reached, the date A.D. 1036 marking the close of the period of active Sino-Indian intercourse[1].

A Chinese account of 749 refers to the Canton river as full of vessels from India, Persia and Arabia and says that in Canton itself there were three Brāhmaṇa temples where Indian Brāhmaṇas lived[2]. The presence of Indians in the Chinese sea can be inferred from two Japanese records which give the credit of introducing cotton into Japan to two Indians carried over to that country by the black current[3].

Indian embassies to China—

Embassies to China sent by Indian states do not appear to have been motivated by simple political considerations but probably cared for commercial gains also. *Tien-chu* or eastern India is recorded to have sent envoys to the T'ang court in 627-650 and 690-692[4]. In 656-658 a number of Indian states, Chan-po (Campāpura), Kan-chih-fo (Kāñcīpura), Shih-li-chün (perhaps the kingdom of the Cāḷukyas) and Mo-la (Malaya in S. India ?), are found reopening official relations with China obviously in recognition of the new possibilities of the Chinese trade[5]. It was in view of the increasing number of embassies to China that an imperial edict of 695 determined the provisions to be supplied to the ambassadors of different countries. The ambassadors of north India and south India were to receive provisions for six months[6]. Chinese accounts preserve notices of embassies to China sent by Śīlāditya of Western India and the Cālukya Vallabha of South India in 692 and the Pallava king Narasiṃhavarman II Rājasiṃha in 720[7].

1 *Age of Imperial Kanauj*, pp. 443-444.
2 K.A.N. Sastri, *Foreign Notices*, p. 19.
3 R.K. Mookerji, *History of Indian Shipping*, p. 174.
4 Chau Ju-kua, p. 111.
5 *J.M.B.R.A.S.*, XXXII, part 2, pp. 74-75.
6 *B.E.F.E.O.*, IV, p. 334.
7 K.A.N. Sastri, *Foreign Notices*, pp. 16-17.

We have the testimony of Al-Mas'ūdī to show that ships from India along with those from Basra, Siraf, Oman, Java and Campā ascended the Khanfu river to reach Khanfu (Canton)[1]. We learn from Sulaimān[2] and Al-Mas'ūdī[3] that the kingdom of Rahma (Bengal) was exporting to China horns of rhinoceros to be made into fashionable and costly girdles. In the Jain text *Samarāiccakahā*[4] we read of a sailor, Suvadana, coming from China and proceeding to Devapura via Suvarṇadvīpa. Sulaimān observes that whereas other ships calling at Kaucamali (Quilon) had to pay from one dīnār to ten, the Arab ships sailing for China were required to pay one thousand dirhams[5]. It would appear from this significant reference that India had not been completely ousted by the commercial rivalry then raging. The king who possessed Quilon probably aimed at safeguarding the interests of his own native sailors and merchants by differential tariff rates. It is in this light that we have to interpret Chau Ju-kua when he observes about the Chu-lién (Cola) country that as the taxes and imposts of the kingdom are numerous and heavy, traders rarely go there[6].

Decline in India's trade with China—

It appears that India's share in the trade with China was gradually dwindling probably because of the competition of Arab and Indonesian merchants. India is not mentioned among the countries which according to the *Sung Annals* were trading at Canton in 971[7]. The *Liang-shu* does not include China in the list of countries with which central T'ién-chu had much sea-trade[8]. Obviously sea-trade with China had ceased to be an important item in India's sea-trade activities. It is significant that Chou K'ü-feī in his list of countries exporting a considerable amount of

1 q. in *Age of Imperial Kanauj*, p. 401.

2 Ferrand, *Textes*, p. 44.

3 Ibid., p. 105.

4 VI, p. 39.

5 Renaudot, *Ancient Accounts of India and China*, p. 9.

6 p. 95.

7 Chau Ju-kua, p. 19.

8 Ibid., p. 113, ll.41f.

merchandise enumerates in order Arabia (Ta-shï), Java (Shö-p'o) and Palembang (San-fo-ts'i) but does not mention India. It is not unlikely that India along with many others belonged to the next rank referred to by Chou K'ü-fei[1].

Indian interest in the trade with China—

But Indian states, especially of the South, occasionally tried to assert themselves. Chau Ju-kua records that in 984-988 there arrived in China by sea a priest who was a native of T'ién-chu. The fact that foreign traders, considering that he was a foreign priest, are said to have vied with each other in honouring him with presents[2] would suggest the presence of some Indian merchants. The *Sung-shi*, however, refers to the arrival, in the same period, of an Indian priest whose native land was Li-tö (Lāṭa)[3].

In his inscriptions the Cola king Rājendra I claims to have captured among other places Kaḍāram (Kedah), Śrīvijaya (Palembang), Mānakkavaram (the Nicobar islands), Malaiyur (Djambi), Pannai (North Sumatra) and Māppappāla (uncertain but probably S. Burma)[4]. It has been suggested by K. A. N. Sastri that this remarkable expedition aimed at keeping open the trade route to China threatened by the growing power of the kingdom of Śrīvijaya[5]. The recently discovered inscription from Tanjore[6] dated in the seventh year of the reign of Rājendra (A.D. 1019) refers to the endowment in terms of Chinese gold made by a certain merchant described as an agent of Kiḍārattaraiyar. It is clear that the Cola kingdom was right there participating in the lucrative trade with China obviously through the intervention of Kiḍāra or the empire of the Śailendras. The Cola empire must have realised the possibilities of this trade if they could have an upper hand on the sea-route.

1 Ibid., p. 23. It should be observed that the term *hu* rendered "foreign" though usually designating the people of Western Asia is sometimes applied to Indians—ibid., p. 114, n. 5.

2 Ibid., p. 111.

3 Ibid., p. 112, ll.39ff.

4 *The Colas*, I, pp. 254ff.

5 Ibid., p. 267.

6 *J.N.S.I.*, XX. 13.

The embassy which Rājendra sent to China in 1033[1] was undertaken probably with a view to improve relations with the state on the other end of the route. It would appear that this commercial policy had been initiated by Rājarāja I but he could not carry it to its successful end. We know that he had built up the Cola navy and had started making naval conquests[2]. This receives support from the fact that the Cola embassy to China in 1015 is said to have been under Lo-tsa-lo-tsa (Rājarāja)[3].

The subsequent kings of the Cola dynasty appear to have followed this policy though not so successfully as Rājendra I. We hear of a Cola embassy to China in 1077[4]. The reference to the conversion of a Cola prince to Buddhism in an inscription from Prome belonging to the period 1084-1112[5] also suggests that the Colas were interested in maintaining maritime contacts with countries to the east.

Stray references indicate that other parts of India from time to time also made attempts to improve relations with China. Thus the *Sung-shī* says that in 1094 people from Mau-li (Mo-lai, Kulam Male or Quilon) brought presents to the Chinese court[6]. Ma Tuan-lin also refers to the arrival of two Malayalis in China[7]. Envoys from sundry kings of India, including one from Kulang (Quilon), are said to have arrived in China in 1282[8]. In 1286 T'swan chau received ships from more than 90 foreign states, among which are several names belonging to southern and western India[9].

Fifteen coins discovered at Tanjore representing almost the entire Sung period[10] go a long way to show that the Arabs had

1 K.A.N. Sastri, *Foreign Notices*, p. 26.
2 *The Colas*, I, p. 220.
3 K.A.N. Sastri, *Foreign Notices*, p. 26.
4 Ibid.
5 Ibid.
6 Chau Ju-kua, p. 124, n. 26.
7 Ibid., p. 90, n. 9.
8 *J.R.G.S.*, XLIV, p. 107.
9 Ibid.
10 *S.I.S.*, I. 164.

not been successful in wresting from India, especially its southern parts, its share of the Chinese trade howsoever it might have dwindled. Significantly enough we find the Chinese government attempting in 1296 to prohibit the export of gold and silver and to limit the value of the trade with Ma'bar (Coromandel), Kulam (Quilon) and Fandaraina (Pantalāyini Kollam) to a relatively small sum of money[1].

Trade with South-East Asia—

It would, however, appear that the activities of Indian sailors and merchants extended in the east mostly only to Indonesia. For this we have the express testimony of both Chinese[2] and Arab[3] sources which mention the ports of Malaya, Java or Sumatra as the farthest limit for ships coming from the west. It may be that these sources which generally think in terms of trade relations between the extreme eastern and western limits of the sea-route failed to take any notice of Indian shipping because of its more or less limited role. But it would be wrong to say that we do not have any foreign testimony to India's maritime relations with Indonesia. We have the unequivocal reference in the *Liang-shu* which states that central T'ién-chu had much sea-trade among other countries with Fu-nan, Jī-nan and Kiau-chī (i.e., Indo-China generally)[4]. This is corroborated by the inscription from Tanjore[5], mentioned already, which speaks of the endowments to a temple at Nāgapaṭṭinam made by a certain Śrī Kuruttan Keśuvan alias Agralekai who was an agent of Kiḍārattaraiyar (the region of Kedah, Malaya).

Literary references to trade with South-East Asia—

There must have been frequent voyages of Indian merchants to the Indonesian lands[6] to have found repeated references in the

1 *T'oung Pao,* XV, pp. 425f.

2 Chau Ju-kua, p. 18. See also ibid., p. 24 for the testimony of Chou K'ü-feï.

3 See Al-Mas'ūdī, *Murūj*, Vol. I, p. 308 q. by Hourani, Op. cit., pp. 75f.

4 Chau Ju-kua, p. 113, ll.41-42.

5 *J.N.S.I.*, XX. 13.

6 Cf. *Tilakamañjarī*, p. 127—*Gṛhītapracurasārabhāṇḍairbhūriśaḥ kṛtadvīpāntara yātraih sahakāribhiranekaiḥ saṃyātrikaiḥ*...........

story books of the period. These texts indicate an improved knowledge of the geography of the area. Thus Kṣemendra in his *Rāmāyaṇamañjarī* substitutes for the vague reference in the *Rāmāyaṇa* a clear mention of Samudradvīpa which obviously has corrupted into the name Sumatra[1]. The *Samarāiccakahā* speaks of Indian merchants going to Mahākaṭāha[2]. From a story in the same text it appears that often merchants used to visit Suvarṇabhūmi for trade[3]. In the *Bṛhatkathāmañjarī* we read of merchants going to Kaṭākṣadvīpa[4], obviously the same as Kaṭāhadvīpa of other references. Stories of merchants going to Suvarṇadvīpa are to be found in the *Bṛhatkathāślokasaṅgraha*[5] and the *Kathākoṣa*[6] also. The *Bṛhatkathākośa* of Hariṣeṇa has references to merchants proceeding to Suvarṇadvīpa[7] and Ratnadvīpa[8]. The *Kathāsaritsāgara* is full of stories about trading voyages to Suvarṇadvīpa and Kaṭāha of which the most significant is that of a father who in search of his lost son and younger sister follows a merchant to Nārikeladvīpa, Kaṭāhadvīpa, Karpūradvīpa, Suvarṇadvīpa and Siṃhaladvīpa[9]. But the most interesting of all these is the *Tilakamañjarī* which describes a naval attack on Dvīpāntara. The descriptions given in this connection are so graphic and realistic as regards the culture and industrial products of the region[10] that they imply a thorough and intimate, if not first-hand, knowledge of these areas. Thus, we see that in all the literary texts of the period the sea-trade

1 R.C. Majumdar, *Suvarṇadvīpa*, I. 54-55.

2 pp. 264ff, 585.

3 Ibid., pp. 398ff.

4 II. 183.

5 XVIII. 428.

6 p. 29.

7 LIII. 3ff; LXXXII. 1ff.

8 LXXVIII. 42.

9 R.C. Majumdar, *Suvarṇadvīpa*, I, pp. 37-38, 51-52. It is however to be recognised that of the above-mentioned works *Bṛhatkathāmañjarī*, *Bṛhatkathāślokasaṅgraha* and *Kathāsaritsāgara* were based on the *Bṛhatkathā* of Guṇāḍhya. As it is difficult to be sure about the additions made by these in the original story we cannot dogmatise about the date to which any reference in these texts applies.

10 pp. 133ff.

of a merchant leads to Suvarṇadvīpa, Kaṭāha, Dvīpāntara or Ratnapura.

Frequent voyages to South-East Asia—

The increasing volume and importance of this trade can very well be realised from the fact that a teacher in Vārāṇasī could have fruits brought from Dvīpāntara[1]. The *Upamitibhavaprapañcākathā*[2] would imply that, besides trade, sight-seeing was another reason for people coming to these islands. The visitors used to take a keen interest in seeing forests, monasteries, gardens and paintings etc. It was the growing familiarity with the Indonesian lands that led Rājaśekhara to observe that in describing things of Dvīpāntara one should be faithful to its dress, customs and other details[3]. Elsewhere he mentions a sojourn in these islands as a qualification of literary men[4]. But at the same time he observes that the poets should not refer too much to the countries and their mountains and rivers lest they become difficult for the ignorant reader to follow[5].

Geographical knowledge of South-East Asia—

We have many indications to suggest that accurate geographical knowledge of the Indonesian lands, resulting from close maritime connections with them, was not confined to the merchants or sailors but was quite widespread. Thus, the *Āryamañjuśrīmūlakalpa*[6] notes the peculiar features of the language in the islands of Karmaraṅga, Nāḍikera, Vāruṣaka (Baros, Sumatra), Nagna (Naked or Nicobar), Vāli (Bali) and Yava (Java). The Purāṇic list of places also includes Pravijaya (Śrīvijaya) which may be identified with modern Palembang in Sumatra[7]. Likewise some of the names in the list of islands found in the *Purāṇas* can be identified with

1 *Uktivyaktiprakaraṇa*, p. 19, l.23.

2 pp. 996-98—....*na ca tasyāsti kānanādau kutūhalam...vihārārāmacitrādidarśane ca mahattamaṃ kutūhalam.* Cf. *Bhavisayattakahā*, LIII. 3-4.

3 *Kāvyamīmāṃsā*, p. 10.

4 Ibid., p. 78.

5 Ibid., p. 94.

6 (ed. T. Ganapati Sastri) p. 332.

7 D.C. Sircar, *Studies in Geography*, p. 28.

places in or near Indonesia[1]. It is significant to note that most of these names are used by Arab travellers to mean islands in the Archipelago[2]. It was the knowledge of the compilers of the *Vāmana*[3] and *Garuḍa*[4] *Purāṇas* about the definite existence of Kaṭāha and Siṃhala that led them to substitute these names for the words *Saumya* and *Gandharva* in the other *Purāṇas*.

The most significant evidence comes from the *Vaijayantī* which gives a list of six small islands (*anudvīpas*) which can all be located in this region[5]. Thus Aṅgadvīpa is the Angadiya of the Arab accounts mentioned immediately after a place on the Siamese coast and located in the Bay of Bengal[6]. Yavadvīpa would obviously refer to Java. It is however not unlikely that Yavadvīpa is a mistake for Yamadvīpa or Yamakoṭi which Al-Bīrūnī places 90° to the east of Laṅkā[7]. Malayadvīpa may be the Malay Peninsula. Śaṅkhadvīpa is the same as the island of Sankhaj which according to Arab writers was a part of the empire of Śrīvijaya and was three days voyage from Malaya[8]. Kuśadvīpa cannot be identified yet. But Varāhadvīpa would be obviously the group of three islands called Barawa by the Arabs and situated at a distance of 100 farsangs from Fansur or Baros on the coast of Sumatra[9].

Regions participating in the trade with South-East Asia—

Tāmralipti in Bengal would appear to have been the chief port for sailing to Indonesia. It is not without significance that in most of the stories of the period the merchants sailing to Suvarṇadvīpa or Kaṭāha are said to start from Tāmralipti[10]. Merchants

1 S. N. Majumdar, Cunningham's *Ancient Geography of India*, pp. 752-54; *I.A.*, 1930, pp. 204ff; V. S. Agrawala, *Kādambarī*, p. 256, f.n. 1 and *Harṣacarita*, p. 169.

2 R. C. Majumdar, *Suvarṇadvīpa*, I. 52-53.

3 XIII. 10.

4 LV. 5.

5 p. 36, ll.26-36.

6 Ferrand, *Textes*, p. 523.

7 I. 303.

8 Ferrand, *Textes*, pp. 194, 346, 377, 381, 395.

9 Ibid., pp. 583f.

10 *Samarāiccakahā*, p. 327; *Bṛhatkathāślokasaṅgraha*, XVIII. 176ff; *Bṛhatkathāmañjarī* II. 183; *K. S. S.* (Tawney), III. 175.

who are said to leave Pāṭaliputra[1] or Campā[2] for a voyage to Suvarṇadvīpa must have sailed from Tāmralipti. We have also references to Buddhist scholars like Dharmapāla (7th century) and Dīpaṅkara (11th century) proceeding from Bengal to Suvarṇadvīpa[3]. From the late eighth century we find influences from northern India, especially from the Pāla dominions, becoming predominant in the culture of South-East Asia. It is reflected not only in the use of the pre-Nāgarī script in a few Indonesian inscriptions[4] but also in the Indo-Japanese bronzes[5] and probably architecture as well[6]. The growth of the Cola power earlier towards the beginning of the eleventh century led to southern India becoming the main Indian influence in Indonesian lands[7]. However, indications are not wanting to suggest that eastern India continued to maintain direct contacts with South-East Asia[8].

The *Samarāiccakahā* mentions **Vaijayantī** as another port from which ships sailed for Indonesian lands[9]. The hoards from the islands of Ramree and Cheduba off the coast of Burma and Siam sometimes contain coins of king Śaktivarman Cālukyacandra of the Eastern Cālukya dynasty of Veṅgī (A.D. 1000—1011)[10]. This points to the direct and intimate contact of the Cālukya dominions with these areas. We have several proofs for the long established and continuous intercourse between the Tamil country and South-East Asia. By far the most significant of these is the inscription from Lobu Tuwa (A.D. 1088) in Sumatra referring to the community of Tamil merchants called the Five Hundred of the Thousand Quarters.[11]

1 *Bṛhatkathākośa*, LIII. 3ff.

2 *Bṛhatkathāślokasaṅgraha*, XVIII. 411.

3 *I. H. Q.*, XIII. 593,596. See also ibid., p. 597 ; R.C. Majumdar, *Champa*, p. xvii.

4 *I. H. Q.*, XIII. 590.

5 *B. K. I.*, XC, pp. 73f.

6 R. C. Majumdar, *Suvarṇadvīpa*, II. 351.

7 Ibid.

8 *I. H. Q.*, XIII. 597.

9 Cf. Moti Chandra, *Sārthavāha*, p. 199. This port cannot be identified.

10 G. Yazdani, *Early History of the Deccan*, p. 804.

11 K. A. N. Sastri, 'A Tamil Merchant-Guild in Sumatra' in *Tijdschrift voor Indische Taal—, Land—, en Velkenkunde*, 1932, p. 314.

Prapañca in his work *Nāgarakṛtāgama* written in Java in 1365 speaks of people among others from Jambūdvīpa (India), Karṇāṭaka (in South India) and Goḍa (Gauḍa), coming unceasingly and in large numbers in ships accompanied by monks and brāhmaṇas[1]. This makes it clear that even up to that late date the trade between the two countries continued to flourish. The fact that besides Jambūdvīpa, Karṇāṭaka and Gauḍa have been mentioned separately would suggest that of all the coastal areas in India these two enjoyed the major share of the trade.

But we cannot minimise the role of the Gujarati traders. Legends in Java preserve the memory of a late wave of emigration from Gujarat[2]. A traditional Gujarati verse which may look back to our period observes that he who goes to Java never returns; if by chance he returns, he brings back money enough to live on for two generations[3]. Some of the tomb-stones of the Sultāns of Samudra-Pase, probably imported from Gujarat[4], also suggest the trade relations between the two areas. Even as late as the time of Albuquerque we find the Portuguese sailors paying a high compliment to the Gujarati sailors who because of their great commerce with the eastern countries knew that route much better than all other nations[5].

Trade with the West—

In the sea-trade with the Muslim countries the areas on the western coast of India had a significant role but the eastern coast does not appear to have much to do with it. The latter would have found voyages to South-East Asia more profitable than covering a long distance to reach the Muslim countries. It is for this reason that the records of this area do not show any awareness of the maritime connections with the Muslim countries. The Chinese

1 *Java in the 14th century* (*The Nāgara-kṛtāgama*) by Rakawi Prapañca of Majapahit, Vol. III, p. 98 (Canto 83, stanza 4).

2 T. S. Raffles, *The History of Java*, II, 87ff.

3 A. K. Forbes, *Rās Mālā*, p. 418.

4 A. K. Majumdar, *Chaulukyas of Gujarat*, p. 268.

5 *J. A.*, 1918, p. 165.

text *Liang-shu* states that central T'ién-chu had much sea-trade among others with Ta-ts'in and An-si (Parthia)[1]. But it is difficult to believe on the basis of the uncorroborated testimony of this text that eastern India had any considerable maritime trade with the Muslim countries.

Abū Zaid would suggest that Indian merchants used to visit Siraf in large numbers and that they had very friendly relations with the Muslim merchants of that place. He says that when one of the principal merchants of Siraf invited the Indian merchants of the place he would serve them food in separate plates. On such occasions there would be about hundred guests[2], most of whom obviously were Indians. The Jewish traveller Rabbi Benjamin writing about 1170 says that the island of Kish[3] was the point to which the Indian merchants bring their commodities[4]. In the time of Ibn Batūta Indian ships coming from Thana, Quilon, Calicut, Fandarina (Pantalayini Kollam), Shaliyat (Chaliam), Mangalore, Fakanor (Barkur), Hinawr (Honavar) and Sindabur (Sadashivagad) called at the port of Aden, where lived a colony of Indian merchants[5]. From Marco Polo it would appear that the Indians were going up to the island of Socotra, mentioned by him as the centre to which Indian pirates brought their loot for disposal[6].

It would follow from the *Jagaḍucarita* that merchants like Jagaḍu had Indian agents at Hormuz and maintained regular trade with Persia, transporting goods in their own ships[7]. In the *Mohrāja-parājaya*[8] we read of Kubera, the business magnate of Anahilvāḍa leaving the port of Bhṛgukaccha for a foreign land in the company of fifty-five merchants and with five hundred ships under him.

---

1 Chau Ju-kua, p. 113, ll.41f.

2 Ferrand, *Voyage du Marchand Arabe Sulayman*, p. 138.

3 The island of Kays is situated in the Persian Gulf at a distance of nine miles from the Persian coast.

4 K. A. N. Sastri, *Foreign Notices*, p. 134.

5 See *The Delhi Sultanate*, p. 648.

6 (Yule) II. 389.

7 A. K. Majumdar, *Chaulukyas of Gujarat*, p. 267.

8 Act III, p. 61.

The western terminus for the Indian ships would appear to have changed from time to time. Thus in the seventh century it was Basra, from where it was transferred to Siraf and then successively to Kish and Hormuz[1]. The dominance of the Arabs would not have left much scope for Indian ships to proceed further to the west. Leaving aside the possibility of an occasional Indian ship venturing ahead in the Red Sea[2] it appears that trade with Mesopotamia, Egypt or the Eastern coasts of Africa was mostly in the hands of the Persians and the Arabs[3].

Indian interest in coastal trade—

The Indian sailors and merchants, forced by the competition of the Arabs and the Chinese, would appear to have concentrated on coastal trade. Indian traders visited the ports on the east and west coast selling their local wares or those brought from foreign lands by foreigners. They geneıally ventured only up to Ceylon. In Indian stories of the period we often have references to Indian merchants visiting Ceylon[4]. An eighth century inscription from Ceylon indicates that Indian traders were trading in Ceylon[5]. The early Bengali merchants generally traded wih Ceylon and Patan in Gujarat and visited Puri, Kaliṅga or Kaliṅgapaṭam, Cilkāculi (Chicacole), Bānpur, Setubandha Rāmeśvar and Nilacca (Laccadives)[6]. In the Arab accounts also we find indications to suggest that sailors from one port of India used to visit other ports for trade. Thus, Al-Idrīsī observes that Debal was inhabited only because it was a station for the vessels of Sind and other countries and refers to the vessels of India coming to it[7]. The same writer refers to vessels from India and Sind casting anchor at Fandarīna (Pantalayini Kollam)[8], and also to Barūh (Broach) being the port for the vessels of Sind[9].

1 *Cathay and the Way Thither*, I. 84-5.

2 Cf. Hourani, Op. cit., p. 82, f.n. 79 for a 10th century reference to Indian ships at al-Qulzum.

3 Cf. Hourani, Op. cit., pp. 79f.

4 *K. S. S.* (Tawney), VI. 211.

5 *J. A. S. B.*, 1935, p. 12.

6 T. C. Dasgupta, *Aspects of Bengali Society*, p. 30.

7 Elliot and Dowson, I. 77.

8 Ibid., 90. 9 Ibid., 87.

Disbursing merchants—

In sea-trade besides the merchants engaged in the actual shipping of merchandise there was a class of disbursing merchants who brought the goods from the foreign merchants and circulated them in the country. It appears that gradually the Indian merchants were leaving the major part of actual shipping to the foreigners and confining themselves to distribution. Thus, for example, Al-Idrīsī observes that at Debal trade was carried on in a great variety of articles and that the rich inhabitants of Debal brought in bulk wares in the vessels of other countries and stored them until they became scarce[1]. Likewise Chau Ju-kua refers to ships from different parts of Sumatra coming to Nan-p'i (Malabar) and Ku-lin (Quilon) taking the products of the latter and bringing their own in exchange[2]. Marco Polo also in speaking of Cambay and Somnath refers to merchants from many lands bringing their merchandise to these places and taking away with them those of these kingdoms[3]. In the *Prabandhacintāmaṇi*[4] we read of a merchant who invests his capital in purchasing sacks of *manjiṣṭhā* imported from abroad.

Muslim merchants on western coast of India—

It appears that the Indonesian merchants had dominance only up to Quilon[5] but the ports to its north were frequented by the Muslims. We have many references to the presence of Muslims on the western coast of India[6]. It appears that their wealth was bringing them importance in society and the state. A reference in the *Prabandhacintāmaṇi* indicates that an Arab

1 Ibid., 77. Cf. Ibn Haukal in Elliot and Dowson, I. 37.

2 pp. 88-89.

3 (A. Ricci and D. Ross) pp. 334, 335.

4 p. 70, ll. 2ff.

5 Chau Ju-kua, pp. 88-89.

6 *E.I.*, XXXII, p. 66, ll. 6-13 ; XXXIII. 236f (the editor does not notice that the merchant is Muslim) ; V. V. Mirashi's article on Chinchani plates in the *J. N. Banerjee Volume*, pp. 96-109 ; Ibn Haukal in Elliot and Dowson, I. 34, 36 ; Al Idrīsī in ibid., pp. 88, 89 ; *P. I. H. C.*, 1939, p. 647 ; *Indian Archaeology*, 1959-60, p. 62.

trader Saida (Sayyad) had become so powerful as to venture to engage in a naval fight with Vastupāla, the minister of the Caulukya state[1].

Arab merchants and the kings on the western coast—

Trading with the Arab merchants must have been a source of large gains to the local merchants and the state. The Arab writers praise the Rāṣṭrakūṭa kings for their sympathetic and considerate regard for the Arabs[2]. This has been lauded by modern scholars as a noble example of religious toleration[3], but no doubt economic factors were equally important. The Arab traders brought rich dividends to the state and the Rāṣṭrakūṭas by patronising them wanted to enjoy the monopoly of the wares brought by the Arab merchants.

The force of the economic factor becomes clear in the story from the *Prabandhacintāmaṇi*[4] which states that when there was a quarrel between the minister Vastupāla and the Arab merchant Saida (Sayyad) at the port of Stambha (Cambay) the latter requisitioned to his help Mahāsādhanika Saṅka from the port of Bhṛgukaccha (Broach). Harihara has composed a historical play *Śaṅkhaparābhava Vyāyoga* to commemorate the ultimate victory of Vastupāla, the governor of Stambhatīrtha, when the port was attacked by Śaṅkha, the son of Sindhurāja, the ruler of Lāṭa[5]. Harihara was associated with Vastupāla and so his contemporary testimony should be accepted for the historicity of the event. It would appear from this that the coastal powers were trying earnestly to attract the Arab merchants to their ports[6], and this gives the clue for the religious toleration on the part of the Rāṣṭrakūṭas.

---

1 p. 102, ll. 10ff.

2 See Sulaimān, Al-Mas'ūdī, Al-Iṣṭakhrī and Ibn Haukal, and Al-Idrīsī—Elliot and Dowson, I. 4, 24, 34, 88.

3 E. g., A. S. Altekar in *The Age of Imperial Kanauj*, p. 17 ; A. K. Majumdar, *Chaulukyas of Gujarat*, p. 267.

4 p. 102, ll. 10ff.

5 *J. O. I.*, VII. 272.

6 See *Prabandhacintāmaṇi*, p. for 103 the policy of Vastupāla.

The powers on the western coast, especially the Caulukyas and the Yādavas, were often clashing for controlling the province of Lāṭa with its ports of Cambay and Broach. The prosperity of the Caulukyas would seem to have been due to their possessing the three ports of Cambay, Broach and Somanātha. The Paramāras being denied any share of sea-trade were comparatively less prospersous. It was with a desire to participate in this lucrative sea-trade that the Paramāras tried and succeeded, though only temporarily, in controlling Broach[1].

It is clear that the states on the western coast tried to regulate the sea-trade so as to get the best out of it. We have a significant indication of this in the accounts of the Jewish traveller Benjamin who records the facilities provided to foreign merchants by the king of Chulam (Quilon). He says : "This nation is very trustworthy in matters of trade, and whenever foreign merchants enter their port, three secretaries of the king immediately repair on board their vessels, write down their names and report them to him. The king thereupon grants them security for their property, which they may even leave in the open fields without guard. One of the king's officers sits in the market, and receives goods that may have been found anywhere, and which he returns to those applicants who can minutely describe them. This custom is observed in the whole empire of the king"[2]. In the *Prabandhacintāmaṇi*[3] also we read of the concern of king Yogarāja that ships coming to the port of Someśvara should not be molested. The *Mānasollāsa*[4] recommends a king to provide protection to shipping and lays down regular licence fees for ships calling at the ports. In his inscription from Motupalli[5] the Kākatīya king Gaṇapatideva guarantees security to the ships visiting his port and mentions the details of the dues to be paid by them. We find the Śilāhāra king Raṭṭarāja also fixing the duty to be paid by the ships[6].

1 A. K. Majumdar, *Chaulukyas of Gujarat*, p. 265.

2 K. A. N. Sastri, *Foreign Notices*, p. 134.

3 p. 14, ll. 3ff.

4 I, p. 62, vv. 374-76.

5 *E. I.*, XII, p. 195.

6 *E. I.*, III, p. 301.

Indian ports—

Our sources speak of a number of ports on the east and west coasts of India. In Bengal Tāmralipti enjoyed the position of one of India's major ports, especially for voyages to South-East Asia. But the silting up of the mouth of the Sarasvatī and the shifting of its course decreased the utility of Tāmralipti and we find Saptagrāma gradually emerging as the major port of Bengal[1]. Other ports on the eastern coast of India mentioned in the early Bengali literature are Puri, Kaliṅga or Kaliṅgapaṭam, Cikāculi (Chicacole), Bānpur and Rāmeśvara[2]. Ma'bar or the Coromandel coast appears to have grown into a virtual clearing-house for the ships coming alike from the East and the West. Wassaf refers to the products of China, India and Sind laden on huge ships constantly coming to Ma'bar and observes significantly that the wealth of the isles of the Persian Gulf and the beauty and adornment of other countries from Irāq and Khurāsān as far as Rum and Europe are derived from Ma'bar which is so situated as to be the key of Hind[3]. Rashiheddin[4] also says the same. Marco Polo[5] speaks of ships from the Persian Gulf and the Arabian coast with goods laden for sale visiting Cail (Kayal). The Arab writers refer to many ports in this area Qayrah (Kāveripaṭṭanam), Manifattan or Malifattan (Nāgapaṭṭanam), Abāṭū (Adirāmpaṭṭaṇam), Taṇḍā (Toṇḍi), Daqtan (Devipaṭṭanam) and Fatni (Kilakarai)[6]. A recently discovered inscription suggests that of these Nāgapaṭṭinam was the most important[7].

Of the ports on the Malabar coast Quilon had become important. From the Arab writers it becomes clear that ships coming from the west called at the port of Quilon for taking in fresh water before sailing for Kalah-bar (Kedah)[8]. The Chinese sources

1 R.C. Majumdar (Ed.), *History of Bengal*, Vol. I, p. 4.

2 T. C. Dasgupta, *Aspects of Bengali Society*, p. 30.

3 Elliot and Dowson, III. 32.

4 Ibid., I. 69.

5 II. 370.

6 Nainar, *Arab Geographers*, Index, s. v.

7 *J. N. S. I.*, XX. 13.

8 Nainar, Loc. cit., pp. 44-45.

likewise state that the Chinese traders going to the country of the Arabs had to tranship at Ku-lin (Quilon) to smaller boats[1]. Abu Dulaf also mentions Kawlam (Quilon) as the port of embarkation for Oman in Arabia[2]. The *Ling-wai-ta* refers to the people of Sumatra and Arabia bringing their wares to trade in the country of Ku-lin (Quilon)[3]. The prosperity of Quilon seems to have continued up to the time of Marco Polo, who refers to merchants from South China and Arabia making profitable voyages to Malabar, in particular the port of Quilon[4].

The Arab writers mention other ports on the western coast which were obviously not so much in use : Kūdāfarīd (Aḷimukam), Sinjilī (Kodungallur), Tandiyūr (Kadalundi), S͟hāliyāt (Chaliam), Fandarīna (Pantalāyini Kollam), Dahfattān (Dharmadam), Buddfatān (Baliapatam), Jurbatan (Srikandapuram), Fūfal (Bekal), Harqilya (Kasargod), K͟hurnal (Kumbla), Manjarūr (Mangalore), Fāknūr (Bārkūr), Bāsrūr (Besrur), Saymūr (Shirur), Barqalī (Bhatkal), Hannūr (Hanovar), Habār (Kārwār), Sindābūr (Sadashivagad), Sandān (Sindhudurg), Tāna (Thana) and Sūbāra (Sopara)[5].

The ports on the Gujarat coast also played an important part in the international sea-trade. It is from the port of Bhṛgukaccha that Kubera, the merchant chief of Anahilvāḍa, is said to have set sail for trading with a foreign country[6]. Al-Idrīsī[7] mentions Baruh (Broach) as a port of call for ships coming from China and Sind. From Marco Polo[8] we learn of the regular export of the products of Gujarat to Arabia and other lands. He refers to the port of Cambay as being visited by merchants with many ships

1 Chau Ju-kua, pp. 24, 91 (n. 17).

2 Nainar, Op. cit., pp. 46f.

3 Chau Ju-kua, p. 91 (n. 16). From Chau Ju-kua we learn that the ships from Sumatra were calling at the port of Quilon (p. 89) and that the products of Nan-p'i (Malabar) were being carried to the different parts of Sumatra (p. 88).

4 II. 390, 376.

5 Nainar, *Arab Geographers*, Index, s.v.

6 *Moharājaparājaya*, III, p. 61.

7 Elliot and Dowson, I. 87.

8 II. 393.

and cargoes[1]. It has been suggested that the Gurjara-Pratihāras developed Cambay or Stambhatīrtha as a rival port to Broach, which was under the Rāṣṭrakūṭas[2]. Somanātha, the famous religious centre, was a third important port in the area. Al-Bīrūnī speaks of its fame as a station for those who went to and fro between Sufala in the country of Zanj (Zanzibar) and China[3].

Debal near the mouth of the Indus was a large mart and the port meeting the needs of an extensive area[4]. Al-Idrīsī observes that ships laden with the products of Oman and the vessels of China and India used to come to this port[5]. He gives a graphic account of the advantages which this naval station possessed: "Merchandise from every country is found here, and is sent on from hence to other countries. It is placed at the extremity of a bay, where vessels can enter and cast anchor. It is well-supplied with water and there is a fine fortress erected by the government of India to prevent the inroads of the inhabitants of the island of Kīsh"[6].

The Arabs received from India much valuable merchandise which they required for their own consumption and which brought them rich profits when exported to the east or the west. The Khalifa Umar was told by a trader that in India the rivers are pearls, the mountains gems and the trees scented water[7]. The Arab traders therefore preferred to sail to India than go towards the west[8]. It would appear that articles exported from India continued to remain the main attraction of the sea-trade of the period. The *Ḥudūd al 'Ālam*[9] gives a list of Indian exports which included perfumes like musk, aloes, amber and camphor, pearls of various varieties

1 II. 398.

2 A. K. Majumdar, *Chaulukyas of Gujarat*, p. 265.

3 II. 104.

4 Elliot and Dowson, I. 37.

5 Ibid., 77.

6 Ibid., 84. Elliot has misread Kanbāya for Daybul—Nainar, Op. cit., p. 52, f.n. 87-88.

7 See S. S. Nadavī, *Araba aura Bhārata ke Sambandha*, p. 54.

8 Abū Zaid in *Ancient Accounts of India and China*, pp. 40ff.

9 p. 86.

and sizes, diamonds, corals, and innumerable kinds of medicinal herb. Ibn Khordadbah[1] mentions diverse species of aloe-wood, sandalwood, camphor and camphor-water, nutmeg, clovepink, cubeb, cocoanut, vegetable stuffs[2], textiles of velvety cotton and ivory as articles exported by India. Benjamin, the Jewish traveller, would suggest that spices were the chief merchandise of India. Speaking of the island of Kish he says that Indian merchants brought there great quantities of spices[3]. According to Marco Polo[4] Indian merchants visiting Hormuz brought with them spices, precious stones, pearls, clothes of silk and gold, elephants' tusks and so forth.

Exports—

The foreign accounts help us to determine the exports of the ports in different parts of India. Thus, we can say on the testimony of Ibn Khordadbah[5] that Sind exported costus, canes and bamboos. According to Chau Ju-kua[6] Gujarat exported to Arabia great quantities of indigo, red kino, myrobalans and foreign cotton stuffs of all colours[7]. Marco Polo[8] mentions pepper, ginger and indigo as the products of Gujarat and very often refers to the delicate and beautiful buckrams and to the export of good buckram and cotton from the province of Gujarat[9]. Ibn Rosteh mentions teak as an export from the Rāṣṭrakūṭa kingdom[10]. Chau Ju-kua mentions fine swords, *tóu-lo* cotton stuffs and common cotton cloth[11] as the

1 Ferrand, *Textes*, p. 31.

2 Ferrand translates it as "des étoffes végétales". But S. S. Nadavī, Op. cit., p. 55 takes it to mean textiles of hemp.

3 K. A. N. Sastri, *Foreign Notices*, p. 134.

4 I. 107.

5 Elliot and Dowson, I. 15.

6 p. 92.

7 Locally manufactured cloth of no great worth was referred to simply as foreign cloth (*fan pu*)—*J. M. B. R. A. S.*, XXXII, Pt. 2 (1959), p. 61.

8 II. 383.

9 II. 379, 385, 388.

10 Ferrand, *Textes*, p. 74.

11 The text uses *tou-lo-mien* which is a composite coinage from Sanskrit *tūla*=cotton and Chinese *mien*=dowry. As contrasted with this other cotton piece-goods are referred to simply as *mien pu* or *pu*—P. Wheatley, *Geographical Notes on some commodities involved in Sung Maritime Trade* in *J. M. B. R. A. S.*, XXXII, Pt. 2 (1959), p. 59.

products of P'öng-k'ie-lo (kingdom of Balhara)[1] and best quality of putchuck[2] and fine white flowered and dotted cotton stuffs as those of Nan-ni-hua-lo (Anhilvada)[3]. Obviously these must have been sent abroad from the ports on the Gujarat coast. We have already shown that there was a regular export of slaves to Persia from the Gujarat coast, so much so that Tejapāla, the minister of Vīradhavala, was seriously concerned to stop it[4].

In some of the Chinese accounts we get lists of the exports of Tiẹ́n-chu[5], but the names of the commodities do not seem to have been from eastern India alone. Thus, we have references to rhinoceros (horns), elephants and ivory, leopards (skin), lions, sables, camels, marmot[6] (? skins), tortoise-shell, gold, silver, copper, iron, lead and tin, sugarcane, sugar, pepper, ginger, sandalwood and other aromatic woods, black salt, all kinds of fruit, gold embroidered (skin) rugs, fine hemps, *po-tié*[7] (white muslin), fine fur garments, handsome rugs called *t'a-töng*, a stone like tale (called *huo-ts'i*) and diamond. The Arab accounts mention aloe-wood and a variety of fine cotton fabrics as the products of Rahma or Ruhmi[8] which is generally identified with the Pāla kingdom[9]. They also mention the horns of rhinoceros as an important export from the kingdom of Rahma to China[10]. It also seems that Rahma was known for its

1 p. 97. P. Wheatley, Op. cit., p. 52 restores P'öng-k'ie-lo as Bangalore and its capital Ch'a-na-chi as Kannada (Karṇāṭa).

2 *Mu-hsiang* or putchuck is one of the most difficult of Chau Ju-kua's aromatics to identify. True putchuck is an Himalayan herb, *Saussurea lappa*, whose bitter root, smelling like a mixture of musk and orris, was used from ancient times as a universal panacea. See P. Wheatley, Op. cit., p. 62.

3 p. 98.

4 See supra p. 73.

5 Chau Ju-kua, pp. 111, 113 (n. 3—for *Hou Han-shu* and *Liang-shu*).

6 The marmot is an animal living in sub-Arctic conditions and hence the present reference is perhaps a mistake.

7 *J. M. B. R. A. S.*, XXXII, Pt. 2 (1959), p. 59.

8 Elliot and Dowson, I. 14, 5.

9 *I. H. Q.*, XVI, pp. 232ff; R. C. Majumdar (Ed.) *History of Bengal*, I, p. 122.

10 Ferrand, *Textes*, pp. 44, 105.

fly-whisks made of *samara* (yak-tail)[1] hair[2]. Sulaimān and Al-Mas'ūdī definitely mention gold and silver as being found in the kingdom of Rahma[3]. We know that these metals are found not in Bengal but in Lower Burma[4]. It would appear that the Arab narratives included both Lower Burma and Bengal in the kingdom of Rahma.

Imports from the West—

We have now to see what India received for the things she exported. The *Vaijayantī* employs the term *turuṣka* for incense[5], suggesting that incense was imported from the Middle East, probably from the coast of Hadharamaut in South Arabia[6]. Likewise the use of the terms *mlecha* for copper[7] and *yavaneṣṭa* for lead[8] would imply that these metals were also in the list of India's imports from the west. We must also note that in this dictionary *yavana* is the word for salt from saline soil[9] and *yavaneṣṭa* for a kind of onion[10]. Ibn Said refers to the import of dates from Basra into Debal in Sind[11]. Al-Mas'ūdī states that ivory was brought from Zanj (Zanzibar) to Oman and from there was shipped to India and China[12]. The dye called *kṛmirāga* (*kiramdana*) was imported from Persia. The Jain texts contain absurd stories about the preparation of this dye[13], which were probably told by the Persian traders to keep the secret of its manufacture and also to emphasise its rarity and high cost. V.S. Agrawala[14] traces a reference to petroleum[15] from the oil fields of

1 Probably referring to Sanskrit *cāmara*.

2 Ferrand, Op. cit.

3 Ibid.

4 Coedes, *Histoire Ancienne des États Hindouisés d' Extrême-Orient*, p. 135.

5 p. 132, l. 221.

6 *The Struggle for Empire*, p. 522.

7 *Vaijayantī*, p. 43, l.49.

8 Ibid., p. 43, l.59.

9 Ibid., p. 133, l.245.

10 Ibid., p. 62, l.414.

11 Ferrand, *Textes*, p. 48, f.n.

12 *Prairies d' or*, III. 7-8 q. in Chau Ju-kua, p. 127, n.4.

13 A. N. Upadhye, *Bṛhatkathākośa*, Introduction, p. 88.

14 *I. H. Q.*, XIII. 226.

15 Petroleum only applies to the very highly refined spirit used in cars etc. It is hardly likely that this was manufactured. Probably the reference is to a heavy thick oil, more like modern lubricating oil.

Persia in the expression *Pārasīkataila* used in the *Vikramāṅka-devacarita*[1].

It would appear from Abū Zaid that formerly India used to get the dinars called Sindiat[2], emeralds from Egypt, coral and the stone dahnaj (a stone resembling emerald). But the cessation of the trade in these things[3] probably indicates that the west no longer gave so much of gold but had found a profitable item of export to India.

It is clear from many references that India spent huge sums on importing horses from the West. With the increasing use of horses in war accompanied by the increase in the number of feudal lords and chiefs there was a growing demand for horses. It becomes clear from a study of Indian texts that foreign breeds of western areas in general and of Vanāyu or Arabia in particular were much valued in India[4]. Indians needed a continuous import of horses because the imported ones could not remain useful for long owing to the ignorance of the Indians of their proper management, training and feeding. These horses could not be bred in India. The Indians had no farriers and the foreign merchants, with a view to preserving the monopoly of their trade, prevented any farrier from coming to India[5]. In the Chinese text *Ling-wai-ta* also we have a reference to the Arabs importing horses to Quilon[6]. In the *Prabandhacintāmaṇi* the cargo of a ship coming to the port of Stambha is said to have included ten thousand horses[7].

But, in order to have an idea of the drain which this import meant to India we must study western sources. It would appear that by the twelfth and thirteenth centuries this trade had reached astounding heights. According to Wassaf[8] an Arab merchant had

1 IX. 20.

2 Most likely because they were minted in Sind.

3 Elliot and Dowson, I. 11.

4 *Abhidhānaratnamālā*, v. 439; *Vaijayantī* p. 111, l. 189.

5 Wassaf in Elliot and Dowson, III. 33-34; Marco Polo II. 340, 345, 450.

6 Chau Ju-kua, p. 91, n. 16.

7 p. 14, ll. 13-19.

8 Elliot and Dowson, III. 33-34.

made an agreement with a Pāṇḍya king to bring to Ma'bar as many horses as he could procure from the islands of the Persian Gulf. Each horse cost 220 dīnārs of 'red gold' (=550 saggi of Marco Polo[1] = 550/6 oz.) and the total number of horses which Ma'bar, Kambayat and other ports received from the ports on the Arabian Sea and Persian Gulf was 14,000 costing 2,2000,000 dīnārs. Marco Polo[2] notes that each of the Pāṇḍya kings every year purchased 2000 horses at the rate of 500 saggi (=500/6 oz.) of gold per horse. Elsewhere Marco Polo[3] observes that each horse imported from the Persian Gulf was sold at 200 livres of Persian money (=£193 according to Yule).

Imports from China—

In the list of exports from China to India Chinese silk naturally occupies an important place. Rashiheddin speaks of Chinese junks bringing to Ma'bar clothes from Chin and Māchin[4]. It would appear from Marco Polo that India received clothes of silk and gold as well as 'sandals' (a silk textile) from China[5]. In Indian literary texts we often have references to the use of Chinese silk (*cīnāṃśuka*)[6]. From these it would follow that the quantity of Chinese fabrics imported to India was quite significant. In the mathematical text *Gaṇitasārasaṅgraha*[7] two problems are set referring to numerous large pieces of Chinese silk. In the *Vaijayantī* the use of the terms *cīnapaṭṭa*[8] for tin and *cīna*[9] for iron would suggest that India imported some amount of these metals from China.

1 Yule, *Marco Polo*, II. 349, f.n.

2 II. 340.

3 I. 83.

4 Elliot and Dowson, I. 69.

5 II. 390. See also ibid., II. 24, 132, 152, 157, 176, 181.

6 *Kuṭṭanīmata*, vv. 66, 344; *Naiṣadhīyacarita*, XXI. 2.

7 IV. 19-20. 300 pieces of 6 *hastas* × 6 *hastas*, 720 pieces of 5 *hastas* × 3 *hastas*, 70 pieces of 5 *hastas* × 9 *hastas* and 525 pieces of 2 *hastas* × 3 *hastas*.

8 p. 43, l.60 China is situated at the northern extremity of the world's most extensive and richest metallogenetic tin province—*J. M. B. R. A.S.*, XXXII, Pt. 2 (1959), p. 115.

9 p. 43, l. 65. See *J. M. B. R. A. S.*, XXXII, Pt 2 (1959), p. 117—iron and ironmongery were amongst the commonest commodities shipped from China to the South Seas.

India would appear also to have received gold and silver from China. In 1296 the Chinese government had to prohibit the export of gold and silver and to limit the value of the trade with Ma'bar, Kulam and Fandaraina[1]. The Chinese accounts significantly remark that in return for the native produce which the Cola embassy of 1077 offered, the Chinese emperor gave strings of cash and taels of silver[2]. A Tamil inscription of the early years of the eleventh century indicates that south India was receiving Chinese gold, probably through Indonesia[3].

Imports from South-East Asia—

Chau Ju-kua gives a list of articles which Nan-p'i (Malabar) received in exchange of its merchandise from Kio-lo Ta-nung (Twala Terang on Perak coast) and San-fo-ts'i (Palembang). These are *ho-ch'ī* silks, porcelain-ware, can.phor (*chang-nau*), rhubarb, bees wax (*huang-lién*), cloves, lump-camphor (*nau-tẓī*), sandalwood, cardamoms and gharu-wood[4]. It was the spices of South-East Asia which formed the chief article of the ancient trade, and the cloves, spikenard and other fine spices which Malabar is said to have received from the East[5] were evidently brought from Java and Sumatra[6]. Al-Kazwīnī[7] also speaks of alọe-wood being brought to Quilon from the islands beyond the equator. In the Indian texts of the period we find elaborate lists of the agricultural products of the region. Thus, we have references to camphor, areca-nuts, betel plants, sandal trees, *lavaṅga*, *lavalī*, cocoanut plantain, *panasa* and *piṇḍakharjūra* besides *rājatālī*, *tamāla* and *mandāra*[8]. In the *Vaijayantī takkola* is the word for the fruit of *Calyptranthes Jambalana*[9].

1 *T'oung Pao*, XV. 425-26.

2 Chau Ju-kua, p. 101, n. 12.

3 *J. N. S. I.*, XX. 13. But there are no Indonesian references to this trade.

4 pp. 88f.

5 Marco Polo II. 390.

6 Ibid., 272, 284.

7 Elliot and Dowson, I. 96.

8 *Samarāiccakahā*, VI, p. 41 ; *Tilakamañjarī*, pp. 133, 135. 137, 140.

9 p. 131, l. 210.

After spices the next important item on the list of imports to India from the south-east Asian islands was that of metals. According to Marco Polo the foreign merchants coming to Cambay brought with them above all gold, silver, copper and blue vitriol[1]. It would appear that the merchants referred to here were those from South-East Asia as Marco Polo himself observes in another context that ships coming to Malabar from the east brought copper in ballast as well as gold and silver[2]. It was the lure of gold which had attracted Indians to these islands. The epithet "the product of Suvarṇadvīpa" applied to gold in the *Vaijayantī*[3] would imply the export of gold from Suvarṇadvīpa to India. A story in the *Samarāiccakahā*[4] would indicate that Indian merchants returning from Suvarṇadvīpa brought with them blocks of gold marked with their names. We read in the *Tilakamañjarī*[5] that one could see in the islands here and there many mines of gems, gold and silver and also an abundance of pearls in the heaps of oysters piled in enormous quantity. Indulging in rhetoric the text adds that even in the houses of the poor could be found innumerable gems fit for kings and that fine gold and silver were neglected as if equal to dust. This seems to be an exaggerated and idealised account of the wealth for which south-east Asian countries were famous. In the stories of the period we often read of merchants going to these islands and obtaining jewels[6].

These islands would appear to have exported fine textiles such as silk to India. The *Mānasollāsa*[7] would seem to imply this when it refers to fabrics of many islands to be used by a king but mentions distinctly those from China and Ceylon. Surprisingly the Chinese text *Ling-wai-ta* mentions the merchants of Kién-pi (Kampar,

---

1 II. 395, 398.

2 II. 390.

3 p. 42, l. 21.

4 VI, pp. 38-39.

5 p. 133.

6 *Upamiti*, pp. 996-8; *Samarāiccakahā*, II, pp. 96f; VI, p. 42.

7 II, p. 90, v. 1040. Also vv. 1018-9. Most silk seems, however, to have been imported from China.

Eastern coast of Sumatra) as bringing every year elephants and cattle to trade in the country of Ku-lin (Quilon)[1].

Imports from Ceylon—

As regards articles coming from Ceylon probably the most important were pearls[2]. The synonyms for dry ginger[3] and tin[4] in the *Vaijayantī* would suggest that India was receiving these articles from Ceylon. The *Mānasollāsa*[5] refers to the fine fabrics from Ceylon as stuffs fit for a king.

Nature of trade—

In order to get an idea of the volume and balance of trade we have to emphasise certain limitations of this trade. As compared with modern trade the trade of our period was extremely slow, limited alike in its volume and variety. No doubt there were some changes in the articles of trade as compared with earlier times. In the lists of imports and exports to different countries we do find increasing importance being attached to certain essentials of daily life like drugs and spices. But the trade was still essentially in luxuries. It has to be realised that in spite of all the progress made in the art of ship-building and navigation the sailors and the merchants were at the mercy of the roaring waves of the unfathomable seas and the unpredictable and unmanagable winds and storms. The fear from the pirates also added to the perils of the sea. In this way the merchant could only concentrate on precious articles of luxury which have comparatively smaller volume and weight. The population of the countries engaged in this trade was still mostly agricultural, and concentrated in economically self-sufficient villages had practically no desire for foreign wares or ability to pay for them. The demand for the foreign merchandise came from the class of rulers and chiefs.

---

1 Chau Ju-kua, p. 91, n. 16.

2 Cf. *Karpūramañjarī*, II.

3 p. 129, l. 150.

4 p. 43, l. 62.

5 II, p. 90, v. 1040.

Volume of trade—

For want of relevant data it is now practically impossible to determine the volume of India's imports and exports, but we can gather some idea of it from stray references. In the Chinese sources we do have some indications but they are marred by our ignorance of the unit of count referred to and of the precise share of the different countries in the trade. However, it has to be noted that from 1049 to 1053 the annual importation of elephants' tusks, rhinoceros horns, strings of pearls, aromatics, incense etc. was over 53,000 units of count which increased in 1175 to over 500,000 units[1]. The accounts of the Cola embassy of 1015, though handed down in an exaggerated form, may be utilised to give an idea of the amount of export. Thus, the Cola king is said to have sent, among other presents, 21,000 ounces of pearls, 60 elephants' tusks, and 60 catties of frankincense; but the gifts actually handed by the envoy are said to have included 6,600 ounces of pearls and 3,300 catties of perfumes[2]. We learn from the same Chinese source that in return for the Indian produce brought by the Cola embassy in 1077 the Chinese emperor gave 81,800 strings of cash and 52,000 taels of silver[3].

Balance of trade—

It has been sometimes suggested[4] that India had an unfavourable balance of trade in this period. We fear we have not enough relevant references to speak in terms of exact figures. No doubt, the balance of India's profits had decreased considerably when compared with earlier times, but this did not amount to an unfavourable balance of trade. A major share of this profit was apparently enjoyed by the ports of southern India, especially those on the Coromandel coast and Malabar coast. The ports in the Gujarat and Cambay area also enjoyed a significant share. In the second rank we may place the ports on the Koṅkaṇa coast and those of

1 Chau Ju-kua, p. 19, n. 4.

2 Ibid., p. 101, n. 12.

3 Ibid.

4 N. R. Ray, *Bāṅgālir Itihās* q. by A. K. Majumdar, *Chaulukyas of Gujarat*, p. 270.

Bengal. Bengal did have maritime connections with south-east Asia but it would appear that, being rather out of way for the direct route which monopolised the lucrative trade between the east and the west, its share was not enviable.

Rate of profit—

The rate of profit in this trade must have been considerable. The very fact that merchants were willing to face the perils of the journey, the danger of loss sustained in it, the dues paid at different ports, and the whims and exactions of the chiefs would suggest that the margin of profit must have been high indeed. This is reflected in a traditional Gujarati verse saying that he who goes to Java never returns and that if by chance he returns he brings back money enough to live on for two generations[1]. Stray references indicate the high profits. Thus, the Arab accounts speak of horns of rhinoceros exported from Rahma to China to be made into fashionable and costly girdles which sometimes fetched 2,000 or even 4,000 dīnārs each[2]. Even though literary accounts have a general air of rhetorical exaggeration it must be observed that in the realistic details of the voyage of a business magnate of Anhil-vāḍa given in the *Moharājaparājaya* it is said that he returned from the foreign land when his takings had swollen to a sum of four crore gold pieces[3].

Decline in India's profits—

As regards the reasons for the decrease in the total profits of India we have already discussed the growing competition of the Arabs, the Indonesians and the Chinese and have referred to Indian traders being generally content to distribute the wares within their country leaving other associated works to foreigners. Another reason seems to be that, as compared to earlier times, India had now a greater demand for imports. It is not unlikely that, with the increasing number of feudal lords and chiefs and the emphasis on show and grandeur, the demand for foreign wares also grew. It would

1 A. K. Forbes, *Rās Mālā*, p. 418.

2 Ferrand, *Textes*, pp. 44, 105.

3 Act III, p. 61.

appear that the patronage of merchants and the consumption of the merchandise brought by them was viewed as an issue of prestige by the ruling chiefs. Thus, a story in the *Prabandhacintāmaṇi*[1] speaks of a merchant, unable to sell his wares in the kingdom of King Vikramāditya of legendary fame, approaching the latter, who purchased the wares in order to remove the bad name which the non-sale of the article would have meant. The *Mānasollāsa*[2] also advises the king to decorate himself with fabrics of many islands. We can easily imagine the increase in the import of luxury articles resulting from this tendency. We have already referred to the drain caused by the import of a large number of horses. Thus it would appear that India did not earn much bullion in this period. It is significant that in some of the stories of the period we read that Indian merchants on reaching foreign markets sold their merchandise and took in foreign wares in exchange[3]. The statement of Abū Zaid that during his time, unlike earlier times, India was not receiving many dīnārs has already been referred to[4]. Chau Ju-kua[5] also speaks of the products of Nan-p'i (Malabar) being exchanged with the goods of Sumatra. In the early Bengali literature also we find lists of foreign articles which the Bengali merchants are said to have received in exchange for their own[6]. No doubt we have some references to Chinese gold coin coming to India[7], but it is significant that so far not a single gold coin of early medieval China has been recovered in India.

---

1 p. 5.
2 II, p. 90, v. 1040.
3 Cf. *Upamitibhavaprapañcākathā*, pp. 870-72—*gṛhītaṃ pratibhāṇḍam*.
4 Elliot and Dowson, I. 11.
5 pp. 88f.
6 T. C. Dasgupta, *Aspects of Bengali Society*, pp. 27-29.
7 See *J. N. S. I.*, XX. 13.

CHAPTER VIII

CREDIT AND BANKING

The anarchy of the period resulting from local wars among the feudal lords, the insecurity on the roads and the menace of the Muslim invasion must have made capital shy. It was, therefore, necessary that the money-lenders should feel secure about the repayment of their money or else have possibilities of higher profits otherwise they would not invest their capital. The *Mitākṣarā*[1] seems to be recognising this fact when it justifies higher rates of interest in case of traders traversing dense forests and sea-faring merchants on the ground of the great danger of the loss of even the principal as the debtors may perish by ship-wreck or from the attacks of robbers and wild beasts.

The commentaries and digests of the period cannot be credited with any newness of approach. They were expected only to harmonize and reconcile the existing authorities[2]. It is, therefore, not strange that Medhātithi upholds the older law relating to usury[3]. But even within this limitation we find a definite tendency towards giving the money-lender greater facilities, especially about the safe recovery of his money.

Responsibility of the heir to pay the debt—

Al-Bīrūnī was informed that the heir had to pay the debts of the deceased, either out of his share or of the stock of his own property even if the deceased had not left any property[4]. No doubt the rules aimed that the interests of the money-lender should not be jeopardised by the death of the debtor, but the laws were not as simple as Al-Bīrūnī would have them. The first three descendants, son, grandson and great-grandson, had to pay the debt if they inherited the ancestral property[5]. The *Vīramitrodaya*,

---

1 On Yāj., II. 38.

2 Medhātithi on Manu, XI. 216; *Mitākṣarā* on Yāj., I. 4-5. Cf. Jaimini, II.1.46.

3 U. N. Ghoshal in the *Age of Imperial Kanauj*, p. 406.

4 II. 164.

5 *Mitākṣarā* on Yāj., II. 51; *Smṛticandrikā*, II. p. 171.

analysing the law on the point, says that even when no ancestral property was received a son was liable to pay the debt with interest, a grandson was liable for the debt without interest, and an unwilling great-grandson was not liable even for the principal[1]. The *Vyavahāranirṇaya*[2] observes that during the life-time of the debtor the sons and not the grandsons are liable, but in case no sons are alive the grandsons become liable. The commentary *Vaijayantī*[3] fixes the graded responsibilities of sons according to their liabilities. The *Vivādaratnākara*[4] modifies the existing law and says that the son was bound to pay at once and not entitled to wait for twenty years if the disease of his father was incurable or if it was certain that he would not return from his journey. Likewise, we find the *Mitākṣarā*[5] supporting the rule making the second husband of a widow liable for the debts incurred by the first husband.

Pressure to realise debt—

Al-Idrīsī has a very interesting reference to the method of the realisation of debt in this period. He says that when a man has a right to demand anything of another, and he happens to meet him, he has only to draw a circular line upon the ground and to make his debtor enter it, which the latter never fails to do, and the debtor cannot leave this circle without satisfying his creditor, or obtaining the remission of the debt[6].

Apparently Al-Idrīsī was either idealising or had misinterpreted the practice. From Abhayatilaka Gaṇi and Hemacandra[7] it would appear that the treatment meted out to a debtor was not so humane. According to Abhayatilaka Gaṇi a creditor unable to obtain payment would take his debtor to a river bank where he would securely tie him with a chain and leave him exposed to the scorching sun. Temporarily deprived of the use of his limbs,

---

1 *Vyavahāraprakāśa*, p. 264.
2 p. 256.
3 On *Viṣṇu Dh. S.*, IV. 30.
4 p. 50.
5 On Yāj., II. 51.
6 Elliot and Dowson, I. 88.
7 *Dvyāśrayakāvya*, III. 40.

the debtor could not like a tortoise and other animals enter the water to quench his thirst.

The creditor could press the debtor for the payment of his money. Even as early as the time of Kātyāyana[1] we have a reference to the custom in some countries of the creditor holding the debtor in restraint openly before an assembly of people until he pays what is due. The *Āpastamba Dharma Sūtra*[2] speaks of the creditor who sits at the door of his debtor to recover his debts (*pratyupaviṣṭa*). In the period of our study there are many references to creditors employing physical pressure to get their money back. As there is no suggestion of any interference by the state it would appear that the creditor was regarded as well within his rights in using such measures. Dāmodara[3], who was associated with the Gāhaḍavāla court, implies that it was quite usual and normal for a money-lender to imprison a debtor for a very long period and to free him only on recovering full payment. The *Upamitibhavaprapañcākathā*[4] also speaks of hard-hearted money-lenders who always confine their debtors in painful imprisonment from which it is difficult to be released.

It is laid down in one of the documents in the *Lekhapaddhati*[5] that if ever a mortgagee needed to get his money back before the due date of payment, in the company of the *bhaṭṭaputras* he could approach the mortgagor and the sureties and realise the principal and the interest. It is significantly added that all the expenses on account of the *bhaṭṭaputras* were to be paid by the mortgagor or his sureties. Apparently the *bhaṭṭaputras* were judicial officers like the *dharmasthas* mentioned in the *Arthaśāstra*[6]. According to Kauṭilya if the mortgagee apprehends any damage (or depreciation in value) of the mortgaged property he can with the permission of the *dharmasthas* sell it in the presence of the mortgagor.

---

1 580-584.

2 I. 6.19.1.

3 *Uktivyaktiprakaraṇa*, p. 23, ll. 16-18.

4 pp. 1019-20.

5 pp. 19-21.

6 III. 12.

Sureties for loans—

From the *Lekhapaddhati* it appears that the practice of requiring sureties for loans had become general. In one case even where a son borrows money out of his share of ancestral property we find a surety besides the witnesses[1]. In the case of mortgages we read of sureties who guaranteed the money on behalf of the debtor.

Many documents in the *Lekhapaddhati* emphasise the responsibilities of a surety and specify his liabilities in detail. The responsibility of the sureties for the payment of the money was equal to that of the debtor himself. The sureties were collectively and severally responsible for the money and it was open to the creditor to realise his money from any of the sureties or from both the sureties and the debtor. It is specifically stated in the documents that the sureties were to regard themselves as debtors. If one of them was approached all were supposed to be approached, and when all were approached collectively each was supposed to be approached personally. It is further laid down that if any of the sureties was approached for the payment, he was not to point to other sureties. If the mortgagee sold the property mortgaged to recover his dues and the proceeds of the sale were not sufficient the sureties had to meet the balance even by selling their own property or by borrowing from others. If the mortgaged property was damaged or destroyed by any natural calamity the sureties were still liable for all the payments and had no right to grumble on this ground[2].

1 p. 56.

2 It has been suggested by A. K. Majumdar (*Chaulukyas of Gujarat*, pp. 280f) that the *ādhipālas* referred to in the *Lekhapaddhati* were villagers who acted as arbitrators in case the mortgagee wanted to foreclose before maturity on grounds of suspected dep reciation in the mortgaged article (It is not correct to say that the functions of *ādhipālas* have been mentioned in only one document—*LP*, pp. 19-20. They appear in others also—*LP*, pp. 41f, 37f). But a study of the documents clearly indicates that the reference is to sureties guaranteeing a mortgage. In the document referred to by Majumdar the expression occurs in connection with the

Contd. on p. 165

Rules favourable to the creditors—

The documents in the *Lekhapaddhati* indicate that deeds were drafted with a view to emphasising the prerogatives of the creditor, but there is hardly anything protecting the debtor from exploitation. The documents generally contain a phrase meaning that whatever is written in them is to be regarded as authoritative even if an additional word is inserted or a word is wanting. We can well realise the implication of this for the poor and often uneducated debtor unable to make out the contents of the deed. In the *Kuṭṭanīmata*[1] we read of a money-lender who used to write ten times the amount lent.

The documents in the *Lekhapaddhati*[2] emphasise the duty of the debtor to repay on or before a certain date, after which the creditor could sell the mortgaged property to recover the amount due. It is stated that the debtor was to pay the money without creating any quarrel and without making any fuss. The debtor or his sureties were not to file a suit against the creditor. Obviously this could have been only a pious wish as the document itself goes on to consider the possibility of a suit being filed in a court of law.

liabilities of the sureties and it is distinctly stated that the surety guaranteeing a mortgage (*ādhipālaka-pratibhūmih*) should pay to the mortgagee the stipulated amount together with interest and other expenses. In another document the reference is more clear (*LP*, pp. 41f). It says that in case the sale proceeds of the mortgaged chattel are not sufficient the mortgagor and the surety guaranteeing the mortgaged property (*ādhipālakena pratibhuvā*) should pay the remaining amount together with interest and other expenses out of their own property. Moreover, whereas one document mentions the *ādhipāla-pratibhūs* as sureties (*LP*, pp. 37f) other documents refer to the *pratibhūs* as fulfilling the same duties (*LP*, pp. 39, 34f). It would therefore follow that in some documents the expression *ādhipāla* has been added before *pratibhū* only to make the sense of their guaranteeing the mortgage more clear, as has been done in one case by adding *dāna* before *pratibhū* (*LP*, pp. 36f) so as to emphasise the responsibility of the surety to pay the money. The *Smṛticandrikā* (II. 150) also quotes Pitāmaha to indicate that *ādhipāla* was a surety.

1 v. 746.

2 pp. 19-21, 36-39.

If the mortgaged property was destroyed by a natural calamity the debtor or his sureties were not to indulge in annoying discussions and controversies. In one of the documents it is laid down that if the mortgaged house collapsed or got damaged in any manner the mortgagee could get it repaired and add the expenses to the original loan[1]. If the mortgagee had any need for his money even before the due date of payment he could sell the property. In case the mortgaged chattel was damaged or depreciated through a natural calamity the mortgagor was to replace it by another one. This is corroborated by the *Mitākṣarā*[2] which observes that it is the duty of the mortgagor to take proper care of the pledged property. The debtor had to make up the amount if the proceeds of the sale of the pledged property were not sufficient. The *Mitākṣarā*[3] also lays down that if the income from a pledged property is not sufficient to meet the interest wholly the debtor has to pay the principal and the unpaid part of the interest before regaining his pledge.

Hypothecation without possession—

Besides the different kinds of mortgages or pledges documented in the *Lekhapaddhati* we have one instance of what may be called hypothecation without possession[4]. Here a man borrows 20 measures of wheat with the stipulation that after the threshing season he would repay 25 measures of wheat. Though the creditor did not possess the field or grains of the debtor it is clear that a charge was created on the standing crops of the debtor. From the definition of *bandha* given in the *Vyavahāramayūkha*[5] it is clear that this was the same as hypothecation without possession. It is explained as an undertaking by the debtor that he will not alienate by sale, gift or mortgage his house, land or other property until the debt due to the creditor is paid off.

1 pp. 36-37.
2 On Yāj., II. 60.
3 On Yāj., II. 64.
4 p. 21.
5 p. 166.

Sub-mortgages—

The *Lekhapaddhati* documents provide significant evidence for the law concerning sub-mortgages. We have two deeds of usufructuary mortgage of buildings of which one lays down that the mortgagee could not sub-mortgage the building by transferring the deed to a new mortgagee[1]. As the other document does not specifically deny the mortgagee the right to sub-mortgage[2] it would appear that normally the right vested with the mortgagee unless specifically stated otherwise.

This is actually what the legal works of the period would indicate. The practice of sub-mortgage, though known from an early time appears to have been recognised rather late[3]. Thus Medhātithi observes that the usufructuary rights of a mortgagee do not create in him the right to sub-mortgage[4]. Kullūka however opposes the interpretation of Medhātithi and adds that it is common practice in all countries for a mortgagee to execute a sub-mortgage of land and the like[5]. Here we see a change in law obviously necessitated by the demand for capital. The *Parāśaramādhavīya*[6] lays down further details about the sub-mortgage. It provides that a sub-mortgage can be made only when the amount due has risen to double the principal, but that if the owner consents a sub-mortgage may be made even before that contingency arises.

Higher rates of interest—

In order to induce the money-lender to invest his money in the disturbed economy of the period it was necessary that he should have some incentive in the form of greater profits. It appears that the money-lenders sometimes found out ways of exceeding the interest permissible under law. Significantly the

1 pp. 37-38.

2 pp. 36-37.

3 Kane, *History of Dharmaśāstra*, III. 429

4 On Manu, VIII. 143.

5 Ibid.

6 III, p. 242.

legal texts appear to recognise and sanction them by taking cognisance of them. Thus Medhātithi[1] mentions two customs which were incongruous with the strict Smṛti law on the point: (a) in some countries grains are lent out during the Spring, and double the quantity is realised during the Autumn and (b) the enjoyment of an usufructuary mortgage remains unchanged even after the total value of the produce so enjoyed is equal to the double the original debt. The *Vivādaratnākara*[2] condemns taking of interest in excess of the prescribed rates but admits that if a Shylock insists on his agreement he can and does recover compound interest and the like. Following Kātyāyana it further observes that if the debtor himself offers a rate of interest higher than the prescribed one, that will be admissible, though not one imposed by the creditor by force[3].

Medhātithi[4] follows the Smṛtis in laying down special rates of maximum interest but allows them upon the profits gained by the debtor with the loan. The *Mitākṣarā*[5] likewise supports the rate of 10% and 20% per month respectively from merchants traversing dense forests and seafaring traders.

The law-books had to admit exceptions to the general rule that whatever the rate of interest and the period of loan the creditor could not realise more than double the principal. Thus the *Mitākṣarā*[6] recognises that if interest is received every day, month or year and is not claimed in a lump sum at one time the total interest received by a creditor may even be several times more than the principal lent. A document in the *Lekhapaddhati*[7] gives a practical instance of how the money-lenders used to avoid the old rule of the debt not increasing beyond double of the principal. The present deed recording the mortgage of a mango-garden was

1 On Manu, VIII. 3.

2 p. 14.

3 Kane, *History of Dharmaśāstra*, III. 421f.

4 On Manu, VIII. 151-52.

5 On Yāj., II. 38.

6 On Yāj., II. 39.

7 pp. 34-35.

drafted when the original loan together with the accumulated interest had become the double of the principal. The legal writers of the period justify the total interest exceeding the principal in case of certain commodities. Thus Medhātithi[1] supports eight-fold interest in the case of liquor as an exception to the general rule. Likewise the *Vivādaratnākara*[2] justifies and explains higher interests—eight-fold in the case of oils, liquors, ghee, raw-sugar and salt, five-fold in the case of metals other than gold and silver and also in case of seeds.

With such increasing demands on capital, it could not possibly be allowed to lie idle or unproductive. Thus the *Madanaratna*[3], a little late in date, lays down rates of interest even in cases where no interest is settled beforehand and where the texts do not specify the rate, implying also loans through friendship, deposit, balance of interest and unpaid purchase money.

Rates of interest—

The legal works try to maintain the traditional rates of interest. Thus Lakṣmīdhara[4] and Caṇḍeśvara[5] approve the traditional rate of 1/80 th of the principal per month on secured debts and of 2% per month on loans without pledge or mortgage. Medhātithi[6] observes that the higher rates of 2, 3, 4 and 5 per cent per month laid down by Manu for brāhmaṇa, kṣatriya, vaiśya and śūdra debtors are for a money-lender who cannot maintain himself at the rate of 1¼% or has only a small capital, or where the borrower is not a righteous person. Al-Bīrūnī also refers to 2 per cent per month as the permissible rate of interest[7]. In all the *Lekhapaddhati* documents which specify rate of interest we have it as 2% per month[8].

1 On Manu, VIII. 140.

2 pp. 17-19.

3 Kane, *History of Dharmaśāstra*, III. 427.

4 *Kṛtyakalpataru*, *Gṛhasthakāṇḍa*, pp. 217-19.

5 *Gṛhastharatnākara*, pp. 446-47.

6 On Manu, VIII. 142.

7 II. 150.

8 pp. 19-21, 33, 38, 55.

In actual practice there must have been wide variation depending upon the needs and status of the two parties and stability of the area. In the mathematical text *Gaṇitasārasaṅgraha*[1] the rates vary between $1\frac{3}{4}\%$ and $13\frac{1}{3}\%$ per month though those between 2% and 6% are predominant. In the *Bījagaṇita*[2] the rates range between 1% and 10% per month whereas the *Līlāvatī*[3] has them between 3% and 5% per month. Many inscriptions from Cāhamāna dominions indicate that generally the rate of interest per annum was 30% though in some cases it may have been $33\frac{1}{3}\%$[4]. In two inscriptions from Jalor a temple of Mahāvīra is said to have paid interest at the rate of 12% and 10% per annum. The lower rates of interest in these cases have rightly been explained on the assumption that the temple with its high credit among rich Jain followers had no need to attract fresh deposits by higher rates of interest[5].

Letters of credit—

That deeds of credit were in frequent use in the period would follow from the space devoted in the *Lekhapaddhati* to the forms of these deeds. The *vyavahārapatra* (deed of debt) recorded loans contracted on the personal security of a surety. In *hastākṣarāṇi* the debtor himself acknowledged the debt though sureties are also mentioned. The *sanmukha-hastākṣarāṇi* recorded loans contracted without any security. Loans on the pledge of chattels are recorded under *ādhau kṛta vastūnāmupari gṛhītadravya-patra-vidhi*. *Ādhipatra* was a deed of mortgage. *Aśvāḍḍāṇakapatra*, *gṛhāḍḍāṇakapatra* and *kṣetrāḍḍāṇakapatra* were deeds for mortgaging horses, houses and fields respectively. *Vṛddhiphalabhogapatra* recorded an usufructuary mortgage. In *valitapatravidhi* the produce of the mortgage itself paid off the debt in course of time. *Gṛhaḍūlipatram* recorded the mortgage of a house which was lost to the debtor if he did not pay the money within the prescribed period.

---

1 IV. 33-V. 78½.

2 pp. 232-248.

3 pp. 31-37.

4 D. Sharma, *Early Chauhān Dynasties*, p. 301.

5 Ibid.

Vṛddhidhānyākṣarāṇi recorded the loan of grain to be paid together with interest in the form of grain.

The examples of bills of exchange in the *Lokaprakāśa* were no doubt revised in the Muslim period, but we can fairly believe that the types enumerated go back to the time of Kṣemendra. The *Lokaprakāśa*[1] mentions bills of exchange (*huṇḍikā*) for cash, for rice, for barley and wheat, for wine (*seya*), for purchase (*kriyākāra*)[2] and for horses (*goṭikā*)[3]. It also referes to *cīrikās* or rememberances which were used as deeds acknowledging debts etc. (*ujjāmacīrikā*). Significantly enough the expression *ujjāmapatrikā* in this very sense (*dhanadhāraṇapatrikā*) appears in the *Samayamātṛkā*[4] of Kṣemendra. The story in this text indicates that such deeds acknowledging debts received had become a regular feature of society. Here a courtesan asks the son of a merchant to sign such a deed for her. The *Lokaprakāśa*[5] mentions these for cash, rice and pledges (*bandha*). In recognition of the importance of the letters of credit Dāmodara devotes the fifth *prakaraṇa* of his *Uktivyaktiprakaraṇa* to a discussion of their rules and forms. Unfortunately the portions of his own commentary on this section of his book has not been recovered otherwise we could have used them for corroborating the *Lekhapaddhati.*

It is difficult to say how far this increased use of letters of credit arose from the paucity of coins in the period. It is however likely that dangers on the road led traders especially those engaged in inter-state trade not to carry much cash.

Loans for unproductive purposes

Until very recent times the common man in India has often been inclined to contract loans for unproductive purposes. That conditions in our period were not very different would appear

1 p. 13.

2 Here *kriya* seems to have been used in the sense of *kraya*. See also ibid., *vikriya-kriyākāra-cīrikā*.

3 Ibid., p. 19, vv. 1-3 indicate that *goṭikā* is a mistake for *ghoṭaka*.

4 VIII. 95-96.

5 p. 13.

from the definitions of the law-books of the period of a *vyāvahārika* debt and its opposite. Thus the *Smṛticandrikā* and the *Vyavahāraprakāśa* give an example of the latter as a debt contracted to pay for drinking wine. Aparārka explains *vyāvahārika* as a just debt (*nyāyyam*) and the *Bālambhaṭṭī* takes it to mean one useful for the family[1]. It would thus appear that in explaining *vyāvahārika* the law-writers were not thinking of commercial activities but of the needs of the family. Loans of clothes, grain, gold, liquor and other articles would appear to have been contracted for consumption[2].

Loans for economic purposes—

It is however not suggested that loans for economic purposes were not recognised by the legal texts. We have already referred to the views of the *Mitākṣarā*[3] on loans contracted by merchants. Medhātithi also takes into consideration the possibility of the debtor growing opulent with the wealth earned from borrowed grain and of the debtor carrying on an extensive business with capital lent to him[4]. In the commentary of Asahāya we read of a merchant taking a loan of ten thousand *drammas*[5]. Two problems in the *Gaṇitasārasaṅgraha*[6] refer to people borrowing money to lend it out at higher rates.

The *Lekhapaddhati* can be made to yield valuable information on the uses of the credit system. A majority of its documents records loans contracted by householders[7] or even state officials[8], in most cases by mortgaging their fields, houses, horses and cattle. But instances are not wanting where a merchant is said to have contracted the loan[9]. In all the documents, irrespective of the

1 Kane, *History of Dharmaśāstra*, III. 447.

2 Cf. Medhātithi on Manu, VIII. 140.

3 On Yāj., II. 38.

4 On Manu, VIII. 151-152.

5 Kane, *History of Dharmaśāstra*, III. 289f, f.n. 395.

6 IV. 55-56.

7 pp. 36-7, 35, 34, 39, 43.

8 pp. 19-21.

9 pp. 21, 38, 42, 37-8, 33.

fact as to who is the debtor, we have a stock expression meaning that the loan was contracted for a work or need of his which had arisen[1]. But it goes without saying that in the case of a merchant the need was not always for family requirements. In one of the documents a merchant borrows 20 measures of wheat with the stipulation to pay 25 measures of wheat at the end of the threshing season[2]. One document, which has been placed with others concerning credits but which is not strictly a case of loan, refers to a son of a merchant borrowing money from his father out of his own share of the ancestral property; this records that the son took five hundred *drammas* for doing the business of lending money[3].

Attitude towards money-lending—

Referring to the stigma attached to usury Al-Bīrūnī observed that it is allowed only to the śūdra and even in his case only as long as the profit does not exceed two per cent per month[4]. However it does not appear that the caste restriction was so strictly respected. A story narrated by the commentator Asahāya speaks of a brāhmaṇa who lent money to a trader[5]. The change of attitude on the part of the law-writers towards money-lending, no doubt resulting from its increased utility for the times, is reflected in the fact that Lakṣmīdhara[6] chooses to quote Bṛhaspati who mentions money-lending as the best means of livelihood for the higher castes.

In all the credit deeds in the *Lekhapaddhati* the creditor is always a merchant who is introduced as one who invests his money for the sake of interest. We have already referred to the document in which the son of a merchant takes five hundred *drammas* from his share of the ancestral property to use in the business of money-lending (*uddhārya-vyavahārārtham*)[7]. Money-lending would appear

1 *Svakāryavaśāt*; *svīya samutpannaprayojanavaśāt.*

2 p. 21.

3 p. 56.

4 II. 150.

5 Kane, *History of Dharmaśāstra*, III. 289f, f.n. 395.

6 *Kṛtyakalpataru, Gṛhasthakāṇḍa*, p. 221.

7 p. 56.

to have been one of the major activities of a merchant (*vaṇik*)[1]. There were people who regularly lent out money on interest. From the *Bījagaṇita*[2] of Bhāskarācārya we learn of the interest from an earlier loan being again lent out.

Rudimentary system of banking—

Medhātithi[3] has a very interesting reference indicating the development in the credit system of the period. It speaks of a man promising to another man to pay him a certain amount of money through a merchant and sending a messenger to notify he latter of this; the payment could not be made on account of the banker's absence or some other reason. It is clear that the man sent to the merchant some form of letter of credit. The reference would suggest a free circulation of money through the frequent use of letters of credit. It is not clear from the reference as to what was the basis of the confidence on the part of the merchant in the man seeking payment through him. Obviously in such a case there could not have been any reliance on a pledge or surety.

But we do not know if, in this case, the merchant served as some sort of a banking institution and the man, who had deposits with him or had earned his confidence in some other manner, could borrow money out of his own deposit or otherwise, to be paid later on.

The modern institution of banking is a highly complex system evolving out of a combination of the two correlated practices of depositing and lending money. To suggest the existence of banking in all its details in our period would be an injustice to the available evidence. But a rudimentary system of banking is suggested in some references. Over and above the system of loans contracted on the basis of pledges or mortgages we find in some cases the practice of borrowing money from time to time

1 *Uktivyaktiprakaraṇa*, p. 14, l. 20—*vaṇije dhanam dhārayate.*

2 pp. 232, 241.

3 On Manu, VIII. 159—*Aham amuṣmādvaṇija etasyeyaddāpaye iti tatra tu manuṣye preṣite kathaṃciddātumaghaṭite' saṃnidhānād vaṇijo' nyato'pi kāraṇāt....*

on a deposit which had been made earlier. Thus we read in the *Kuṭṭanīmata*[1] that the maid servant of a courtesan deposited with a merchant a pearl necklace and received 30 *kedaras*; she took 30 *kedaras* a second time and also camphor, saffron, sandal and incense from time to time. In the *Rājataraṅgiṇī*[2] we read of a man who deposited a lac of *dīnāras* with a merchant and for some 20 or 30 years took from him money to meet his expenses. It has however to be emphasised that in both these cases the merchant with whom the deposit was made was to treat it as a trust or pledge without using it himself and the depositor was not to receive anything by way of interest from it. But we must also note that in the *Rājataraṅgiṇī* the merchant was made to pay interest on the deposit because it was found that he had been using it. It would therefore follow that if the merchant-banker used the money of the deposit he had to pay interest on it. But, as we shall see, merchants generally accepted deposits as pledges or trusts and were not expected to use them or pay interest on them.

Collective banks—

We notice a significant change as regards collective banking in this period. There are very few references to guilds in northern India accepting deposits or endowments and paying regular periodical interest on them. We read in the Siyadoni inscription of A.D. 912[3] that 1350 *Śrīmadādivarāhadrammas* donated by a merchant named Nāgāka were invested with the distillers of spirituous liquor. The reason for the paucity of such references is to be sought in the disturbed conditions of the time. It is also likely that the frequent migration of population from one place to another that resulted from the interminable wars of the period did not leave the guilds stable and permanently established in one place. The definite downgrading of industrial labour which we find in the period also affected the status of the guilds[4]. In

---

1 vv. 605-9.

2 VIII. 123-158.

3 *E. I.*, I. 173 ff.

4 See supra Ch. IV 'Guilds' p.81

some Cāhamāna records we find temples accepting endowments and paying interest on them[1]. It is likely that the sanctity attached to the property of a temple led people to find more stability in the temples than in other bodies.

Hoarding—

In India the common man does not think much in terms of employing his surplus for further gains. His main concern is to have his money safe. This explains the popularity of the practice of hoarding money in India. In the *Dhūrtaviṭasaṃvāda*[2] wealth is said to have only three courses open for it—gift, consumption and hoarding. Here hoarding is criticised, but it is clear from the reference that it prevailed widely in society. In the stories we often read of people chancing to find hoarded money[3]. *Khanyavāda* was the science of determining the location of hidden treasures[4]. The *Mānasollāsa*[5] requires the king to find out hoards from various signs.

Deposits as sacred trusts—

Under such circumstances the safe custody of deposits was in itself a great obligation. As the bailee did not receive any advantages from the deposit it must have been only a pious duty for him to protect it[6]. It may be easily realised that it would have been difficult to find a willing bailee, especially in a period of political insecurity such as the one we are studying. It was with a view to encourage people to accept deposits that the law-writers of the period granted favourable rules to the bailee. Thus we find from Haradatta[7] that sons were not liable for the misappropriation or loss of a deposit or bailment made to their father or other

1 D. Sharma, *Early Chauhān Dynasties*, p. 301.

2 *Caturbhāṇi*, II, p. 24.

3 *Upamitibhavaprapañcā*, pp. 865, 957; *Prabandhacintāmaṇi*, p. 56, l. 20. Also ibid., p. 36, l.8.

4 *Upamitibhavaprapañcā*, p. 60; *Aparājitapṛcchā*, p. 122, vv. 39-42.

5 I, p. 59, vv. 333-61.

6 Cf. *Kuṭṭanīmata*, v. 455.

7 On Gautama, XII. 39.

ancestor provided that they themselves had not joined or helped in the embezzlement or loss. Likewise the *Vivādaratnākara*[1] observes that in case the deposit is not sealed and the bailee uses it for some time and then replaces it, no blame or liability attaches to him.

Terms for deposits—

For deposit three terms used rather loosely are *nyāsa*, *nikṣepa* and *upanidhi*. The *Mitākṣarā*[2] explains *nikṣepa* as deposits counted in the presence of the depositary, *nyāsa* as handing over in the absence of the head of the house and *upanidhi* as a deposit sealed in the presence of the depositee but without being counted. It appears that there was much confusion as regards the precise significance of these three terms. Thus the *Abhidhānaratnamālā*[3] uses *nikṣepa* and *upanidhi* in the same sense. The *Vaijayantī*[4] also mentions *nyāsa*, *upanidhi*, *sthāpya* and *nikṣepa* as synonyms. Kṣīrasvāmin[5] explains *upanidhi* and *nyāsa* as an open deposit and *nikṣepa* as the delivery of some goods to a craftsman for being worked up. The legal works of the period also reflect this uncertainty about the true import of these terms. As against the *Mitākṣarā*, Viśvarūpa[6] takes *nyāsa* to mean an open deposit for safe custody and *nikṣepa* as the delivery of one's article for handing over to a third party. In the *Samayamātṛkā*[7], in connection with a deposit of jewels in a sealed box, the words *nikṣepa* and *nyāsa* are used indiscriminately. In literary references *nyāsa* is the term generally used and implies a sacred trust to be protected but not to be enjoyed by the depositary[8]. *Upanidhi* was sometimes used as a general term for a deposit[9]. It would appear that the deposit called *nikṣepa* could be used by the depositary[10].

1 pp. 86-87.

2 On Yāj., II. 67 ; *Vyavahāraprakāśa*, p. 280.

3 v. 82.

4 p. 124, l. 24.

5 On *Amara*, II. 9.81.

6 On Yāj., II. 69.

7 VIII. 65, 87.

8 *Kuṭṭanīmata*, v. 455 ; *Prabandhacintāmaṇi*, p. 95, l.20.

9 *Prabandhacintāmaṇi*, p. 108, ll. 8-9.

10 Cf. *Kumārasambhava*, V. 13.

Merchants accepting deposits—

In this period the merchants appear regularly to have received deposits. *Nikṣepa-vaṇikas* or merchants accepting deposits are referred to in the *Naiṣadhīyacarita*[1]. Kṣemendra refers to the social type of a merchant who turns deaf when approached for the recovery of property deposited with him[2] and becomes opulent by confiscating deposits made with him[3]. Kalhaṇa records a story of a merchant refusing to return a deposit and observes, "A merchant in a law-suit relating to the embezzlement of a deposit is more to be dreaded than a tiger; because he shows a face smooth as oil, uses his voice but very little and shows a gentle appearance"[4]. Elsewhere also he exposes the hypocrite merchants who having embezzled deposits show themselves ever eager to listen to the recital of sacred texts[5]. The combined testimony of Kalhaṇa and Kṣemendra indicates that the dishonesty of the deceitful merchants was quite a normal phenomenon. Obviously it must have seriously affected the credit system of the period.

---

1 III. 43.

2 *Samayamātṛkā*, V. 53-58.

3 *Deśopadeśa*, VIII. 14 : *Narmamālā*, III. 71 ; *Kalāvilāsa*, II. 4, 23-24.

4 *Rāj.*, VIII. 123-160.

5 Ibid., 706-710.

CHAPTER IX

COINAGE SYSTEM

The coins of the early medieval period have so far not received a systematic and comprehensive analysis and study. There is no catalogue covering all these coins and after Cunningham's book in 1894 there have been only occasional discussions about some isolated points.

As against the originality, artistic excellence and wide variety found in the coin-types of the Gupta period, those in our period are restricted in number and with a few exceptions there is no newness or originality about them. These types are imitations of older ones and are very crude in execution.

Weight standard of the coins—

The coins of the early medieval period afford a poor substitute for the coins of the earlier period even in respect of their weights. Now the coins follow a definitely lighter weight standard. Whereas in the earlier period the gold coins weighed 120 grains and tended to approximate to 146 grains those of our period generally weigh in the neighbourhood of 60 grains. A similar depreciation of weight can be noticed in the case of silver and copper coins also.

This is not to imply that the coins of this period had no weight-scheme to follow. A careful analysis reveals that they were made to approximate to some regular and definite weight standard. We can discern two parallel systems in these coins. Most of the coins seem to be based on the standard of a Greek drachma weighing 67·5 grains. It appears that not only the silver coins but also the gold and copper coins of most of the dynasties of our period followed the weight standard of the drachma. Another widely prevalent weight scheme appears to have followed the weight prescribed for the traditional denomination *purāṇa* which weighed 32 *rattīs* or 58·56 grains.

Indo-Sassanian coins—

According to Cunningham[1] the silver coins of the Indo-Sassanian type generally weigh upwards of 60 grains. In the coins illustrated by him we find a typical Indo-Sassanian piece of silver weighing 65 grains[2], whereas a similar copper piece weighs 66 grains[3]. Bidyabinod[4] gives 41·3 grains as the minimum and 61·7 grains as the maximum of these coins. The coins of the Piplaj hoard made of impure silver considerably alloyed with copper and lead have 61 grains as their average weight[5]. The weight of silver pieces catalogued by Smith[6] under the north-western type ranges between 52·6 and 64 grains, mostly approximating to 63 and 58 grains, and pieces less than 56 grains are few in number. The flat pieces of *gadhaiyā* coins catalogued by him weigh between 61 and 64·2 grains whereas the thick transitional pieces are between 59·7 and 63·8. Thick dummy pieces of silver in the *gadhaiyā* variety appear to have a tendency towards over weight being between 62·3 and 74·5 grains, but the copper pieces weigh between 52·2 and 65 grains[7]. Among the *gadhaiyā* pieces with the legend *Oṃkāra* noticed by H. V. Trivedi the silver ones vary in weight between 61 and 65 grains, whereas the two copper coins weigh 60 and 45 grains[8]. The silver pieces with the legend *Śrī Vi* or *Śrī Vigra* catalogued by Smith as forming the eastern or Magadha type are found to weigh between 52·7 and 60 grains[9]. But among the coins of this type illustrated by Cunningham[10] we see that a copper piece weighs 65 grains, while a silver one weighs 62 grains. As regards the pieces with the *Ādivarāha* type we find that the silver coin illustrated by Cunningham[11] weighs 62 grains. The

1 *C. M. I.*, pp. 47f.
2 Ibid., p. 53, no. 7.
3 Ibid., no. 8.
4 *Supp. Cat. Ind. Museum*, I. 59.
5 *J. N. S. I.*, VII. 98, 100.
6 *C. C. I. M.*, I, pp. 237-39.
7 Ibid., pp. 240f.
8 *J. N. S. I.*, XIII. 205.
9 *C. C. I. M.*, I, pp. 239f.
10 *C. M. I.*, p. 54, nos. 15, 16.
11 Ibid., no. 20.

copper coins of this type catalogued by Smith weigh 61 and 57·9 grains whereas the silver ones range between 51·9 and 63·4 grains[1]. The coins of Vināyakapāladeva are found to weigh between 62 and 69 grains[2]. Cunningham gives 65 grains as the weight of the silver coins with the legend *Śrī Somala deva.* According to him the copper coins of this king have the horseman device on them and are in three sizes of 65, 33 and 17 grains[3]. The copper coins with the legend *Śrī Tri-vi* are found weighing 16 and 19 grains[4].

It becomes clear from the above that the Indo-Sassanian coins of copper and silver alike were intended to approximate to the weight 67·5 grains. Coins recorded as weighing more than this standard are few in number. Generally there is a depreciation of some 7 grains in the weight of the coins which may also be regarded as excusable, because anything nearing perfection is neither seen nor expected in the coins of ancient times. It is however equally possible that the depreciation in some cases was deliberate, especially where we find that the coins weigh some 12 grains less than their standard. We would suggest that the pieces weighing in the neighbourhood of 50·62 grains were intended to pass as three-fourths of the standard coins. Likewise it would appear from some pieces weighing 33 and 17 grains that there were half (33·75 grains) and one-fourth (16·87) denominations of this weight standard.

Coins of the Ṣāhis—

The silver coins of Spalapatideva of the Ṣāhi family of Ohind weigh between 45·3 and 54 grains, whereas the weight of the copper pieces ranges between 38·8 and 45 grains[5]. The silver coins of Sāmantadeva catalogued by Smith weigh between 45·2 and 51·2 grains[6]. But Cunningham illustrates two silver coins which

1 *C. C. I. M.*, I, pp. 241f.

2 *J. N. S. I.*, X. 29.

3 *C. M. I.*, p. 53.

4 Ibid., pp. 54 f.

5 *C. C. I. M.*, I, pp. 246f.

6 Ibid., p. 247.

weigh 50 and 33 grains. As regards his copper coins with the humped bull and horseman device Smith catalogues pieces weighing between 45·4 and 54·2 grains, whereas copper coins of the elephant and lion type range between 30·7 and 37·5 grains[1]. According to Cunningham[2] the latter type is found on coins of three sizes weighing about 42, 14 and 7 grains. Likewise, in the case of the copper coins of Vakkadeva, whereas Smith records pieces ranging between 29·1 and 39·1 grains[3], Cunningham mentions these coins as being of three sizes 52, 42 and 18 grains[4]. The silver coins of Aśatapāla recorded by Smith[5] weigh 45 and 45·5 and his copper pieces illustrated by Cunningham[6] are 48 grains in weight. The silver pieces of Khudavayaka noticed by Smith[7] range between 44·5 and 49·7 grains. The silver and copper coins of Bhīmadeva respectively weigh 50 and 24 grains[8]. The solitary coin of Kamara weighs 30·3 grains[9].

An analysis of these weights would indicate that the coins of the Ṣāhi kings did not follow the weight scheme of a drachma but in the case of copper and silver pieces alike were made to approximate to the weight of a *purāṇa* or 58·56 grains. But these coins were depreciated in weight. They are not found weighing more than 54·2 grains and often are 52, 50, 48 or 45 grains, which indicates that the depreciation ranged between 4 and 13 grains. Pieces weighing 42 grains or even 33, 37, 38 or 39 grains can be recognised as three-fourths of the standard weight (43·92) with a depreciation of 2 to 11 grains, but the weight 33 grains is found only for a solitary piece. Coins weighing 30·7, 30·3 or 29·1 grains are to be treated as one-half pieces (29·28). Coins weighing 24 and 18 grains are also to be classed as one-half pieces with a

1 C. C. *I. M.*, I, p. 248.
2 C. *M. I.*, p. 64.
3 *C. C. I. M.*, I, pp. 248f.
4 *C. M. I.*, pp. 62f.
5 *C. C. I. M.*, I, p. 249.
6 *C. M. I.*, p. 65.
7 *C. C. I. M.*, I, p. 249.
8 *C. M. I.*, pp. 64f.
9 Ibid., p. 62.

depreciation of 5 and 11 grains. Coins weighing 14 and 7 grains can clearly be recognised respectively as one-fourth (14·64) and one-eighth (7·32) of the standard coins.

Coins of Gāṅgeyadeva—

The gold coins of Gāṅgeyadeva generally weigh about 60 grains[1]. V. V. Mirashi illustrates one of his gold coins weighing 61 grains[2]. According to Cunningham[3] his gold coins weigh 62, 30 or 14 grains. The gold coins of Gāṅgeyadeva catalogued by Smith[4] range between 59·3 and 63 grains and there are solitary pieces weighing 14·6 and 5·6 grains. The top weight of his gold coins in the Lucknow Museum is 65 grains. It is clear that these gold coins follow the weight prescribed for a drachma. The depreciation in their weight ranges between 2·5 and 8·2 grains, usually some 6 grains. The pieces weighing 30, 14 or 5·6 grains are to be regarded respectively as one-half (33·75), one-fourth (16·87) and one-eighth (8·43) denominations. It would appear that the silver and copper coins of Gāṅgeyadeva also follow the weight standard for a drachma. Thus Cunningham[5] mentions his silver coins as weighing 61 and 7 grains, which may be taken to correspond to the weight of a drachma and its one-eighth. Cunningham[6] gives 61 grains as the weight of the copper coins of Gāṅgeyadeva. The three copper pieces noted by Smith[7] weigh 59·2, 48·7 and 48·3 grains. In this case we find not only a piece having the weight of a drachma but also one of three-fourths (50·62) that weight.

Coins of the Candellas—

The Candella kings, who borrowed the coin-type started by Gāṅgeyadeva, also adopted the weight-standard of the latter's coins. The gold coins of Kirtivarman approximate to 63 or 31

1 *J. N. S. I.*, XVIII. 110-11.

2 *C. I. I.*, IV, p. clxxxii.

3 *C. M. I.*, p. 72.

4 *C. C. I. M.*, I, p. 252.

5 *C. M. I.*, p. 72.

6 Ibid.

7 *C. C. I. M.*, I, p. 253.

grains and thus are to be recognised as being equal in weight respectively to a drachma and its half[1]. Smith[2] catalogues two gold coins of Madanavarman weighing 62·2 and 62·3 grains and one weighing 15·6 grains. These clearly approximate to the weight respectively of a drachma and its one-fourth. Eight gold coins of Madanavarman found in the Rewa State weigh between 13·16 and 16·07 grains[3] and are equal to one-fourth of a drachma. The reign of Paramardi is represented by a solitary gold piece weighing 61·4 grains[4] and obviously intended to represent the weight of a drachma. The gold coins of Sallakṣaṇa are of two types according as their weight approximates to those of a drachma or a quarter drachma. His copper coins also have a weight approximating to a drachma. For the reign of Jayavarman we have copper coins weighing 60 grains which were most likely intended to correspond to the weight of a drachma. A. S. Altekar[5] mentions a solitary copper piece of Jayavarman weighing 30 grains and hence representing a half of the standard weight. The copper coins of Pṛthvīvarman also correspond to the weight standard of a drachma. One of his copper coins which weighs 16·2 grains can be easily recognised as representing one-quarter of the weight of a drachma. For the reign of Trailokyavarman we have gold and copper coins alike approximating to the weight of a drachma. Viravarman is represented by two gold coins weighing respectively 62·5[6] and 46[7] grains. We can easily recognise in these pieces the weight standard of a drachma and its three-fourths (50·62).

---

1 *I. A.*, XXXVII, pp. 147f.

2 *C. C. I. M.*, I, p. 253.

3 *J. A. S. B.*, N. S. XXII. 131. There is a solitary silver coin of Madanavarman in the collection of Mr. Hoey which weighs equal to the quarter of a drachma. But it is not unlikely that like many gold pieces of the Candellas very heavily alloyed with silver the present piece was officially intended to pass as being of gold.

4 *J. A. S. B.*, 1889, p. 34.

5 *J. N. S. I.*, V. 33. A silver coin of Jayavarman noticed by Cunningham in the collection of the British Museum is not traceable now.

6 *C. C. I. M.*, I, p. 254.

7 *J. N. S. I.*, XVI. 236-8.

The above survey makes it clear that the coins of the Candellas, irrespective of their metal, were made to approximate to the weight standard of a drachma, though they usually show a depreciation of some 5 to 7 grains.

Coins of the Kalacuris—

The coins of the Kalacuris of S. Kosala reveal two different weight standards. The two gold coins of Jājalladeva illustrated by V. V. Mirashi[1] weigh 61 and 15·5 grains. These can be recognised as approximating to the weight of a drachma and its one-fourth. But the coins catalogued by Smith[2] range either between 56·3 and 59·9 or between 13·3 and 14 grains. Thus the maximum depreciation in the two series would be respectively 11·2 and 3·57 grains. The gold coins of Ratnadeva noticed by V. V. Mirashi[3] weigh 62 and 15·5 grains. But Smith[4] catalogues one piece weighing 60·5 grains and others ranging between 12·5 and 13·9 grains. Thus the maximum depreciation in the gold coins of Ratnadeva works out as 7 and 4·37 grains. The gold coins of Pṛthvīdeva also follow the weight standard of a drachma. V. V. Mirashi[5] illustrates two gold coins of this king weighing respectively 61 and 15 grains. But Smith[6] catalogues only pieces approximating to the weight of a drachma and ranging between 59 and 60·2 grains thus indicating a maximum depreciation of 8·87 grains.

But the copper coins of the Kalacuris of S. Kosala are difficult to fit into the weight standard of a drachma. The copper coin of Jājalladeva illustrated by V. V. Mirashi weighs 43·5 grains[7]. The two copper coins of Ratnadeva weigh 100 and 23·5 grains[8]. The four pieces of Pṛthvīdeva are found to weigh 99·5, 68, 99·5 and 73

1 *C. I. I.*, IV, p. clxxxv.
2 *C. C. I. M.*, I, pp. 254f.
3 *C. I. I.*, IV, p. clxxxvi.
4 *C. C. I. M.*, I, p. 255.
5 *C. I. I.*, IV, pp. clxxxvi-vii.
6 *C. C. I. M.*, I, p. 254.
7 *C. I. I.*, IV, p. clxxxv.
8 Ibid., p. clxxxvi.

grains[1]. The two coins of Pratāpamalla weigh 38 and 29 grains[2]. These copper coins seem to have been based on the standard weight of a *karṣa* or 80 *raktikas* or 146·4 grains laid down for a *paṇa*[3]. It is significant that there is no piece corresponding to the full weight of a *paṇa*. This is typical of the coins of this period, which reveal considerable depreciation, most likely deliberately made. The coins weighing 100 and 99·5 may be regarded as the three-fourths of a *paṇa* (109·8) with a depreciation of 9·8 grains; those weighing 73 and 68 grains are to be taken as one-half of a *paṇa* (73·2); the 43·5 and 38 grains pieces to be one-third of a *paṇa* (48·8); those of 29 grains to be one-fourth of a *paṇa* (36·6) and those of 23·5 grains to be one-sixth of a *paṇa* (24·4).

The only king of the family who seems to have struck silver coins is Pṛthvīdeva. But even these are very rare and L. P. Pandeya has so far been able to secure only three of them[4]. One piece illustrated by V. V. Mirashi[5] weighs only 6 grains which was probably intended to pass as one-eighth of the standard piece of weight equal to a drachma.

Coins of the Gāhaḍavālas—

An analysis of the Gāhaḍavāla coins also indicates the use of two different weight standards, the *purāṇa* standard of weight for silver and copper coins and the drachma standard for the gold coins. The reason for this differenciation is to be found in the prototypes of these two series. The silver and copper coins of the Gāhaḍavālas are of the horseman and bull type, ultimately derived from the coins of the Ṣāhi kings of Ohind which followed the *purāṇa* standard of weight. On the other hand, the gold coins of the Gāhaḍavālas are of the seated goddess type, and,

1 Ibid., p. clxxxvi-vii.

2 Ibid., p. clxxxvii.

3 The suggestion seems to receive support from the fact that the Kaman Stone Inscription (*E.I.*, XXIV. 335) seems to use *paṇa* as the term for a copper coin.

4 C. *I. I.*, IV, p. clxxxvii.

5 Ibid., p. clxxxvi (no. 14 in Plate A).

being copied from the coins of Gāṅgeyadeva, adopt the weight standard of a drachma.

The silver coin of Madanapāla catalogued by Smith[1] weighs 45·3 grains whereas his copper pieces range between 46·6 and 50 grains. The copper coins of Govindacandra noticed by Smith weigh 37, 40·7 and 49·3 grains. The depreciation in the case of the silver coin of Madanapāla is 13·26 grains while in the case of his copper coins it ranges between 11·96 and 8·56 grains. The copper coin of Govindacandra weighing 49·3 grains indicates a depreciation of 9·26 grains. His coins weighing 37 and 40·7 grains are to be regarded as three-fourths of the standard weight (43·92) thus showing a depreciation of 6·92 and 3·22 grains. The two gold coins of Govindacandra weigh 58.8 and 68 grains. These pieces can be taken to follow the weight standard of a drachma. The weight of these coins show a clear tendency to form two groups. approximating to 68 and 61 grains. The first group may testify to an attempt on the part of the Gāhaḍavāla king to be faithful in following the weight standard whereas the second group indicates the regular tendency of depreciation in the coins of the period.

Coins of the Tomaras—

As regards their weight standard the coins of kings described by Cunningham and Smith as belonging to the Tomara dynasty unfold a tale similar to that of the coins of the Gāhaḍavāla kings. The copper coins of the dynasty follow the bull and horseman type not only in type but also in the weight scheme and thus approximate to the weight standard of a *purāṇa*. Likewise the gold coins of the dynasty are of the seated goddess type, borrowed from the coins of Gāṅgeyadeva, whose drachma standard is also adopted by the coins of the Tomaras.

The two copper coins of Sallakṣaṇapāla noticed by Smith[2] weigh 48·9 and 50·6 grains thus having a depreciation of respectively 9·66 and 7·96 grains. The copper coins of Aṇaṅgapāla range

1 *C. C. I. M.*, I, pp. 260f.

2 Ibid., p. 259.

between 45·7 and 50·2 grains mostly clustering round 50 grains with one piece weighing 43·7 grains. The coin weighing 43·7 grains may be regarded as representing three-fourths (43·92) of the standard weight of a *purāṇa*, while the remainder were intended to approximate to a *purāṇa* with a depreciation ranging between 12·86 and 8·36 grains. The two copper coins of Mahīpāla[1] weigh 47·5 and 46 grains. They were also made after the *purāṇa* standard but the depreciation in these cases is 11·06 and 12·56 grains. On the other hand the gold coins of Kumārapāladeva weigh 61·7 and 62·7 grains[2]. We may take these as approximating to the weight standard of a drachma.

Coins of the Cāhamānas—

The copper and silver coins of the Cāhamānas also borrow the bull and horseman type started by the Ṣāhi kings of Ohind. The weight standard of these coins of the Cāhamānas also follows the weight standard used by the Ṣāhi kings i.e., a *purāṇa* weighing 58·56 grains. Thus the copper coins of Someśvaradeva noticed by Smith[3] weigh 41, 48·1, 50 and 52·7 grains. The last three appear to have been intended for a piece weighing a *purāṇa* whereas the first represented its three-fourths. In the case of the *purāṇa* pieces the depreciation ranges between 10·46 and 5·86 grains whereas in the case of the three-fourths piece it is only 2·92 grains. The copper coins of Pṛthvīrāja[4] approximate to the weight of a *purāṇa* more closely, ranging between 50·6 and 53·5, thus narrowing down the depreciation to between 7·96 and 5·06 grains. Only one piece has an unusually small weight of 47·4 grains with a depreciation of 11·16 grains. His silver coin illustrated by Smith and weighing 52 grains may easily be regarded as following the weight standard for a *purāṇa*, with a depreciation of 6·56 grains.

Coins of the kings of Narwar—

The coins of the kings of Narwar including Malayavarman, a Pratihāra chief of the place, and the kings of the Jājpella dynasty

1 Ibid., p. 260.
2 Ibid., p. 259.
3 Ibid., p. 261.
4 Ibid., p. 262.

follow the weight standard of a *purāṇa* These coins are of the horseman and the bull type and the kings of Narwar seem to have borrowed the weight standard along with the coin-type from the Ṣāhi kings of Ohind. The three copper coins of Malayavarman noticed by Smith[1] weigh 57, 51·1 and 44 grains. The first two may be regarded as approximating to the weight of a *purāṇa* while the last one represents a three-quarter piece (43·92). The copper coins of Cāhaḍadeva approximate very closely to the standard weight of a *purāṇa.* The weights of his coins catalogued by Smith are 49·7, 51, 51·8, 53·5, 54·8, 54·9 and 57·5 grains[2]. It is clear that, leaving aside his three pieces approximating to 51 grains, most of his coins are in the vicinity of 54 grains, while one piece is almost identical in weight to the standard.

Coins of Pīpala, Pithi and Kīrtti—

The bull and horseman type of coins with the names of Pīpala, Pithi (Pṛthvī) or Kīrtti[3] also adopt the standard for the weight of a *purāṇa,* most likely because the issuer of these coins borrowed the weight standard as well as the type from the coins of the Ṣāhi kings. Thus, the copper coins of Pīpala weigh 52·1 and 52·4 grains while those of Pithi weigh 52 and 52·2 grains. The silver coin of Kīrtti weighs 50·5 grains. Thus the depreciation in these three types of coin ranges between 8·06 and 6·16 grains.

Coins of Śiva and bull type—

The copper coins with the Śiva and bull type are recovered mostly from East Punjab and Delhi area and are described by Cunningham as having circulated in the period between 500 and 800 A.D.[4] The weight as recorded by Smith in the case of some of these pieces is 58·4, 66·3, 70 and 78 grains. It is difficult to determine the weight scheme followed by these coins. The two latter weights, especially the last would suggest that these are not based on the drachma standard. We may suggest that as the de-

1 Ibid.,

2 Ibid., pp. 262f.

3 Ibid., p. 263.

4 *C. M. I.*, pp. 48f.

vice is to be traced to the coins of the Kuṣāṇa king Vasudeva, the present coins adopt their weight standard also, but the depreciation in the weight will have to be recognised as very wide. Another possibility is that these coins follow the traditional weight of a *kārṣāpaṇa* as 80 *rattīs* or 144 grains but were minted only to weigh half of its standard weight.

Coins of Kashmir—

Stein[1] has discussed the weight standard of the Kashmir coins very thoroughly. The coins with the name of Toramāṇa which initiate the typical coins of Kashmir of the early medieval period range between 83·8 and 111·5 grains, mostly clustering around 100 grains. The coins with the names of Pratāpāditya, Vinayāditya, Yaśovarman or Vigraha on them, which form a separate category because of the debasement of their device, have a higher upper limit, weighing from 83·8 to 123·5 grains. The long series of typical Kashmir coins of the period beginning with the reign of Śaṅkaravarman are lighter in weight, ranging between 71·5 and 97·5 grains.

Relative value of gold, silver and copper—

The texts of our period having any bearing on the currency system do not mention the ratio in the value of gold, silver and copper[2]. A.S. Altekar[3] has tried to determine the relative value of the three metals on the basis of the tables of coins. According to the *Līlāvatī*[4] of Bhāskarācārya 16 *paṇas* were equal to one *dramma* and 16 *drammas* were equal to one *niṣka*. The coin denominations *paṇa*, *dramma* and *niṣka* may be taken to refer respectively to copper, silver and gold coins. But the text does not mention the weight of the *dramma* and *niṣka* coins. So any calculation about the ratio in the value of gold and silver will be only tentative. If we believe that *dramma* and *niṣka* refer respectively to the silver

1 *Rāj.*, Vol. II, note H; *Num. Chron.*, 1899.

2 The *Śukranīti*, IV. 2.181-82 gives the relation as being 1 unit of gold=16 units of silver, and 1 unit of silver=80 units of copper.

3 *J. N. S. I.*, II. 1-14.

4 p. 1, no. 2.

and gold coins of early medieval period, which were equal in weight, being based on the weight of the drachma of the Attic standard, we can infer the ratio between gold and silver as having been 1:16.

In the *Jñāneśvarī*[1], composed in 1290, we have a definite statement to the effect that gold is 15 times in price of the same weight of silver. It is interesting to compare this with the ratio between the two metals prevailing in earlier periods. On the basis of the reference in the Nasik inscription of Uṣavadāta dated 120 A.D.[2] Rapson[3] calculated the ratio of gold and silver as 1:10. But the Baigram plate of the reign of Kumāragupta I[4] makes 16 *rūpakas* equal to 1 *dīnāra*. The ratio between gold and silver would therefore be 1:8[5]. We have therefore to postulate, besides regional differences, fluctuations in the ratio in different periods. This much however is clear that gold in our period was dearer in relation to silver than in earlier periods. We do not know the precise reason for the increase in the value of gold. In the earlier period India received a considerable quantity of gold from its trade with the west, but this supply seems to have dwindled in the early medieval world.

In the *Līlāvatī* 16 copper *paṇas* are equated with one silver *dramma*. This equation is also supported by the *Medinīkośa*[6]. On the assumption that a silver *dramma* of our period weighs 50 grains (with an alloy of 20% the actual silver content is taken to be only 40 grains) and a copper *paṇa* 140 grains, A.S. Altekar[7] infers the ratio between silver and copper to be 1:56. But in case the copper *paṇa* of the *Līlāvatī* is taken to be equal to 20 *māṣas*[8]

1 XVII. 322.

2 *Select Inscriptions*, pp. 157ff.

3 *Catalogue of the Coins of the Andhra Dynasty*, p. clxxxv. Bhandarkar, *A.I.N.*, p. 192 calculated the ratio as 1: 14.

4 E. *I.*, XXI. 81f.

5 S. K. Maity, *Economic Life in the Gupta period*, p. 172. In the *History of Bengal*, Vol. I, pp. 665f it is calculated as 1 : 4·6.

6 *Pa—dvika*, v. 92.

7 *J. N. S. I.*, II. 13.

8 *Māṣo viṃśatitamo bhāgaḥ paṇasya parikīrtitaḥ*, q. by the *Mitākṣarā* on Yāj., I. 365. Also *Kṛtyakalpataru*, *Gṛhastha*, pp. 218f.

and not 16 *māṣas* the ratio between the two metals turns out to be 1:70[1]. However, we do not know the precise weight of the copper and silver coins referred to in the *Līlāvatī*. It is not unlikely that the table in the *Līlāvatī* does not take into consideration the existing coins but simply mentions the traditional equations, only with the difference that it substitutes *dramma* for the earlier and more common *purāṇa*[2]. But we do not want to brush aside the possibility that the traditional table was applicable in later periods also with slight variations in the coins of the different regions introduced to suit the relative value of the metals in the localities concerned.

Coins mentioned in the epigraphic and literary records—

So far there has been no systematic attempt to identify the coins mentioned in epigraphic and literary records of our period. Among literary records the *Dvyāśrayakāvya* and the *Prabandhacintāmaṇi* are the most important as referring to many types of coins. The names mentioned in the *Dvyāśrayakāvya* are *bhāgaka*, *rūpaka*, *viṃśatika*, *kārṣāpaṇa*, *niṣka*, *sūrpa* and *dramma*[3], whereas the *Prabandhacintāmaṇi* refers to *dīnāra*, *niṣka*, *dramma*, *viṃśopaka* and *ṭaṅka*[4]. In the *Bṛhatkathākoṣa* of Hariṣeṇa we have references to *kapardaka* or *akṣa*, *dramma* and *dīnāra*[5]. These same names are found in other literary works also but those which are most frequently mentioned are *rūpaka*, *dīnāra*, *niṣka* and *kārṣāpaṇa*.

The coin names occurring in the Paramāra inscriptions are *rūpaka*, *ardharūpaka*, *dramma* and *viṃśopika*[6]. The Caulukya records mention *dramma*, *viṃśopaka*, *rūpaka* and *kārṣāpaṇa*, the *Vīsalapriyadramma* and the *Bhīmapriyadramma*[7]. In the Pratihāra

1 D. Sharma, *Early Chauhān Dynasties*, p. 305 states that the ratio varied between 1 : 60 and 1 : 80.

2 *Kṛtyakalpataru, Gṛhastha*, p. 219 ; ibid., *Vyavahāra*, p. 280. See also *Gṛhastharatnākara*, p. 447.

3 XVII. 79-81, 84, 94 ; XX. 10. See also A. K. Majumdar, *Chaulukyas of Gujarat*, p. 271.

4 A. K. Majumdar, *Chaulukyas of Gujarat*, p. 271.

5 *J. U. P. H. S.*, XIX. 85.

6 D. C. Ganguly, *Paramāra Dynasty*, p. 243.

7 A. K. Majumdar, *Chaulukyas of Gujarat*, p. 271.

inscriptions we find the names of *dramma*, *pāda*, *rūpaka*, *viṃśopaka*, *paṇa* and *kākiṇī*[1]. According to D. Sharma the chief coins circulating in the area under the Cāhamānas were *dramma*, *viṃśopaka*, *lohaḍiyā*, *rūpaka*, *raupya-ṭaṅka*, *jītal* and *dīnāra*[2]. In the Siyadoni inscription[3] alone we find *pañcīyaka-dramma*, *Vigrahapāla-dramma*, *Vigrahatuṅgīyadramma*, *Śrīmadādivarāha-dramma*, *viṃśopaka*, *kākiṇī*, *varāṭaka* and *kapardaka*.

Drammas—

It is clear from the numerous references to *dramma* in the inscriptions of the early medieval period[4] that it was the most common coin. The name is variously spelt, and is sometimes abbreviated as *drā* or *dra*[5]. The term *dramma* is derived from the Greek drachma. These coins were called *dramma* because they adopted the weight standard for a drachma. We know that the weight of a drachma is followed by coins which are generally described as the Indo-Sassanian or *gadahiyā* coins. The term *dramma* would appear to have originally and mostly denoted this series of coins and later on came to be applied to other coins which adopted the drachma weight standard. A general support for this is to be found in the close resemblance in the geographical distribution of the Indo-Sassanian coins and the areas covered by the inscriptions referring to *drammas*. These include Rajasthan, Marwar, Gujarat, the northern parts of the Rāṣṭrakūṭa empire, Central India and U.P[6].

The term *dramma* though originally connected with a weight scheme does not seem to have been used in the epigraphic records for coins of different metals; on the contrary it appears to have

1 B. N. Puri, *Pratihāras*, pp. 134-36.

2 *Early Chauhān Dynasties*, pp. 302ff.

3 See *E. I.*, I, pp. 168f.

4 *J. N. S. I.*, XVII. 66-68; D. Sharma, *Early Chauhān Dynasties*, p. 303; B. P. Mazumdar, *Socio-Economic History*, p. 216.

5 *J.N.S.I.*, XVII, 68f.

6 The coins with the name *Śrī Vigraha* are found in east up to Magadha. It is however significant that *dramma* is mentioned also in the Bodhgaya inscription of Dharmapāla—*J. A. S. B.* (N. S.), IV. 101.

mostly been used for silver coins with this weight[1]. In one inscription *dramma* is distinguished from *suvarṇa*[2] which obviously denoted a gold coin, while in some others it is differentiated from *paṇa*[3], most likely a copper coin. The *Līlāvatī* of Bhāskarācārya[4] gives the following equations : 16 *paṇas*=1 *dramma*, 16 *drammas*=1 *niṣka*. It would appear from this table that *paṇa*, *dramma* and *niṣka* signified respectively copper, silver and gold coins. There are also other indications to suggest that *dramma* denoted basically a silver currency. Thus, the *Bṛhatkalpabhāṣya* of Kṣemakīrti describes the *drammas* of Bhillamāla as being of silver[5]. An inscription from Dhod (Mewar) dated 1171 A.D. specifically refers to the *drammas* with the name of Ajayadeva as being of silver[6]. In the *Upakeśagacchapaṭṭāvali* the *gadahiyā-mudrā* which stands for the Indo-Sassanian coins or the *drammas* of the inscriptions is said to have been made of silver[7].

Drammas of gold—

We know that, following the example of Gāṅgeyadeva, many dynasties struck their gold coins after the weight standard of a drachma. No doubt, so far as the weight of these coins is concerned it will be convenient to describe their several denominations in terms of *drammas*. But it does not appear likely that *dramma* occurring in the records of northern India in the early medieval period denoted gold coins. The only exception to this is found in the Kanheri cave inscription of the ninth century[8] which,

---

1 Bhagwanlal Indraji, *J. B. B. R. A. S.*, XII. 325-8 ; D. R. Bhandarkar, *A. I. N.*, pp. 207, 209 ; V. V. Mirashi, *J. N. S. I.*, III. 36f. *C. I. I.*, IV, p. clxxxiv.

2 *E. I.*, VII. 40.

3 *E. I.*, XXIV. 329ff.

4 I. 2-4.

5 *Rūpamayaṃ vā nāṇakaṃ bhavati yathā Bhillamāle drammaḥ* q. in *J. N. S. I.*, XIV. 109.

6 *Nāgarī Pracāriṇī Patrikā*, XLV. 358.

7 *J. N. S. I.*, XX. 18.

8 *I. A.*, XIII. 136.

scholars believe[1], refers to *kāñcanadrammas*. As the gold coins with the seated goddess device and adopting the drachma weight standard are known to have been initiated by Gāṅgeyadeva, the present reference could not have been to coins of this series. Either *dramma* is to be taken here as a general term for a coin or else we have to postulate that the Indo-Sassanian coins were struck of gold also[2]. Recently V. V. Mirashi[3] has pointed out that the relevant reading in the inscription is *ekaṃ dramma-śataṃ*, and not [*kāṃcana*]-*dramma-śataṃ*.

It has been suggested by A. K. Majumdar[4] that, as in the northern provinces of the Rāṣṭrakūṭa empire[5], *dramma* in the Caulukya records also was applied to both silver and gold coins. To prove that *dramma* sometimes denoted a gold coin he relies on the Timana grant which mentions the grants of a *rūpaka* and a *dramma* made to a temple[6]. He argues that as here there is a reference to a daily grant of one *rūpaka* and an annual grant of one *dramma*, *dramma* denoted a coin of greater value most probably a gold coin. But the inscription refers to two different grants and there is nothing to suggest that they stand for the same grant in terms of a daily and annual award[7].

It has been suggested in a recent study[8] that there were gold *drammas* known after the name of king Vīsaladeva. This is evidently based on the Bhinmal inscription of V. S. 1345[9] which mentions

1 D. R. Bhandarkar, *A. I. N.*, p. 209; A. S. Altekar, *Rāshṭrakūṭas and their times*, pp. 364ff, 64f; V. A. Smith, *C. C. I. M.*, I, p. 251. See also *I. A.*, XXXVII. 147ff; *J. N. S. I.*, XVII. 77.

2 Mr. Nagar of the Lucknow Museum claims to have found a gold coin of Bhoja (B. N. Puri, *History of the Gurjara-Pratihāras*, p. 153, f. n.) who is known to have struck the Indo-Sassanian coins of the *Ādivarāha* type of silver and copper.

3 *J. N. S. I.*, XXV. 238-40.

4 *Chaulukyas of Gujarat*, pp. 273f. See also *J. N. S. I.*, XVII. 77f.

5 A. S. Altekar, *Rāshṭrakūṭas and their times*, pp. 364f.

6 *I. A.*, XI. 337. The reference is probably to Plate II, ll. 1-3.

7 *J. N. S. I.*, XIX. 118f. See also V. V. Mirashi, *J. N. S. I.*, XXV. 239.

8 *J. N. S. I.*, XVII. 78.

9 *Bombay Gazetteer*, I, pt. 1, p. 488.

raukma Vīsalaprī dra 200. This is the solitary instance of its kind against which a case of general improbability is created by the fact that hitherto no such gold coins have been discovered. We would suggest that *raukma* is a mistake for *raukya* meaning cash which is also used in the *Lekhapaddhati*[1] in connection with money transactions in terms of the coins in circulation.

Ādivarāha drammas and Vigrahapāla drammas—

Our records mention certain types of *drammas*[2] named after the king who issued them. The *Śrīmad Ādivarāha dramma* mentioned in the Siyadoni inscription[3] and the *Varāhamudrā* of the *Dravyaparīkṣā*[4] is to be identified with the Indo-Sassanian coins with the legend *Śrīmadādivarāha*, issued by the Pratihāra king Bhoja I[5]. The *drammas* variously described in the Siyadoni inscription as *Vigrahapālīya dramma*, *Vigrahapāladramma*, *Vigrahapāla-satka dramma* and *Vigraha dramma* can easily be recognised as the Indo-Sassanian coins with the name of *Śrī Vigraha* on them, though it is difficult to be dogmatic about the king who struck them. The Siyadoni inscription also refers to the *Vigrahatuṅgīya drammas* which are generally identified with the *Vigrahapālīya drammas*[6]. S. Ray[7] proposes to identify these with the Kashmir coins of Vigrahatuṅga. But the coins from Kashmir are not known to have been based on the drachma standard of weight and hence the name *dramma* can be applied to them only if *dramma* is treated as a general term for coins. Some coins of the typical Kashmir device of debased standing king and goddess have on them the name of *Śrī Vigraha* but are not known to have circulated outside Kashmir.

---

1 pp. 25, 34, 35, 36, 41, 56.

2 I have taken much help from the article on the subject by Mr. R. C. Agrawal—*J. N. S. I.*, XVII. 69-76.

3 *E. I.*, I. 169.

4 *J. N. S. I.*, X. 29.

5 See the Kaman inscription (*E. I.*, XXIV. 332) for a reference to *drammas* circulated by king Bhojadeva.

6 *J. N. S. I.*, III. 38 ; XIV. 125, f. n. 3.

7 *J. N. S. I.*, XIV. 125-7.

Bhīmapriya drammas—

The *Purātana-Prabandha-Saṅgraha*[1] variously spells a coin as *Bhīmapriya-dramma*, *Bhīmaprī dramma*, *Bhīmapuri drāma* and *Bhīmasena dramma*. These may be identified with *Bhimapuri* coins mentioned in the *Dravya-parīkṣā*[2] and were probably struck by one of the Caulukya kings with the name of Bhīma. But we have yet to find a coin with this name.

Vīsalapriya drammas—

In the epigraphic records there are references to *Vīsalaprī dra*, *Vīsalapriya-dramma*, *Vīsa dra*. and *Vīsalapurī dra*[3]. The *Lekha-paddhati* calls these both *Viśvamallapriya* and *Vīsalapriya dramma*[4]. These coins have most likely to be ascribed to king Vīsaladeva of the Vāghela dynasty. But no such coins have yet been recovered.

Ajayadeva drammas—

The *Ajayadeva drammas* mentioned in an inscription from Dhod (Mewar) dated 1171 A. D.[5] have been described as *Ajayapriya rūpakas* in the *Pṛthvīrāja-vijaya Mahākāvya*[6]. These coins were struck by the Cāhamāna king Ajayadeva and have been recovered from Rajasthan.

Pāruttha drammas—

The records of the early medieval period reveal the names of several other coins with the name of *dramma* attached to them. *Poruthi dra* and *pāruttha dra* are mentioned in an inscription of Aparāditya II dated 1184 A.D.[7] An inscription of Śilāhāra king Someśvara dated 1260 A. D. refers to *poruttha dramas*[8] (sic). In the *Purātana-*

1 pp. 33, 34, 65, 95; *J. N. S. I.*, XVII. 71.

2 *Bhīmapriya-daśa-viṃśopaka* mentioned in the Juna (Marwar) Inscription of V. S. 1352 (*E. I.*, XI. 59) also implies the existence of *Bhīmapriya drammas*.

3 *J. N. S. I.*, XVII. 72f.

4 For *Viśvamallapriya drammas* see pp. 33, 37, 39, 55; for *Vīsalapriya drammas* see p. 42.

5 *Nāgarī Pracāriṇī Patrikā*, XLV. 538.

6 V. 88-89.

7 *J. B. O. R. S.*, XXIX. 211-15, ll. 10-11.

8 *E. I.*, XXIII. 280, ll. 13-15.

Prabandha-saṅgraha these coins are called *pārūthaka*[1] or *pārutha*[2]. The *Kharataragaccha-bṛhadgurvāvali* mentions these as *paruttha drammas*[3]. The *Lekhapaddhati* gives the name as *pāraupatha*[4] or *pārupathaka*[5].

It is not possible to explain the name of this coin or to identify it. The references suggest that it was circulating in Rajasthan, Malwa, Gujarat, Konkan and Marwar areas. A. K. Nairne[6] suggested these to be Parthian *drammas* mentioned as Khurāsāni dirhams by Abul Fida and as Tātariya or Tahiriyeh dirhams by Al-Mas'ūdī and Sulaimān. But the *pāruttha drammas* appear to have been in regular and common circulation in Marwar and Konkan and so it would not be safe to identify them with any foreign currency[7]. In all the references to this coin in the *Lekhapaddhati* they are said to have been struck at the mint of Śrīmāla.

C. D. Dalal[8] takes *pāraupatha* to represent a proper name. The *Lekhapaddhati* uses the adjectives *śreṣṭha* and *śrīmat* before *pāraupatha*. But these do not necessarily imply that *pāraupatha* was a personal name. The adjective *śreṣṭha* is for the coin and refers to its good condition, while *śrīmat*, if not used for the coin, does not by itself make *pāraupatha* the name of a king because the *Lekhapaddhati* is literally full of cases of the use of *śrīmat* before the name of a city.

It is not unlikely that the name of the coin was derived from the place of its origin or minting, which seems to receive support from the forms *pārupathaka* and *pārūthaka*[9]. V. S. Agrawala[10]

---

1 pp. 53, 128.

2 p. 78.

3 pp. 2, 13.

4 pp. 34, 41f, 35, 36f.

5 p. 43.

6 *B. G.*, 1896, I, pt. II, p. 21, f. n. 6.

7 *J. N. S. I.*, XVII. 75.

8 *Lekhapaddhati*, p. 114.

9 In the Bilhari Stone Inscription (*C. I. I.*, IV, pp. 209ff, v. 81) *paura* appears to have been the name of a coin used in connection with a tax on the sale of elephants and horses in the local market. See also vv. 79 and 80 of the same inscription.

10 *J. N. S. I.*, XII. 201.

seems to have been right when he identified the *pāraupatha drammas* with the *Bhillamāla drammas* or the *Śrīmālīya drammas*. The name *Śrīmālīya dramma* would appear to be supported by the *Lekhapaddhati* which always refers to the *pāruthaka* coins as minted at the Śrīmālīya mint. In the *Purātana-Prabandha-saṅgraha*[1] it is the *pārūthaka drammas* which alone are said to have circulated in the kingdom of Jalor near Bhinmal. Śrīmāla and Bhillamāla evidently refer to the same city. Kṣemakirti in his commentary on the *Bṛhatkalpa Bhāṣya* refers to the *drammas* of Bhillamāla[2].

But we would emphasise that there were no coins with the names of *Bhillamāla* or *Śrīmālīya drammas*[3]. The excavations at Bhinmal in 1954 did not yield any such coin[4]. Śrīmāla or Bhillamāla was the name of a mint city and there is no justification for supposing that only one solitary type of coin was struck at this mint. In the *Lekhapaddhati* we have references to the minting at Śrīmāla of not only the *pāraupatha drammas* but also the *Viśvamallapriya drammas*[5] and *drammas* in general[6].

The *Purātana-Prabandha-Saṅgraha*[7] equates 8 *drammas* with one *pārutthaka*. But even this clue does not help us in identifying the *pārutthaka* coin. The higher value attached to the *pārutthaka* coins could have been due to either their higher weight or superiority in metal. But as we do not know of any coin weighing 540 grains the first possibility is ruled out. It is not unlikely that in contrast to the highly debased or billon pieces the *pārutthaka* coins were of very pure silver or were silver coins plated with gold[8].

1 p. 53.

2 *J. N. S. I.*, XIV. 109.

3 *Contra* see *J. N. S. I.*, XVII. 74.

4 Ibid.

5 pp. 33, 37, 39, 42, 55.

6 p. 34.

7 p. 53.

8 D. Sharma, *J. N. S. I.*, XXII. 196 regards the *pāruttha drammas* as a silver coin on the basis of the *Lekhapaddhati*, pp. 34, 43. But we do not find any indication of it in any of the references to this coin in this text. Probably D. Sharma bases his view on the term *raukya* used in some cases. But *raukya* means cash and refers to the cash payment of these coins in the transactions recorded in the documents.

Ṣaḍboddika drammas—

The Jaunpur brick inscription of A. D. 1215[1] mentions a mortgage in terms of *ṣaḍboddika drammas*. V. S. Agrawala suggests that it was a copper coin equal in value to six *boddikas* or 3/32 silver *kārṣāpaṇa*[2]. This can be accepted only when we take *dramma* as a general name for coins. If *dramma* here signifies the Indo-Sassanian coins of silver weighing 67·5 grains then *ṣaḍboddika dramma* implies an inherent contradiction as a *dramma* cannot be equal to six *boddikas* in value. We learn from the *Līlāvatī*[3] that a *dramma* is equal to 64 *kākiṇīs*, which is another term for a *boddika*.

Cunningham[4] connected *boddika* with *pādika* or one-fourth of the ancient *kārṣa* being 11·2 $\left(\frac{44{\cdot}8}{4}\right)$ grains in weight and hence a *ṣaḍboddika dramma* is made equal to 67·2 grains (11·2 × 6) and thus is said to represent the *gadhaiyā* coins of the period[5]. Cunningham's interpretation of *boddika* is however doubtful. *Boddika* is to be connected with *boḍḍi*, *boḍiā* or *boḍī* which was used for a *kākiṇī* and was equal to 80 cowries.

We would interpret *ṣaḍboddika-dramma* on the analogy of *kapardaka-voḍḍi*[6] and *kapardaka-purāṇa*[7] as a *dramma* calculated in terms of 6 *boḍis*[8]. In the *Līlāvatī*[9] we find the equations 4 *kākiṇīs* (i.e., *boḍis*) = 1 *paṇa* ; 16 *paṇas* = 1 *dramma*. It would therefore appear that ordinarily a *dramma* was calculated in terms of a *paṇa* of 4 *boḍis*. In opposition to the common *drammas* which were *catur-boddikas* and equal to 64 *boḍis*, the *ṣaḍboddikas* were higher in value being equal to 96 *boḍis*.

---

1 *J. U. P. H. S.*, XVIII. 196.

2 Ibid. ; *J. N. S. I.*, XII. 202.

3 I. 2-4.

4 *Archaeological Survey Reports*, IX. 176 ; *C. M. I.*, p. 50.

5 *J. A. S. B.* (Num. Supp.), 1930, p. 34 ; Rapson, *Indian Coins*, p. 34 ; B. P. Mazumdar, *Socio-Economic History*, p. 217.

6 *E. I.*, XXIII. 140, l.6.

7 In many Sena grants e.g., *I. B.*, III. 99ff.

8 *J. N. S. I.*, XX. 39.

9 I. 2-4.

A comparison of the tables in the *Līlāvatī*[1] and Śrīdhara's Gujarati commentary on the *Gaṇitasāra*[2] indicates that there were two types of *drammas* with two different values. The *dramma* in the *Līlāvatī* is worth 1280 (16 × 4 × 20) cowries, whereas according to the commentary on the *Gaṇitasāra* it was equal to 2000 (5 × 4 × 5 × 20) cowries thus being worth 1½ times the former. Significantly enough this is the relation between an ordinary or *caturboddika dramma* and a *ṣaḍboddika dramma* and it is therefore not unlikely that the *dramma* contemplated in the Gujarati commentary was a *ṣaḍboddika dramma.* We have seen that some of the available Indo-Sassanian coins show a very wide difference in weight between 50 and 70 grains. It is not unlikely that the heavier pieces represented the *ṣaḍboddikas.*

Pañcīyaka drammas—

The Siyadoni inscription[3] mentions *pañcīyaka drammas.* It has been suggested on the analogy of the *ṣaḍboddika dramma,* that it consisted of five *boddikas* and connecting *boddika* with *pādika* weighing 11·2 grains, the *pañcīyaka drammas* are said to weigh 56 (11·2 × 5) grains[4]. This weight scheme was adopted by the Ṣāhi kings and by others who struck coins after those of the Ṣāhis, and thus it is further claimed that *pañcīyaka drammas* are to be regarded as one of the two principal types of coins on the basis of their weights. But as we have pointed out *boddika* is to be connected not with *pādika* but with *voḍi* or *kākiṇī.* Moreover the term *pañcīyaka* is not the same in form as the *ṣaḍboddika*, since it makes no mention of the *boḍi.*

B. N. Puri[5] has put forward the ingeneous suggestion that these coins were introduced by the local *goṣṭhī* or *pañcāyat.* But the term for such corporate bodies in the records of the period is *pañcakula* and not *pañca.* Then, as rightly shown by A. K. Majum-

1 Ibid.
2 *J. N. S. I.*, XX. 40.
3 *E. I.*, I. 169, ll. 6, 37.
4 *J. A. S. B.* (Num. Supp.), 1930, pp. 34ff.
5 *Pratihāras*, p. 134.

dar[1] the *pañcakula* did not represent the modern *pañcāyat* but rather denotes a body of five men to assist various ministers and officers. Even if it is conceded that such local bodies existed in the period, there is no independent evidence to show that they possessed the important right to mint coins in their name.

V. V. Mirashi[2] has pointed out that in the Siyadoni[3] inscription a cess of ¼ *Ādivarāha dramma* is subsequently put down as *paṃ dra.* It therefore follows that a quarter *dramma* was known as a *pañcīyaka dramma*, most probably because it was equal in value to 5 *viṃśopakas.* We have seen elsewhere[4] that there are many coins which weigh about the one-fourth of the standard weight of a drachma. These may have been *pañcīyaka drammas.*

Thus in this case the term *dramma* would appear to have been used rather loosely and did not denote a coin weighing 67·5 grains. The *pañcīyaka drammas* no doubt were connected with the *dramma* coins being a sub-division of the *drammas* and so were justified in retaining the name of *dramma.* It is however to be noted that in the Siyadoni inscription itself there is a reference to a quarter of a *pañcīyaka dramma* (*pañcīyaka-dramma-pāda*)[5]. If this refers not to the abstract value but to some specific coin having that value, then this would represent 1/16 of the drachma weight standard. This would be a tiny coin, especially in view of the usual depreciation in the coins of this period, and we have yet to recover a coin with such a weight. In this case it is not unlikely that *pañcīyaka dramma* did not represent a coin weighing one-fourth of a *dramma* but a coin having that value, and it probably contained considerable copper[6].

---

1 *Chaulukyas of Gujarat*, pp. 236-42.

2 *C. I. I.*, IV, p. cxxxiv.

3 *E. I.*, I. 175-77, l.37.

4 See supra pp. 179-90.

5 *E. I.*, I. 173, l.6.

6 *Drā Ela* coins of the inscriptions (*E. I.*, IX. 51-2; *Jain Inscriptions*, I, p. 229, no. 884) may refer in abbreviations to some kind of *drammas*—*J. N. S. I.*, XVII. 75f. But it is not possible to explain their nature.

Dvivallaka drammas—

In the *Kharataragaccha-bṛhadgurvāvali* and the *Lekhapaddhati* we find references to *dvivallaka drammas*[1]. C. D. Dalal[2] and V. S. Agrawala[3] explain these as coins having a mixture of two *valas* or six *rattis* of base metal. Recently D. Sharma[4] has pointed out that the *dvivallaka dramma* may be a Muslim coin introduced into Rajasthan and Gujarat after these territories were conquered by the Khaljīs, there being no reference to the actual use of this coin before 1323. He explains these coins as having two parts of base metal for one of precious, i.e., having silver and copper in the ratio of 1 : 2. He shows that the *aṭhagānī* coins of the *dramma* class belonging to the reign of Qutbuddīn Mubārak as described by Ṭhakkura Pheru have twice as much copper as silver. This seems convincing. But if *vallaka* is taken as a weight then the *dvivallaka drammas* may be explained alternatively as a sub-denomination of a *dramma* weighing 2 *vālas* or 6 *rattis* or 10·98 grains. It is not unlikely that some smaller coins approximating to this weight represented the *dvivallaka drammas.*

Sub-multiples of drammas—

There are epigraphic references to half (*drammārdhika* or *drammārdha*), three-quarters (*dramma-tribhāga*) and a quarter (*pāda*) *drammas*[5]. We have elsewhere[6] seen that there are coins which are equal to the above-mentioned fractions of the weight of a *dramma*. Though there is no reference to one-eighth of a *dramma,* such coins have actually been recovered[7]. In an inscription from Ahar (Udaipur) of A.D. 952 there is a reference to a cess as being 1/40th part of a *dramma* (*drammārdhaviṃśaka*)[8]. No coin of such a weight is known and unless it is taken to refer to a copper coin,

---

1 *J. N. S. I.*, XXII. 197.
2 *Lekhapaddhati*, p. 118.
3 *J. N. S. I.*, XII. 202f.
4 *J. N. S. I.*, XXII. 197-200.
5 *J. N. S. I.*, XVII. 79f.
6 See *supra* pp. 179-90.
7 *J. N. S. I.*, XVII. 82.
8 *I.A.*, LVIII. 162.

it most likely stands for an arithmetical value and not for any specific coin.

Viṃśopakas—

The coin called *viṃśopaka* is sometimes spelt as *vaṃsopaka, visovaka, visopaka, piṃsopaka, viśopaka, visopaga* and *visovaga.*[1] It is clear from the Bhinmal inscription dated A.D. 1182[2] that this was a coin considerably lesser in value than a *dramma.* This inscription refers to a tax of one *vi* on every *dramma.* D. R. Bhandarkar[3] regarded *viṃśopaka* as a copper coin equal in value to 1/20th of a *dramma.* This suggestion is supported by the Siyadoni inscription[4] which mentions a monthly tax of half a *Vigrahatuṅgīya dramma* then abbreviates this as *vi* 10 i.e., 10 *viṃśopakas.* The *Gaṇitasāra* of Ṭhakkura Pheru also equates 20 *viṃsopakas* with one *dramma*[5]. As suggested by V. V. Mirashi[6] the coin was so named because it formed the twentieth part of a *dramma.* Bhandarkar seems to be justified in regarding *viṃśopaka* as a copper coin, because a silver coin weighing 1/20th of a *dramma* has not yet been recovered and would have been so tiny as to be inconvenient to handle. There are a few epigraphic references where *viṃśopakas* are not converted into their equivalent *drammas.* But this does

---

1 *J.N.S.I.*, XVII. 80.

2 *B.G.*, I, pt. I, pp. 47f—*teṣāṃ prati dra vi* 1 *labhya.*

3 *E.I.*, X, p. 19, f.n. 3. Originally he identified *viṃśopaka* with *paṇa* or *māṣa* which according to Kātyāyana's table represents 1/20th of a silver *kārṣāpaṇa* which in turn Bhandarkar identified with *dramma.*

4 *E. I.*, I. 173f, 1.20.

5 D. Sharma, *Early Chauhān Dynasties*, p. 319.

6 *C. I. I.*,IV, p. clxxxix, f. n. 7. B. N. Puri, *History of the Gurjara Pratihāras*, p. 135 identifies *viṃśopaka* with ancient *viṃśatika* mentioned by Patañjali. He probably bases his suggestion on the similarity between the two names. Sandesara (*J. N. S. I.*, VIII. 143) regards *viṃśopaka* as identical with *bīsā* mentioned in the Gujarati commentary on the *Gaṇitasāra.* But as pointed out by D. Sharma, *Early Chauhān Dynasties*, p. 304 *viṃśopaka* is to be equated with *lohaṭika* and not *bīsā* of the table. According to the table a *dramma* is equal to 100 *bīsās* or 20 *lohaṭikas.* Hara Govindadas Trikamchand explains *visopaga* or *visovaga* as the 1/20th part of a cowrie-shell—*Pāia Sadda Mahaṇṇavo*, IV, p. 1007.

not affect the relation between the two coins, because such a way of representing the figures might have been regarded as more convenient as is sometimes the practice in modern times[1].

In the epigraphic records we find references to *viṃśopakas* associated with *Vigrahadrammas*, *Varāha-drammas* and those named *Bhīmapriya*[2]. The *Vṛṣa-viṃśopakas* referred to in the Arthuna inscription dated 1079 A.D.[3] may have been either those with the bull and horseman device or else those of the bull and Śiva type.

Ṣoḍaśikās—

In the Bilhari inscription[4] there is a reference to a coin called *ṣoḍaśikā* which V. V. Mirashi[5] regards on the analogy of the *viṃśopaka* as a copper coin worth 1/16 of a *dramma*. The *Līlāvatī*[6] makes one *dramma* equal to 16 *paṇas*. It is therefore not unlikely that *ṣoḍaśikā* was another name for the copper coin commonly known as *paṇa*. But we learn from the *Śārṅgadharasaṃhitā* that the coin was called *ṣoḍaśikā* because it weighed 16 *māṣas*[7].

Rūpakas—

Rūpaka is another term which is very often referred to in the literary and epigraphic records of the period[8]. The references to *suvarṇa rūpakas* in the *Rājataraṅgiṇī* and *Kathāsaritsāgara*[9] indicate that in literary works *rūpakas* sometimes denoted coins in general. But *rūpya rūpaka* basically and generally stands for a silver coin[10].

---

1 *J. N. S. I.*, XVII. 81; D. Sharma, *Early Chauhān Dynasties*, p. 303, f. n. 45. The Dandhapur (Sirohi) Inscription of V. S. 1233 records a gift of 36 *viṃśopaka* and not 1 *dramma* and 16 *viṃśopakas*. In the Gundoch inscription of V. S. 1288 the rate of interest is given as 1/20 *dramma*.

2 *J. N. S. I.*, XVII. 81.

3 *E. I.*, XIV. 295ff.

4 *C. I. I.*, IV, pp. 209ff, v. 79.

5 Ibid., p. clxxxix.

6 I. 2.

7 *C. I. I.*, IV, p. clxxxix.

8 *J. N. S. I.*, XIX. 116ff.

9 Ibid., 119.

10 Ibid., 117.

In the *Pṛthvīrājavijaya*[1] the *drammas* struck by king Ajayadeva are called *rūpaka.*

But *rūpaka* often referred to a specific silver coin and hence was distinguished from the *drammas*. The Ahar inscription belonging to the reign of the Guhila king Allaṭa records the tax of one *dramma* on the sale of an elephant and two *rūpakas* on that of a horse[2]. It is clear from this that *rūpaka* was different from and lower in value than *dramma.* B. N. Puri[3] suggests that its value was between $\frac{1}{4}$ and 1/20 of a *dramma.* According to the Gujarati commentary on the *Gaṇitasāra* one *dramma* was equal to five *rūpakas*[4]. It is not unlikely that some of the silver coins of our period which weigh about 13·5 grains were meant to be used as *rūpakas.* Viṣṇugupta as quoted in Hemādri's *Vratakhaṇḍa* equates 70 *rūpakas* with a *suvarṇa* and 28 *rūpakas* with a *dīnāra*[5]. We learn from the commentary on the *Uttarādhyayana Sūtra* that one *rūvaga* (=*rūpaka*) was equal to 8 *kākiṇīs*[6].

The Anjaneri plates of Bhogaśakti dated A.D. 710-11[7] refer to the *rūpakas* of Kṛṣṇarāja. These are to be identified with the silver coins weighing between 30 and 34 grains and struck by king Kṛṣṇarāja (c. A. D. 555-575) of the Kalacuri family[8].

Bhāgakas—

The *Dvyāśrayakāvya* mentions a coin called *bhāgaka* which has been explained by Abhayatilaka Gaṇi as a term representing the half of a *rūpaka*[9]. It may be concluded from this that Abhayatilaka Gaṇi treated *bhāgaka* as standing for a theoretical coin-value and not some specific coin. In another place also he refers to *rūpakārdha*[10]. It is, however, not unlikely that there were actually

1 V. 88-89.
2 *I. A.*, LVIII. 162.
3 *Pratihāras*, p. 136.
4 *J. N. S. I.*, VIII. 144.
5 *J. N. S. I.*, XIX. 116.
6 *J. U. P. H. S.*, XVIII. 67, f. n. 104.
7 *C. I. I.*, IV, pp. 149 ff, ll. 38, 39.
8 *J. B. B. R. A. S.*, XXI, pp. 213f.
9 XVII. 94, p. 389—*bhāgaśabdo rūpakārdhe.*
10 Ibid., XVII. 93—*rūpakārdha-drammapañcakādi.*

coins weighing 6·75 grains or 1/10 of a *dramma*. A coin of Gāṅgeyadeva weighs 5·6 grains[1] and may have been struck as a *bhāgaka*.

Viṃśatika—

On the basis of a reference in the *Dvyāśrayakāvya* as explained by Abhayatilaka Gaṇi[2] *viṃśatika* is taken to be a coin worth 20 *rūpakas*[3]. As there is no silver coin weighing 270 grains (13·5 × 20), it has been suggested that *viṃśatika* was a gold coin[4]. But we would argue that *viṃśatika* was not the name of any specific coin, but merely represented twenty times the value of a given coin. It was not connected with any specific coin but could be used for all alike. The commentary by Abhayatilaka Gaṇi clearly implies this when it explains *viṃśatika* as being twenty times the value of the *rūpaka* and other coins.

Sūrpas—

Another coin name in the *Dvyāśrayakāvya*[5] which is not referred to in any other source is *sūrpa*. It appears to have been a coin of very little value, but it is not possible to say anything definite about it or to identify it.

Kārṣāpaṇas—

In the literary records and also some of the inscriptions we find references to *kārṣāpaṇas*[6]. *Kārṣāpaṇa* is explained as a silver coin weighing a *karṣa* or 80 *raktikas*[7] or 146·4 grains. But it is to be noted that no known silver coin of the early medieval period is based on this weight standard. Hence the references to *kārṣāpaṇas* in this period are to be explained as survivals from earlier times or else as referring to weights of silver. It is also possible that in this period when coins were usually struck of a lesser weight than those of earlier times, the silver

1 *C. C. I. M.*, I, p. 251, no. 9.

2 XVII. 81, p. 382—*viṃśatī rūpakādīni mānam-asya viṃśatikam.*

3 *J. N. S. I.*, XIX. 119 ; A. K. Majumdar, *Chaulukyas of Gujarat*, p. 271.

4 *J. N. S. I.*, VIII. 145.

5 XVII. 84.

6 *Dvyāśraya*, XVII. 79, 84.

7 *J. N. S. I.*, XIX. 117.

coins adopting the drachma weight standard were commonly referred to as *kārṣāpaṇas*[1]. This would receive support from the fact that the *Līlāvatī* equates 16 *paṇas* with one *dramma*, since we know that this was the original relation between *paṇas* and *kārṣāpaṇas*. Another possibility is that *kārṣāpaṇa* was used to denote silver coins which in this period were struck according to the weight standard of a *purāṇa*. In some sources like the Gujarati commentary on the *Gaṇitasāra*[2] one *purāṇa*, like the ancient *kārṣāpaṇa*, is described as equal to 16 *paṇas*.

In the Kaman Stone inscription of Bhojadeva we have a reference to *paṇas* along with *drammas*[3]. *Paṇa* is used for a copper coin as opposed to *rūpya* or *rūpaka* for a silver coin[4]. We have seen above that 16 *paṇas* are equated alike with *purāṇa*, *dramma* and *kārṣāpaṇa*. The *paṇa* coins weigh a *karṣa* or 146·4 grains[5]. We find that some copper coins of the early medieval period are based on the *karṣa* standard of weight and are to be treated as *paṇas*. On the basis of the equation 80 cowries =1 *purāṇa* as given in lexicons and of 16 *paṇas*=1 *purāṇa* in the *Gaṇitasāra* A. K. Majumdar[6] deduces that one *paṇa* is worth 5 cowries. This may be regarded as one of the traditions about the value of a *paṇa*. But he does not take notice of the fact that in most of the tables on coins we have the equations 20 *varāṭakas* or *kauḍas*=1 *kākiṇī* or *boḍī* and 4 *kākiṇīs*=1 *paṇa*[7]. Thus the usual and common value of a *paṇa* was 80 cowries.

Dīnāras—

In the literary works of our period we generally find gold coins referred to as *niṣka*, *suvarṇa* and *dīnāra*. Of these *dīnāra* in

1 D. R. Bhandarkar, *A. I. N.*, p. 210 had originally suggested it but subsequently he changed his opinion—*E. I.*, X, p. 19, f. n. 3.

2 *J. N. S. I.*, VIII. 141ff.

3 *E. I.*, XXIV. 329ff.

4 *J. N. S. I.*, XIX. 117.

5 E. g., *Vaijayantī*, p. 189, 1.79.

6 *Chaulukyas of Gujarat*, p. 272.

7 *Līlāvatī*, I. 2-4; Gujarati commentary on the *Gaṇitasāra*—*J. N. S. I.*, VIII. 141ff; Bengali arithmetical table—*J. U. P. H. S.*, XVIII. 196.

many cases came to stand for coins in general. Thus Jonarāja in his commentary on the *Pṛthvīrāja-vijaya Mahākāvya*[1] explains the silver coins of Ajayadeva called *rupaka* as a special kind of *dīnāra* (or coin). In the *Rājatarangiṇī*[2] we have a reference to *dinnāras* of gold, silver and copper. Stein[3] observes that if the *dinnāra* was more than a mere abstract unit of account, it could not well have been represented by any other token than the cowrie. The term *dinnāra* is derived, through the Greek, from the Latin *denarius*, which was a silver coin, but in Sanskrit lexicons it is treated as a name for a gold coin. It is not unlikely that the term sometimes denoted a gold coin struck in the Gupta period.

Suvarṇas—

According to Viṣṇugupta, as quoted in Hemādri's *Vratakhaṇḍa* 70 *rūpakas*=1 *suvarṇa* and 28 *rūpakas*=1 *dīnāra*[4]. Thus the relation between the values of a *dīnāra* and a *suvarṇa* will be 2 :5. But Nārada and Kātyāyana treat *suvarṇa* and *dīnāra* as being synonymous[5]. According to the *Līlāvatī* 16 *drammas* are equal in value to a *niṣka*, whereas a *karṣa* (146·4 grains) of gold is called *suvarṇa*[6]. Excepting a few stray pieces the gold coins of this period are not found adopting the weight standard for a *suvarṇa*.

Niṣkas—

It is likely that some of the gold coins of our period which appear to have been based on the drachma standard of weight were sometime called *niṣkas*. From the *Dvyāśrayakāvya*[7] we learn that *niṣka* was a gold piece weighing 108 *palas*. As one *pala* is equal to 4 *karṣas* the weight of a *niṣka* becomes too great to form a convenient coin and hence the *niṣka* of the present reference is to be regarded rather as a metallic weight.

---

1 V. 88-89 ; *J. N. S. I.*, XIX. 117f.

2 VII. 950.

3 *Rāj.*, Vol. II, p. 323.

4 Kane, *History of Dharmaśāstra*, III, p. 122, f. n. 162.

5 Ibid.

6 I. 2-4.

7 XVII. 84.

Taṅkas—

In the *Kharataragaccha-bṛhadgurvāvali* there are references to *hema-ṭaṅka* and *raupya-ṭaṅka* which D. Sharma regards as Muslim coins introduced by the *Khaljīs* after the conquest of Rajasthan and Gujarat[1]. Gold *ṭaṅkas* are mentioned by Jīnamaṇḍana and also in the *Prabandhacintāmaṇi*[2]. *Ṭaṅka* originally seems to have been a simple weight being equal to 4 *māṣas* or 8 *rattīs* or 14·64 grains[3]. But as the derivation of the term suggests it was also used as a general name of a coin. That *ṭaṅka* was a very common name of a coin, whether general or of a specific type or metal, would follow from the coins of Mahmūdpur (new Lahore) struck by Mahmūd of Ghazni which have the name dirham in the cufic legend and *ṭaka* (or *ṭaṅka*) in the Brāhmī legend[4]. Ṭhakkura Pheru in his *Gaṇitasāra* equates 50 *drammas* with one *ṭaṅka*[5]. It is clear that the coin denoted by *ṭaṅka* here was a gold coin. In the Rewa Stone Inscription of Vijayasiṃha[6] there is a reference to *ṭaṅkakas* stamped with the effigy of Bhagavat (*Bhagavanmudrayā*). V. V. Mirashi[7] explains this as referring to the gold coins of Gāṅgeyadeva bearing the figure of Bhagavatī or Lakṣmī. He thus argues that gold coins of the period were called *ṭaṅkas*. This is also indicated by some of the references given above. But as this name is not found in in any other inscription it may be suggested that some of the existing names for gold coins like *niṣka*, *suvarṇa* and *dīnāra* which technically were applicable to gold coins of specific weight were also used to refer loosely to the gold coins of the period.

Gadyāṇakas—

Another term which in the early medieval period denoted a gold coin was *gadyāṇaka*. In northern India it is found only

1 *J.N.S.I.*, XXII. 197.

2 p. 15; A. K. Majumdar, *Chaulukyas of Gujarat*, p. 271.

3 *J.N.S.I.*, XXII. 200.

4 Thomas, *Chronicles of the Pathan kings of Delhi*, illustration 7; *J.A.S.B.* (Num. Supp.), 1930, p.40.

5 D. Sharma, *Early Chauhān Dynasties*, p. 319.

6 *C.I.I.*, IV, no. 67, ll.20-21.

7 Ibid., p. clxxxiii.

in the records of the Gāhaḍavālas[1]. V. V. Mirashi equates *ṭaṅkas* and *gadyāṇakas* and adds that the larger gold coins of the Gāhaḍavālas weighing between 59 and 68 grains may be taken to be *gadyāṇakas*[2]. The weight of a *gadyāṇaka* according to the *Līlāvatī*[3] is 48 *rattīs* or 87·84 grains. It would therefore appear that even the larger coins of the Gāhaḍavālas were not based on the *gadyāṇaka* standard but were the result of the desire on the part of their issuer to be faithful to the standard weight of a *dramma*. Thus these Gāhaḍavāla coins are to be named as *gadyāṇaka* only when the term is taken to refer to a gold coin in a very loose manner.

Cowries as medium of exchange—

It appears that for daily transactions cowries had come to be very largely used in our period. Fa-hsien[4] observes that even in his period Indians were using cowries in buying and selling commodities. The records for the early medieval period indicate that cowries were in regular use.

Varāṭaka—

The *Līlāvatī*[5] equates 20 *varāṭakas* (cowries) with one *kākiṇī* and four *kākiṇīs* with one *paṇa*. The same equations are given in the Gujarati commentary on the *Gaṇitasāra* but it uses the name *kauḍa* for *varāṭaka* and mentions *boḍī* as another term for *kāgiṇī* (or *kākiṇī*)[6]. We find the same equations in Bengali arithmetical table but as another term *gaṇḍā* is also introduced the equations are 4 *karās* (*kaurīs*) = 1 *gaṇḍā* ; 5 *gaṇḍās* = 1 *buṛi* (*boḍiā*) ; 5 *buṛis* = 1 *paṇa*[7].

1 See B. P. Mazumdar, *Socio-Economic History*, p. 242, n. 74.
2 *C.I.I.*, IV, p. cxxxiii.
3 I. 3.
4 (Legge) p. 43.
5 I.2.
6 *J.N.S.I.*, VIII. 141ff.
7 *J.U.P.H.S.*, XVIII. 196. V. V. Mirashi (*C.I.I.*, IV, p. clxxxix) suggests that *kaparda* was identical with *kākiṇī* and was equivalent to 20 cowries. But we think that *kaparda* itself was a term for cowrie. The *kauṛī* of modern Hindi is derived from *kaparda*. This is supported by the Gujarati commentary on the *Gaṇitasāra* which uses the form *kauḍa* for cowries—*J.N.S.I.*, VIII. 141ff. Kṣemakīrti also in commenting on *Bṛhatkalpabhāṣya* paraphrases *kavaḍḍa* as *kapardaka*—ibid., Vol. II, p. 573. The *Vaijayantī*, p. 247, ll.11-12 equates a *kākaṇī* with 20 cowries (*kapardas*) and adds that sometimes it is taken to be equal to one *kaparda*. It would appear that though generally a *kākiṇī* was regarded as worth 20 cowries in some particular area *kākiṇī* and *kaparda* were treated as synonyms.

Varāṭaka and kapardaka—

The Siyadoni inscription refers to both *varāṭaka* and *kapardaka*[1], but as the references are not in the same context it does not affect their being synonyms. In the Bilhari (M.P.) inscription one *kapardī* is mentioned as a cess to be paid to the Śaiva ascetics by each shop[2]. The Tezpur (Assam) rock inscription of Harjjara lays down a penalty of 100 cowries for the infringement of certain state regulations[3].

Kapardaka-purāṇas—

In the copper plate grants of the Sena kings there are references to *purāṇas* and *kapardaka-purāṇas.* But these are not two different coin-denominations. From the references in the grants they appear to have been interchangeable terms. *Kapardaka* was prefixed to *purāṇa* with a view to make the identity of the coins clear[4]. D. R. Bhandarkar[5] explained the term to refer to a silver coin (*purāṇa*) shaped like a cowrie (*kapardaka*). But not a single coin of this shape has been recovered from any part of India; and such a coin besides the difficulty in fabrication would mark a retrogression in the evolution of coinage[6]. S. K. Chakravortty[7] convincingly argues that *kapardakapurāṇa* was a mere theoretical unit of account representing the value of a *purāṇa* counted in cowries and not an actual coin. Thus payments would appear to have been made in cowries which represented the prevailing currency and though the silver *purāṇa* was regarded as the standard coin it was not in general use and a certain number of cowries came to be equated to the silver coin.

---

1 *E.I.*, I, pp. 173ff, ll.45, 20.

2 *C.I.I.*, IV, pp. 209ff, v. 80. Here *kapardi* seems to have been differentiated from *dyūtakaparda.*

3 *J.B.O.R.S.*, 1917, pp. 508f.

4 *History of Bengal*, I, pp. 668f.

5 *A.I.N.*, pp. 139, 176.

6 *I.H.Q.*, IX. 596.

7 Ibid., 599.

Kapardaka-voḍīs—

In the Shergadh (Kotah) inscription there is a reference to a coin-denomination called *kapardaka-voḍī*[1]. A. S. Altekar[2] corrected *voḍī* into *voḍrī*, which he regarded as equal to the fourth part of a copper *paṇa*, and concluded that *kapardaka-voḍī* must have been equal to 20 cowries. But it would appear from many other references in diverse sources that the name *voḍḍi* was more common in use[3]. However, his surmise about the value of a *voḍī* is supported by the Gujarati commentary on the *Gaṇitasāra*[4] which equates 20 *kauḍas* with one *kāgiṇī* or *boḍī*. What is significant in the present inscription is the form *kapardaka-voḍī*. As it would be absurd to explain the expression as meaning a *voḍī* equal to a *kapardaka* it is to be analysed as meaning a *voḍī* calculated in terms of *kapardakas*[5]. On the analogy of the *kapardaka-purāṇa* the present expression is to be taken to indicate that the *voḍī* was not a coin in actual use but was a theoretical monetary value. The term *kapardaka* was prefixed to *voḍī* to make it clear that *voḍī* was really calculated and paid in terms of cowries. This also suggests that round about the Kotah state in Rajasthan cowries were the usual currency.

Use of cowries—

A. K. Majumdar[6] holds that the mention of cowries does not necessarily mean that the shells were actually in use as a medium of exchange and that for the sake of convenience in calculation the coins of higher denominations were converted into cowries. But the doubt is not well-founded because we have besides the mathe-

---

1 *E.I.*, XXIII. 140, l.6.

2 Ibid.

3 Hemacandra's *Prakrit Grammar*, IV. 335 : *boḍḍi* ; *Mṛcchakaṭika*, VIII. 40 : *voḍia* ; Gujarati commentary on the *Gaṇitasāra*—*J.N.S.I.*, VIII. 141 ff : *boḍi* ; Jaunpur brick inscription—*J.U.P.H.S.*, XVIII. 196 : *boḍḍika*.

4 *J.N.S.I.*, VIII. 141ff ; also Bengali arithmetical table—*J. U. P. H. S.*, XVIII. 196.

5 *J.N.S.I.*, XX. 39.

6 *Chaulukyas of Gujarat*, p. 272.

matical tables and inscriptions other references to the use of cowries as medium of exchange. The testimony of foreign travellers and writers is also very clear on this point. Chau Ju-kua makes a general statement about the people of T'ién-chu (India) that they use cowries as a medium of exchange[1]. We learn from the *Tabaqāt-i-Nāsirī*[2] that when the Muhammadans first came to Bengal they did not find the people using a money currency, but cowries. Ibn Batūta also records that the people of Bengal used cowries as money and purchased them from the inhabitants of the Maldives[3]. All doubts on the subject are set aside by the recent discovery of a treasure trove from Bhaundri village in Lucknow district which contained, besides the coins of the Pratihāra king Vināyakapāla, 9834 cowries[4].

That the cowries were objects of value and were used for exchange in economic transactions follows from the *Uktivyakti-prakaraṇa* of Dāmodara Paṇḍita, who was associated with the Gāhaḍavāla court. The text has a reference to a merchant hoarding cowries in his house[5]. Elsewhere it speaks of cowries being counted[6]. The *Kṛtyakalpataru* of Lakṣmīdhara, who also belonged to the Gāhaḍavāla kingdom, mentions *kapardakas* as typical objects which are counted and are used in economic transactions (*gaṇimam*)[7]. There are literary references also which speak of cowries as being used in daily transactions; though they are in many cases mentioned as being of very little value, there is no suggestion that they were mere theoretical monetary values[8]. Cowries are known to have been used in India even during the nineteenth century.

1 p. 111. Earlier (p. 97) he states that the people of P'ön-k' ie-lo (Balhara i.e., the Rāṣṭrakūṭa kingdom) use pieces of white conch shells ground into shape as money.

2 (Tr.) p. 556.

3 K.A.N. Sastri, *Foreign Notices*, p. 122.

4 *J.U.P.H.S.*, XIX, p. 85.

5 p. 51, l. 8—*Vaṇijo gṛhe kaparddakān nikṣipyati.*

6 p. 41, l.7—*Kaparddakān gaṇayati.*

7 *Vyavahāra*, p. 124.

8 *Bṛhatkathākośa*, LXXVI. 23, 43; XXX. 29; *Kalāvilāsa*, II. 5.7; *Samayamātṛkā*, VIII. 80; *Narmamālā*, I. 103; *Kuṭṭanīmata*, v. 633; *Dhūrtākhyāna*, V. 71; *Dohākośa*, XIV, 86 (p. 331).

Barter system—

The question next to be answered is the extent to which the early medieval period had a regular currency. It has to be emphasised at the very outset that even until recently barter played a considerable part in the economy of India, at least in rural areas. This should serve as a caution for any claim or expectation of a very highly developed money economy in the early medieval period. In this period also barter[1] can be assumed to have covered most transactions in the villages. It would appear from Medhātithi that merchants and traders also sometimes found it convenient to resort to barter. Medhātithi[2] explains that *paṇya* (merchandise) is the substance (*dravya*) that is sold for money, or is exchanged for some other substance. In some of the story books of our period also we read of merchants visiting distant parts of the country and exchanging their own merchandise with the wares of those regions[3]. The mathematical texts of the period[4] mention the rule for determining the value in the case of a barter (*bhāṇḍa-pratibhāṇḍaka*).

Paucity of gold coins—

The main thing which strikes the student of the numismatics of this period is the extreme paucity of gold coins. The Indo-Sassanian coins are not known to have been struck in gold. The Ṣāhi kings also struck coins only of silver and copper[5]. The coins of Kashmir reveal a boring uniformity, being only in copper. The solitary exception is that of Harṣa (A.D. 1089-1101) who issued gold and silver coins[6]. Among earlier kings the coins with the name of Pratāpāditya, Vinayāditya, Yaśovarman and Vigraha are often made of an alloy probably intended to pass as base gold[7].

1 *Vaijayantī*, p. 123, l.12; p. 128, l.141.

2 On Manu, V. 127.

3 *Samarāiccakahā*, VI, p. 16; *Triṣaṣṭiśalākā*, Vol. I, pp. 7ff.

4 *Līlāvatī*, p. 35 (no. 85); *Gaṇitasārasaṅgraha*, IV. 37-38.

5 *C.M.I.*, pp. 62 ff; *C.C.I.M.*, I, pp. 246 ff.

6 *C.M.I.*, p. 34.

7 *C.C.I.M.*, I. 266.

Gold coins in northern India were first struck, after a gap of many centuries following the Guptas, by Gāṅgeyadeva, the Kalacuri king of Tripuri. His gold coins are not scarce[1]. But it would appear that his successors did not issue coin of any kind[2]. The gold coins of Kīrtivarman, the first Candella king to issue coins, are limited in number[3]. For the reign of Madanavarman, whose coins are the most numerous of all Candella kings, we have in all only 59 coins[4]. We have only one coin of base gold for the reign of Paramardi[5]. The gold coins of Hallakṣaṇa are also few, and we have none for Jayavarman and Pṛthvīvarman[6]. There are a few gold coins of Trailokyavarman and two pieces only for Vīravarman[7]. As compared with other dynasties the gold coins of the Kalacuris of Dakṣiṇa Kosala make an impressive list[8]. Among the Paramāra kings we find only a solitary gold coin for king Udayāditya (A.D. 1060-1087)[9]. The only Caulukya king whose gold coins have been recovered is Jayasiṃha Siddharāja (A.D. 1098-1143) but these are only two in number[10]. There are two gold coins of Vīrasimha of the Kacchapaghāta dynasty of Nalapura[11], five gold coins with the device of a cow suckling a calf[12] and a unique gold

1 22 gold coins from Azamgarh—*J.N.S.I.*, XVII. 111 ; 3 gold coins—Cunningham, *A.S.R.*, X. 25 ; *C.I.I.*, IV, p. clxxxiii.

2 Eight gold coins with the name of Gāṅgeyadeva found at Isurpur in Saugor district differ in fabric from the other coins of Gāṅgeyadeva and hence are taken by V. V. Mirashi to have been struck by Karṇa, the son and successor of Gāṅgeyadeva—*J.N.S.I.*, III, p. 26.

3 *I.A.*, XXXVII, p. 148.

4 Mitra, *Early Rulers of Khajuraho*, pp. 183f.

5 *J.A.S.B.*, 1889, p. 34.

6 Mitra, Loc. cit., p. 183.

7 Ibid., 184.

8 600 gold coins from Bilaspur—*J.A.H.R.S.*, XII. 169 ; 36 gold coins from Orissa (9 from Puri and 27 from Sonepur)—*J.N.S.I.*, XVII. 58ff ; 56 coins from Sarangarh in Chhattisgarh—*Proc. A.S.B.*, 1893, p. 92.

9 *J.A.S.B.*, N.S., No. XXXIII. 203. K.P. Rode reports the discovery of a coin of king Jagadeva of the Paramāra dynasty—*J.N.S.I.*, IX. 75. But the details about the coin are lacking.

10 *J.A.S.B.*, N.S., VII.47.

11 *I.H.Q.*, XVIII. 71.

12 *J.N.S.I.*, XXII. 278-80:

coin of king Devapāla of the Pāla dynasty[1]. Among the kings whom Cunningham assigns to the Tomara dynasty only two, Kumārapāladeva and Mahīpāla, are found to have issued gold coins, but even these are scarce. As against the coins of the kings and dynasties noticed above we find that the gold coins of king Govindacandra of the Gāhaḍavāla dynasty are really abundant though they are extremely debased. Thus in 1887 some 800 of his gold coins were recovered from one single hoard in Bahraich district[2].

Considering the area and time covered by them these gold coins are miserably meagre in number. If we prepare an exhaustive list of the amount of gold and the number of gold coins which the early Muslim invaders are said to have obtained by way of loot, ransom and penalty much of the paucity of gold coins can be explained.

But even this cannot account for the fact that many dynasties and many kings do not appear to have struck any gold coin at all. It is obvious that, in view of the cheapness of commodities in the period when cowries were sufficient for daily transactions, the gold coins would have been very high in value and would not have been ordinarily needed. The feudalisation of the state-structure that took place in the period would have dispensed with much of the need for higher denominations of coins which in earlier periods might have been required to remunerate or reward important functionaries of the state.

It is also not unlikely that coins struck in earlier periods continued to be in circulation in this period. It is significant that after the Guptas no gold coins appear to have been issued for over 450 years. We may suggest that during this period the gold coins of the Kuṣāṇas and Guptas continued to be used but as in course of time many of these were melted down, some of the kings from the eleventh century onward following the example of Gāṅgeyadeva felt the need for issuing gold coins.

---

1 *J.N.S.I.*, XIII. 123-25.

2 *C.C.I.M.*, I, p. 257.

Specimens of highly debased gold coins and pieces which were made of silver but had a gold plating indicate that such coins were legel tender in at least the kingdom of the king issuing them. If they were meant to be treated according to their metallic contents there would not have been much sense in debasing them. It would appear therefore that they were intended to represent a value more than that indicated by their metallic contents.

But gold coins must have been also used in larger transactions like inter-state trade. It goes without saying that a merchant coming from an area outside the empire of a certain king would not be willing to accept at its intended value a debased gold coin issued by that king. Thus in inter-state and foreign trade relations gold coins were used according to their real weight and purity of metal. The mathematical texts of our period have a full section dealing with rules relating to calculation of the weight, purity and value of gold and in the illustrations they mention how merchants by combining gold pieces of different purity and exchanging them for other pieces obtain profit[1].

In such circumstances kings usually would not have taken the trouble of minting gold coins but would have left it to the big merchants and trading concerns to issue their own gold coins. The *Jāmi 'ul-Hikāyāt* of Muhammad 'Aufī records that during the reign of Yamīn-ud-daula Mahmūd some sharp men of India brought out a dirham of great purity and placed a suitable price upon it. Time passed on and the coin obtained currency. Merchants coming from Islamic countries used to purchase these dirhams and carry them to Khurasan. When the people had grown accustomed to the value of the coin, the Indians began by degrees to debase the standard and the merchants unaware of the depreciation, under the impression of deriving a profit brought silver and gold to exchange for the debased coins of copper and brass[2]. Even though the historicity of this particular affair may be doubted, it does reflect the prevailing practice.

---

1 *Gaṇitasārasaṅgraha*, V. 169-212; *Līlāvatī*, pp. 43-45 (nos. 101-9), 30 (no. 77).

2 Elliot and Dowson, II. 188.

On this point we have a significant reference in the *Rājataraṅgiṇī*[1] which says that a good minister under king Ananta (1028-1063 A.D.) abolished the royal privilege of marking the gold according to quality and price, in order to remove the chance of oppression by later kings. We do not have any parallel reference for any other part of northern India. But on the basis of the reference from Kashmir we can say that theoretically a king had the right to examine the gold coins struck by the bankers before they were allowed to circulate. Some of the kings and dynasties must have actually exercised this right. But this was regarded as a source of much trouble to the bankers in case an oppressive king had a mind to exploit it.

Gold coins are amazingly numerous in the Kuṣāṇa and Gupta periods. This gold currency was issued most likely to meet the requirements of the brisk trade relations which existed between India, Central and Western Asia, Egypt and Rome. In the early medieval period the paucity of coins is to be connected with the comparative decline in the volume of this foreign trade.

Paucity and debasement of silver coins—

The silver coins of the period reveal a state of affairs which is by no means encouraging even when compared with that indicated by the gold coins of the period. Some kings and dynasties did not issue any silver coins, while others had to resort to heavily debased or billon coins. Thus in Kashmir the only king to issue silver coins was Harṣa. The Indo-Sassanian or *gadahiyā* coins are mostly of very base silver, so that at times it is difficult to be sure whether a given coin was meant to be circulated as a copper coin or a silver one. It has been suggested that the so-called copper pieces were originally silver-plated and were meant to be used as silver coins[2]. This is however going to the other extreme. There are no doubt many coins which can easily be recognised as honest copper pieces. The coins of the Ṣāhi kings of Ohind were issued in both silver and copper. The analysis of one of the silver

1 VII. 211-12.

2 *J.N.S.I.*, X. 218.

coins of this family reveals that it contains $\frac{894 \cdot 6}{1000}$ silver, the balance being copper, with a trace of gold[1]. As compared with the silver coins of other kings of northern India these form a really satisfactory series. V. A. Smith[2] doubts if the Kalacuris either of Tripuri or of Ratnapura or the Candellas issued a silver currency. Their gold coins are generally so largely alloyed with silver that they can hardly be distinguished from silver coins and hence it is not unlikely that coins which appear to have been of silver were officially intended as gold coins. Among the Candella kings we have a solitary doubtful specimen of a silver coin of the reign of king Madanavarman. But this may have been intended to circulate as gold, like the heavily alloyed gold coins of the Candellas[3]. Likewise, though the coins of the Kalacuris of Ratnapura are found quite abundantly, there are only three silver coins all belonging to the reign of Pṛthvīdeva[4]. If these are honest silver coins, we can say that Pṛthvīdeva made a weak attempt to introduce a silver currency. He did not issue a large number of silver coins and the scheme had to be dropped by other kings of his family. The bull and horseman coins issued by the Tomaras, the Gāhaḍavālas, the Cāhamānas, the kings of Narwar and other unidentified Rajput kings[5] are mostly composed of billon, a mixture of silver and copper. The ratio of the two metals in these coins varies so much that the coins range from fairly good silver to merely pure copper. But the number of coins which can be classed as honest silver coins is limited indeed and most of the coins of these kings are to be branded as of highly debased silver or of billon.

The general paucity and debasement of silver coins may be connected with the decrease in the amount of silver which India could receive. In those times before the discovery of America

1 *Proc. A.S.B.*, 1889, p. 198.
2 *C.C.I.M.*, I, p. 252.
3 Mitra, *Early Rulers of Khajuraho*, pp. 183f.
4 *C.I.I.*, IV, p. clxxxvii.
5 *C.C.I.M.*, I, pp. 259-63.

the chief source of silver was Central Asia. The rise of the Arab power under the vigorous impact of Islam and the political disturbances which resulted in Central Asia must have affected the trade relations between India and these parts of Asia, with the consequent decline in the quantity of silver coming to India[1].

The above survey must have made it clear that there was a general paucity of coins in this period which we have seen may have been due to the general cheapness of price, the feudal conditions of society and polity, the larger use of cowries for daily transactions and the draining of a considerable amount of coined monev by the Muslim invaders. Side by side we find that the coins of the period, show a debasement in metal as in weight. This we may connect with a general paucity of gold and silver in the period.

Sometimes these features of the early medieval coins are traced to the unfavourable balance of trade which India is supposed to have suffered from in the period[2]. But though there was a general decline in the amount of India's foreign trade in this period, it is difficult to believe that the evidence indicate an unfavourable balance of trade. And, as has been rightly pointed out by A. K. Majumdar[3], it is highly debatable if the economic forces, such as balance of trade, which operate in the modern world, had any influence in those days, when the mode of trading was entirely different.

Right to mint coins—

In the early medieval period we find that though some of the major dynasties did not issue a regular currency and appear not to have minted many coins, some of the insignificant dynasties or kings issued considerable quantity of coins judged according to the conditions of the period. The Sena kings are not known to have issued any coins at all. For the Pālas we have only a very limited number of coins and their ascription is doubtful. We have only

1 C.J. Brown, *Coins of India*, p. 53.

2 N.R. Ray, *Bāṅgālir Itihās* q. by A. K. Majumdar, *Chaulukyas of Gujarat*, p. 270.

3 Loc. cit.

three copper coins of a unique type from Paharpur which are tentatively assigned to the early Pāla empire[1]. Scholars do not agree about ascribing the coins with the legend *Śrī Vigra* to king Vigrahapāla of the Pāla dynasty[2]. Recently a unique gold coin of king Devapāla has been discovered[3]. The coins of the Caulukyas, Paramāras and Kacchapaghātas are very few indeed and belong to the reigns of only one or two kings of these dynasties. For the Pratihāras, the Candellas, the Kalacuris of Tripuri and Ratnapura, the Gāhaḍavālas, the Cāhamānas and the Tomaras also we do not find coins for all the kings of the dynasties. As against this the comparatively insignificant dynasty of the Ṣāhi kings of Ohind issued an abundant currency.

What is even more remarkable is the fact that even the kings or dynasties who issued coins did not aim at a complete currency. Their coins are found only in one metal or two and then it is seldom that all the smaller denominations of a particular coin of a given weight standard seem to have been issued. The only exception to this general rule is provided by the coins of Gāṅgeyadeva which are in all the three metals and are found in smaller denominations also[4].

We would suggest that the issuing of coins was viewed by kings as a matter of convenience. If there was already in circulation a sufficient number of coins or if the economic needs of the kingdom did not require fresh coins, the kings refrained from issuing them. We know that Gāṅgeyadeva was the only king of the Kalacuri family of Tripuri to mint coins[5]. It is likely that by his time it was felt that the existing currency is not sufficient and hence he introduced a complete coinage system. But as his successors thought that Gāṅgeyadeva's coins were enough for the kingdom they gave up issuing coins.

---

1 *History of Bengal*, I. 667.

2 Cunningham, *C.M.I.*, p.49; *History of Bengal*, I, pp. 667f; *J.N.S.I.*, XIII. 124.

3 *J.N.S.I.*, XIII. 123f.

4 *C.M.I.*, p. 72.

5 *J.N.S.I.*, III. 26. V. V. Mirashi ascribes eight gold coins with the name of Gāṅgeyadeva from Saugor district to Karṇa.

Sometimes coins were issued to proclaim some conquest on the part of the king concerned. Thus the Candella coins, which were struck after the coins of Gāṅgeyadeva, were most likely initiated by Kirtivarman to signalise his victory over the Kalacuri king Lakṣmīkarṇa. Likewise the adoption of the seated goddess type by the Gāhaḍavāla king Govindacandra was done to proclaim some such victory achieved by the Gāhaḍavālas.

This apathy on the part of the ruling kings does not amount to their giving up the right to mint coinage. It is clear however that people in this period did not always view the issuing of coins as the necessary sign of an independent ruler. Issuing of coins was an important function of the state but it was viewed according to the requirements for new coins and the fact that a certain king or dynasty did not issue any coin was not interpreted as bringing down their status.

References in the *Rājataraṅgiṇī* indicate that coined money was the right, privilege and concern of the state, though at times it did not perform the function or else gave a free hand to private concerns especially in the matter of gold coins. We have already referred to a minister under king Ananta as abolishing the royal privilege of marking the gold according to quality and price, in order to remove the chance of oppression by later kings[1]. Another passage in the same text speaks of a City Prefect as remedying the long-standing abuse of the disuse of cash in commercial transactions[2]. The reference to false *rūvagas* (=*rūpakas*) in the *Āvaśyaka-cūrṇi*[3] of Jinadāsa written in c. A.D. 676, also makes a case for the coins being issued by the ruling authority and according to a certain standard of weight and purity of metal. Muhammad 'Aufi speaks of a certain Rai of India who conferred on his brother the chieftainship of Nahrwāla. This brother was of a wicked disposition and made counterfeit dirhams and circulated them in different parts of the country. The Rai on learning of this

1 VII. 211f.

2 VIII. 3334 ff.

3 p. 550 q. in *J.N.S.I.*, XIV. 108.

dishonest act sent an army and captured his brother[1]. This may indicate that the issuing of coins was the right of the sovereign king and he had to keep proper control over the currency circulating in his kingdom. The reference may also be made to show that the feudatory chiefs had no right to mint coins.

It would appear that in actual practice some of the merchants and bankers had also the permission to mint coins, mostly gold coins. We have seen above that this fact is mentioned in a passage in the *Rājataraṅgiṇī*[2] and also in the *Jāmi 'ul Hikāyāt*[3]. The coins issued by any king carried with them a presumption and surety about their value. But it would appear that where large amounts were involved all coins were alike evalued according to their real value. In the *Lekhapaddhati*[4] the *drammas* involved in the transactions, even though they are mentioned as issued by king Viśvamalla (Bīsaladeva) and hence forming the regular currency, are referred to as being thrice examined (*triparīkṣita*). Significantly enough in an inscription from Dhod (Rajasthan) dated A.D. 1170[5] 16 *drammas* with the name of Ajayadeva are said to have been tested before being accepted as the price of a house. Thus in actual practice, especially where large amounts were involved, the coins, whether of the local ruler or those issued by a king of another locality or dynasty, were alike tested and their value determined accordingly. Under such circumstances the coins minted by bankers had not much disadvantage. In an inscription from Chinchani (Thana) belonging to the middle of the tenth century[6] we find the transaction recorded in terms of money coined by a trader named *Śreṣṭhin* Gambhuvaka who was most likely a banker of repute and trust.

---

1 Elliot and Dowson, II. 168.

2 VII. 211f.

3 Elliot and Dowson, II, p. 188.

4 pp. 34, 43.

5 *An. Rep. Rajputana Museum*, Ajmer, 1922-23, p. 2.

6 *E.I.*, XXXII, p. 60, ll.35-47.

CHAPTER X

CONCLUSION

Periods of Indian history—

The periodisation of history is very desirable, because it helps to proper understanding by analysing the stages in its evolution. Though broad divisions are not difficult to make, real problems are created when one seeks sharp dividing lines. History is a continuous process and so should not be divided into water-tight compartments. Any given tendency or institution has a long history before it finally emerges in a recognisable form, and likewise it continues to live in some form even after it seems to have ceased to exist. Thus in periodisation one can generally have only rough approximation and should not expect to find fixed dates.

In Indian history there is no completely agreed upon system of periodisation. It is fashionable with some text books to resort to the rough division into Hindu, Muslim and British periods on the basis of the people who had the predominant political power in the period. Another convenience in such a division is from the standpoint of teaching because of the difference in the language of the important source material for the three periods. This division implies several misconceptions of a basic nature and has therefore been rightly criticised[1] even though it has an air of rough simplicity.

Sometimes attempts have been made to apply such a division more strictly by taking a narrow interpretation of the term Hindu. Thus C. V. Vaidya[2] speaks of three periods in the early history of India, Aryan (c. 4000 or 2000 B.C.—300 B.C.), Aryo-Buddhist or Buddhist (c. 300 B.C.—600 A.D.) and Hindu (c. A.D. 600—1200 or 1300). A similar suggestion is made by V. A. Smith who divides his *Early History of India* into three sub-periods, Ancient India (from the earliest times to c. 322 B.C.), Hindu India (c. 322 B.C.—

1 U. N. Ghoshal, *Studies in Indian History and Culture*, pp. 245ff.

2 *History of Mediaeval Hindu India*, Vol. I, Preface, p. 1.

647 A.D.) and Mediaeval Hindu Kingdoms or the Hindu period (c. A.D. 647—1200 or 1300). But the use of the term 'Hindu' may give a wrong orientation and is, therefore, not happy.

Marxist view—

The Marxist historians envisage fixed and definite periods having universal applicability, each characterised by productive relationships corresponding to a definite stage of development of the material productive forces. Without entering into a discussion of the soundness of the Marxist viewpoint, which sadly emphasises a part for the whole, we can praise it for focussing attention on the economic life of a country or people in a given period which has often been neglected by earlier historians. In a purely economic study it is undoubtedly advantageous and desirable to keep in mind the Marxist approach. That the periods postulated by him do not strictly apply to Indian conditions was tacitly accepted by Marx himself when he referred to "the Asiatic mode of production". This however has not deterred an official party-line Marxist in India from distorting facts to fit them in the general scheme of periods[1]. It is conceded by an open-minded Marxist that "India showed a series of parallel forms which cannot be put into the precise categories, for the mode based on slavery is absent, feudalism greatly different from the European type with serfdom and the manorial economy"[2]. It is therefore interesting to find this scholar observing that "Marxism is far from the economic determinism which its opponents so often take it to be" and that "the adoption of Marx's thesis does not mean blind repetition of all his conclusions at all times"[3].

Ancient, medieval and modern periods—

Generally, following the practice in European history, the history of India is divided into Ancient, Medieval and Modern periods. Here we are not concerned with the last period, but the line of demarcation between the first two is by no means easy to fix.

---

1 S. A. Dange, *India from Primitive Communism to Slavery.*

2 D. D. Kosambi, *An Introduction to the study of Indian History*, p. 15, n. 14.

3 Ibid., p. 10.

Starting point for the medieval period—

Rapson[1] took the establishment of the Kuṣāṇa dynasty to represent the dividing line between the Ancient and Medieval periods. But this suggestion ignores the fact that the Gupta period, which represents the classical age of ancient Indian culture, comes after the Kuṣāṇas. The Kuṣāṇas did not bring about such fundamental changes as to mark the transition from the ancient period to medieval. Sir John Marshall[2] and F. J. Richards[3] seek to find in the rise of the Guptas the division between Ancient and Medieval India. This implies a wrong notion about the nature of the Gupta period, which, no doubt, was an age of the efflorescence and even of the culmination of some earlier tendencies but does not represent any violent break or significant transition from the preceding centuries. Some scholars regard the death of Harṣa as marking the change from the ancient to medieval times[4]. V. A. Smith regards the year 647 A.D. as marking an epoch in the history of India. But in recent studies this suggestion has been rejected, for it is based on the misconception that Harṣa was the last emperor in Indian history and that during the period after the death of Harṣa everything, including polity and religion, declined[5].

H. C. Ray[6] accepts A.D. 916 as the line of demarcation between the two periods in the history of northern India because it saw the beginning of the break-up of the Gurjara-Pratihāra empire, the last great empire of northern India, after which we find a medley of petty states. He seems to have based his view on the fact that the Rāṣṭrakūṭa ruler Indra III sacked Kanauj about the year 916. But this in itself does not mean much, because the Rāṣṭrakūṭas achieved similar successes even during the reigns of powerful

1 *Ancient India*, p. 147.

2 *Guide to Sanchi*, p. 7.

3 *Indian Antiquary*, 1930 February.

4 Ishwari Prasad, *History of Medieval India*.

5 Cf. H. C. Ray, *Dynastic History of Northern India*, Vol. I, Introduction, pp. xxxiv-xxxix.

6 Ibid., pp. xxxviii-xxxix.

kings like Vatsarāja and Nāgabhaṭa II. Moreover, Al-Mas'ūdī, who visited India in the year 915-16, testifies to the power, prestige and wide extent of the Pratihāra kingdom[1]. Though the Rāṣṭrakūṭa invasion undermined the prestige of the Pratihāras, the latter seem to have recovered at least a major part of their dominions, which even up to the middle of the tenth century extended from Surāṣṭra to Banaras in the east and Chanderi (Narwar) in the south[2]. No doubt after their disappearance there did not arise any empire in northern India which could compare with that of the Pratihāras, but we cannot ignore the imperial families of the Candellas, Paramāras, Caulukyas, Gāhaḍavālas and Cāhamānas. H. C. Ray[3] himself recognises 916 A.D. to be a weak dividing line when he describes the establishment of Muslim rule in most parts of northern India as "the final act of the drama" to which the incidents during the period of about three hundred years (c. A.D. 916 to 1200) may be taken to be only a prelude. The year 916 may be conceded to have some political importance, though not of such a magnitude as to herald the beginning of a new period in the long history of India, but it can hardly be credited as having introduced any significant change in cultural life.

K. M. Munshi[4] regards A.D. 997 as the fateful year with which Ancient India ended and Medieval India began. In that year Mahmūd, son of Sabuktigīn, captured Ghaznī. The conquests made by Mahmūd led to the ultimate establishment of Muslim rule over northern India. Afghanistan and Punjab were brought under Muslim authority thus paving the way for its rapid extension. But it was only with the Mamlūk Sultāns of Delhi that Muslim power definitely established itself; for the intervening period of two hundred years the Muslims did not attempt an effective conquest of India to the east of Punjab. If the establishment of Muslim rule

1 Elliot and Dowson, I, p. 21.

2 *The Age of Imperial Kanauj*, p. 36.

3 Op. cit., p. xxxviii.

4 *The Age of Imperial Kanauj*, Foreword, pp. vii, xxiii. In his Foreword to *the Struggle for Empire*, p. viii he gives 1000 A. D. as the date dividing Ancient from Medieval India. In that year Mahmūd of Ghaznī first invaded India.

is to be treated as ushering the Medieval period the dividing line is to be placed towards the close of the twelfth and the beginning of the thirteenth century[1].

Early and late medieval period—

We feel that in the absence of sharp divisions it would be safer to use round dates for dividing Indian history into convenient periods. We can profitably speak of an early Medieval period covering roughly five hundred years from A.D. 700 to 1200 and the Medieval period proper or late Medieval period which synchronised with the establishment of Muslim rule and may be said to have lasted until the establishment of British rule. In many respects the early medieval period prepared the ground for the later period, which basically represents a continuation of tendencies in the earlier one. The one fundamental difference between these two sub-periods is the presence of Muslims as rulers in the later period, and this accounts for most of the apparent differences. The fact that in the early medieval period the Muslims were not the dominant political power has often led scholars to bracket it with the Ancient period. The division of sections in the Indian History Congress seems to have been based on this idea. Thus Ancient India is divided into two sections the first up to A.D. 711 and the second from 712 to 1206, whereas Medieval India has two sections, 1206—1526 and 1526—1764. There is no basic difference between the two sections under Medieval India except the minor political consideration that before 1526 the political power was in the hands of the Turk and Afghan Sultāns and that year saw the establishment of the Mughal dynasty in India.

Establishment of Islamic power—

We feel that the period roughly from A.D. 700 to 1200 has more affinities with the subsequent centuries than with the preceding ones. There is of course the glaring difference that after 1200 Muslims were the politically dominant class. But even when viewed in the light of the question of the establishment of Muslim

1 U. N. Ghoshal, *Studies in Indian History and Culture*, pp. 252f.

rule the period between 700 and 1200 can be regarded as the necessary prelude to subsequent times. The successful penetration of Muslim arms in India was a gradual process spread over many years. The beginning of the early Medieval period roughly synchronises with the first success achieved by the Muslims on Indian soil. The Arabs conquered Sind in 711-12. The early Medieval period witnessed the persistent effort of Muslims to conquer India and the success achieved in 1206 could not have been possible without the conquests of Sabuktigīn, his son Sultān Mahmūd of Ghaznī and Sultān Muhammad of Ghor. Thus the story of the establishment of Muslim power has to be traced back to 712; it does not begin abruptly in the year 1206.

Decline in culture—

V. A. Smith had observed that there was a general decline in everything from about 647[1]. The statement is a little exaggerated and is therefore rightly criticised[2]. In the early medieval period there are important names in the different fields of art and scholarship who compare favourably with their counterparts in earlier times. What is however significant and which is often overlooked is the fact that their was not much original and creative activity in most aspects of cultural life. It was an age mostly of commentaries and digests and not of original works. The emphasis seems to have been on the preservation and explanation of the existing fund of knowledge. This tendency is found in legal writings, philosophical literature and works on astronomy, medicine and other similar technical branches. The literary works also do not reveal any freshness, but, bound to earlier conventions, excel in laboured and pedantic imitation of the past masters. The output in the field of art and architecture, though imposing in size and volume, is formal and conventional in approach, without much life and vigour. The intrusion of Islam accelerated the process of the decline of Indian culture which had started in the early medieval period. Unlike other foreign invaders of earlier periods

1 *Early History of India*, pp. 371f.

2 H. C. Ray, *Dynastic History of Northern India*, Introduction, pp. xxxv-xxxvi.

the Muslims were not absorbed in the fold of Indian culture. On the contrary their cultural and religious antagonism expressed itself in persecution and proselytisation, and forced the Hindus to retire into protective shells. Naturally therefore the Hindus aimed rather at preserving their past cultural heritage than at attempting original and creative work. The resulting stagnation brought in its train cultural decadence. Thus we can interpret the late medieval period as another more advanced stage of the cultural decline which characterises the early medieval period.

Feudal tendencies—

There is another important consideration which indicates that the period roughly from the eighth century is to be studied as forming a unity with the priod after the establishment of Muslim rule. We can describe the age of feudalism in Indian history as really beginning with the eighth century. It is in this sense that the period from 700 to 1200 A.D. is to be separated from the earlier centuries. Feudal tendencies appear no doubt towards the closing years of the Gupta rule, but clear references to the feudal practice of assigning fiefs to officers first appear in the reign of Harṣa. The period of confusion and absence of a strong central power after Harṣa probably favoured the rise of petty local chiefs. The inscriptions and literary records of the early medieval period clearly indicate that even imperial dynasties had not much military power of their own and relied on the help of their feudatories, failing which they found themselves in a very miserable condition. If considered from the point of view of their feudal character the Gurjara-Pratihāras did not differ much from the subsequent dynasties, and so it would not be correct to place the beginning of the early medieval period in 916 as done by H. C. Ray.

The Muslim rule, alike under the Turko-Afghan Sultāns and the Mughal emperors, was based on the system of feudal assignments. The early Muslim rulers of necessity had to continue the existing Hindu machinery of administration. Even the later kings did not introduce much innovation in the details of the administration. Thus in its broad outline the administrative machinery in general and the feudal system in particular of the Muslim period were but a continuation of the early medieval institutions.

D. D. Kosambi[1] seems to have realised this fundamental unity of the period from Harṣa to the establishment of the British rule when he discussed the entire period under the head "feudalism from below". However, he over simplifies the situation by bringing under this heading different types of feudalism, that of the early medieval period, that of the later Rajput period and that associated with the Turko-Afghan Sultāns and the Mughal kings. We would emphasise that Kosambi's expression "feudalism from below" is not a happy term. It conveys the impression that the establishment of feudal estates was generally independent of the authority of central government. Though there are no doubt some references to suggest that such a tendency was not altogether absent, we find that the creation of a landed aristocracy was generally the result of the policy of the central authority to grant villages to officers and feudatories besides brāhmaṇas and religious institutions. We may use the term feudalism, without qualification, because, though there are certain important differences between Indian institutions and European feudalism, in their broad outline they show remarkable resemblance, and because even in Europe the feudal institutions differed so much from one place to another that F. W. Maitland was averse to calling feudalism a system and preferred to describe it as a complex[2].

× × × ×

We now attempt a brief estimate of the general economic life in our period and its importance in the economic history of the country. It goes without saying that economic conditions were not uniform in all parts of the country. The differences in the climatic conditions, the economic products, and the political life in different areas created regional differences in the economic life. Likewise there must have been ups and downs in different periods. But we have not enough evidence to undertake a study

1 *An Introduction to the Study of Indian History*, Chs. IX and X.

2 *The Constitutional History of England*, p. 143.

of the regional and periodical differences in the economic life of the times.

It has been pointed out in a recent study that in the Gupta age "beneath the facade of outward splendour were the toiling masses on whose efforts the whole edifice depended"[1]. But this is a historical truism applicable to all ages of ancient and medieval history not only of India and Oriental countries in general but of all human societies. It is however not to be denied that strangely enough this basic and commonplace fact is sometimes lost sight of even by scholars and so needs to be emphasised.

Standard of living—

On the basis of the degree of economic prosperity society of our period may for the sake of convenience be classified into the commonly used divisions of upper, middle and lower classes, without implying that any such divisions were actually recognised in those times, and with the reservation that these three classes had many gradations.

Upper class : Kings—

The upper class included the kings, feudal chiefs, ministers and state officers, big merchants and prosperous brāhmaṇas. We get an idea of the splendour and the luxury at the court and the magnificence associated with the life of kings from the *Mānasollāsa*, though strictly speaking this text does not belong to the geographical limits under consideration. According to this text the royal palace should have one to nine stories, should be whitewashed, should have in some parts latticed passages and in others dark passages illuminated by jewelled lamps, should have an ivory fencing and pillars of gold or sandal-wood, floor of glass or crystal and walls of crystal mirror-like slabs[2]. The text discusses elaborately the different aspects of the life of a king, his luxurious dress and toilet, his rich dietary and sumptuous banquets and his recreations and pastimes which all reveal luxurious and expensive magnificence.

1 S. K. Maity, *Economic Life in the Gupta period*, p. 190.

2 III. 123-29.

We have ample references from other sources confirming this account of royal pomp and grandeur. Thus the *Naiṣadhīyacarita*[1] gives a vivid picture of the splendour and luxury of the royal palace. Bilhaṇa in his *Vikramāṅkadevacarita*[2] describes how the recreations of a king were made to vary according to different seasons. A royal palace included a concert hall, a theatre, a gymnasium, a dancing hall and a picture-gallery[3]. The works of Rājaśekhara reflect the pomp and ostentation in the royal palace. He describes the costly ornaments and unguents and perfumes used by the royal ladies[4] and refers to such objects of luxury in a palace as a plantain-arbour with a raised emerald seat[5], a sleeping-chamber with perforated columns and a jewelled quadrangle and a crystal house with pictures on the walls[6]. In describing the court of the Cāhamāna king Pṛthvīrāja the *Kharataragaccha-paṭṭāvalī* refers to the throne as being rainbow-shaped and embedded with jewels of various colours and to the walls and the floors of the court as shining with bright jewels and precious stones[7]. Kalhaṇa makes pointed reference to royal ostentation in Kashmir, which seems to have attained its climax under king Harṣa (A.D. 1089-1101). His numerous palaces shone forth with wonderful splendour and had golden *āmalaka* ornaments and buildings which reached the clouds[8]. Of these the palace of hundred gates was especially remarkable for its grandeur[9]. The ladies in the harem of Harṣa used costly garments and unguents and covered their bodies with gold ornaments[10]. Nobody in his court was seen without brilliant dress, without gold ornaments, with a small following or without a resolute bearing. On journeys the ministers would always be

---

1 XVIII. 5-27.

2 XII. 50-78.

3 *Samarāṅgaṇasūtradhāra*, XV. 18f.

4 *Karpūramañjarī*, II ; *Viddhaśālabhañjikā*, II and III.

5 *Karpūramañjarī*, II.

6 *Viddhaśālabhañjikā*, I.

7 *Hindustānī*, 1940, pp. 82ff.

8 *Rāj.*, VII. 938.

9 *Rāj.*, VII. 1550.

10 *Rāj.*, VII. 928-31.

mistaken for the king. King Harṣa introduced the bright and gaudy court costumes fashionable in south India[1].

Feudal chiefs—

The petty feudal chiefs imitated the pomp and grandeur of emperors. But the luxuries which they enjoyed were dependent on the resources which they could command and hence their magnificence could only reflect the royal splendour on a smaller scale. The ministers and other high state officers who often received villages differed little from the feudal chiefs and lived a similar life of luxury and show.

State officers—

The *Kuṭṭanīmata*[2] describes the dress and bearing of a young son of an officer in the king's service which may be taken to represent the class of petty landed chiefs and state officers. He wears finger rings and ear-rings of a distinctive type and has thin golden threads around his neck. His limbs are yellowish with the saffron rubbed on his body. His shoes have ornamental designs. His clothes dyed yellow with saffron have a gold border. Whenever he comes out in public he is accompanied by a number of attendants, including a betel-casket bearer and five or six armed men.

Big merchants—

The big merchants of this period rivalled the kings in their affluence and their way of living was quite royal. The *Moharāj-aparājaya*[3] of Yaśahpāla describes the oppulence and grandeur of the mansion of a millionaire (*koṭīśvara*) merchant under the Caulukya king Kumārapāla. Huge banners with ringing bells were hoisted over the mansion to proclaim the owner's status as a *koṭīśvara*. He maintained alms-houses and owned a large number of horses and elephants. The main building was approached by a stair-case of crystal. The mansion included a temple with crystal floor and with walls, which were adorned with religious paintings

1 *Rāj.*, VII. 881-3, 895, 994, 946-9.

2 vv. 61-70.

3 Act III, pp. 53ff.

and which enshrined an image in emerald. Even the king when he visited the mansion was wonder-struck to see the rich stores of gold, silver and jewels.

Cultured man of resources—

The *Kāvyamīmāṃsā*[1] of Rājaśekhara describes the ideal surroundings for a poet. In this we can easily see the comfortable life which a cultured man of good resources was expected to live in this period. He should have his nails properly cut, should chew betel-leaves, anoint his body with unguents, put on costly, though not gaudy, garments and deck his head with flowers. His residence should have arrangements suiting the requirements of different seasons. It should have a garden-house with an awning of numerous trees, a miniature hill, tanks and ponds, a collection of tame birds and animals, a shower-house with paved floor, a creeper-bower and also swings and hammocks.

High standard of living—

In the records of our period we have several references to indicate that the general standard of living was high and people were used to many items of comfortable and prosperous living. The literary references show that golden and jewelled ornaments for the different parts of the body were much in vogue[2]. The sculptures of this period also reveal a marked tendency for massive ornamentation and elaborate jewellery[3]. We get a general idea of the amenities which were associated with the concept of a comfortable life from the *Upamitibhavaprapañcākathā*[4] which mentions couches with soft cotton sheets, seats filled with goose feathers, gowns and other soft garments, upper garments, woollen-cloth, silks, including Chinese, musk, aloes, sandal, and other unguents as things delightful to the touch.

1 X, p. 49.

2 *Kāvyamīmāṃsā*, VI, p. 27.

3 Cf. S. Kramrisch in *Journal of the Indian Society of Oriental Art*, XV, pp. 178 ff.

4 p. 220.

The literary works are full of references to the luxurious behaviour of ladies changing their cosmetics according to the different seasons. Thus we learn that at the end of the winter and the beginning of the spring season the maidens start using sandal-juice and give up the use of bees' wax for their lips, fragrant oil for their hair and thick saffron for their mouths[1]. In the evening the jewelled roof-terraces and the picture galleries are opened for pleasure, the couches are spread out by the attendants and the maids-in-waiting move their fingers on the silks[2]. At the rise of the full moon aloes are burnt as incense at the pleasure-houses where rare pearls are suspended as festoons and charming pleasure-couches are prepared[3]. In summer people delighted in rubbing themselves with sandal-paste at midday, playing in bathing-pools until nightfall, and drinking cool liquor at evening[4].

The *Ratirahasya*[5] testifies to the popularity of excursions to gardens (*udyānayātrā*), excursions for drinking (*pānayātrā*) and water-sports (*jalāvatāra*). The description of the spring revels found in the *Upamitibhavaprapañcākathā*[6] reveals a spirit of joy and abandon which reflects a prosperous society. On the appointed day people flocked to the garden outside the city and engaged themselves in different sports, while gallant lovers drank with their mistresses goblets of scented wine from bejewelled drinking vessels. People sang and danced and formed themselves into many drinking parties or else engaged in amorous sports. Later on the king also came to join the festivity and revelry and was welcomed with song, dance, play of musical instruments, the sprinkling of sandal and saffron juice and similar exuberant manifestations of gaiety. Medhātithi[7] mentions the professions of several personal servants, catering for the needs of a man of means who wants to live a luxurious life.

1 *Karpūramañjarī*, I.

2 Ibid.

3 Ibid., III.

4 Ibid., IV.

5 XIII. 93.

6 pp. 590-603.

7 On Manu, IX. 76, 143.

General prosperity—

The general prosperity in our period can easily be inferred from the references to the use of objects of luxury some of which we have noticed above. There is nothing to suggest that there was any appreciable decline in agriculture or industries[1]. On the contrary we have good evidence[2] about the advanced knowledge of the technique of cultivation. Some of the industries such as textiles, working of metals, especially iron, copper and bronze, the art of jewellery, leather work, wood-carving, stone-work and ivory-carving had achieved a degree of technical skill[3]. We have seen that in this period India still exported many articles to neighbouring countries and Indian merchants carried a profitable trade with them[4]. The Muslim accounts also show the prosperity of northern India at the time of the Muslim invasions. Arab geographers also refer to the prosperity of the different parts of northern India. Al-Idrīsī speaking about the general conditions in India observes that "provisions are abundant, and the taxes are light, so that the people are in easy circumstances"[5]. Some of the indigenous records also speak of the prosperity of specific regions in particular periods[6].

But this is not to imply the idealised generalisation that the prosperity was shared by all the sections in society. It has been pointed out that the poorest man of the time seems to have been fairly well off, for some images at Khajuraho also show some crude

---

1 *The Age of Imperial Kanauj*, pp. 399-404; *The Struggle for Empire*, pp. 516-24.

2 E.g., the *Kṛṣiparāśara* and the sayings of Khanā. See *University of Allahabad Studies*, Ancient History Section, 1963-64, pp. 1-38.

3 *The Age of Imperial Kanauj*, pp. 400f; *The Struggle for Empire*, pp. 517-20.

4 See supra pp. 131-43, 149-52, 157-60.

5 Elliot and Dowson, I, p. 82.

6 E.g., a private inscription from Mallar says that under the Kalacuris the country was well-governed and was free from the infestation of troubles, and the people were happy—*C.I.I.*, IV, no. 97, ll. 9-10. Cf. the account of the prosperity of Rājā Māṇikacandra's subjects as found in the *Maināmatī* songs which reflects the conditions in the days of Hindu rule—T. C. Dasgupta, *Aspects of Bengali Society*, pp. 86f.

jewellery on their persons[1]. It is however not safe to base an inference on this evidence. The art of this period, including sculpture was to a great extent conventionalised[2] and so is not very faithful in reflecting the minute details of social life. Moreover the ornaments depicted on the persons of the poor are not to be interpreted as being valuable ones. The literary works of the period make this point quite clear. The ornaments used by the lower class are often described as being of cheap metals or objects. Thus we find that the betel-casket bearer, who in the *Kuṭṭanīmata* is said to accompany the young son of an officer, uses a garland of thick glass beads around his neck and conch-shell bangles on his wrist[3]. There are other references also to women of poor class using ornaments made of conch-shell[4].

Low cost of living—

Nevertheless the general condition even of the lower classes could not have been very bad because prices in general were low. Prices continued to be low in any case upto the time of Ibn Batūta[5]. We get some idea of the cost of living in our period from the Kolhapur Plates of Gaṇḍarādityadeva dated 1126 A.D[6]. It would follow from this inscription that two *nivartanas* of land were sufficient to provide for twelve brāhmaṇas rich food with cooked rice of white grains (*śvetavrīhyodana*), with broth (*sūpa*) made of *āḍhakī* and other pulses, with ghee, whey (*takra*) and four vegetables and betel-leaves (*tāmbūla*).

Differences in standard of living—

There are certain indications to suggest wide differences in the standard of living among the social groups. Thus we learn from the *Rājataraṅgiṇī* that whereas the courtiers ate fried meat

1 *Uttara Bhāratī*, II, No. 2, p. 164.

2 K. De B. Codrington, *Medieval Indian Sculptures*, p. 17.

3 vv. 66-67.

4 E.g., *Subhāṣitaratnakoṣa*, v. 1152.

5 Yule, *Cathay*, IV. 80-82.

6 *E.I.*, XXIII. 30-32.

and drank wine cooled and perfumed with flowers[1], the common people had to be content with rice and *utpalaśāka* (a wild vegetable of bitter taste)[2]. Likewise, whereas the rich enjoyed luxurious theatre-halls, filled with leather-cushioned couches[3], the common man witnessed theatrical performances under an open sky and in case of a downpour had to disperse[4]. The *Sandeśarāsaka* points out that men of taste sometimes being hard-pressed find betel-leaves beyond their reach and have to console themselves with the modest *śatapatrī*[5]. From the *Dāyabhāga*[6] it appears that sometimes housewives found the earnings of their husbands insufficient and had to take to spinning, weaving or some other mechanical art. In the story books we often read about the hardships which a poor man or woman had to face[7]. The *Triṣaṣṭiśalākāpuruṣacarita*[8] relates the story of the miserable lot of a woman afflicted with poverty, who earned a living by working in other people's houses, spent the whole day in threshing, grinding, carrying water, sweeping the house, smearing the house with cow-dung and similar work and took her food after the whole day had passed.

It would appear that even the most benevolent king would sometimes fail to appreciate the miserable lot of the poor and would add to their existing difficulties. Thus the *Prabandhacintāmaṇi*[9] records a tradition that in his desire to establish learned men in his capital king Bhoja ordered the weavers and fishermen to be removed from their localities where houses were to be built for the scholars.

---

1 VIII. 186f.

2 V. 49.

3 *Kuṭṭanīmata*, v. 68.

4 Rāj., VII. 1606.

5 v. 18.

6 p. 85.

7 *Bṛhatkathākośa*, XLII. 4f; *Prabandhacintāmaṇi*, pp. 10 (l.13), 12 (ll.2f), 93 (l.21), 109 (ll.25f).

8 (Tr.) III, p. 248.

9 p. 29, l. 17.

Suffering poor people—

We learn from the literary sources of the period that in spite of the general prosperity some people suffered abject poverty and had to resort to begging in order to maintain themselves[1]. In the disgusting picture of the Kali age as given in the *Bṛhannāradīya Purāṇa*[2], which reflects the existing conditions to some extent, people are said in general to have little property. Medhātithi refers to gleaners, who, after wandering about several villages, earned just enough to serve as food for the day[3]. Elsewhere Medhātithi refers to the starving condition of the family as one of the main causes which led people to commit offences[4]. The *Uktivyaktiprakaraṇa* has by way of illustration a sentence which means that a certain person is starving due to hunger[5]. As these illustrations were about things which were quite well-known to young boys for whom the text was meant, it would also follow that poverty bordering on starvation was by no means unknown.

Hemacandra in his *Triṣaṣṭiśalākāpuruṣacarita*[6] notices the truism that generally the women of the poor conceive quickly. Such an appreciation could not have been the result of imagination or theorisation, but reveals a realistic knowledge of the phenomenon of poverty and one of its underlying causes. Kṣemendra, who is known for his genius in presenting faithful sketches of the representative characters of his time, makes occasional references to the behaviour of poor men. Thus in his *Aucityavicāracarcā*[7], he refers to a stranger who sits uninvited in the middle of the line of many people taking food but is found out at last and proves himself a source of shame and disgust. He quotes Māgha to the effect that hungry stomachs cannot live upon grammar nor can thirsty mouths drink the juice of poetry and that nobody ever

1 Cf. *Abhidhānaratnamālā*, vv. 348, 351, 359-61 for such terms.

2 XXXVIII. 34—*alpārthāśca bhaviṣyanti.*

3 On Manu, VIII. 260.

4 Ibid. 126.

5 p. 51, l. 14—*Bhūkheṃ sukhā* (Skt. *Bubhukṣayā śuṣyati*).

6 I. 1.533 (Tr. I, p. 53)—*prāyeṇa hi daridrāṇāṃ śīghragarbhabhṛtaḥ striyaḥ.*

7 p. 22.

rescued a family by learning, hence all the arts are useless and one should earn gold alone[1]. In his *Suvṛttatilaka*[2] he points out that the poor, who have limited resources, cannot enjoy a festival.

Even in some of the big cities there were many people who had no regular income and had to support themselves by the most degraded devices. The *Bṛhatkathākośa*[3] of Hariṣeṇa has a story about the miserably unhappy poor man who lived in a separate locality in the city of Ujjayinī. Of these a certain Viṣṇudatta with great difficulty supported his family by beating his heart and head with hard stones in his hand, by holding bundles of grass with his teeth in the centre of the market place or by entertaining people with sweet songs. The realistic details of these methods, which such people adopt in modern India also, suggest that the author knew these social groups well and had not produced them out of his imagination.

Poor brāhmaṇas—

It has been recently pointed out by D.D. Kosambi that the poverty of his particular class seems to be the only reality with which the poets of the classical period came to grips[4]. In the *Subhāṣitaratnakoṣa* there are some verses referring to the miserable plight of a poor brāhmaṇa. For his sustenance he has to humour a farmer by praising him so that he may give him a handful of chaff[5]. With a tattered umbrella in his hand and tormented by hunger a brāhmaṇa acolyte returns home with tired legs after wandering for the whole day for his meagre alms[6].

Here we are not concerned with the propriety of a class theory being the suitable guide to the excellence of a literature[7]. Though

1 Ibid., p. 26.

2 III. 26.

3 III. 3-6.

4 *Subhāṣitaratnakoṣa*, Introduction, p. xliii. See also D. D. Kosambi, *Śatakatrayādisubhāṣitasaṃgraha*, Introduction, p. 81.

5 v. 305.

6 v. 1170.

7 H. H. Ingalls, Preface to the *Subhāṣitaratnakoṣa*, p. x.

Indian literature does not aim at realism in the restricted sense of an awareness of the clashes of the bourgeois and the proletariat[1], it would be incorrect to say that it is unrealistic as not reflecting the existing institutions. Sanskrit poetry has its own ideas and ideals and in achieving them it abides by certain conventions and sometimes encourages laboured effects, but does not always sacrifice spontaneity[2]. The accounts are sometimes consciously overdrawn and exaggerated, but they cannot be said to be devoid of a substratum of truth. Even the *Subhāṣitaratnakoṣa,* which belongs to the class of *subhāṣita* literature intended primarily for amusement (*vinoda*)[3], about which the remark of Kosambi has special applicability, has many graphic pen-sketches of a highly realistic character[4]. The poverty of a section of the brāhmaṇas is a historical reality for all periods of Indian history. The *Prabandhacintāmaṇi* has some stories about poor brāhmaṇas, whose only means of subsistence was begging[5] or whose only possession was an aged bull[6] or a tattered wrapper[7]. Another brāhmaṇa tells his woeful tale : he has no wrapper for protection against cold or a brazier for fire ; his back is bruised from sleeping on the ground ; there is nothing to stop draught from entering his hut ; he has not even a handful of rice to eat ; he has no peace of mind for a single moment and is harassed by his creditors[8].

Life of a villager—

There are several indications to suggest that the life of a villager, in particular of a cultivator, was by no means an enviable one and he had to be satisfied with basic necessities only. The *Subhāṣitaratnakoṣa* has a number of verses reflecting the poverty

1 Cf. S. P. Bhattacharyya in *J. N. Banerjea Volume*, p. 135.

2 Ibid., pp. 134f.

3 Ibid., p. 134.

4 See vv. 1176, 1179, 1181, 1162, 300 for descriptions of some aspects of village life.

5 p. 42, l. 16.

6 p. 8, l. 25.

7 p. 103, l. 12.

8 p. 29, ll. 13f.

of the villagers. The family of a householder has many members, but a single ox, the only possession of the family, is too exhausted to get up, making the future all the more gloomy[1]. An entire family has just one room which contains the kitchen, the mortar, the household furniture and the householder and his children; above all this the housewife will provide an addition to the family within a day or two and has to spend her labour time in that very room[2]. A poor housewife is in real trouble in her old house when it rains heavily; with a piece of broken winnowing basket on her head, she dries *śaktu* which has become lumped, consoles crying children, throws out water in a broken earthen pot and protects the bed made of grass[3]. Another poor householder has to bear the sight of his children looking like corpses with bodies emaciated with hunger; his relatives are scornful; the worn out water-jar leaks and his wife daily begs from the neighbour the loan of a needle to mend her torn garment, only to receive sarcasm and anger[4]. A famished householder consoles his wife with the wishful thinking that with their pumpkins which they will grow without labour by their hovel at the end of the summer season they will feed themselves like a king[5]. A housewife relies only on pumpkins for her family but does not get a bounteous crop because the water which she borrows from well-wishers leaks through the cracked pot and she cannot water them[6]. The shy children of the poor are said often to cast greedy glances at richer people eating their meals[7]. A poor mother wishes that the night might never pass and thus stop the worries about food which she will face tomorrow[8]. Another mother with emaciated body and torn clothes whose children clamour for food wishes fervently that one *māna* of rice may suffice for them for one hundred

1 v. 1317.
2 v. 1310.
3 v. 1312.
4 v. 1307.
5 v. 1306.
6 v. 1315.
7 v. 1320.
8 v. 1311.

days[1]. In two verses of the *Subhāṣitaratnakoṣa* a traveller on approaching a house for food and shelter finds the householder in abject poverty and so returns without expressing his request[2]. In the *Sūktimuktāvalī*[3] of Jalhaṇa belonging to the early part of the thirteenth century humble dwellings and harrowing poverty were often regarded as characteristic of village life. That such descriptions had some realistic basis and were not the result of poetic conventions would follow from a poem of Ḍheṇḍanapāda, a mystic saint. He speaks of his house as standing on a solitary hillock, with no rice in the earthen pot and all the inmates very hungry[4].

The *Avadānakalpalatā*[5] of Kṣemendra presents a peasant as the veritable embodiment of poverty and misery. He is working hard in his field. His hair is tawny with dust; his hands and feet are cracked; he is tormented with hunger and thirst and he is pained by the cuts he has received in the course of his work. Kṣemendra further speaks of the sons of well-to-do householders who are forced by poverty to accept slavery and who, emaciated with hunger, toil wearily in the fields[6]. In the *Caryāgīti* we have a reference to peasants in tattered wrappers who are too poor to buy ploughshares[7]. The economic backwardness of the cultivator affected his social status. For Vācaspatimiśra[8], the Sāṃkhya philosopher of this period, the peasant with his feet covered with dust was the best example of the mentally undeveloped[9].

Low standard of living—

A villager was satisfied with very little and did not seriously try to obtain the amenities and comforts of the well-to-do townsmen.

---

1 *Saduktikarṇāmṛta*, p. 310.

2 vv. 1314, 1328.

3 p. 441.

4 *Bauddha Gān O' Dohā, pada*, no. 33.

5 XXIV. 94-96.

6 Ibid., XVII. 14.

7 *Dohākośa*, p. 333.

8 *Sāṅkhyatattvakaumudī*, p. 17, ll. 1-3—*Tatra vyaktaṃ svarūpataḥ pāṃsulapādako hāliko'pi pratyakṣataḥ pratipadyate.*

9 *I.A.*, 1933, p. 17.

The conception of a happy life in a village which we find in the works of this period indicates that the standard of living in the country was really low. Thus in the *Prabandhacintāmaṇi*[1] a householder who owns four bulls and two cows and has a sweet-tongued wife is said to be really fortunate. Babbara, the court poet of the Kalacuri king Karṇa, describes the ideally happy villager as having saintly, obedient, meritorious and learned sons with minds fixed on their *dharma*, a pious-minded, faithful and modest wife, absorbed in virtuous deeds, loyal servants, and a neat and clean house with high walls and well thatched[2]. According to the same source the food of such a fortunate farmer consisted of hot rice on green plantain leaf, with cow's ghee and milk, fish and *nāliya* (*nālitā* = *Arum Colocasia*) vegetable[3].

Causes of poverty—

We can safely conjecture that some of the general causes which are responsible for reducing people to poverty in other countries and periods existed in our period also. We have seen in some of the references quoted above that the poor man describes himself as harassed by his creditors. Probably the high rates of interest and the exacting ways of the merchant-creditors were responsible for much distress. Thus the *Kuṭṭanīmata* tells of a man losing his fortune through the exactions of usurers[4]. Likewise Medhātithi refers to the practice in some parts of the country of the debtor repaying the debt by selling himself[5].

Famines—

The popular imagination, divorced from historical reality, which seeks solace from present sufferings by projecting an idealised golden age of plenty in the past, likes to believe that famines were non-existent in earlier times[6]. The paucity of relevant evidence[7]

1 p. 24, l. 3.

2 R. Sāṅkṛtyāyana, *Hindī Kāvya Dhārā*, p. 314.

3 Ibid., p. 316.

4 v. 615.

5 On Manu, VIII. 46.

6 *I. A.*, 1923, p. 108.

7 Ibid., pp. 192f.

may appear to corroborate this. But a proper analysis will reveal that famines were far more frequent and distressing in effect than those in modern times. Famines and the sufferings accompanying them seem to have been quite a common phenomenon[1]. In describing the typical condition of the Kali age, in which is reflected the contemporary life, the *Bṛhannāradīya Purāṇa* says that people will be gravely distressed by famine and will migrate to countries rich in wheat and barley[2]. The *Triṣaṣṭiśalākāpuruṣacarita* refers to famines "terrible with universal destruction"[3]. The *Aparājitapṛcchā*[4] realises the tremendous loss brought about by famines. Under the stress of famines *dharma* declines, and the subjects and the rulers alike suffer. The literary works of the period often refer to famines lasting for twelve years[5].

In one of the documents in the *Lekhapaddhati*[6] a son addresses his father as one who supports members of his caste during famine and also as one who provides food to people during famine. It would appear from this that famines often visited different parts of the country. Firishta refers to a famine of 1033 which raged in Hindustan with considerable violence and as a result of which many countries were entirely depopulated[7]. The *Prabandhacintāmaṇi*[8] mentions a famine which visited Gujarat during the reign of the Caulukya king Bhīma. Another famine in this region is recorded in the *Jagaḍucarita*[9] as having occurred under Vīsaladeva. From the *Rājataraṅgiṇī* we learn of two dreadful famines in Kashmir

---

1 Cf. Russelkonda (Ganjam) Plates of Neṭṭabhañja, *E. I.*, XXVIII. 262—*kalikalahaḍimva-ḍammara-taskara-durbhikṣa-rogāpagata* ; *Prabandhacintāmaṇi*, p. 35, l. 26 ; *Samayamātṛkā*, II. 60 ; *Uktivyaktiprakarana*, p. 39, ll. 3-4 , *Upadeśataraṅgiṇī*, vv. 137f q. *in Hindī Kāvya Dhārā*, p. 392.

2 XXXVIII. 87.

3 (Tr.) I, p. 331.

4 p. 187, v. 24.

5 *Prabandhacintāmaṇi*, p. 34, l. 7. See also *Kathākoṣa*, p. 169. J.W. Spellman, *J.A.O.S.*, 1962 November.

6 pp. 30f—*durbhikṣe svajātipoṣakān* and *durbhikṣe pālanaparān*.

7 Briggs, *History of the Rise of Muhammadan Power*, I, p. 103.

8 p. 30, l.20.

9 VI. 71-90.

in 917-18 during the reign of Pārtha[1] and in 1099-1100 under Harṣa[2].

Causes of famines—

Generally famines resulted from drought[3]. The *Aparājita-pṛcchā* regards this as the most important cause of famines and hence advises kings to provide for irrigation so that their kingdoms may be free from the fear of famines[4]. The *Bṛhannāradīya Purāṇa*[5] in its description of the Kali age says that people will have fear of drought and with eyes directed towards the sky will apprehend the sufferings of hunger; through drought they will lead the life of ascetics, eating only roots, leaves and fruits and will even commit suicide.

But the *Agni Purāṇa*[6] attaches equal importance to absolute drought and excessive rain as causes of famine and mentions *mantras* to be recited on the occasion of a river's changing its former channel, or receding from, or encroaching upon the site of a village or a town, or on the occasion of a fountain, tank, pool or any other natural reservoir of water running dry. Even to-day, when so much effort has been made to keep them in control, the rivers in northern India often swell, to spread devastation, misery and famine. The *Kathākoṣa*[7] refers to famines coming from too much rain. The *Viśeṣa-śataka* of Samayasundara Gaṇin[8] speaks of an entire *janapada* being completely flooded as a result of incessant rains for fifteen days. The two dreadful famines of Kashmir which we have referred to above were the direct consequence of devastating floods.

1 V. 270-78.

2 VIII. 1206ff.

3 *Prabandhacintāmaṇi*, p. 30, 1.20.

4 pp. 187-88, vv. 21-41.

5 XXXVIII. 80f.

6 CCLXIII. 19-21.

7 p. 161.

8 q. by Pran Nath, *A Study in the Economic Condition of Ancient India*, p. 47, f.n. 4.

Relief measures during famines—

In those days of slow communication the famine-stricken areas could not expect early relief from other areas. We find no reference to any system to prevent famines and economic institutions were not adjusted to withstand the reverses resulting from the natural calamities. We read about charitable help which magnanimous merchants extended to the sufferers[1] but these could have been at the best in the nature of providing them with food and clothing and could hardly be expected to have aimed at rehabilitating them. The responsibility of the king to provide relief on these occasions is clearly recognised in the texts of the period[2]. Medhātithi[3] speaks of the king supporting his subjects by giving them corn from his granary. But the state did not think in terms of strengthening the financial reserves of the people, and of the peasants in particular, to enable them to escape the evil consequences of the failure of the crops.

Anti-social activities during famines—

Moreover, there were some anti-social elements who wanted to exploit the famines for greater gain and who thus added to the sufferings of the people. Kṣemendra in his *Deśopadeśa*[4] describes a typical avaricious and miserly merchant of his times who hoards but does not sell paddy and other grains, even though he has kept it for sixty years; at the time of drought or excessive rains he dances with joy and welcomes a famine or any other public calamity because he can then get good money for his hoarded grain.

Likewise some hard-hearted kings did not realise their duty at the time of famines and instead increased the hardship of the people by their oppressive measures. The *Aparājitapṛcchā*[5] recognises the possibility that famines become particularly horrible if

1 *Lekhapaddhati*, pp. 30f; *Jagaḍucarita*, VI. 71-90.

2 Cf. *Aparājitapṛcchā*, pp. 187f.

3 On Manu, V. 93.

4 II. 33f.

5 p. 187, v. 27.

the ruling king is cruel, probably implying that he not only did not arrange any welfare measures but did not remit the state dues and tried to exploit the suffering people. The history of Kashmir in this period substantiates this fear. We learn that on the occasion of the famine of 917 the king's minister and the *tantrins* became wealthy from selling stores of rice at high prices; the king would take that person as minister who raised money by selling the wretched subjects. King Harṣa had imposed fresh imposts over and above the existing ones. When the great famine of A. D. 1099-1100 occurred, he did not reduce his rigorous taxation and continued to exact heavy fines. Kalhaṇa very aptly remarks that the heavy taxes were just like a boulder placed on an old bullock worn out by dragging the plough[1].

Impact of feudalism on economic life—

The feudalisation of the state structure in our period and the emergence of petty feudal chiefs was bound to have an adverse effect on the economic system in general. We have abundant evidence to prove that the burden of the taxation system was heavy.

Burden of taxes—

In the inscriptions of the period we find revenue terms such as *akṣapaṭalaprastha*, *pratīhāraprastha*, *cauroddharaṇa*, *duhsādhyādāya*, and *talārābhāvya*[2]. These stand for dues which the villagers had to pay to the officers named in these expressions, over and above the different dues which they paid to the state. This indicates the feudal practice of the period of remunerating state officers in terms of land-grants and assignments of revenue. The *Deśīnāmamālā*[3] mentions *grāmaroḍā* and *koḍio* as people who enjoy villages by deceitful manipulation. These represented a class of chieftains who, taking advantage of the central authority, established their power and realised dues from villagers, though they were not recognised by the established authority.

---

1 Rāj., VII. 1225.

2 See supra pp. 57-8, 60-1, 63, 65.

3 IV. 48, 90.

Though in general the vassals were required to collect the dues and to pay tributes or periodical dues to their overlord, there is some evidence to indicate that the tax-collecting rights of the kings and their subordinate chiefs were not mutually exclusive and the poor farmer had to pay separate dues to the latter. The *Dvyāśrayakāvya*[1] shows that the village lord (*grāmapati*) and the king realised separate shares of the produce after the harvest. The resulting burden on the taxation system can be realised from the fact that the records of the period indicate several grades of rulership and of sub-infeudation[2].

The feudatories needed money. They had to pay tributes to their overlord, had to maintain a strong army not only for self-preservation in those days of frequent internecine wars but also for expanding their territories. In addition they tried to maintain a high show of luxury and grandeur in imitation of the highest rulers of the times. The *Vikramāṅkadevacarita*[3] of Bilhaṇa indicates how the feudatories needed money for their armies and wars. A feudatory of king Vikrama, who was his own brother, wanted to increase his army with a view to successfully rebelling against his overlord, and thus amassed a treasure by extortion.

The feudatory rulers appear to have been on the look-out for new methods of realising money from their subjects and exploited every opportunity to do so. Two inscriptions from the Caulukya kingdom show that the prohibition of the killing of animals on certain days which king Kumārapāla promulgated out of sincere religious conviction was utilised by two of his feudatories for raising money by imposing fines on those who disobeyed the orders[4]. The *Vastupālacarita*[5] tells of a *māṇḍalika* who extracted heavy presents and bribes from the people. The *Udayasundarīkathā*[6]

1 III. 2. See also Bṛhat-Parāśara III (Jivananda, p. 113).

2 Ratanpur stone inscription of the reign of the Caulukya king Kumārapāla.—P. Peterson, *Collection of Prakrit and Sanskrit Inscriptions*, p. 206. See also *Lekhapaddhati*, p. 7.

3 Sarga IV.

4 *Prakrit and Sanskrit Inscriptions*, pp. 172f, 206f.

5 p. 100.

6 p. 56.

of Soḍḍhala refers to a feudal chief who imprisoned rich people to extract money from them. The *Bṛhannāradīya Purāṇa*[1] in its description of the Kali age observes that the servants of the state torture even the brāhmaṇas for the sake of money. In the *Laṭakamelaka*[2] of Śaṅkhadhara, Saṅgrāmavisara, who typifies a *rājaputra* chief (*rāuttarāja*) enjoying the assignment of a village (*grāmapaṭṭaka*), is said to have made money even from sparrows, dead-birds, pig-dung and the shrouds of dead bodies. The *Kathāsaritsāgara*[3] also refers to the exactions from people by a petty *sāmanta* and the obnoxious rules and regulations promulgated by him.

It appears from Al-Bīrūni[4] that in order to escape the heavy burdens of taxation villagers concealed their property from royal officers. We can infer the usual ways of a feudal chief from the unusual concessions which the benevolent king Kālaketu of the *Caṇḍīkāvya* offers to a new settler. "I won't seize your produce from the field, but shall wait till you pay me off in cowries at your convenience and shall not depute any tax-collector to realise taxes from you. If you really mean to remain in Gujarat, I won't demand anything in the shape of *selāmis*, *bānsgāris*, *pāravanis* and *pañcaks*, and also I won't charge boat-tax, salt-tax, loom-tax and paddy cutting tax or demand anything on the plea of mistakes in the account-books. However much you may sell of your good paddy, I won't covet a share...I won't take any house-rent from those of you who are new settlers in my city"[5].

The oppressive taxes could not but adversely affect the economy of the villages, bringing the villagers to a very low level of subsistence. A verse in the *Subhāṣitaratnakoṣa*[6] describes the ruined condition of a village which was depopulated as a result of exactions by the feudal chief. The description of the Kali age in the *Bṛhannāradīya Purāṇa*[7] speaks of people fleeing from exorbitant taxation to

1 XXXVIII. 50.

2 Act II, p. 18.

3 *Lambaka* 3, *taraṅga* 18. Cf. Kṣemendra's *Bṛhatkathāmañjarī*, III. 200f.

4 II. 149.

5 T. C. Dasgupta, *Aspects of Bengali Society*, pp. 312f.

6 v. 1175.

7 XXXVIII. 87.

countries rich in corn. The baneful effects of the burdensome taxes of the period are best reflected in the *Maināmatī* songs which describe the evil consequences for Māṇikacandra's subjects who were very opulent before a new chief came to rule the land under king Māṇikacandra. This man imposed exorbitant taxes with the result that people sold everything including ploughs and other agricultural implements, and even their own children ; the widows and the poor suffered all the more terribly. Ultimately the *tāluks* were turned into jungles[1].

We find no reference to suggest that the overlords made any serious efforts to stop these exactions of the feudal chiefs. As the central authority in the period had declined considerably and had to depend on the levies sent by the feudal chiefs, it could not afford to interfere with their high-handed exploitation. It would appear that the overlords were aware of the heavy taxes imposed by the chiefs and gave them some degree of approval by recognising their existence. In the land-grants of the period we sometimes find the terms *niyatāniyata*[2], *ucitānucita*[3] and *bhaviṣyat*[4] suffixed to the lists of taxes which a donor king transferred to the grantee. These terms amount to a recognition of the possibility of new taxes being imposed in the future, and of their being unjust in some cases. The legal opinion also appears to have been modified a little to suit the new conditions and to provide some sanction for the feudal exactions. Thus, we find Medhātithi[5] observing that the vaiśyas are very wealthy and hence the officers appointed to extract money from them are not to be punished even if they do them wrong.

As we have already shown[6], the feudal chiefs indulged in loot and plunder, thus creating difficulties for the merchants carrying on inter-state trade.

1 T. C. Dasgupta, *Aspects of Bengali Society*, p. 86.

2 *E.I.*, X, p. 99.

3 *J.U.P.H.S.*, XXIII. 228-50.

4 *J.B.O.R.S.*, XVII. 1ff, II. 37-49.

5 On Manu X. 119—*Vaiśyā mahādhanā bhavanti. Tatastathākaraṇe niyuktāḥ kṛtāparādhā na hanyante.*

6 See supra pp. 102-3.

Destruction from feudal wars—

The frequent feudal wars of the period were also responsible for much destruction of the economic prosperity of the country. The records of the period indicate that the invaders often attempted to cripple the economy of their enemy and to destroy the lives and property of their subjects. Thus, Medhātithi[1] advises a king to invade the enemy territory during the months of Phālguṇa and Caitra, because thus he can injure the other party by destroying standing crops. Likewise in the case of a siege the same authority recommends that the invading king should harass the territories outside the fortress occupied by the enemy by kidnapping the inhabitants and persecuting them in various ways[2]. The *Mānasollāsa*[3] speaks of the destructions which a king could inflict on his enemy. He could cut down the forests, destroy the water-reservoirs and burn the villages (*deśanāśaka*), or capture by force all the cattle (*go̊graha*), or snatch all the grain whether stored in granaries, markets or threshing-floors or still in the fields, and thus cause famine (*dhānyaharaṇa*) ; he might capture and imprison the householders, cultivators and rich bankers and merchants (*bandigrāha*), or encircle the villages with soldiers and forcefully take the inhabitants' gold (*dhanādāna*) ; if he had a large army he might besiege cities and take everything (*sarvasva-haraṇa*).

It is claimed in an epigraphic record of the period that in the battle of Rohaḍavāpika (*Rohaḍavāpikottha-samare*) the subjects (*prajā*) of a certain ruler named Maṇḍalika struck with spearheads by the Cāhamāna king Pṛthvipāla's troopers left far away their shame, sons, wives, mothers as well as property, and fled away in all directions[4]. We learn from the *Rājataraṅgiṇī*[5] that during the reign of Sussala the *ḍāmaras* set fire to a temple in which many people of the neighbourhood had sought asylum with their women, children, animals, rich stores and property. It would follow

1 On Manu, VII. 182.

2 Ibid. 195.

3 I, pp. 122f, vv. 1038-47.

4 D. Sharma, *Early Chauhān Dynasties*, pp. 188ff at p. 190, ll.17-18.

5 VIII. 971-1004.

from a reference in the *Triṣaṣṭiśalākāpuruṣacarita*[1] that it was very common in this period for kings to destroy each others' village-lands.

Sacking of cities—

The sacking of cities seems to have been a common feature of the wars of this period[2]. Ānanda, the governor of Kramarājya, advised king Uccala to proceed to Śrīnagara and plunder the neighbouring towns and villages[3]. In the *Rājataraṅgiṇī*[4] we read on many occasions of cities and villages being burnt and pillaged by rebels. We can easily imagine the nature and amount of ruin and economic dislocation resulting from these wars. We have already referred to a passage from the *Mānasollāsa*[5] which speaks of an invading king as confiscating all the grain in the kingdom of the enemy with the result that famine visited the invaded country. The *Rājataraṅgiṇī*[6] gives a vivid description of the ruin brought about by the sack of Śrīnagara. The entire city was reduced to a heap of earth, full of swollen decomposing corpses. The ground was white with fragments of human skulls. The granaries were consumed by fire. The famishing people, scarcely able to walk, appeared like scorched wooden posts.

Dislocation of life—

These feudal wars must have meant a tremendous strain for both parties and dislocated the economic and cultural life of the vanquished country. People could not pursue their normal callings for some time because of the resultant chaos. Medhātithi[7], therefore, advises the conqueror to consolidate his power over the conquered territory and to proclaim that henceforward every one among the people was free to take to his own calling. When

1 Vol. I, p. 198.

2 Cf. *Upamitibhavaprapañcakathā*, p. 629. See also B.P. Mazumdar, *Socio-Economic History*, p. 245.

3 *Rāj.*, VII. 1323-5.

4 VII. 1325 ; VIII. 734, 1127, 1169-85.

5 I, p. 122, vv. 1041-42.

6 VIII. 1184-1212.

7 On Manu, VII. 201—*yathāsvaṃ svaṃ vyāpāram anutiṣṭhantu.*

Pālī waş captured and sacked by the Caulukya king Kumārapāla in A.D. 1149, a Jain monk named Sthiracandragaṇi, who was copying a text at the time, had to flee to Ajmer where he completed the work[1]. As we have pointed out earlier trade and commerce in particular suffered much from existing feudal anarchy[2].

March of an army—

Whatever might have been the ideal, it appears that the march of the army often brought destruction to the people living in the villages through which it passed, and thus the subjects suffered at the hands of the army of their own ruler[3]. It would follow from the works of Bāṇa that even in the time of Harṣa the marching armies meant considerable damage to the crops and much physical labour and strain to the villagers[4]. The *Tilakamañjarī*[5] which belongs to the period under study, also vividly describes the destructions which an army inflicted on a village which was situated on the path of its march. The soldiers carried away all the chaff from the threshing-floors, and robbed the villagers of their valuables and their fodder; elephant riders sometimes directed their elephants against villagers who took to flight; vegetable gardens and sugarcane plantations were looted; some peasants were forcibly turned out by *ṭhakkuras*, who could not get accommodation, and with their possessions in their hands went from house to house in search of shelter. The peasants did their best to conceal their corn, and even their dried cowdung was not safe from looting; the poorer peasants hid their valuables in the houses of their wealthier neighbours where they were better protected.

This darker aspect of the economic life of the times, especially the disastrous effects of the feudal polity, is often neglected in

1 *Catalogue of MSS in the Jaisalmer Bhandars*, p. 7.

2 See supra pp. 101-3.

3 According to Aparārka on Yāj., II. 163 (A.S.S., p. 771) the horses and elephants belonging to the king are simply to be warded off and no redress is possible for the harm caused by them to the crop.

4 Cf. V. S. Agrawala, *Kādambarī*, pp. 125f and *Harṣacarita*, p. 201.

5 pp. 119f.

studies of the subject[1]. This gives an incorrect notion of the stages in the economic life of the country.

Stages in the economic decline of India—

The common belief among Indians is that the present poverty of India is the result of economic exploitation during two hundred years of British rule. We do not aim at challenging the truism that much of India's wealth and her raw-materials were drained by the British rule. But a study of the economic history of India suggests that it would be wrong to blame the British alone for the economic backwardness of India. The question must be judged in its true historical perspective. We find that the economic decline of India has a history spreading over many centuries. Our present analysis has shown that the feudal polity in the early medieval period affected the economic prosperity of the country adversely and reduced the cultivators to a low state of subsistence. India still remained prosperous; but the prosperity was monopolised by the rulers, including the feudal chiefs, the merchants and the temples. The common villager of our period was often in a miserable condition.

Muslim invasions and Muslim rule—

The effects of the Muslim invasions and of Muslim rule in general are often not realised in a study of this question[2]. As the question is outside the chronological scope of our study we discuss only some important aspects of it.

The early Muslim invasions of Muhammad bin Qāsim, the Ghaznavides and the Ghūrids drained India of much wealth. If we made a list of all the recorded amounts obtained during these invasions as spoil, ransom or tribute, it would reach a fabulous sum. As contrasted with later periods when the Muslims had established themselves in India all these amounts were taken to countries beyond the frontiers of India.

1 Cf. Chapters on Economic Life in *The Age of Imperial Kanauj* and *The Struggle for Empire*.

2 Cf. R. C. Majumdar in *The Age of Delhi Sultanate*, p. 623 for a comparative estimate of the Muslim rule and British rule.

Since almost all the sources which pertain to the early Muslim rule are Muslim in origin, it is difficult to get an unbiased picture of those times. Sometimes in order to laud the victorious arms of Islam, these narratives present an exaggerated picture. Even then we can form some idea of the enormous economic loss and ruin and the dislocation of economic life which the Muslim invasions meant. Thus Al-Bīrūnī says that "Mahmūd utterly ruined the prosperity of the country, and performed there wonderful exploits, by which the Hindus became like atoms of dust scattered in all directions, and like a tale of old in the mouth of the people"[1]. The chronicles dealing with the early Muslim invasions are full of references, too many to list, of destruction and ravage[2].

As in the case of earlier invasions, Indian literature does not take any detailed notice of the foreign invasion[3] and so we cannot describe the destruction and ruin which the people had to suffer nor can we corroborate the Muslim narratives. But we do get some incidental references which indicate that the invaders inflicted heavy losses on the people. The *Ādi Purāṇa*[4] describes the oppression of the people at the hands of *Asuras* who are said to have been born out of *Yavanas*. The description would suggest that the author of the text knew of the tyranny of the Muslims. It says that these people will be addicted to immoral ways, will oppress the people and will snatch and collect all the

---

1 I. 22.

2 Cf. *The Struggle for Empire*, pp. 499f. See e.g., *Tabaqāt-i-Akbarī*—Bakhtyār Khaljī conquered the fort of Bihar, plundered and ravaged the whole of the country, and acquired much booty (B.I., p. 50). The recent excavations at Lal-Kot, Delhi reveal a deposit of burnt ash and earth mixed with the debris of fallen structures—*Indian Archaeology*, 1957-58, p. 25.

3 Cf. Medhātithi on Manu II. 22—Āryāvarta was so called because the Āryas sprang up in it again and again. Even if it was overrun by the Mlecchas, they could never abide there for long.

4 XIV. 139f—*Asurā yavanāṃśeṣu jātā lokopatāpinaḥ.*
Anītiniratāḥ sarve saṃgrahe ca prabuddhayaḥ.
Palāyamānāsteṣāṃ hi prajāḥ syurapi pīḍitāḥ.
Prāpurdeśāntaraṃ cāpi kvacinna sukhitābhavan.

wealth and that many people will flee to other lands. The *Kānbaḍade Prabandha* of Padmanābha (c. A.D. 1456) describes the destructive effects of the armies of 'Alā-ud-dīn Khaljī and we can safely utilise it to indicate the nature of ruin spread by the earlier invading armies of Muslims. The text says that "the conquering army burnt villages; devastated the land, plundered people's wealth, took brāhmaṇas, children and women of all castes captive and flogged them with thongs and rawhide, carried a moving prison with it, and converted the prisoners into obsequious Turks"[1]. The popular impression about the devastation which accompanied Muslim invasions is reflected best in a document of the *Lekhapaddhati*[2] which speaks of a *rājaputra* girl, who left her village, when, as a result of the plunder by the invading Muslims, famine visited the place; and, as the families of her parents and in-laws were now reduced to beggary, in order to keep alive she wandered from village to village until at last she had to accept slavery on most depressing terms.

Even after establishing themselves as rulers the Muslims did not change their policy basically. They aimed at oppressing the subjects and extracting money from them for their luxuries. The only difference which we notice was that now not much of the loot and plunder went beyond the frontiers of India but was enjoyed by the ruling class in India. We have referred above to the devastations which accompanied the invasions made by 'Alā-ud-dīn Khaljī. The Muslim rulers did not care much about the prosperity of the people; they were content merely to extort money for themselves and sometimes did not bother much about local administration. On the contrary, we definitely know at least in the case of 'Alā-ud-dīn Khaljī that he deliberately wanted to reduce the Hindus of Doab to such a state of abject poverty that they might devote all their time and energy merely to feeding themselves[3]. Even if we allow for the element of exaggeration we can realise the amount of destruction from the description of

---

1 q. by K. M. Munshi in his Foreword to *The Struggle for Empire*, pp. xiv-xv.

2 pp. 45-7.

3 *An Advanced History of India*, p. 308.

Hindusthan as given by Amīr Khusrav, a liberal Muslim. He says "The whole country, by means of the sword of our holy warriors, has become like a forest denuded of its thorns by fire... The strong men of Hind have been trodden under foot, and all are ready to pay tribute...Had not the law granted exemption from death by the payment of poll-tax, the very name of Hind, root and branch, would have been extinguished"[1].

There is some evidence to suggest that even after the establishment of Muslim rule those parts which did not come under their dominance continued to enjoy a fair degree of prosperity, compared with which the areas ruled by Muslims were economically not well off. In this connection we have to notice that the richest architectural remains of our period belong to southern India or to those parts of north, such as Orissa and central India, which were not much affected hy Muslim invasion. Though we have to allow due margir for the iconoclastic fury of the Muslims, it is not without significance that we do not get any indication that any Hindu monument worth its name was constructed in the areas conquered by Muslims[2]. The *Ta'rīkh-i-Fīrūz-Shāhī* of Shams-i-Sirāj gives a glowing picture of the prosperity and happiness of the country of Jājnagar (Orissa) before it was invaded by Fīrūz Shāh in 1360; "the inhabitants had spacious houses and fine gardens, they had even gardens and walks within their houses, and fruit trees, flowers, etc., were cultivated therein"[3]. The way in which the amazed writer describes the prosperity of Orissa implies, by way of contrast, that such a state of prosperity was not known in those parts of northern India which were under Muslim occupation. The known history of the period does not show any economic advantage possessed by Orissa over other parts of northern India to explain its prosperity. On the contrary the general impression is that it was one of the areas which formed economic backwaters in the period. The only possible difference

1 Elliot and Dowson, II, p. 546.

2 The recent excavations at Nevasa (Ahmadnagar) indicate that the medieval period which saw the establishment of Muslim rule was one of decline in the prosperity of Nevasa—*Indian Archaeology*, 1955-56, p. 11.

3 q. in *D.H.N.I.*, I, pp. 491f.

which we can notice is that it had so far been free from Muslim invasions and depredations. To bring home the point we must refer to the testimony of the Russian traveller Afanasii Nikitin, who was in India from 1469 to 1472 and whose journal is regarded by competent scholars as a reliable source[1]. His account reveals a grim contrast between the selfish pomp and luxury of the Sultān and his nobility, and the extreme poverty of the common people[2]. Nikitin is the first foreign visitor to India to refer to its poverty. It would therefore appear that though the economic exploitation of the country took place on a large and systematic manner later on, India had become poor after the establishment of the Muslim power.

---

1 *J.A.O.S.*, Vol. 81, p. 128.

2 R.H. Major, *India in the fifteenth century*, p .14.

APPENDIX I

SĀMANTA—ITS VARYING SIGNIFICANCE IN ANCIENT INDIA

In the epigraphic and literary records of medieval Hindu India the term *sāmanta* is used to mean vassals and nobles. Thus the *sāmantas* were vitally connected with the structure of Indian society. But, in spite of its importance, the term has not received a full-length study.[1]

According to its derivation the term *sāmanta* is an adjective and means 'being on all sides', 'neighbouring' or 'bordering'. In earlier works we find it used in this sense.[2]

It also occurs in connection with the rules on boundary disputes.[3] Almost all these rules require boundary disputes to be decided in the first instance by the *sāmantas*. It has been supposed that the *sāmanta* was the feudal lord and his right to decide a boundary dispute arose out of his ownership of land. But such an interpretation does not stand scrutiny. Firstly, the traditional interpretation of the term is against such a view. The commentary of Kullūka on Manu[4] and that of Vijñāneśvara on Yājñavalkya[5] very clearly maintain that *sāmanta* means the villagers living on the four sides.[6] The rules themselves show that the word stands

---

1 Among the most important studies of the term is that of V.S. Agrawala, *Harṣacarita: Eka Sāmskṛtika Adhyayana*, pp. 217–220.

2 In *Kātyāyana śrautasūtra* (1.7.25) it is used in connection with rites performed on all sides of the sacrificial fire (*āvṛttisāmanteṣu pradakṣiṇam*). In Pali works *sāmanto* means 'neighbouring', 'bordering', or 'in the neighbourhood', 'closely'.

3 *Vasiṣṭha Dharmasūtra* (XVI, 13–15), *Arthaśāstra* (III, 8, 9), *Manu* (VIII, 258-263), *Yājñavalkya* (II, 150-152), *Nārada* (XI, 2–4), *Kātyāyana* (737, 743–745, 749–751); *Pañcatantra* (of Pūrṇabhadra), pp. 188-89 and *Agnipurāṇa* (CCLVII, 1-3).

4 VIII, 258—*samantabhavāḥ sāmantāstadvāsinaḥ;* also VIII, 259, 262, 263.

5 II, 150—*samantādbhavāḥ sāmantāḥ catasṛṣu dikṣvanantaraṁ grāmādayaste ca pratisīmaṁ vyavasthitāḥ.*

6 Cf. texts quoted by the *Mitākṣarā* on *Yājña*, II, 150—'*grāmo grāmasya*

for the neighbouring cultivators[1] who were given the power to decide such cases, because being men on the spot they were better able to verify the boundaries with the help of boundary marks.[2] If *sāmanta* was the feudal lord with some abiding claim on the land, it is not clear why he should be given a very slender right to decide such issues,[3] still less how he could be punished for a wrong judgment.[4]

In an inscription of 592 A.D. a certain king Viṣṇuṣeṇa granted to a community of merchants his *sthitipatra*, containing important rules that formed the law of the land. The 34th rule[5] of this list reads: *sthāvaravyavahāre sāmantaiḥ avasitasya vinayo rūpakaśatam aṣṭottaram*. Dr. V. S. Agrawala[6] takes this to mean that the final settlement of land cases was beyond the jurisdiction of *sāmantas*, who were liable to a fine of 108 silver coins if they disposed of them. But the sentence has to be interpreted in the light of the traditional rules on boundary disputes as expounded in the legal texts. Here also the cultivators from the neighbouring villages have been authorized to decide such cases; the rule empowers them even to impose a fine of 108 silver coins.[7] This inscription would thus

---

sāmantaḥ kṣetro kṣetrasya kīrtitaṁ/gṛham grahasya nirdiṣṭaṁ samantātparibhāvayet//' and '*ye tatra pūrvaṁ sāmantāḥ paścāddeśāntaraṁ gatāḥ/tanmūlatvāttu te maulā ṛṣibhiḥ parikīrtitāḥ//*'

1 The rule that the boundary should be settled by an even number of *sāmantas*, four, eight or ten, and inhabitants of the same village (*Yājña*, II, 152; *Manu*, VIII, 258) ill suits the position of a *sāmanta* as the single lord of his feudal estate.

2 *Manusmṛti* (VIII, 258–60) indicates that *sāmantas* mean the neighbouring cultivators. The rule aims at relying at first on the evidence of those who are nearer to the field, and in their absence to widen the scope of men included in the term *sāmanta*.

3 *Vasiṣṭha Dharmasūtra* (XVI, 13–15; cf. *Śaṅkhalikhita* q. in *Vivādaratnākara*, p. 208) shows that the right of the *sāmantas* was of a very elementary nature and there were many others who had a stronger jurisdiction in such cases. The *sāmantas* could settle cases only as long as they had not grown complicated and a just judgment could be reached on the basis of spot inspection—*Nārada*, XI, 11; *Yājña*, II, 153.

4 *Nārada*, XI, 7; *Manu*, VIII, 263.

5 *JRASB.*, XVI, p. 115.

6 *Harṣacarita*, p. 219.

7 This suits better the construction of the phrase '*sāmantaiḥ avasitasya vinayo*'. Moreover, the next rule, apparently related to it, runs: '*saṁ-*

show that *sāmanta* in the sense of 'neighbouring villagers' was still in use up to a very late period. The compilers of the Smṛtis use the term in this sense, and under their influence it retained the meaning even when some others also had been evolved.

Another reference often taken to support the theory that the word *sāmanta* means a feudal lord is the rule allowing *jñātisāmantadhanikāḥ* in respective order the right of priority in the purchase of land.[1] But there is no reason to suppose that the right of *sāmantas* here refers to the claims of feudal lords. It seems that as land was the basis of the economy of the country, it was intended that outsiders should not intrude and disturb the economy of an autonomous and corporate village by laying their hands on the fields. The rule grants priority in buying land to blood relations and then to neighbouring villagers, and only on their not buying the land was it to be sold to an outsider.

Mr. Ellis[2] takes *sāmanta* in a verse quoted by the *Mitākṣarā*[3] to mean a feudal lord and not a neighbour. He quotes a commentary, known as *Tarkapañcanīyam*, composed in the 19th century, which uses the word in the sense of king or lord. He further argues that in this passage the use of the word in the sense of neighbour would be manifest tautology. But to base any

---

vadane rūpakāḥ catuṣpañcāśat'. According to the interpretation suggested by Dr. Agrawala the second rule would mean that if information had duly been given to the king about the case, the fine was only 54 silver coins. It is not quite understandable why a *sāmanta* should make decisions in cases on landed property if he had no jurisdiction and why the two claimants should come to him for settlement. A happier sense is indicated by the second interpretation. In that case it would mean that a fine of 54 silver coins only was to be paid by the party that had itself invited arbitration in a boundary dispute but was defeated. If the cultivator had not asked for the arbitration, it indicated that he had a false title to the land and so had to pay the double of 54 silver coins. Further, the rules that follow these two refer to fines or sums to be paid by the parties in a dispute. It would appear that the rule 34 was also of this nature.

1 *Artha.* III, 9. Also Vyāsa, Bhāradvāja and Bṛhaspati q. in *Vyavahāranirṇaya*, p. 355 f.

2 *Replies*, p. 23ff q. by A. Appadorai, *Economic Conditions in Southern India*, p. 326 ff.

3 On *Yājña*, II, 114: 'Land is conveyed by six formalities, by the assent of townsmen, of kindred, of neighbours and of heirs, and by the delivery of gold and water.'

theory on so late a work, while disregarding earlier commentaries like the *Mitākṣarā*, is quite contrary to the canons of history. The point raised by Mr. Ellis has been explained by the *Mitākṣarā*.[1] The word *sāmanta* has been used not because a *sāmanta* had any claim to the ownership of the land necessitating his assent, but because he had to know of any change in the ownership of lands adjoining his own to enable him to decide justly any boundary dispute arising in the future.

It has again been contended that the word *sāmanta* in the seventh book of the *Arthaśāstra*[2] should be translated not as a 'king'[3] but as 'independent noble'.[4] We have seen above that in the *Arthaśāstra* the term *sāmanta* signifies a neighbouring cultivator.[5] There are instances[6] in which the forts and ambassadors of a *sāmanta* are spoken of and a *sāmanta* appears as a power to be reckoned with. But a study of the inscriptions of Aśoka would show that *sāmanta* in such contexts means a neighbouring king.[7]

---

1 *Ibid.* The *Mitākṣarā* says that these are not absolutely necessary formalities of a sale, but they are recommended for the sake of greater caution and convenience, and that the assent of the villagers is to be secured for the publication of the transaction of sale, as a text says that acceptance, particularly of immovables, should be public, so that the consent of neighbours should be secured to obviate any dispute concerning the boundary.

2 The word *sāmanta* is not confined to the seventh book of the *Artha-śāstra—Index Verborum to the Arthaśāstra*, Vol. III pp. 264–66.

3 The commentary by T. Ganapati Sastri (Vol. II, pp. 272, 278, 301; III, p. 87; also I, pp. 48, 85; II, pp. 210, 219, as also the one contained in the edition of Jolly and Schmidt (Vol. II, pp. I, 2 etc.) explain *sāmanta* as the king of the neighbouring territory.

4 Pran Nath, *Economic condition of Ancient India*, p. 132 f.

5 Cf. also *Artha*, III, 8, 9.

6 *Artha*, I, 10, 13, 17, 18, 21; V, 4, 6; VI, 2; VIII, 4; IX, 3, 6, 7; XII, 4; XIII, 3, 4.

7 In the Second Rock Edict (*CII.*, I. p. 184 ff.) Aśoka refers to his benevolent deeds in the domains of Antiochus and other kings who were his *sāmaṁtas* (*ye vā pi tasa Aṁtiyokasa sāmaṁtā rājāno*). The Girnar version of the Second Rock Edict has '*sāmipā rājāno*' for *sāmaṁtā rājāno* (Ibid., p. 2, 1.3; *Select Inscriptions*, p. 18. l. 3; f.n. 3). The kings of southern India and the Greek kingdoms to the west of India have been mentioned in the Second Rock Edict as *pracantas* (*pratyantas*) (*Select Inscriptions*, p. 18, 1.2). In the thirteenth Rock Edict Aśoka speaks of his *dhammavijaya* in these neighbouring territories (*aṁteṣu*) (Ibid., p. 37, 1.8). The second separate Kaliṅga Edict is addressed to the

There is no warrant for the view that *sāmanta* denoted a vassal or noble in the Mauryan period. The term *sāmanta* when applied to villagers had the sense of a cultivator from a neighbouring village and when used in connection with kingdoms denoted a neighbouring king.

The *maṇḍala* theory in the *Arthaśāstra* is also taken to suggest that India was then divided into many petty estates. But this theory is a piece of political speculation[1] and not a mirror of the existing political condition.[2] Hence it cannot be construed to show that the *sāmantas* were owners of petty estates and not rulers of kingdoms.

The term *sāmanta* appears at several places in the *Nītisāra* of Kāmandaka[3] assigned by Winternitz[4] and Jolly[5] to the 8th century A.D. But the general opinion of scholars, in view of recent researches, favours an earlier date for the work.[6] Moreover, the work cannot be taken to represent the condition of its time, for in the introductory verses the author describes it as a scholar's compilation based primarily on the *Arthaśāstra* of Kauṭilya, whose views are collected with convenient titles.[7] So it would not be safe to think that Kāmandaka has given his impression of the working of the different institutions of his own time. Thus, evidently the

---

people of the *aṁta* territories (Ibid., p. 46, 11.2, 4, 15). The first Pillar Edict refers to *aṁtamahāmātā* or the *mahāmātras* for the frontier kingdoms (Ibid., p. 55 f.). It is apparent that the terms *sāmantas*, *antas* and *pratyantas* are similar in import and alike mean 'neighbouring kings'.

1 The fact that any state, whatever its extent, may have an unfriendly neighbouring state which it tries to win or appease has been developed into the *maṇḍala* theory, permuting all possible combinations of relations with neighbouring states, some friendly others antagonistic.

2 *Artha*, VI, 2; cf. *Manu*, VII, 155–157; *Kāmandaka*, Chs. VIII, XII, XIII; *Mbh.*, XIII, 59, 70–71; *Viṣṇudharmottara*, II, 145, 11–15; *Agni*, CCXL, 4-5; CCXXIII, 21-22; *Sarasvativilāsa*, pp. 30–41; *Mit.* on *Yājña*, I, 345; *Nītivakyāmṛta*, p. 318 f. It is not possible to decide which of these descriptions reflects the conditions of its time.

3 (Ed. J. Vidyasagar) XI, 6; XIII, 29; XIV, 22; XV, 51.

4 *GIL.*, III, p. 526 q. in the *Classical Age*, p. 300.

5 Introduction to the *Kauṭaliya Arthaśāstra*, pp. 6–8.

6 R.L. Mitra, Preface pp. 1, 4ff; T. Ganapati Sastri, Preface pp. v-vi. K.P. Jayaswal, *History of India*, p. 118 f; *JBORS.*, XVIII, pp. 37–39; *IA.*, 1918, p. 159; V R.R. Dikshitar, *The Gupta Polity*, pp. 12–15.

7 I, 2–8.

word *sāmanta*, as used by him, has the same sense as that assigned to it in the *Arthaśāstra* of Kauṭilya.[1]

It appears, however, that towards the close of the 5th century the word came to be used also for a subordinate ruler. The Kasare plates of Sendraka Nikumbhāllaśakti dated in A.D. 482[2] are addressed among others to *rājasāmantaviṣayabhogika*. The reference in the Devagiri plates[3] of Yuvarāja Devavarman is more explicit. In it the Kadamba King Kṛṣṇavarman (*c*. A.D. 475–485) is described as *sāmantarājaviśeṣaratna*. Indeed inscriptions containing orders addressed to *sāmantas* and others as well as those describing the feet of the king as coloured by the pollen of the flowers or rays of the gems in the crowns of *sāmantas* are numerous and cover a very long range of dates. Besides, there are some other inscriptions in which a certain *sāmanta* appears as the *dūtaka* or executor of the grant.[4] Though these references may, when read in the light of other inscriptions, afford valuable material, in themselves they do not contain much to remove the mist surrounding the term *sāmanta*. There are, however, certain other inscriptions in which certain *sāmanta* kings record their own grants. The earliest inscriptions of this type recovered so far are those of Dhruvasena I (A.D. 525–545)[5] of the Maitraka dynasty. The number mentioning Mahāsāmantarājas becomes quite considerable in the later period.[6] These inscriptions clearly employ the

---

1 In Bhartṛhari (*Śatakatrayādi-Subhāṣitasaṅgraha, Vairāgya* p. 66 f, verse 169) also *sāmanta* in '*Bhrātaḥ kaṣṭamaho mahānsa nṛpatiḥ sāmantacakraṁ ca tat*' refers to the kings circling a kingdom according to the theory of *maṇḍalas*.

2 *EI*., XXVIII, 34 (B).

3 *IA*., VII, p. 33.

4 In the Gunaighar inscription of Vainyagupta dated A.D. 507 (*Select Inscriptions*, p. 333 f) the executor Mahārāja Śrīmahāsāmanta Vijayasena probably entrusted the business to the Kumārāmātya Revajjasvāmin and two other officers. Also Valabhi plate of Dharasena II dated somewhere between A.D. 571 and 588 (*JBBRAS*., I, p. 24), Coras plates of Dhruvasena III of A.D. 633 (*Ibid*., I, 17, p. 57) and Madhuban grant of Harṣavardhana (*EI*., VII, 22. Also XXIII, 42A).

5 Palitana Plate dated A.D. 525—*EI*., XI, 9 (p. 108); Kathiawad Plate—*EI*., XVIII, p. 110.

6 Sunaokalo plates of Mahāsāmanta Mahārāja Saṁganasiṁha (*EI*., XI, p. 74) dated A.D. 540. In the Barabar Hill inscription Anantavarman (*CII*, III, 48) calls Śārdūlavarman one of his ancestors the *cūḍāmaṇi* among *sāmantas*. Cf. Palitana plates dated A.D. 574 (*EI*.,

term *sāmanta* in the new sense. There may be some sense in a king claiming another king as his neighbour but none in a king calling himself a neighbour without indicating whose neighbour he was. By this time the term *sāmanta* had undergone a change of meaning, and indicated a state of subordination.[1]

Thus by a process of association the term *sāmanta*, which originally meant a neighbouring king, had come to be applied to those neighbouring kings who had been made subordinate.

There are facts, however, which show that these *sāmantas* were not petty nobles but rulers of considerable importance in their respective regions. Titles and terms indicating rulership are used.[2]

XI, 2 p. 18) of Sāmanta-mahārāja Siṁhāditya; inscriptions of the Gūrjara kings of Nāndīpurī (*Bhandarkar's list* Nos. 1209-1213); inscription of Mahāsāmanta Mahārāja Viṣṇuṣeṇa (A.D. 592) and Sāmanta Avanti (A.D. 605 or 676) (*IHQ.*, XXV, pp. 287-291), Rohtasgadh seal matrix of Śrīmahāsāmanta Śaśāṅkadeva (*CII*, III, 78); Nirmand Plates of Mahāsāmanta Mahārāja Samudrasena (ibid., 80).

1 In his two copper plates from Midnapore (*JRASBL.*, XI, pp. 1–9) as well as the inscriptions of the Śailodbhava kings of Orissa (*JAHRS.*, X, pp. 1–15) Śaśāṅka has been given full imperial titles. The Rohtasgadh seal indicates earlier times when Śaśāṅka was a subordinate ruler, no matter whether of Mahāsenagupta (*Classical Age*, p. 78) or of the Maukharis (*IHQ.*, XII, p. 457). The earlier rulers of the Maitraka family are referred to by the title of *Mahāsāmanta Mahārāja*. Sometime during the reign of Guhasena (A.D. 556–567) they discontinued the payment of allegiance to the Guptas. The Wala plates of the year A.D. 588 (*IA.*, VI, p. 11) mark the period of transition. Whereas in the text of the grant king Dharasena II is mentioned with his titles of *mahāsāmanta mahārāja* the royal signature towards the end of the plate contains the title of *mahādhirāja*. After some changes of fortune the dynasty emerges as completely sovereign under Dharasena IV, who ascended the throne in A.D. 644. This is indicated by the high title of *cakravarti* which he assumed.

2 The title of *mahārāja* for *sāmantas* is quite common (*IA.*, VII, p. 33; *EI.*, XI, p. 74, l. 18; *CII*, III, 80). The Nirmand Plates (ibid., 80) use *abhikhyātanarapativaṁśajaḥ* for Mahāsāmanta Samudrasena. Inscriptions and literary works in describing the feet of a sovereign as touched by the heads of defeated rulers employ for the latter *nṛpa* and *sāmanta* without any discrimination—*EI.*, XVIII, 27; XXVIII, 3, 34 (A and B); XXII, 6; XVII, 21; XIII, 9; XII, 17; XII, 10; IX, 28; VII, 13; *Gupta Inscriptions*, 40. *Pañcatantra* (Ryder tr.), pp. 12, 351; *Ibid.*, p. 120 (Hertel p. 102 f.); *Raghu*, IX, 13; IV, 88; *Vāsavadattā* (Gray tr.), p. 47, *Harṣacarita* (tr.), p. 59. The Mundesvari inscription (*EI.*, IX, 41) uses *rājye* for the kingdom of Mahāsāmanta Mahārāja Udayasena.

Instances of grants of villages and revenues by *sāmantas,* a royal prerogative, make it clear that *sāmantas* when making such grants exercised their rights as rulers. It appears that when rulers were defeated and made *sāmantas* or subordinate kings, their right to rule over their particular territories was not taken from them. They retained all their rights, powers and functions as kings,[1] only with the difference that they had to acknowledge the suzerainty of the overlord.

It appears that such subordinate neighbouring kings were regarded as having a status equal to that of a governor and were often reinstated in the territory which they already possessed. It was natural that, with the inclusion of a *sāmanta's* territory into a conqueror's empire, he should be treated as an officer governing a part of that empire. In the inscriptions[2] the list of officers to whom the grants are addressed includes *sāmanta* together with *rājā* before *kumārāmātya, viṣayapati* and *bhogika*. These references suggest that the *sāmantas* were treated as the officers of the state. Their being addressed even before governors and other high officers of the state indicates their status.[3]

A *sāmanta* was thus a ruler distinct alike from a sovereign king and from a governor. His emblems and other paraphernalia indicated this dual position of superiority over appointed governors and subordination to the Emperor. The use of the *pañcamahāśabdas* (the sound of five musical instruments) was an honour awarded to subordinate rulers by the sovereign king to indicate their privileged status.[4] Probably there were specific banners,

1 All those officers who are addressed in the grants of sovereign kings also find mention in the records of *Sāmanta* kings. Cf. the inscription of Sāmanta Viṣṇuṣeṇa which contains a list of rules according to which he governed his subjects (*JRASB.*, XVI, p. 11 f). These rules show that he exercised the same powers and had the same jurisdiction as any ruler might be expected to possess.

2 Badakhimedi plates of Indravarman (*EI.*, XXIII, 13); Bugude plates of Mādhavavarman (*EI.*, III, 6); Patiakella grant of Mahārāja Śivarāja (*EI.*, IX, 40); Kasare plates of Sendraka Nikumbhāllaśakti (*EI.*, XXVIII, 34 (B)); Tipperah grant of Lokanātha (*EI.*, XV, 19).

3 Cf. *EI.*, XVIII, 7—*Tatpādānudhyātaśrīsāmantanārāyaṇabhadrasyaudumvarīkaviṣayasambhogakāle.*

4 Baloda and Rajim grants of Tīvaradeva (*EI.*, VII, 13; *CII.*, III, p. 294 ff); Kasare plates of Sendraka Nikumbhāllaśakti and Ellora grant of Dantidurga. Cf. *EI.*, XXII, 15. Also *EI.*, XXVIII, 34 B; *EI.*, XXV,

umbrellas and horse-crests for a *sāmanta*, which the *sāmanta* could use only with the permission of his suzerain.[1]

Dr. V. S. Agrawala[2] thinks that a *sāmanta* was a vassal enjoying an approximate annual income of one lac of silver *kārṣapaṇas*. He bases his opinion on the list given in the *Śukranīti*,[3] which he regards as a work of the Gupta period. The account of the *Śukranīti* would mean that the *sāmantas* manned the entire administration and possessed all the land in the country. But this is not the picture we form of the Gupta period from other sources. It seems that the *Śukranīti* is not a unitary work. It was revised from time to time and data from different periods are combined in it. The references to guns and gunpowder[4] would make it a very late work.[5] Moreover, the word *sāmanta* is found at least in three instances in the works of Kālidāsa.[6] The meaning assigned by Dr. Agrawala ill suits these references. The contexts show that the term means neighbouring kings who had been subdued and made to pay *kara*.[7] Kālidāsa thus seems to belong to the transitional period when the term *sāmanta* was coming to mean a subordinate ruler in place of a neighbouring king. The *Mānasāra* also presents a picture different from that envisaged by Dr. Agrawala. The nine

---

p. 25; Tiwarkhed Plate of Nannarāja (*EI.*, XI, 27 (p. 279)). Baudh grant of Raṇabhañjadeva (*EI.*, XI, 36 (B)) and Sankheda grants of Dadda IV Praśāntarāga (*EI.*, V, 5); *EI.*, XII, 13. Cf. *IA.*, IX, p. 126—Vijayāditya Satyāśraya is said to have acquired for his father the tokens of the river Yamunā and the *pālidhvaja*, and the insignia of the *dhakkā* drum and the *mahāśabda*, and rubies and elephants.

1 In a Devagiri inscription dated A.D. 600 Mahāsāmantādhipati Śāntivarman who had acquired the *pañcamahāśabdas* is said to have employed the *Nandanavana* umbrella, the horse crest and the mirror banner (*EI.*, XI, p. 6). The inscription is undoubtedly spurious. But as it has nothing irreconcilable with the known history of the region for its true period (*EI.*, XI, pp. 3–4) the information may be utilized as it is in line with other references in the inscriptions of this period.

2 *Harṣacarita*, p. 219.

3 I, 365–384. B. Prasad, *Theory of Government in Ancient India*, p. 252.

4 IV, 7, 389–418.

5 After writing this paper the author came to the conclusion that the *Śukranīti* was a work of the 19th century. His views are published in *BSOAS.*, xxv, 524–56, which see for earlier theories on the date of text.

6 *Raghu*, V, 28; VI, 33; *Vikramorvaśī*, III, 19.

7 The commentary of Mallinātha also derives the term *sāmantānāṁ* as *samantādbhavānāṁ rājñām*.

ranks of kings enumerated in the *Mānasāra*[1] are the *cakravartin, mahārāja, narendra, pākṣaṇika, paṭṭadhara, maṇḍaleśa, paṭṭabhaj, prahāraka* and *astragraha. Sāmanta* does not find a place in this list, though if *sāmanta* meant to the author of the *Mānasāra* what it signified to Śukra, he would have included it. If *sāmanta* meant at the time a neighbouring king then its omission from the *Manasāra* list is easily explained. Another negative argument of great importance is the omission of the term *sāmanta* from dictionaries compiled during this period. To Amarasiṃha *sāmanta* had no technical or special meaning to deserve a separate mention. The word *sāmanta*, however, does occur at one place in the *Amarakośa*: '*rājā tu praṇatāśeṣasāmantaḥ syādadhīśvaraḥ cakravartī sārvabhaumaḥ...*'[2] The context shows that here the *Amarakośa* mentions not a series of grades of rulership but two types of rulers. A *cakravartī* is one who has defeated all kings and established his universal sovereignty: a *rājā* is one who has established his claim over his territory by defeating neighbouring kings. The meaning of *sāmanta* as neighbouring king has the sanction of the different commentaries on the *Amarakośa*.[3] The word cannot be traced in the *Anekārthasamuccaya* of Śāśvata, who has been assigned to a period about the end of the sixth and the beginning of the seventh century A.D.[4]

What was responsible for neighbouring kings being reduced to the status of subordinate kings and governors? I would ascribe it to the working of the peculiar Indian doctrine of *dharmavijaya*. This discouraged the annexation of a conquered territory but recommended the acceptance of subordination by the defeated king. It was not a principle of purely academic interest, but seems to have actually been followed.[5] This tendency is very old and deep-rooted in the Indian tradition. The word *samrāj* occurring several times in the *Ṛgveda*[6] implies a suzerain with many kings

1 XLII, 2–5 ff. The list also appears elsewhere in connection with the description of crowns (ch. XLIX), thrones (ch. XLV), etc.

2 II, 8, 2.

3 Cf. Bhanuji Dikshit (p. 447)—*Saṁlagno'nta ekadeśo'syāḥ samantāyāḥ svadeśavyavahitabhūmerime rājānaḥ, praṇatā aśeṣāḥ sāmantāḥ svadeśānantararājā yasya,.*

4 K.G. Oka in his Introduction p. vi.

5 Cf. the observation of Sulaiman the Arab merchant—Elliot and Dowson Vol. I, p. 7.

6 *Vedic Index*, II, 433.

under him. The terms *rājya*, *sāmrājya*, *bhaujya*, *svārājya*, *vairājya*, *pāramasthya*, *māhārājya*, *ādhipatya* and *svāvasya* in the *Aitareya Brāhmaṇa*[1] seem to refer to gradations of sovereignty. The *Aitareya Brāhmaṇa*[2] describes the dominion of a *samrāṭ* as extending right up to the natural boundaries, up to the very ends. The description suggests that the *samrāṭ* exercised suzerainty and not actual administration over such a large dominion. This notion of an empire follows even from the descriptions of the details connected with the four royal sacrifices known as the *Aindra Mahābhiṣeka*, *Aśvamedha*, *Rājasūya* and *Vājapeya*.[3] These sacrifices suggest some claims of superiority by their performer. The *Śrauta sūtra* literature[4] also reveals the difference between *rājya* and *sāmrājya*.

The policy of *dharmavijaya* or *digvijaya* is to be compared with *lobhavijaya* or *asuravijaya*. The former type of conquest was not accompanied by territorial aggrandisement or the annihilation of the conquered king, but only aimed at establishing a general suzerainty over powers subdued. The two *digvijayas* of Duryodhana and Yudhiṣṭhira described in the *Mahābhārata* did not result in the annexation of the defeated territories. The *Rājasūya* performed by Yudhiṣṭhira at the end of his conquest was attended by the kings acquiescing in subordination.[5]

A similar policy of *dhammavijaya* is advocated in the Buddhist texts. Kings accept the suzerainty of the righteous conqueror impelled by his peity and religious superiority. All other details resemble the Brahmanical view. Even according to the Buddhist theory the conquest and the consequent subordination are real. Here also the sovereign allows the subdued king to enjoy his territory as before.[6] The theory was evidently a norm from which there were many deviations,[7] but the principle of *dharmavijaya* was always there.[8]

Aśoka, in his inscriptions, detailed a policy of *dhammavijaya*

1 VII, 3, 14; VIII, 12, 4–5; VIII, 14, 2–3.
2 VIII, 4, 1.
3 Cf. *Aitareya Br.*, XXXIX, *Śatapatha Br.*, IX, 3, 4, 8; V, 1, 1, 3, 13–14.
4 B. Prasad, *State in Ancient India*, p. 59 f.
5 *Mbh.*, II, 45. Also II, 25, 3; II, 5; XV, 6, 16; III, 25.
6 *Dīgha*, III, p. 62 f—*Yathābhuttañca bhuñjathā ti.*
7 *Jātaka*, III, 13, 116, 153; V, 425.
8 *Jātaka*, V. p. 316.

which he enjoined his successors to follow.[1] His ideal of righteous conquest amounted to gaining influence in neighbouring lands by creating trust and bestowing happiness.[2] In Rock Edict XIII[3] Aśoka describes his *dhammavijaya* among his neighbouring States in terms of spreading his 'ordinances based upon the Law of Piety and his instruction in the law'. The Rock Edict II[4] refers to the healing arrangements made by Aśoka in these neighbouring countries.

This principle also received the sanction of the Smṛtis.[5] The *Arthaśāstra* differentiates between *dharmavijaya* and *lobhavijaya* or *asuravijaya*. A *dharmavijayī* was satisfied with mere obeisance or surrender on the part of the conquered.[6]

The theory finds elaborate expression in the works of Kālidāsa, who seems to regard universal dominion as the highest goal of kingship. His *Raghuvaṁśa* and *Mālavikāgnimitra* describe the performance of the horse sacrifice. The *Raghuvaṁśa*[7] has a detailed account of the conquest of all regions at the hands of Raghu. But nowhere is Raghu said to have attempted the annexation of conquered territory. The passage in the *Raghuvaṁśa*,[8] stating that Raghu deprived Mahendra of his glory but did not rob him of his territory, though brief, is the best description of the policy of *dharmavijaya*.

This is not to imply that there were no instances of military conquest in ancient India. The Buddhist canonical works reveal the existence of four great kingdoms in the Buddha's time.[9] The growth of the Magadha empire reveals a gradual process of conquest and assimilation of different States into one unity. The *Purāṇas* in describing Mahāpadmananda as *sarvakṣatrāntaka*

1 Cf. reference to Śāliśuka in the *Gārgisaṁhitā* (*JBORS.*, IV, p. 261)—*sthāpayiṣyati mohātmā vijayaṁ nāma dhārmikam.* This ideal has to be interpreted in line with the Buddhist view of a *cakkavatti* described in the *Cakkavatti Sīhanāda Sutta* as consisting of conquest not by the sword, but by righteousness—*Dialogues of the Buddha*, Part III, p. 59.

2 Separate Kaliṅga Edict II—*Select Inscriptions*, p. 46.

3 *Ibid.*, p. 37.

4 *Ibid.*, p. 18.

5 *Manu*, VII, 202; *Viṣṇu*, III, 30.

6 *Artha*, XII, 1.

7 Ch. IV.

8 IV, 43.

9 Cf. Raychaudhuri, *Political History*, p. 199 ff.

refer to this change in Indian polity which, though enunciated by Magadhan powers in particular, was gradually adopted by a number of powerful kingdoms that arose in India in the subsequent centuries.

But references to the performance of *Aśvamedha* reveal that the original ideal of a paramount empire was always there. The *Śatapatha Brāhmaṇa*[1] enumerates kings who performed the *Aśvamedha* sacrifice. Puṣyamitra Śuṅga, who founded an empire on the ruins of the Maurya dynasty, is said to have performed two *Aśvamedha* sacrifices.[2] The Nanaghat Cave inscription of Nāganikā[3] refers to Gautamīputra Sātakarṇi as performing two such sacrifices though the account of one sacrifice has been lost. Other historical kings who performed these sacrifices are Pārāśarīputra Sarvatāta,[4] Vāsiṣṭiputra Śrīcāṁtamūla Ikṣvāku,[5] Śivaskandvarman Pallava,[6] Kṛṣṇavarman Kadamba,[7] Devavarman, Śālaṅkāyana,[8] and the Vākāṭaka king Pravarasena.[9] The Nāga kings also are said to have performed *Aśvamedha* sacrifices.[10] The Poona Plates of the Vākāṭaka queen Prabhāvatīguptā[11] and the *Aśvamedhaparākrama* coins of Samudragupta[12] clearly establish that Samudragupta also performed a horse-sacrifice.[13]

The Allahabad Pillar inscription[14] reveals Samudragupta as following this ideal. No doubt he uprooted many petty States in northern India and created a consolidated empire. But this policy of suppression was not applied in the case of the kings of southern

---

1 XIII, 5, 4, 1–23.

2 Cf. *Senāpateḥ Puṣyamitrasya dviraśvamedhayājinaḥ—Select Inscriptions*, p. 96; *Mālavikāgnimitra; Harivaṁśa*, III, 2, 40; *Iha Puṣyamitraṁ yājayāmaḥ*— Patañjali (*IA.*, 1872, p. 300).

3 *Select Inscriptions*, p. 186 ff.

4 *Ibid.*, p. 91.

5 *Age of Imperial Unity*, p. 224.

6 *Select Inscriptions*, p. 437.

7 *Classical Age*, p. 272.

8 *Ibid.*, p. 205.

9 *Select Inscriptions*, pp. 407, 419.

10 *Ibid.*, p. 419.

11 *Ibid.*, p. 412.

12 Allan, *Gupta Coins*, p. 21 ff.

13 Cf. Allan, *Gupta Coins*, p. xxxi and *JRAS.*, 1901, p. 102 for a seal and a stone figurine suggesting this *Aśvamedha*.

14 *Select Inscriptions*, p. 254 ff.

India and of the five kingdoms and nine tribal territories located on the borders of his kingdom. Of these the inscription specifically calls the five kingdoms *pratyantas*. The relations of Samudragupta with certain foreign States on the border throw welcome light on the status of subordinate kings. These States are described as serving him by personal visits, offers of daughters in marriage and requests for charters confirming the possession of their territory. For defeated kings would appear to have been reinstated in their kingdoms by a royal charter. These charters did not create any new rulership. Whereas formerly a king ruled in his own right, as a subordinate he required a charter issued in his favour.

A study of the nature of the Gupta empire reveals that it was largely formed by States subdued in pursuance of the policy of righteous conquest. The Allahabad pillar inscription suggests that the Sanakānikas had been subordinated. But the Udayagiri cave inscription[1] records the grant of a cave by a certain Sanakānika Mahārāja. This shows that subordinate neighbouring States were allowed to exist. We find many ruling dynasties existing even within the boundaries of the Gupta empire.[2] In Malwa, for instance, ruled a dynasty to which belonged Jayavarman, Siṁhavarman and Naravarman[3] and probably also Viśvavarman of the Gangdhar stone inscription[4] and Bandhuvarman mentioned in the Mandasor stone inscription of Kumāragupta.[5] Again in the Bundelkhand region we find the dynasties of the Parivrājakas and the Uccakalpas ruling as subordinate kings. The brief notices of Hsuan Ṭsang about the political status of the different States visited by him suggest that this form of empire had become the order of the day. He refers to several countries as having no

1 *Select Inscriptions*, p. 271.

2 Cf. the picture in Kālidāsa—B.S. Upadhyaya, *India in Kālidāsa*, p. 114. It is this characteristic of the Gupta empire which B. Prasad (*State in Ancient India*, p. 285 ff) describes by calling it a feudal-federal organization. But here the terms feudal and federal are to be used only in a restricted sense. The empire was a federal organization only in the sense that it comprised a number of states. Likewise the empire cannot properly be called feudal in character because *sāmantas* in India denoted a class of rulers and not of landlords.

3 *Ibid.*, p. 377 ff.

4 *Ibid.*, p. 379 ff.

5 *Ibid.*, p. 288 ff.

independent rulers but as being dependencies of some other country.[1]

During the later years of Gupta rule the process seems to have been reversed. Now the governors, with the growth of their power, began claiming to be *sāmantarājas*.[2] The Maitrakas provide the most clear picture of this process of transformation. In the records of this dynasty its first two members have the title of *senāpati*, suggesting for them the status of military officers appointed to rule the region. But the subsequent members of the family are styled *mahārājas* or *mahāsāmantarājas*. Another instance of this process comes from Orissa. Here Somadatta, an officer of Śaśāṅka, originally ruled as governor.[3] Later we find this very Somadatta ruling the provinces of Utkala and Daṇḍabhukti as *sāmanta-mahārāja*.[4]

There were both bigger and smaller *sāmantas*, differentiated by the terms *mahāsāmanta* and *sāmanta*.[5] The bigger *sāmantas* had a privileged position at the court. Their words carried weight and could not be lightly brushed aside.[6] Some bigger *sāmantas* appear to have had their own *sāmantas*.[7] In the inscriptions of the medieval period these big *sāmantas* are called *mahāsāmantādhipati*.[8] The smaller *sāmanta* was subordinate to a bigger one, who, in his turn, accepted the suzerainty of the emperor.[9]

---

1 Cf. *Si-yu-ki* I, pp. 90, 91, 98, 136, 143, 163; II, 193, 268 f, 274, 275, 276.

2 Whereas during the reign of Kumāragupta, the Governor of Puṇḍravardhana was called *uparika*, in the inscriptions from the time of Budhagupta onwards, he assumes the title of *uparika-mahārāja*—*Select Inscriptions*, pp. 284, 295, 324, 328, 338.

3 *EI*., XXIII, 32 (B and C).

4 *JRASB*. (L), XI, p. 7 f.

5 *Mahāsāmantaśrīsāmanta* in the list of officers addressed to in grants—*EI*., XXIII, 13; III, 6; XV, 19; XXVIII, 41.

6 *Harṣacarita*, p. 153—*Anatikramaṇāvacanairupasṛtya pradhānasāmantair vijñāpyamānaḥ*.

7 Cf. the expression *samatikkrāntakīrttiranekasāmantottamāṅgāvanatamukuṭamaṇimayūkhavicchūritacaraṇāravindayugalaḥ* applied to Mahāsāmantamahārāja Śrīvaruṇasena—*Gupta Inscriptions*, 80. Some of the grants of our period made by *sāmantas* are also addressed, among others, to their own *sāmantas*.

8 Cf. *EI*., XII, 31. The term is mentioned in the spurious inscription from Devagiri dated A.D. 600 (*EI*., XI, 1, p. 6).

9 Thus the Maitrakas had their own *sāmantas* (*EI*., XI, 17—the Gārulaka family). See also Eran stone pillar inscription of the time of Budha-

The nature of the relation between the subordinate and sovereign states depended upon the comparative strength and size of the two states. A *sāmanta* king paid his allegiance only as long as the suzerain was powerful. On the least sign of the weakness of the empire the *sāmantas* tried to shake off the subordination. The *sāmantas* were always on the lookout to declare their independence and the paramount power had to bring them to submission from time to time. It was the fear of the might of the paramount lord that kept them loyal.[1]

The *sāmantas* used to accompany the emperor in his wars. Rājyavardhana, when he went to meet the Hūṇas, is said to have been attended by his devoted *sāmantas*.[2] Bāṇa, on first meeting Harṣa at the camp in the village of Maṇitārā, found a large number of the *sāmantas* of the enemy kings[3] who fighting for their overlords were defeated and captured.

---

gupta—*Select Inscriptions*, p. 326 f. Pṛthivīvigraha ruling over Kaliṅga under the suzerainty of the Guptas had Mahārāja Dharmarāja as his subordinate (*IHQ*., XXVI, p. 75).

1 The inscriptions of the Parivrājakas (*Gupta Inscriptions*, 21–23; *EI*., XXI, 20), the Uccakalpas (*Gupta Inscriptions*, 26, 27) and Mahārājas Lakṣmaṇa (*EI*., II, p. 364; *ASI*., 1936-7, p.88) and Subandhu (*EI*., XIX, 44) have only a very veiled reference to their overlords the Guptas. Cf. the early history of the Maukharis, the Vardhanas and the Aulikaras. The inscription of king Mānadeva of Nepal (Indraji No. 1) describes how subordinate rulers used to raise the banner of revolt at the first sign of confusion after the death of the sovereign king. Prabhākaravardhana is compared with Mandāra for churning, like an ocean, the whole ring of feudatories drunk with the intoxication of valourous frenzy (*Harṣacarita*, p. 155). The inscriptions also almost invariably refer to kings as having subdued their *sāmantas* by their might (*EI*., XXIII, 15; XII, 13, 7; VI, 29; IX, 45; XXVI, 5A; IX, 50; VIII, 24) or won them over by the pre-eminence of their three-fold powers (*EI*., XXIII, 42A; XV, 14; XXVI, 23). It was a common belief that the *sāmantas* remained loyal only through fear of the might of the sovereign. The Aihole inscription of Pulakeśin (*EI*., VI, 17) remarks that the Lāṭas, Mālavas and Gūrjaras subdued by Pulakeśin's splendour became as it were teachers of how *sāmantas*, subdued by force, ought to behave.

2 *Harṣa*, p. 121. The Aihole inscription of Pulakeśin II in referring to the defeat inflicted by Pulakeśin on Harṣa describes Harṣa's feet as arrayed with the rays of the jewels of the diadems of hosts of feudatories prosperous with unmeasured might (*EI*., VI, 1). It is likely that Harṣa's army was swelled by contingents of soldiers supplied by his *sāmantas*.

3 *Ibid*., p. 74.

The *sāmantas* had to pay the sovereign lord certain dues.[1] But the references do not reveal the nature of these *karas*.[2] Was a fixed sum paid annually or periodically, had the paramount sovereign the right to extort as much money as possible, or was the *sāmanta* merely expected to pay something in the nature of a present? We cannot establish if the king went out to collect this sum from the *sāmantas* or if the *sāmantas* paid it at the time when they presented themselves at the court.

One of the duties of the *sāmantas* was to report at the court personally, and to win the favour of the king by personal service. References, both epigraphic and literary, often describe the feet of sovereign kings as being coloured by the rays from the gems in the crowns of *sāmanta* kings as they bowed down to reverence the feet of their overlord.[3] The ways in which a *sāmanta* performed obeisance and personal service are elaborated best in the passage[4] where Harṣa, after resolving to conquer all the kings, commanded them either to become his vassals or to be prepared to fight. The *sāmantas* had to wave chowries and with staff in hand to serve as doorkeepers. There were many forms of obeisance. Sometimes the *sāmanta* simply joined his palms; at others he bowed his head. Or he might touch the feet of the king with his head. Or he might put the dust of the king's feet upon his own head. The passage also refers to the payment of taxes by defeated and subdued kings. The *sāmantas* were also required to obey the orders of the king. As their husbands served the king, so the wives of the *sāmantas* had to serve the queen. In the *Harṣacarita*[5] Queen Yaśovatī claims that she used to be bathed in water by the wives of countless *sāmantas*.

---

1 In the *Harṣacarita* (p. 74) king Puṣyabhūti is said to have made the *sāmantas*, defeated by the might of his arm, pay taxes.

2 *Pañcatantra*, I (tr.) p. 85—the envoys from King Valour, monarch of the south, go to collect yearly tribute from the king of the Sugar-cane city but on not receiving the customary honour, grow indignant and remark, "Come, king! Payday is past, why have you failed to offer the taxes due".

3 Cf. *Kathākośa*, p. 136—*Tatra rājñaḥ samīpe sevākaraṇārthaṁ sāmanta-mahāsāmantaśrīkaraṇavyayakaraṇapramukhasabheṣūpasthiteṣu.*

4 *Harṣacarita*, p. 168 f. The *Harṣacarita* has many references to the presence of *sāmantas* in the capital or at the court—*Ibid*., pp. 121, 126, 144, 156.

5 p. 140.

Thus a *sāmantarāja*, even if allowed to rule his own territory, had often to visit the court to attend upon the king. Some *sāmantas* resided permanently at the court. Economically unproductive, they formed an idle and worthless class. Bāṇa in his *Kādambarī*[1] paints a lively picture of thousands of subordinate crowned kings (*mūrdhābhiṣiktena sāmantalokena*), seated in the assembly hall of a palace. 'Some were playing at dice; some were practising the game of chess; some were playing on the seven-stringed *parivādinī* lute; some were conversing about poems; some were indulging in jocular talk; some were making out the syllables corresponding to the dots of *bindumatī*; some solving the poetical riddles known as the *prahelikās*; some considering the fine sayings in the poems composed by His Majesty; some reciting stanzas in the *Dvipadī* metre; some praising or appreciating the merits of poets; some busy drawing ornamental decorations on the ground; some talking with the numerous courtesans present there; and some listening to the songs of the bards.' But there were also some *sāmantas* who occupied administrative posts.[2] How did these two classes of *sāmantas*—one doing nothing productive and enjoying the luxuries of the court and the other holding offices under the sovereign come to exist? Perhaps the term *sāmanta* now denoted a mere honorific title; certain *sāmantas* may have become bankrupt and come to the court, where they received maintenance; or perhaps the title of *sāmanta* was claimed not only by direct successors but also by collaterals, from which group people went to the court to eke out a living, as their own petty States were not sufficient to hold them all.[3] The meagre data does not warrant a conclusive solution of the problem. Some *sāmanta* rulers may have been reduced to a

---

1 pp. 193–4.

2 In some records a *sāmanta* appears as the *dūtaka* of the grant made by a king (*Select Inscriptions*, p. 333 f; *JBBRAS*., I, 5, p. 24; I, 17 p. 57; *EI*., VII, 22). In the Madhuban grant of Harṣa, Sāmanta Skandagupta and Sāmanta Īśvaragupta appear respectively as *mahāpramatāra* and *mahākṣapaṭalādhikaraṇādhikṛta*—*EI*., VII, 22. Cf. *bhāṇḍāgārādhikṛtamahāsāmanta-Divākaraprabhaḥ*—*EI*., XII, 13. The Mundesvari inscription of Mahārāja Udayasena (*EI*., IX, 41) calls him both *mahāsāmanta* and *mahāpratihāra*. The Sarangarh grant mentions a Mahāsāmanta Indrabalarāja as the *sarvādhikārādhikṛta* of king Sudevarāja of Śarabhapura—*EI*., IX, 39. Cf. *EI*., XXIII, 13; XVIII, 32.

3 Cf. the reference *mahāsandhivigrahiśrīsāmantasūnunā Khaṇḍena*—*EI*. XXIII, 42(A).

pitiable condition, having exhausted their resources in extravagant luxuries; but whether this was common we cannot be sure. About the other two possibilities unless relevant evidence is available nothing definite can be said. It has to be realized that such offices were often sinecures, in the nature of an honour conferred by the king. Even *sāmantas* actually ruling their respective kingdoms have been found in charge of some office, obviously under the sovereign king.[1] Such offices would then appear to have shown the suzerain's appreciation of the loyalty of a *sāmanta*.

In medieval times *sāmanta* no doubt denoted a chieftain or noble having the right to enjoy a certain fixed income.[2] The *Kathāsaritsāgara*[3] refers often to individuals being made *sāmantas* by kings who gave them villages, gold, umbrellas and vehicles. Sometimes the king, becoming displeased with *sāmantas*, dismissed them and appointed others in their place.[4] So it is clear that *sāmantas* were no longer a class of subordinate rulers, but virtually a class of privileged nobles enjoying landed properties.[5] Such a class depended upon the goodwill of the king. The references in Baṇa and a passage of the *Mālatīmādhava*[6] to the feet of the minister Bhūrivasu as coloured by the pollen of the flowers in the crest-chaplets of many a *sāmanta* indicate that the tendency towards a further change in the meaning of the term had started in the 7th century. *Sāmanta* in the *Mālatīmādhava* would appear to represent the period when the term was coming to mean a chieftain. The practice of some *sāmantas* residing at the imperial court with permanent mansions at the capital[7] suggests that the new development had already begun.

---

1 The Mundesvari inscription of Udayasena refers to his reign and also describes him both as *mahāsāmanta* and *mahāpratihāra*—*EI.*, IX, 41. Also see Kanas Plate of Bhānudatta—*EI.*, XXVIII, 51 (B).

2 *Aparājitapṛcchā* of Bhuvanadeva, LXIX, 35–44; LXXVIII, 3–7, 32–34; LXXXI, 1–4.

3 XVIII, 126–130; XXX, 137-138; XLIX, 61–62; LIII, 72.

4 XLII, 115.

5 Cf. *Rājataraṅgiṇī* (ed. Pandit), V, 250—the ministers, *sāmantas*, *tantrins* and *ekāṅgas* assemble to invest some fit person with the regal power. See also III, 232; IV, 556, 643; V, 224, 343, 355, 395.

6 VI, p. 77—*Iyamaśeṣasāmantamastakottaṁsaparāgarañjitacaraṇāṅguleramātyabhūrivasoḥ*. Cf. also *Harṣacarita*, p. 205 for a reference to an *āṭavikasāmanta*; *EI.*, XV, 19—grant made to a brāhmaṇa *mahāsāmanta*.

7 Cf. *Bṛhatsaṁhitā*, LIII, 8—*Nṛpasacivāntaratulyaṁ sāmantapravararājapuruṣāṇām. Nṛpayuvarājaviśeṣaḥ kañcukiveśyākalājñānam.*

APPENDIX II

TECHNIQUE OF AGRICULTURE

Irrigation and Rains:

The responsibility of the king to provide for irrigational facilities in his kingdom is traditional and very old in origin. The failure of rains was often ascribed to some sin or fault on the part of the king. Medhātithi[1] says that it is the nature of the rainy season that there should be rain, and yet, on account of the faulty action, either of the king or of the kingdom itself, there is sometime drought. It was as a result of this notion that the kings undertook the excavations of wells, tanks and canals. The *Aparājitapṛcchā*[2] advises that crops should be protected for maintaining the kingdom, and that water reservoirs should be provided for the crops. It was the recognition of the practical importance of irrigational works which led Lakṣmīdhara, the Gāhaḍavāla minister, to defy conventional notions and class such works of public utility separately under *dāna* and not under *iṣṭāpūrta* and ascribe them a high spiritual efficacy. It was a change of real significance and the lead has been followed by subsequent writers on the subject.[3]

The most remarkable irrigational project implying ingenious engineering skill comes from Kashmir and belongs to the reign of king Avantivarman. Under him the minister Suyya dammed the river Vitastā (Jhelum) to save Kashmir from devastating floods of the Mahāpadma lake. Suyya deepened the bed of the Vitastā at its two ends, cleaned the river bed at its bottom after constructing a temporary stone dam at all threatened points, and built protective stone embankments for seven *yojanas* along the river bank. Thus, he was able to shift the junction of the Vitastā and the Sindhu from its old to its existing position. On the land raised

1 On Manu, I, 30.

2 p. 186, v. 9—*Rājyārthaṃ dhāryate śasyaṃ śasyārtham tu jalāśayaḥ.*

3 K.V.R. Aiyangar in his Introduction (p. 114) to the *Dānakāṇḍa* of the *Kṛtyakalpataru.*

from the water he founded many villages protected by circular dykes and constructed extensive projects. Kalhaṇa notices the prosperity resulting from the work and showers unstinted praise on the great engineer.[1] Another king of Kashmir, Lalitāditya Muktāpīḍa reclaimed many hitherto water-logged areas by making an arrangement at Cakradhara for conducting the water of the Vitastā and, by constructing a series of water-wheels, distributing it to various villages.[2] King Harṣa excavated the big Pampā lake, identified by Stein with the modern Pamba Sar.[3]

We find king Kelhaṇa of the Naḍḍula branch of the Cāhamānas and Ajayasiṃha, a son of his feudatory, constructing wells.[4] A sister of Pūrṇapāla, a Paramāra ruler of Abu, also claims to have constructed tanks.[5] Bhoja, the Paramāra king, also appears to have been energetic in building reservoirs.[6]

The Caulukyas of Gujarat have many important irrigational works to their credit. It would appear that even the first king of the dynasty, Mūlarāja I, paid due attention to irrigation. Śrīdhara in his *praśasti* claims that one of his ancestors was appointed by Mūlarāja I to dig *vāpis*, wells and tanks.[7] From the *Prabandhacintāmaṇi* we learn that Udayamatī, the queen of Bhīma I, excavated a very large reservoir at Pattana.[8] According to popular tradition the step-well known as *Rāṇī-kī-vav* also owes its construction to this queen.[9] Merutuṅga credits her son king Karṇa with the excavation of a large tank called Karṇasāgara.[10] Mayaṇalladevī, the wife of king Karṇa, is generally regarded as having excavated the still-existing Mansar lake at Viramgam.[11] But

1 *Rāj.*, V, 84–121.
2 *ibid.*, IV, 191.
3 *ibid.*, VII, 940.
4 *D.H.N.I.*, II, p. 1119.
5 *E.I.*, IX, p. 15.
6 *I.A.*, XVII, pp. 350–2.
7 *E.I.*, II, 438. Cf. *P.I.H.C.*, VII, p. 643 for the grant of an *arghaṭṭa* by king Bhīma II.
8 p. 54, 11. 3-4.
9 A.K. Majumdar, *Chaulukyas of Gujarat*, pp. 389, 390. Cf. Burgess and Cousens, *Architectural Antiquities of Northern Gujarat*, p. 112 for a description of the *vav* of Vyad.
10 *Prabandhacintāmaṇi* (Tawney), p. 78. Cf. Forbes, *Rās Mālā*, 1, 104.
11 *A.S.W.I.*, VIII, ii, 91.

tradition reserves the highest praise for the Sahasraliṅga lake built by Siddharāja.[1] Archaeology testifies to the high engineering skill employed in this irrigational project. The lake received water from the river Sarasvatī with which it was connected by a 300 ft. long channel. Excavations have revealed stone sluices through which also water was conducted to the lake.[2] The *Prabandha-cintāmaṇi* informs us that Tejapāla, the minister of king Vīradhavala, also had to his credit the construction of many tanks.[3]

The extant records indicate that under the Kalacuris many feudatories and ministers excavated tanks and wells. Thus, Malayasiṃha, a feudatory, is reported to have dug a tank in A.D. 1192.[4] *Rāuta* Vallāladevaka, another feudatory, excavated a water channel.[5] We likewise read of the digging of tanks and wells in the Raipur-Bilaspur area by the Tuṃmāna Kalacuri feudatory Brahmadeva[6] and ministers Puruṣottama[7] and Gaṅgādhara.[8] In the Berar region we find Gamiyaya, a minister of king Hemādrideva, excavating a tank and a well.[9]

A number of tanks existing even to this day bear eloquent testimony to the concern of the Candella kings for irrigation facilities. Rahilya Sagar, Kirat Sagar (1½ miles in circumference), Madanasagar (3 miles in circuit), Vijayasagar and Kalyansagar have been ascribed respectively to Rahila, Kīrtivarman, Madanavarman, Vijayapāla and Kalyāṇadevī. A tank in Ajayagadh is said to have been excavated by Paramardi.[10] In the Khajuraho inscription dated 1011 of the Vikrama era we read of the construction of embankments to divert the course of a river.[11]

---

1 *Sarasvatī Purāṇa*, XVI, 212; *Dvyāśrayakāvya*, XV, 120-21; cf. *P.I.H.C.*, 1939, p. 479 for other references.

2 A.S. Gadre, *Archaeology in Baroda*, 1934 47, p. 8. See *Annual Reports Baroda State*, 1934–35, p. 18 for an epigraphic reference to the water of the river Sarasvatī having been canalised to fill up the lake.

3 p. 99, 1.27.

4 *E.I.*, XIX, 298 f.

5 *I.A.*, XVIII, 213.

6 *E.I.*, XXVI, 262.

7 *ibid.*, XXVII, 283.

8 *ibid.*, XXI, 164.

9 *ibid.*, XXI, 132.

10 *I.A.*, XXXVII, 132; *A.S.R.*, II, 439 f referred to by N.S. Bose, *History of the Candellas*, p. 147.

11 *E.I.*, I, 122, v. 26.

Śrīharṣa refers to the charitable provisions for wells etc. made by the hero of the *Naiṣadhīyacarita.*[1] Paṇḍita Dāmodara, associated with the Gāhaḍavāla court, refers in his *Uktivyaktiprakaraṇa* not only to the cleaning of wells[2] and digging of tanks[3] but also to a state official named Sūrapāla supervising the digging of a tank, his head shaded by an umbrella.[4] This reference is in line with what we have for the reign of king Mūlarāja I of the Caulukya dynasty and indicates that the Caulukya kings were not alone in commissioning officers to dig wells and tanks in their kingdoms. Lakṣmīdhara, the minister, lauding the merit of constructing a special type of reservoir called *dvārībandha*, observes that the merit which accrues from the Vedic sacrifices of the cow, man and the horse, is excelled by that accruing from the construction of such a dam.[5] *Dvārībandha* means the damming of a mountain spring and thus forming a high level reservoir useful for irrigation. Where the bund is a long one sluice gates are to be provided for draining of excess water.[6] On the basis of the suggestion of Lakṣmīdhara that flights of steps may be built into it, and gardens and temples near the bund K. V. R. Aiyangar[7] rightly says that the description seems to be based on an irrigation dam actually existing at the time.

Gaṅgādhara, a minister of king Rudramāna, is said to have excavated a tank in the Gaya district of Bihar.[8] The *Rāmapāla-carita*[9] refers to the reservoirs constructed by king Rāmapāla. In the *Pavanadūta* we find a mention of an embankment that commemorated king Vallālasena. The Bhuvanesvar inscription records the excavation of a tank by Bhaṭṭa Bhavadeva, the minister of Harivarman, and refers to the advantage resulting therefrom.[10]

Besides these irrigation works which owed their construction

1 *E.I.*, IV, 310.
2 p. 46, 1.14.
3 p. 49, 1.22.
4 p. 21, 11.15-16.
5 *Kṛtyakalpataru, Dānakāṇḍa*, p. 296.
6 *ibid.*, p. 292.
7 *ibid.*, introduction pp. 116-17.
8 E.I., II, 338.
9 III, 42, p. 108.
10 *Inscriptions of Bengal*, III, p. 40.

to the state, there must have been many others built by private individuals. Digging of wells and tanks has been propagated in India as a charitable work of merit. We have many records testifying to the actual hold of this precept on the Indian masses. Well-to-do persons such as merchants built tanks and wells to reap the merit accruing from them. If we make allowance for cases in which the patrons of such works did not care to have their memory recorded on lasting material, and also for many more, records of which have been lost or not recovered so far, we can form an idea of the extent of charitable work of this type. In the mathematical text *Līlāvatī* we have a whole section devoted to the problem of measuring an excavation (*khāta-vyavahāra*),[1] which must have been included because of its practical importance for the excavation of reservoirs.[2] Hemacandra mentions *uḍḍo* as the term for a man who digs wells etc.[3] The *Upavana-vinoda* has a separate section for the examination of the soil where wells can be dug.[4] In the *Agnipurāṇa* we have a list of asterisms auspicious for the excavation of tanks.[5]

That there were tanks and wells in the villages follows also from the land-grants of the period, which, in enumerating the boundaries of fields or villages granted, often mention canals, tanks, wells and embankments.[6]

Recognising the importance of irrigational works the *Agnipurāṇa* says that for forts and fortified cities that land is to be preferred which does not depend upon rains but has at its disposal water (in the form of reservoirs etc.).[7] The *Aparājitapṛcchā* says that famines do not visit the land where crops grow even with a little rain, that crops grow quickly if people have reserves of water with them or have built reservoirs, and that he who has collected water has achieved all his ends.[8] Medhātithi explains the term

1 pp. 93–95, nos. 217–23.

2 p. 94, no. 222.

3 *Deśīnāmamālā*, I, 85.

4 pp. 77–81, vv. 94–146—*Kūpārtham bhūmiparīkṣā.*

5 CCLXXXII, 5-6.

6 See, for example, Mitra, *Early Rulers of Khajuraho*, p. 180—*nālā, puṣkariṇī, bhiti;* Barua, *Cultural History of Assam*, p. 70—*gaṅgīnikā, jala, garta, ḍobā.*

7 CCXII, 2—*Adevamātṛko bhaktajalo deśaḥ praśasyate.*

8 p. 188, vv. 32-33, 40.

sasyapradā (fertile) as productive of rich harvests and not dependent entirely upon rain.[1]

The *Mānasollāsa* enumerates nine kinds of water according to the source.[2] The *Aparājitapṛcchā* mentions rivers, streams, wells, *vāpīs*, tanks, river-dams, machine-wells and canals as the usual means of irrigation.[3] Of the different means of irrigation in the plains of the northern India rivers naturally occupy the foremost place. This is implied by the reference in the dictionaries of two kinds of countries, those living on river water and those depending on rains.[4] The Arab geographers Al Istakhrī[5] and Ibn Haukal[6] notice how seed is sown in Sind after the river Mihrān, having inundated the land, has subsided. The *Tilakamañjarī* also refers to the fertile banks of a certain river Sarāvatī whose water was canalised to many neighbouring villages.[7] In the *Agnipurāṇa* we read of arms of rivers made to run into tanks.[8]

The *Mānasollāsa* gives a very simple account of the reservoirs classifying them into *kūpa* (well), *vāpikā, puṣkariṇi, dīrghikā* and *taḍāga*.[9] Elsewhere it describes a *miśra* tank (*tāḍāka*) as one which every year receives fresh water channels and is bound up with embankments.[10] It obviously refers to the tanks, so popular and useful in the plateau of the Deccan, in which rain water is stored from year to year. The classification in the *Aparājitapṛcchā* is quite elaborate. It refers to ten categories of wells, *śrīmukha, vijaya, prānta, dundubhi, manohara, cūḍāmaṇi, digbhadra, jaya, nanda* and *śaṅkara*, which varied from four to thirteen hands in length, each being one hand long than that preceding it. It calls small wells *kūpikās* and mentions two types of them respectively three and two hands long. It then goes on to enumerate four

1 On *Manu*, VII, 212—*Bahusasyādevamātṛkā ca.*
2 II, p. 136, v. 1605—*Divyāntarikṣaṃ nādeyaṃ nairjharaṃ sārasam jalam. Bhaumaṃ caundam ca tāḍākam-audbhidaṃ navamaṃ smṛtam.*
3 p. 188, vv. 34–36.
4 *Abhidhānaratnamālā*, II, 161; *Vaijayantī*, p. 38, 11.92-93.
5 Elliot and Dowson, *History of India*, I, 30.
6 *ibid.*, I. 40. Cf. Al Idrīsī (*ibid.*, I, 81) about Tūbarān.
7 p. 181. Cf. *Aparājitapṛcchā*, p. 188, v. 37—*Setubandhabhavā nadyāḥ śasyobhavataṭodbhavāḥ.*
8 CCLXXII, 4—*Praveśayen-nadivāhān puṣkariṇyāṃ tu kārayet.*
9 I, p. 8, vv. 71-72.
10 II, p. 137, v. 1613.

classes of *vāpīs* and four classes of *kuṇḍas*. It enumerates *sara, mahāsara, bhadraka, subhadra, parigha* and *yugmaparigha* as the six types of tanks, but then further classifies them as *jyeṣṭha, madhyama* and *kaniṣṭha,* according to the length and width of their fences (*pāli*).[1] Even if we make allowance for the academic emphasis on minute classification, we can utilise the list to form an estimate of the role of reservoirs. The dictionaries contain terms for a reservoir, a deep water reservoir, a pond, a small pond, a large pond, a natural pond, an artificial pond, a small tank, a large oblong tank, a dug spring, a natural spring and a well.[2] The *Upamitibhavaprapañcākathā*, though implying others also, mentions by name only three reservoirs, *dīrghikā, guñjālikā* and *yantravāpikā.*[3] In the *Deśīnāmamālā* we have the term *uttūho* for a steep well and *ulittaṃ* for a well in a high place.[4] We can understand the working of tanks and reservoirs from the problems in mathematical texts of the period. The *Līlāvatī*, for example, refers to the regulation of fountains (*nirjharāḥ*) for filling a cistern (*vāpī*).[5] The *Gaṇitasārasaṅgraha* gives the rule to determine the time taken to fill a *vāpī* when any number of optionally chosen channels (*praṇālikās*) are together allowed to fill it.[6] The latter text also refers to water flowing out of a *vāpī* through a pump (*yantra*).[7]

We can get an idea of how the wells worked from the dictionaries of the period which give terms for the cover or facing of a well, a small post near the well, the rope and bucket, water channel and a drain.[8] Hemacandra in his *Deśīnāmamālā* explains *āgattī, ukkā, ukkaṃḍī, ukkaṃtī, ḍheṃkā, ṇelicchī* and *vaḍḍhitā* alike as *kūpatulā*[9] or a contrivance for raising water from a well in which a horizontal beam, from one end of which a bucket hangs, see-saws on a vertical post. We cannot say whether these are the different

1 pp. 183–85, vv. 2–36.

2 *Abhidhānaratnamālā*, vv. 675–677; *Vaijayantī*, p. 154, ll. 9–15.

3 p. 56.

4 I, 94, 89.

5 p. 39, no. 95.

6 VII, 32½–33.

7 IV, 28–30.

8 *Abhidhānaratnamālā* (*Halāyudhakoṣa*), Ed. Jayaśaṅkara Jośi, vv. 684–85; *Vaijayantī*, pp. 154-55, ll. 16–18, 40–42.

9 I, 63, 87; IV, 17, 44; VII, 36.

names of the same appliance or whether they stood for slightly differing but similar appliances. The *Aparājitapṛcchā*[1] speaks of strong machines fitted to wells. In the dictionaries *araghaṭṭaka* is the name of a wheel or machine for raising water from a well.[2] The revolving movements of the buckets in the wheel of *araghaṭṭa* have often been referred to in literary works, mostly of a philosophical type.[3] The *arghaṭa* or *arhaṭa* occurs in land-grants, sometimes as an object of gift[4] and sometimes in connection with the enumeration of boundaries.[5] But it does not appear likely that the *arghaṭa* was within the reach of a common cultivator with ordinary means. *Arghaṭas* as irrigational works must have been quite valuable objects to have been donated as gifts. Significantly enough they appear to have been owned mostly by kings, feudatories,[6] ministers and in some cases by opulent merchants. The *Upamitibhavapraprañcākathā*, which gives elaborate similes connected with irrigation with the help on an *araghaṭṭa*, mentions the landlord together with his cultivators, workers and servants,[7] suggesting thereby that it was only an opulent agriculturist who could have this luxury.

From Medhātithi we learn about the way in which cultivators used irrigational works. In this connection he explains the term *yantra* to mean the building of embankments for regulating the flow of water.[8] He also refers to water being drawn from the well or the tank and preserved in a cistern and similar small reservoirs.[9]

---

1 p. 214—*Kūpaśca dṛḍhayantrair-alaṅkṛtaḥ.*

2 *Abhidhānaratnamālā*, v. 685; *Vaijayantī*, p. 155, 1.42. For a detailed discussion of references to *ghaṭīyantra* and *araghaṭṭa* as indicating Persian Wheel see our *Aspects of History of Agriculture in Ancient India* (Varanasi, 1980). pp. 114-68.

3 *Upamitibhavaprapañcākathā*, pp. 66, 418, 723; *Prabandhacintāmaṇi*, p. 40, 1.24; p. 24, 11. 5-6—*Tvaṃ kiṃ na paśyasi ghaṭīr-jalayantracakre riktā bhavanti bharitāḥ punar-eva riktāḥ. Pañcatantra*, IV (Hertel), pp. 231, 244.

4 *P.I.H.C.*, VII, 643; *E.I.*, XIV, 186, 1.26.

5 *E.I.*, XI, pp. 28 f.

6 The Partabgarh Ins. (*E.I.*, XIV, 182 ff) refers to a field of the Provincial Governor Mādhava which was irrigated by it. P.I.H.C., VII, 643—grant of an *arghaṭṭa* by Bhīma II.

7 pp. 984–6.

8 On *Manu* XI, 62—*Yantrāṇi setubandhādīni jala-pravāhaniyamārthāni.*

9 On *Manu*, XI, 162—*Uddhṛtodakasyeraṇādisthasya.*

Elsewhere he refers to cutting the embankments and taking the water to irrigate the field and to obstructing the water-courses by closing the source from which the water-flows.[1] A story in the *Prabandhacintāmaṇi* relates how workers were filling in water from one field to another.[2] A stock example in the Vedānta school of philosophy speaks of the water of a reservoir issuing from sluices and flowing through a small channel (*kulyā*), on entering the fields, assuming rectangular and other shapes.[3]

The *Samarāṅgaṇasūtradhāra* describes four water-machines (*vārī-yantra*) to bring water down (*pāta*), to raise it first and then to bring it down (*ucchrāyasamapāta*), to bring it down and then to raise it (*pāta-samocchrāya*) and to raise it (*ucchrāya*).[4] No doubt mechanical contrivances in ponds are often referred to in literary works.[5] But it is highly improbable that these devices were regularly utilised for the irrigation of agricultural crops. The *Samarāṅgaṇasūtradhāra* refers to their use for recreation[6] and for practical purposes and requires them to be installed in *vāpīs*, wells and *dīrghikās*.[7] Obviously to suggest that they were used by the common cultivator will be nothing short of absurdity. Even in the case of an opulent noble or merchant it is not likely that they were used in agriculture; at best he utilised these marvels in his gardens.[8]

In the period under study we find that with the growth in the claims and powers of the state there was a distinct attempt on the part of the ruling powers to establish their ownership over irrigational water. The list of rights and privileges which the land-grants transfer to the donee and which, therefore, existed earlier in the donor king or feudatory include the ownership of water (*sajala*).[9] The authority quoted by Bhaṭṭasvāmin also distinctly observes that those well versed in the *śāstras* view the king as the

1 On *Manu*, III, 153.
2 p. 56, 11.14-15.
3 *Vedāntaparibhāṣā*, p. 23.
4 I, pp. 178-79, vv. 109–114. Cf. *ibid.*, p. 175, vv. 75-76 for a device to convey water into a field and also to pour it out from it.
5 e.g., *Karpūramañjarī*, III, 20; IV, 10, 13; *Kuṭṭanīmata*, v. 684.
6 I, 178, v. 109—*Krīḍārthaṃ kārya-siddhyai ca.*
7 I, p. 179, v. 114.
8 Cf. *Ibid*, I, 178, v. 110–*Vāṭikādi-prayojanam.*
9 *E.I.*, XIV, 186, l. 24: XV, 295 ff: XXVIII, 327-28: *C.I.I.*, IV, 324–31.

owner of the land and water.[1] But in ancient India the state never thought of deriving any income from its ownership of irrigation works. It was regarded as a pious duty on the part of the king to provide such works of public utility.[2] However the many demands on the purse of the feudal state led it, in its desire to tap new sources of revenue, to utilise its ownership of irrigational works as a separate source of income. We find the Gāhaḍavālas imposing a *jalakara*,[3] for the first time in Indian history. It is likely that, pressed by the inroads of the Muslims, they resorted to all possible avenues for collecting money.

But this is not to suggest that all the wells, tanks and ponds etc. in the village were owned by the state. It is obvious that the man who had a well dug on his own land was its natural owner.[4] In the same manner references are not wanting to show that machine wells called *araghaṭṭas* were owned by private individuals.[5]

It would thus appear that the claim of the state to the ownership really amounted to its rights over natural ponds, lakes or rivers or streams situated in or passing through the village. Medhātithi would suggest that for all practical purposes this right vested in the village as a whole which enjoyed it on behalf of the king. An example of *saṃsthā* (laws) given by him is "this water should not be given for purposes of irrigation of crops to such and such a village until we have secured such and such a benefit from it in return".[6] Elsewhere referring to the compacts formed by the villagers he says that if the inhabitants of a village decide to oppose those of a neighbouring village diverting the water course and to be of one mind in case of a riot or legal suit, any one who is a party to the decision would be punished on his backing out of it on some inducement offered by the headman of the other village.[7]

But it is clear that all this irrigational activity going on in the

1 On *Artha*, II, 24; *J.B.O.R.S.*, XII, p. 138—*Rājā bhūmer-patiḥ dṛṣṭaḥ śāstrajñair-udakasya ca.*

2 *Dīgha*, I, 135; *Rāma*, II, 100, 48; *Mbh.*, II, 5, 78; V, 61, 17; V, 147, 26; *Artha*, IV, 3; *Raghu*, XVI, 2.

3 *E.I.*, IV, no. 11 (O); VIII, no. 14 (D); X, no. 23; XIII, no. 20.

4 Cf. *Agnipurāṇa*, CCLVII, 8.

5 Cf. *Upamitibhavaprapañcākathā*, pp. 984-86.

6 On *Manu*, I, 21.

7 On *Manu*, VIII, 219.

country could little affect the ultimate dependence of Indian agriculture on the rains. Paṇḍita Dāmodara expresses the helplessness of the common cultivator at many places in his *Uktivyaktiprakaraṇa*. He says that the clouds by their timely rains make the world new, as it were,[1] that fields yield crops only when the nature is kindly,[2] and that if God produces rains then there will be grains.[3] Medhātithi, echoing the same sentiment, says that if God were to give rain many persons would take to cultivation.[4] The arrival of rains was a source of pleasure to everybody and people looked to it with eagerness.[5] The *Aparājitapṛcchā* also shudders to think of the fate of the world if there are no timely rains or there is drought or only a little rain.[6] The picture of the Kali age painted by the *Bṛhannāradīya* is that of people threatened with drought and with their eyes drawn towards the sky.[7] In support of all this we have the testimony of Abū Zaid who describes Indian rains or Fasara (=Skt. *varṣā*) during the three months of summer as "the life of the Indians; were they to fail, they would be reduced to the deepest want. For their fields sown with rice, are watered only by rains, and are fecundated thereby."

These sources indicate that the coming of the rains was always a subject of anxiety lest they should be inadequate as regards time, place and quantity. No doubt there are references to rivers swelling from the rains,[8] but the main fear was its paucity or absence especially when needed. In his helplessness the cultivator could but pray the heavens for rain. Of course the Vedic sacrifices had ceased to be very popular with the masses; even then when threatened with drought people must have performed sacrifices. Medhātithi refers to the sacrifices like the *kārīrī* per-

---

1 p. 22, l. 18—*Parjanyaḥ kurute viśvaṃ kābhiḥ punar-navam?—vṛṣṭibhiḥ*.

2 p. 35, l. 29—*Sukāle annaṃ niṣphāyate*.

3 p. 9, ll.15-16—*Yadi devo vṛṣṭim akariṣyat, tadānnam abhaviṣyat*.

4 On *Manu*, II, 45—*Devaśced varṣed bahavaḥ kṛṣiṃ kuryuḥ*. Cf. Bṛhat—Parāśara (Jivananda Vidyasagara, *Dharmaśāstra-saṅgraha*, II, p. 109)—*Deva-parjanya-bhū-sīra-yogāt kṛṣiḥ prajāyate*.

5 *Kathākośa*, pp. 3, 11.

6 p. 187, v. 28. Cf. *Kathākośa*, p. 162—how shall the world manage to subsist if the moon shall withdraw her digit, if the giver tribute, the cloud rain.

7 XXXVIII, 80-81.

8 *Uktivyaktiprakaraṇa*, p. 40, l. 14; *Kathākośa*, p. 3.

formed by men desiring rain.[1] The *Agnipurāṇa* says that by casting libations into the fire with the *mantra Apām garbham* etc., a man is sure to bring down a good shower of rain, while by performing a *homa* ceremony with the *mantra Apaḥ piba* etc., a man is sure to inundate the earth with a continuous downpour.[2]

Side by side with these there was an attempt to study the natural phenomena accompanying rains and to create a somewhat ordered knowledge out of it. Parāśara in his *Kṛṣiparāśara*, referring to the importance of rain for cultivation, and of the latter for human existence, observes that one should first of all carefully acquire knowledge about rains.[3] An old text, still unpublished, variously called the *Mayūracitraka, Meghamālā* or *Ratnamālā* and ascribed to Nārada contains "indications of coming rains, famine or plenty, etc., from the appearance of the atmosphere."[4] The *Śakunajñāna* section of the *Śārṅgadharapaddhati* has a sub-section on the question of rains.[5]

The technique of forecasting weather involved the study of astronomy and depended on the experience and observation of natural phenomena accumulated over centuries. The *Kṛṣiparāśara* shows how the two approaches were utilised for predicting monthly, yearly and immediate rainfall. In the first instance the text describes the rainfall in any year according to the planets who happen to be its king, minister, superintendents of water and crop.[6] Later in the text we read about rainfall or drought in any year as determined by the movement and position of the planets.[7] It classifies clouds into four, *āvartta, saṃvartta, puṣkara* and *droṇa,* and describes annual rainfall according as one of them is supreme in the year.[8] Then it gives directions for predicting rainfall on the basis of observations made in different parts of the

---

1 On *Manu*, II, 10 (Vol. I, p. 71).

2 CCLX, 50-51.

3 v. 10.

4 *I.A.*, XLVII, 262; see *J.O.I.*, IX, p. 408, f.n. 2 for four MSS. of the *Meghamālā*. The *Gurusaṃhitā*, a text on weather-maxims, edited by us (Varanasi, 1981) was composed towards the end of the early medieval period.

5 vv. 2372-77.

6 vv. 12–22.

7 vv. 71–78.

8 vv. 23–25.

year. By dividing the 30 days of Pauṣa into 12 equal parts of $2\frac{1}{2}$ days each, corresponding to the 12 months in order, one can know the rainfall in the 12 months by observing the course of the wind in their corresponding parts of the Pauṣa month as ascertained by the flag attached to a post.[1] Another device is to divide each day of Pauṣa into 12 parts of 5 *daṇḍas* each, and to observe the rainfall throughout the month; rainfall in the earlier or later half of those parts will indicate rainfall by day or by night respectively in the corresponding month.[2] Then follow indications of rainfall in the rainy season as they may be gathered from the climatic conditions, wind, lightning, rain, fog, clouds etc., in the months of Pauṣa, Māgha and Phālguna.[3] In Caitra the rainfall on the first day of the bright half of the moon is taken to foretell the annual rainfall according to the week day on which it happens to occur. The position of the *nakṣatra* Citrā in Caitra also suggests the amount of rainfall.[4] By putting into a river a stick with certain marks on it in the month of Vaiśākha one can ascertain the amount of rainfall and flood-water.[5] A shower in the months of Jyaiṣṭha and Śrāvaṇa in certain *nakṣatras* is said to indicate the nature of the rainy season.[6] The direction of the wind during the full-moon in Āṣāḍha also forebodes the weather in the rainy season. Rain on the ninth day of the bright half of Āṣāḍha also foretells the rainy season.[7] In Śrāvaṇa rain in certain *nakṣatras* indicates the nature of the rainy season.[8] In the month of Bhādra also rains are predicted on the basis of the *nakṣatras.*[9] Then, the *Kṛṣiparāśara* mentions the behaviour on the part of living beings as indicating immediate rainfall viz., a water-spout near or in the water, the rising of ants from their holes with eggs, the sudden croaking of frogs, cats, ichneumons, serpants, other beings living in holes and moths running in an excited condition,

---

1 vv. 30-31.
2 vv. 32–33.
3 vv. 34-43.
4 vv. 44–47.
5 vv. 48–56.
6 vv. 57-58.
7 vv. 59–61.
8 vv. 62–64.
9 p. 17—found only in the Vaṅgavasī edition of the *Kṛṣisaṅgraha* or *Kṛṣiparāśara.*

boys making bridges with sand, dancing by peacocks, pain in the body of men afflicted with wounds or rheumatism, snakes climbing to the tops of the trees, acquatic birds drying their wings in the Sun, and the noise of crickets.[1]

It is not to be supposed that all this knowledge was only stored in books without being put to practical use. The very fact that books on the subject were composed in Sanskrit suggests their usefulness to the class which knew the language and at the same time was interested in the practical aspect of agriculture. The *Kṛṣiparāśara* merely collects the fund of knowledge which cultivators at that time possessed. Such practical knowledge transmitted from generation to generation when once acquired is generally not allowed to be relegated to oblivion.[2] The popular aphorisms ascribed to Khanā indicate that such knowledge was actually possessed by the cultivators, who remembered it and quoted it in the form of pithy sentences. It indicates how the weather was foretold on the basis of natural indications like cloud, winds, rainbows and rain on particular days and months.[3] Some of these sayings of Khanā would indicate that the knowledge of weather forecasting on the basis of astrological calculations or the position of planets was not altogether denied to the common cultivator.[4] That these aphorisms were meant for the guidance of the cultivators would appear from some of these in which the cultivators are directly addressed or a house-wife addresses her father-in-law worrying about rains and cultivation.[5]

All this knowledge must have been of great help to a cultivator. He could time the sowing, ploughing etc., according to it. It must have been useful in arranging for other means to water the fields. The knowledge of the amount of rainfall may have helped in the selection of crops for different regions. As early as

---

1 vv. 65–70.

2 Cf. Medhātithi on II, 6 (Vol. I, p. 63)—*Pipīlikāṇḍāsañcāreṇa hi bhaviṣyantīṃ vṛṣṭim-anumimate; Rāj.*, VIII, 722 refers to the cows looking above, serpants ascending trees, and ants moving with their eggs as foretelling an immediate rainfall. Also Khanā quoted by T.C. Dasgupta, *Aspects of Bengali Society*, pp. 230ff, no. (f).

3 T.C. Dasgupta, *Loc. cit.*, pp. 230–36.

4 Cf. *ibid.*, pp. 225-26, nos. (b) and (d).

5 Cf. *ibid.*, pp. 230 ff, no. (d); G.P. Majumdar, *Vanaspati*, pp. 211-12.

the *Arthaśāstra*[1] we have a reference to the use of a bowl with its mouth as wide as an *aratni* (24 *aṅgulas*) as a rain-gauge. The passage indicates the way in which this branch of knowledge was developing, but in the absence of other references to rain-gauges, we cannot trace the evolution of or perfection attained in the construction of such an instrument. The *Kṛṣiparāśara* refers to a crude way of determining rainfall. It defines *āḍhaka* as a vast expanse of water a hundred *yojanas* wide and thirty *yojanas* deep.[2] Likewise, the *Meghamāla* also states that a continuous rain for seven nights together was called *droṇa*.[3] The *Kṛṣiparāśara*[4] does not give us any idea of the comparative amount of total rainfall in different parts of India. It simply says that of the total rainfall sea, mountains and earth respectively receive water in the ratio of 10, 6 and 4.

Soil, Manure, Seed and Sowing:

It is needless to emphasise that the first thing of importance in agriculture is the soil. It was the realisation that the fields near rivers are more fertile which must have led people to attach importance to them.[5] A knowledge of the qualities of the soil is implied when Medhātithi[6] explains *ūṣara* as that part of the land where, on account of the defects of the soil, seeds do not spring. The advance in the technical knowledge about the properties of soil is best indicated by the use in the dictionaries of different terms for an ordinary field, a fertile field suitable for every crop, a

1 II, 5.
2 vv. 26–28.
3 See *J.O.I.*, IX, p. 418.
4 v. 29. The *Agnipurāṇa*, CXXX, 1–11 mentions the asterisms belonging to the belt of fire under whose influence the food grains stand perched in the fields and rainfall of the year is abnormally below the average as affecting the seven divisions of the Uttarāpatha viz., Saindhava, Yāmuna, Gurjara, Bhoja, Bāhlika, Jālaṃdhara and Kāśmīra. Likewise it observes that the asterisms of the belt of wind affect the countries of Ḍāhala, Kāmarūpa, Kaliṅga, Kośala, Ayodhyā, Avantī, Koṅkaṇa and Andhraka.
5 Cf. *Kavīndravacanasamuccaya*, no. 210—*Prāyaḥ stana-taṭībhūmiḥ prakāma-phala-dāyinī yasyām-agre karaṃ dattvā yojyate nakha-lāṅgalam.*
6 On *Manu*, II, 112.

field unfit for cultivation, fallow land, an area with saline soil, desert, firm ground, clay, excellent soil, an area green with young grass and one abounding in reeds.[1] In the land-grants we have references to different types of land such as *sāra* and *ūṣara*,[2] *kṣetra* and *khila*[3] etc. which indicate that these terms coined to indicate the fertility and other features of the soil were not merely academic but were much used in connection with cultivation. It appears that the characteristics of the soils in the different parts of the country were also understood. The dictionaries have terms for countries with black or yellowish soil.[4] It was also realised that the properties of the soil made certain fields eminently suited for certain crops. Thus, we find terms for fields named after the crops grown in e.g.,[5] those of *mudga, kodrava, yava, vrīhi, śāli, ṣaṣṭi, tila* etc. In the sayings of Khanā we find specific details about the type of soil required for certain crops. "You worthy cultivator, your aim will be fulfilled if you grow *pāṭol* (*Trichosanthes dioica*) in sandy alluvial soil." "The sandy soil is fit for the cultivation of *āus* paddy and clayey soil for that of jute." "If you grow *arum* on the bank of a river, it will grow to the height of three cubits i.e., it will flourish well."[6]

For agriculture the knowledge and use of manure to maintain the fertility of soil is very essential. There seems to have been some recognition that howsoever rich in chemical contents land may be, in due course of time it becomes unproductive[7] because every crop takes away from it certain elements. That the Indian cultivator was using manure gets the undoubted testimony of the *Uktivyaktiprakaraṇa*.[8] The *Kṛṣiparāśara* recognises the importance of manure for crops and says that without manure, the paddy simply grows up, but does not yield any fruit.[9] It describes the way in which cow-dung, the chief form of manure in India, was

1 *Abhidhānaratnamālā*, 158-59, *Vaijayanti*, p. 124, 11. 34-36.
2 Cf. Mitra, *Early Rulers of Khajuraho*, p. 165.
3 Cf. Choudhury, *Hist. of Assam*, p. 298.
4 *Abhidhānaratnamālā*, 160; *Vaijayantī*, p. 38, 1.89.
5 *Vaijayantī*, p. 124, 11. 37–41.
6 G.P. Majumdar, *Vanaspati*, pp. 212-13.
7 Cf. *Deśīnāmamālā*, VI, 63 for consumed land—*Polaccā kheṭitā-bhūmiḥ*.
8 p. 39, 1. 17—*Hālikaḥ kṣetraṃ pasayati*.
9 v. 111—*Vinā sāreṇa yaddhānyaṃ varddhate phala-varjitam*.

formed and used. It says "In the month of Māgha the heap of cow-dung should be worshipped faithfully and on an auspicious day the dung should be dried in the sun, and made into small balls. In the month of Phālguna these balls are to be placed into pits dug in every field and at the time of sowing the manure is to be spread over the field."[1] Without suggesting that the passage implies a knowledge of the component elements in which modern science analyses cow-manure we can hold that it indicates an awareness of its fertilising property and an appreciation of the way in which this property could be preserved and augmented. R. Gangopadhyay analyses this method of preparing dung-manure to show that the injunction not to disturb the dung-heap reduces to a minimum the loss of nitrogen, the chief fertilising element, that of drying dung into balls results in reducing active ammonia which may be injurious to the plants, while that of placing the dung balls in pits increases the humus that contributes to the fertility of the soil.[2]

It has generally been observed that the modern Indian farmer does not make a proper and full use of manure. We have to see how far does the present practice represent the conditions in the period under study. It is undoubted that cow-dung was used as a fuel.[3] It was recognised that dried cow-dung increases fire[4] and so dried dung-cakes were often collected in large numbers.[5] The *Deśīnāmamālā* has many words for a fire of dry cow-dung: *kouā*,[6] *pouā*,[7] *phuṃphuā*[8] and *mummuro*.[9] In the *Aucityavicāracarcā* a fire of dry cow-dung is said to be as pleasant as the anger of a newly wedded wife[10] and there are several other definite references to its use.[11] But we are not to suppose that cow-dung was used as

1 vv. 109–11.
2 *Agriculture and agriculturists in ancient India*, pp. 58-59.
3 *Vaijayantī*, p. 10, l. 40; p. 231, l. 35.
4 *Vaijayantī*, p. 91, l. 193.
5 *ibid.*, p. 187, l. 25.
6 II, 48.
7 VI, 61.
8 VI, 84.
9 VI, 147.
10 p. 6.
11 In a verse from the *Subhāṣitaratnakoṣa* (v. 302) we read of the woman-folk in the hamlet enjoying the fire of dried cow-dung (cf. *ibid.*, v.

fuel to such an extent as to render it unavailable for use as manure. At that time when huge forests surrounded the villages there was no dearth of fuel as there is today; thus the cultivator must have found it advisable and profitable to use the cow-dung for manuring the fields. It is only in modern times, when forests have been cleared, that the farmer has resorted to such a large use of cow-dung for fuel. Bāṇa indicates that cow-dung and rubbish formed the usual manures. In one of his graphic pictures he describes how a cultivator carried rubbish and cow-dung in carts drawn by oxen to fields that had become unfertile.[1]

Some of the manures used in the period are referred to in the sayings of Khanā.[2] "Those things (e.g., rotten cow-dung) which injure man cure the plants." "If some water, in which a fish has been washed, is poured at the root of a gourd plant, then the plant will surely be benefited from it." "The land which contains rotten paddy as manure is fit for the rearing of chillis." "Betel-nut plants require cow-dung as manure for their growth." "Pieces of rotten straw or chips of wood should be used as manure at the roots of *arums*."

In agriculture much depends upon the quality of the seeds sown. The *Kṛṣiparāśara* says that if the seeds are unproductive the efforts of other factors in cultivation become futile; the seeds are at the root of the crops, hence one should pay attention to the seeds.[3] Medhātithi mentions sowing of unripe seed as one of the faults on the part of the farmer which may hamper the crop.[4] Elsewhere he says that the corn, left over after consumption, when sown next year does not reproduce.[5] The *Prabandhacintāmaṇi* of Merutuṅga at one place says that seeds, which have been burnt, do not sprout.[6] The commentary of Nīlakaṇṭha explains the

307). A very clear proof of cowdung being used as fuel is furnished by Bāṇa, a little earlier than the period of our study, who describes the houses of his kindred as filled with heaps of cow-dung and fuel. *Harṣacarita*, p. 33—*Indhana-gomaya-piṇḍa-kūṭasaṅkaṭāni*.

1 *ibid.*, p. 202—*Purāṇa-pāṃsūtkira-kariṣa-kūṭa-vāhinīnāṃ..Śakaṭa-śreṇīnāṃ saṃpātaiḥ saṃpādyamāna-durbalorvī-virūkṣa- kṣetrasaṃs-kāram.*

2 T.C. Dasgupta, *Aspects of Bengali Society*, pp. 236–39.

3 vv. 166-67.

4 On *Manu*, VIII, 243—*Nidānam -ayogya-bīja-vāpaḥ.*

5 On *Manu*, IX, 37—*Tadapi hi punarupabhuktaśeṣam-upyamānam—aparasmin-vatsare..nānuvartate.*

6 p. 82, 1.21—*Dagdhānāmiva bījānāṃ punarjanma na vidyate.*

pulākā grains mentioned in the *Mahābhārata* as grains rendered incapable of growing through the excessive heat of the soil.[1] Likewise, Nīlakaṇṭha observes that *kākayava* is the term for seeds separated from their outer skin and thus rendered unproductive.[2] The *Kṛṣiparāśara* has a detailed note on how to collect and preserve seeds.[3] It advises that all kinds of seeds should be collected in the month of Māgha or Phālguna. They are then to be well dried in the sun and exposed to dew at night. The seeds are to be kept in small bundles (*puṭikās*). Mixed seeds (presumably seeds of more than one species sown together) result in bad crops and seeds of the same class yield a rich harvest; hence one should collect with care seeds of the same class. After placing the seeds in it, the bundle should be closely tied up, and the seed should be purged of grass particles, otherwise the crop will be full of grass. The *Kṛṣiparāśara* then requires the seeds to be kept away from impure associations. These suggestions though superstitious, by attributing a degree of sanctity to the seeds, emphasized their importance in agriculture. It is thus said that the seeds should not be kept on an ant-hill, in a cow-shed, a room where a woman has given birth, or a house inhabited by a barren woman. Seeds should never be allowed to come in contact with the remnants of food, a woman in her menses, a barren woman, a pregnant woman or a woman who has just delivered a child. Then follow some practical suggestions for preserving the seeds. A farmer should not even unknowingly place ghee, oil, whey, a lamp or salt over the seeds, and should avoid using seeds affected by lamps, fire, smoke and rain, and also those placed in pits. One should never sow seeds which have already germinated or mixed seeds.

Sowing had grown to be a technical and specialised procedure demanding careful attention. To bring home the importance of the process the *Kṛṣiparāśara* converts it into a veritable ritual.[4] The proprietor of the field should himself sow three handfuls of seeds moistened with cold water, with a pure and concentrated mind and meditating upon Indra. He should invoke the goddess of earth (*vasundharā*) for the rich growth of crops, seasonal rain-

1 On XII, 181, 7.
2 On II, 77, 13.
3 vv. 168–81.
4 vv. 177–81.

fall and the welfare of the cultivators. He should then feed the cultivators with ghee and other delicacies. These details would appear to be supported by the *Deśīnāmamālā* when it uses the term *maṅgalasajjhaṃ* for a field ready for sowing seeds.[1]

Sowing has to be done on scheduled dates. Medhātithi implies that untimely sowing affects the yield of the crop.[2] The *Kṛṣiparāśara*, thinking in terms of paddy cultivation, observes that for sowing of seeds Vaiśākha is the best, Jyaiṣṭha middling, Āṣāḍha bad, and Śṛāvaṇa worst. It also mentions those *nakṣatras* which are auspicious for sowing and those which are less so. Saturdays and Sundays are to be avoided and certain *tithis* and special periods are not auspicious for sowing.[3] We can never know how much of this advice was mere superstition and how much was the result of actual experience in the climatic conditions of the period and region of the text concerned. Khanā seems to be full of directions on this point.[4] "By sowing paddy in the month of Āṣāḍha one gets a full harvest, in Śrāvaṇa only leaves and no fruits in Bhādra only husks and in Āśvina nothing." "Sow paddy to your hearts content throughout the whole of Śrāvaṇa and the first twelve days of Bhādra." "During the last four days of Bhādra and the first four days of Āśvina sow *kalāi* (*Phaseolus var. radiatus*) as much as you can." "One should sow peas after the first 19 days of Āśvina and within the first 19 days of Kārtika". "Khanā directs, good cultivator, sow mustard towards the end of Autumn". "The cultivator, who does not plant, either in the month of Bhādra or Āśvina and idles away his time and then too late in the month of Kārtika and Agrahāyana sets grown-plants in the field, is fated to see them perish from an attack of mildew and his barns empty". "Sow turmeric in Vaiśākha and Jyaiṣṭha ......" "This is the direction of Varāha's son Mihira: Excepting Caitra and Vaiśākha plant brinjals very cheerily throughout the other ten months ...." "Plant betel in Śrāvaṇa and the product will be too much to be chewed up even by Rāvaṇa." "*Pātols* will doubly grow if planted in Phālguna."

1 VI, 126.
2 On *Manu*, VIII, 243—*Akāle vāpanaṃ*.
3 vv. 168–76. Cf. *Agnipurāṇa*, CXXI, 49.
4 G.P. Majumdar, *Vanaspati*, pp. 214-15. Cf. *I.H.Q.*, VII, 23-24.

A cultivator was expected to know the requirements of his field as regards seeds.[1] This probably includes knowledge not only of the seeds likely to grow well in a particular field[2] but also the amount of seeds required for it. In the *Vaijayantī* we find terms for naming the fields which require *droṇa*, *āḍhaka*, *khāri* etc. measures of seeds[3] to be sown in them. This knowledge would appear to have been quite common in this period. Actually we find that in many land-grants of the period the donated field is described in terms of its seed capacity.[4]

The cultivator was also required to know how seeds of particular types were to be sown, thickly or sparsely.[5] Generally, it appears, the seeds were scattered in the field by the hand.[6] It was after the field had been ploughed that seeds were generally sown,[7] but sometimes the field was ploughed after sowing.[8] Medhātithi, however, refers to seeds being sown with the help of the plough etc.[9] This probably refers to some such device by which a cultivator used to sow the seeds in the line of tilling through a cone attached to the pole of the plough.

A pertinent question is to what extent the cultivator made use of the system of rotation of crops or resorted to the practice of leaving the fields fallow after one crop. No doubt, from as early as the times of the *Taittirīya Saṃhita* we find references to two

---

1 *Kṛtyakalpataru*, *Gārhasthyakāṇḍa*, p. 256—*Svakṣetrabījaguṇasya vettā syāt.*

2 Medhātithi on *Manu*, IX, 330—*Idaṃ bījamasmin kṣetre prarohatīdaṃ na.*

3 p. 124, ll. 42-43.

4 *E.I.*, V, no. 5 (I and II)—*Vrīhipiṭakavāpaṃ kṣetram* and *Vrīhidaśa-prasthavāpaṃ kṣetram; E.I.*, V, no. 16 (A)—*Dvādaśakhaṇḍikako-dravabīja-saṃsthānaṃ kṣetram; E.I.*, XVIII, no. 6—*Viṃśati-khaṇḍī-kāvrīhi-bīji-parimāṇaṃ kṣetram; E.I.*, X, no. 11—*Vāpagatya koraḍe sārddha-droṇa-sapta-parikalitā.*

5 Medhātithi on IX, 330—*Idaṃ bījaṃ vistṛtamupyata idaṃ saṃhatamupyata itthenāmuptiṃ viṃdyāt.* Cf. *Kṛtyakalpataru*, *Gārhasthyakāṇḍa*, p. 256—*'Bījānāmuptivit' samyak sasyotpatyanukūlaghanavirala-bījavapanavettā.*

6 Cf. *Vāsavadattā* (Gray's tr). pp. 100, 120.

7 Cf. Medhātithi on *Manu*, IX, 36—*Vapanakāle upapādite kṛṣṭasamīkaraṇādinā saṃskṛte.*

8 *Vaijayantī*, p. 124, l. 46.

9 On *Manu*, II, 112—*Śubhaṃ śreṣṭhaṃ vrīhyādikaṃ lāṅgalādinopyate.*

seasonal crops[1] with the possibility of a third.[2] Khanā would suggest that a system of rotation was known, especially when she observes "My worthy cultivator, plant radish towards the end of the third season of the year, sow mustard towards the end of autumn, and if you mind to take money, sow maize in the following month of Caitra."[3] But against this we have the testimony of the *Yuktikalpataru*[4] which would imply that the system was not much in vogue. It says that land loses fertility from cultivation year after year; when one plot of land loses in fertility, cultivation should be done elsewhere. The word *khila*, which stands for a fallow land,[5] often occurs in the inscriptions. It would, therefore, follow that often plots of land were left to recover their fertility. However, we should also avoid the other extreme of suggesting that rotation of crops was little utilised. In the inscriptions of the period we find references to fields called *śāradyagraiṣmikakṣetrādi*, *graiṣmikakṣetrādi* and *śāradyakṣetrādi*.[6] It is clear from these that there were fields which had two crops in a year in Śarada and Grīṣma, obviously implying a practical application of the principle of rotation. But the reference to fields which had only one crop either in Grīṣma or Śarada would suggest that, as in modern times, the cultivators followed the system of rotation or keeping fallows according to the wealth of properties that their fields possessed, and also as their own resources permitted and their needs required.

Agricultural Implements:

The *Kṛṣiparāśara*, emphasising the need for proper implements, says that they should be firm, otherwise the cultivator faces difficulty at each step.[7] In proportion to the importance of

---

1 *Tai. Saṃ.*, V, 1, 7, 3; *Gobhila* G.S., I, 4, 29; *Artha*, II, 24; *Mbh.*, XII, 100, 10-11; *Bṛhatsaṃhitā*, XXXIX, 13-14; Megasthenes (McCrindle), pp. 32, 55.

2 *Tai. Sam.*, VII, 2, 10, 2; *Artha*, IX, 1; Pāṇini, IV, 3, 44–46.

3 *I.H.Q.*, VII, p. 24.

4 p.6—*Tathā varṣeṣu varṣeṣu karṣaṇād bhūguṇākṣayaḥ. Ekasyāṃ guṇahīnāyāṃ kṛṣimanyatra kārayet.*

5 *Abhidhānaratnamālā*, v. 158; *Vaijayantī*, p. 124, l. 36.

6 Dabok inscription dated A.D. 813—*E.I.*, XX, 13.

7 vv. 119-20. Cf. Devala q. in the *Jyotiṣatattva* (*Smṛtitattva*, I, p. 687)—*Halādibhirdṛḍhaiḥ kṣemaṃ kudṛḍhairna śubhaṃ vadet.* Bṛhat-Parāśara (Jivananda, II, p. 107), likewise, after giving the measure-

the plough the *Kṛṣiparāśara* devotes considerable space to the different parts of the plough and their measurements. These are[1] (1) *yuga* (yoke) which is described as extending upto the ears of the oxen,[2] (2) *aḍḍacalla* or the pins of the yoke where the bullocks are tied which measure 12 *aṅgulas* (9 inches), (3) *yotra* or yoke-tie which is to be 4 *hastas* (6 feet), (4) *rajju* or string 5 cubits (*karas*) long (7 feet 6 inches), (5) *īṣā* or the pole of the plough to be 5 *hastas* (7 feet 6 inches) long, (6) *niryola* or the rod of the plough exclusive of the pole and the share and measuring 1½ *hastas* (2 feet 3 inches), (7) *śaula* or an extra piece of wood that tightly fixes the *niryola* to the pole and measures an *aratni* (cubit),[3] (8) *ābaddha* or a rod of iron which prevents the *niryola* from getting out of the pole is circular in shape (*maṇḍalākāraḥ*) and is 54 *aṅgulas* (3 feet 4½ inches) in length, (9) *niryolapāśikā* or the plates that fix the ploughshare to the *niryola*[4] and measure 12 *aṅgulas* (9 inches), (10) *phāla* or ploughshare which is 1 *hasta* and 5 *aṅgulas* (1 foot 9¾ inches) or 1 *hasta* (1 foot 6 inches) long [Ploughshares of a smaller size (*phālikā*) measured only 9 *aṅgulas* (6¾ inches) and resembled an *arka* (*Calotropis gigantea*)-leaf in shape], and (11) *halasthāṇu* (the handle of a plough) or a piece of wood fixed to the *niryola* at the end opposite to which the ploughshare is fixed, which the cultivator holds while ploughing and which measures 5 *vitastis*[5] (3 feet 9 inches). The *Kṛṣiparāśara* requires the goad (*paccanī* or *paccanikā*; in local dialect in W. Bengal it is called *pāñcanbārī*) to be of strong bamboo with an iron top and measuring 12½ or 9 *muṣṭis* (fists) in length. The terms for some of the parts, such as the ploughshare, yoke-tie, pin of a yoke, pole and the goad, are to be found in the dictionaries of the period.[6] It may be that distinctive terms for other parts were still in the

ments of a plough, observes that it should not be in any way less than what has been mentioned.

1 vv. 111-20. Cf. the descriptions in *Mānasāra*, V, 56–77 and Bṛhat-Parāśara (Jivananda, II, p. 107) which differ in the terms used and the measurements of the parts. Either these were earlier or were not the product of a man like the author of the *Kṛṣiparāśara* who had an intimate knowledge of agricultural details.

2 *Karṇasamānakam*. It may also mean "of the shape of an ear".

3 The distance between the elbow and the tip of the little finger.

4 Monier-Williams explains it is "a strap of leather on a plough".

5 Monier-Williams equates one *vitasti* with 12 *aṅgulas*.

6 *Abhidhānaratnamālā*, vv. 575, 577; *Vaijayantī*, p. 125, 11. 53–56, 58.

process of evolution or else the dictionaries confine themselves to the words in common use. These dictionaries employ the term *śamyā*[1] in place of the *aḍḍacalla* of the *Kṛṣiparāśara*. Likewise the *Deśīnāmamālā*[2] has *javaṇaṃ* for the *halasthāṇu* of the *Kṛṣiparāśara*. These facts may be taken to suggest regional variations in terminology.[3]

The *Kṛṣiparāśara* also mentions two other implements, which appear to have been used as harrows. Of these *viddhaka* said to have 21 spikes (*śalyas*) and *madikā* (=*mai* of Bengali usage) is described as measuring 9 hands (13 feet 6 inches) in length. In the dictionaries we find terms for some other agricultural implements whose connection with agriculture is indicated even by their position in the texts.[4] Thus, we have *matya* for a roller to level the sown field; *koṭīśa* for a harrow to break clods of earth; *khanitra* or *avadāraṇa* for a spade or hoe; *godāraṇa* or *kundāla* for a scraper or shovel of which the main part was known as *abhriḥ* or *kṣūḥ* and *dātra, lavitra* or *asida* for a sickle of which the handle was called *vaṇṭaka*. The digging hoe (*kuddāla*) is also referred to.[5]

Ploughing:

Ploughing being the first process in cultivation naturally receives careful attention from a cultivator. The *Kṛṣiparāśara*[6] lays down the performance of the ceremony called *hala-prasāraṇa* before the commencement of ploughing and observes that he who starts cultivation without performing *hala-prasāraṇa* does it in vain. The ceremony consists in invoking a number of deities and worshipping them with offerings and also in whetting the ploughshares and besmearing them with honey and also besmearing with

1 *Abhidhānaratnamālā*, v. 575; *Vaijayantī*, p. 125, 1. 55.

2 III, 41.

3 Cf. T.C. Dasgupta, *Aspects of Bengali Society*, p. 230 for names of agricultural implements in early Bengali literature.

4 *Vaijayantī*, p. 125, 11. 56–60; *Abhidhānaratnamālā*, vv. 576, 577.

5 *Prabandhacintāmaṇi*, p. 108, 11. 1-2; *ibid.*, p. 109, 1. 16. Cf. Medhātithi on *Manu*, IX, 293.

6 vv. 121–56. *Halaprasāraṇaṃ naiva kṛtvā yaḥ karṣaṇaṃ caret. Kevalaṃ baladarpeṇa sa karoti kṛṣiṃ vṛthā*—v. 153. Bṛhat-Parāśara, Ch. III (Jivananda, II, pp. 107-108) describes the ceremony in detail under the name *halasya yojanam*.

butter and ghee both the sides of the faces of the oxen. The *Agnipurāṇa* gives details for worshipping the Sun and the gods of the element and observes that these ceremonies are to be performed before transplanting or mowing down the rows of paddy plants, the unfastening of the ploughshare or removing the threshing plank.[1]

From the *Kṛtyakalpataru* of Lakṣmīdhara it is clear that the need for thorough ploughing was realised.[2] In the dictionaries of the period we find terms for fields cultivated twice, thrice or a greater number of times.[3] The *Kṛṣiparāśara*[4] requires the furrows to be continuous and without break and to be one, three or five in number. By the number of the furrows the text probably means the number of times the field is to be ploughed. Khanā[5] has many practical tips for ploughing. "One should plough the soil sixteen times for radish, half the number of times for cotton, half of that for paddy and none for betel." "One should cultivate the soil for radish making it as soft as cotton and for sugarcane plough it to the dust."

The *Kṛṣiparāśara* refers to the nature of soil and its suitability for ploughing at different periods of the year.[6] Having paddy cultivation in mind he regards Hemanta as the best season and the rainy season the worst. The *Kṛṣiparāśara* requires actual ploughing to be commenced on an auspicious occasion. It gives a long list of *nakṣatras*, days, *tithis* and *rāśis* (zodiacal signs) auspicious for this purpose and goes on to add another list of days, *tithis* and *rāśis* which are inauspicious, noting their evil effects on the farmer and his bulls and crops and even on other people.[7] Such superstitious ideas appear to have had quite a hold on the minds of the cultivators. Khanā likewise requires the cultivator to begin the ploughing from the east and to avoid the days of the full moon and the new moon for the commence-

---

1 CCLIX, 43–47.

2 *Gārhasthyakāṇḍa*, p. 195—'*Dvihalakṛte' punaḥ karṣaṇāya*, *Ibid.*, p. 182—*Taddhastāttrir-upahatāni svakṛṣṭāni.*

3 *Vaijayantī*, p. 124, 11. 43–45; *Abhidhānaratnamālā*. v. 576.

4 vv. 142–43.

5 G.P. Majumdar, *Vanaspati*, p. 213.

6 vv. 154–55.

7 vv. 121–30. Cf. *Agnipurāṇa*, CXXI, 46–48.

ment of ploughing.[1] The *Kṛṣiparāśara*[2] mentions a number of superstitions concerning the effects suggested by some portents in the course of ploughing e.g., the raising of a tortoise by the plough when it is driven across the field,[3] the breaking of the ploughshare, plough, pole, yoke, *śaula*, or yoke-tie, exhaustion of the cultivator or falling down, sudden running, bellowing, the licking of their noses or the passing of dung or urine by the oxen drawing the plough.

Plough-oxen:

The utility of a good plough depends upon the oxen that draw it.[4] The *Kṛṣiparāśara* gives much space to the proper upkeep of cows and bulls.[5] Bṛhat-Parāśara repeatedly emphasises the role of oxen. It observes that the world lives on the crops produced by the oxen: they produce the grains, crush them and carry them: they are really objects of worship; the merit of keeping one ox is ten time that spoken of by the sages for keeping a cow; they are to be cared for properly; he who yokes them without care goes to hell.[6] The *Kṛṣiparāśara* also requires cultivation to be carried without cruelty to the oxen. If one earns a fourfold crop by oppressing the oxen he is reduced to the condition of a pauper by their sights.[7] The ideal of a humane treatment of the oxen[8] was at the base of the suggestion to increase the number of oxen yoked to a plough. Thus, the *Kṛṣiparāśara* remarks that a plough should have eight oxen yoked to it: one who yokes six is just a business-man: those who employ four are cruel, while those employing two are but beafeaters.[9] A verse in the *Atrisaṃhitā* reads: plough-oxen are to be employed for one quarter of the day when they are strong and two per plough; if the number of the oxen yoked to a plough is four they are to be engaged for half the day; if the

1 G.P. Majumdar, *Vanaspati*, p. 213.

2 vv. 144–51.

3 Cf. *Samarāṅgaṇasūtradhāra*, I, p. 33, vv. 63-64—significance of wood, brick, stone or bone coming out of earth during ploughing.

4 Cf. Bṛhat-Parāśara, Ch. III (Jivananda, II, p. 102)—*Kugavairna kṛṣim kuryāt*.

5 vv. 84–108. Cf. Bṛhat-Parāśara (Jivananda, II), Ch. III.

6 Ch. III (Jivananda, II. pp. 110, 105).

7 v. 85.

8 Cf. *Kṛtyakalpataru, Gārhasthyakāṇḍa*, p. 192.

9 v. 96. Cf. *Parāśarasaṃhitā*, II, 3-4.

number is six, for three quarters of the day, and if the number is eight, for the whole day.[1] These considerations of compassion and pity imply the realisation that the larger the number of the oxen the better is the ploughing. It is, however, not clear how far this knowledge led to the practice of deep ploughing by using more oxen. It is not unlikely that in a few cases more than two oxen were yoked to a plough,[2] but the modern practice would suggest that the six or eight oxen in the texts referred to above were to be used by rotation or relay.

The *Kṛṣiparāśara* favours black or red or black-and-red oxen and discards those having big waists, or with their tails and ears cut off or all-white ones. He realises the practical need of keeping the oxen, like the cultivator, free from discases.[3] Bṛhat-Parāśara says that one should not yoke a bull, with defective limbs, or one diseased, lifeless, weak, hungry, thirsty or tired. The bull should be able-bodied, free from disease, well-fed, hearty, not impotent or insolent but full of life and vigour. Bulls are to be yoked only for half of the day and after that they should be bathed.[4] After ploughing their horns are to be smeared with oil or ghee and then they should be sent to graze and at night they should be given fodder.[5] The *Kṛṣiparāśara* advises strength-giving fodder for the oxen and observes that if they are allowed to graze in the morning and evening they always thrive.[6] It enumerates the *nakṣatras* and days auspicious and otherwise for a cow's *yātrā* and *praveśa*, probably referring to its going out to the field and entering the cow-shed for the first time.[7]

The *Kṛṣiparāśara* appears to be full of concern for the welfare of cows and bulls. It provides for a fairly spacious cow-stall in clean and hygienic condition. Its interest in the welfare of cattle is reflected in some of the superstitions it records including those on the auspicious periods for constructing cow-stalls.[8] It describes

1 vv. 218-19.

2 Cf. *Abhidhānaratnamālā*, v. 283.

3 vv. 134, 141.

4 Ch. III (Jivananda, II, pp. 101 f, 110). Cf. *Parāśara-saṃhitā*, IV, 2.

5 Bṛhat-Parāśara, Ch. III (Jivananda, II, p. 110).

6 v. 86.

7 vv. 105–8. Cf. *Agnipurāṇa*, CXXI, 44-45.

8 vv. 87–95.

certain festivities which performed on the *tithi* called *laguḍaprati-pat* are supposed to render cows free from diseases for one year.[1] On this occasion the cows were marked with heated iron and their tails, hairs and ears were slightly cropped. Bṛhat-Parāśara requires that the nose of the bull should be pierced with a wooden plug twelve fingers long.[2]

Agricultural Processes:

From the *Kṛṣiparāśara* and other texts of the period we learn about the details of the different processes of cultivation.

The *Kṛṣiparāśara* requires that after the sowing of seeds the field should be levelled with a harrow otherwise the growth of the plants is not even.[3]

The text says that if a sown field is not hoed, the crops cannot grow in abundance, nor yield a good harvest. It adds that if hoeing is done in the month of Śrāvaṇa or Bhādra, the harvest is doubled, even if grass grows again, and that if another hoeing is done in the month of Āśvina, corn grows plentifully.[4] Medhātithi also refers to the weeder cleverly preserving the corn and plucking out the weeds though the two grow together and are in close touch with one another.[5]

Animals, birds and insects have to be checked from devouring or destroying the crops.[6] Bṛhat-Parāśara advises that fences, which animals cannot cross, should be erected.[7] In the *Prabandha-cintāmaṇi* we read of the watchmen collecting the branches of thorny shrubs,[8] obviously for fencing the fields. Sometimes a scarecrow of grass was set up. The *Deśīnāmamālā* uses the expression *avaḍao,*[9] *jharaṃko* and *jharaṃto*[10] for these grass-men.

1 vv. 99–104.
2 Ch. III (Jivananda, II, p. 106).
3 v. 182. Medhātithi on *Manu*, IX, 36 suggests that after ploughing and before sowing the field was prepared by levelling—*Kāle varṣāḍau vapanakāla upapādite kṛṣṭa-samī-karaṇādinā saṃskṛte.*
4 vv. 189–92.
5 on *Manu*, VII, 110.
6 Cf. *Uktivyaktiprakraṇa*, p. 46, 1. 30.
7 Ch. III (Jivananda, II. p. 112).
8 p. 77, 11. 19–20.
9 I, 20.
10 III, 55.

The *Subhāṣitaratnakoṣa* gives a graphic picture of a herd of pigeons some how overcoming their fear of the scarecrow and eating the seed in a corner of the field.[1] For protecting the field the watchmen had often to live in the fields,[2] keeping awake at night.[3] A verse in the *Subhāṣitaratnakoṣa* refers to the platforms raised on the boundaries of the fields from which the watchmen scared away wild boars.[4] The noise made by the watchmen to scare away animals and birds is called *hiṃdolayaṃ, hilloḍaṇaṃ*[5] *hiṃḍolaṇaṃ* and *hiḍolaṇayaṃ*[6] in the *Deśīnāmamālā*. According to Hemacandra the expression *hiṃḍolaṃ* is also used to signify a contrivance to scare away birds etc. from fields.[7] Even in modern times Indian cultivators strike a horizontal hollow bamboo pole with a vertical one by pulling it with a rope while lying in their hut or in the midst of their work in other parts of the field. The use of the term *hiṃḍolaṃ* meaning swing suggests that Hemacandra had in his mind some such device.

Indian cultivators, rightly renowned for their superstitious nature, are found resorting to many such practices for protecting their crops. Thus, in the *Śārṅgadharapaddhati* it is said that if sand in a pot empowered with *mantras* is thrown in the field insects, cranes, parrots, boars, deer, rats and hares keep away.[8] The *Kṛṣiparāśara*[9] has an interesting *mantra* which if written on the leaf of *ketakī* and fastened in the north-east corner of the field is said to protect the crop from diseases, insects and animals. The incantation requests Rāma to direct Hanumān to drive away from the field with his tail the insects, birds and animals, of which many are named, which destroy the crops. The *Kṛṣiparāśara*[10]

1 v. 264.
2 *Deśīnāmamālā*, VI, 26.
3 *ibid.*, III, 32. In the *Vaijayantī* the term for a field hut is *gangarī* (p. 161, 1. 54).
4 v. 285.
5 VIII, 69.
6 VIII, 76.
7 *Deśīnāmamālā*, VIII, 69.
8 vv. 3017-18.
9 Pages 48f. Cf. *J.B.O.R.S.*, III, p. 562 for a similar practice in vogue in Bihar with the difference that here the notice is addressed directlp to the insects.
10 vv. 198-205.

further requires that on the occasion of the *Kārttikasaṃkrānti* a cultivator should plant a leafy reed at the north-east corner of the field and worship it with suitable offerings to ensure a uniform and luxuriant growth of crops.

The *Agnipurāṇa* mentions auspicious occasions for harvesting.[1] Khanā gives many practical tips in connection with reaping.[2] "Corn ripens within 20 days after the first appearance of the ear, and one should cut and thresh the corn in 10 days more." "The corn ripens 30 days after the first appearance of the spike, 20 days after the first appearance of flowers and 12 days after the ears bend like a horse's head......" Before the actual commencement of reaping, the *Kṛṣiparāśara*[3] requires the performance of the ceremony called *muṣṭigrahaṇa* when the cultivator after worshipping the plants cuts off two and a half handfuls of plants in the north-east corner of the field and returns home with the plants on his head. Non-observance of the rite is said to create difficulties for the cultivator at every step and to lead to the loss of the crops.

The expression used in the *Kṛṣiparāśara* for threshing (*mardayitvā* = *maṇāi* in Hindi and *malan* in Bengali) refers to the process of separating grain from straw by making oxen tread on the corn. In the dictionaries of the period we have, besides terms for a threshing floor, the word *methi* which stands for the post of the threshing floor round which cattle turn to thresh out the grains.[4] In the *Rāmacarita* we read about the threshing floor where the reaped crops were spread out and were threshed by bullocks which went round and round over them.[5] The *Kṛṣiparāśara* attaches a great significance to the threshing post and describes in details the rites accompanying the fixing up of the post. It enumerates trees which are auspicious and inauspicious for making the post and also notes the days on which the rite is to be performed.[6] Threshing was sometimes done by human foot,[7] probably when the crops were not abundant or when the farmer could not afford to have it done with the help of cattle.

---

1 CXXI, 50. Cf. Medhātithi on *Manu*, VIII, 243.
2 G.P. Majumdar, *Vanaspati*, pp. 215-16.
3 vv. 206–13.
4 *Abhidhānaratnamālā*, v. 578; *Vaijayantī*, p. 125, 1.61.
5 (ed. R.C. Majumdar, R.G. Basak and N.G. Banerji) *Kavipraśasti*, 13.
6 vv. 214-20.
7 *Deśīnāmamālā*, VI, 40; III. 37; cf. *ibid.*, VI, 34.

For separating the grain from the husk the corn was first pestled and then winnowed.[1] The *Vaijayantī* has distinct terms for unhusked rice, husk, eye of corn, dust of clean rice, clean rice-water and rice-powder.[2] In the *Deśīnāmamālā* we find many words for a pestle and a mortar.[3] It explains *kaṃcī* as the name for the metal ring at the end of a pestle.[4] Some other utensils used in this connection were the sieve[5] and the grinding stone.[6] The room for rice cleaning and pounding was called *kṣaṇā* or *buśālī*.[7]

Kṛṣiparāśara requires that after all this has been done the grains are to be measured and kept in the granary.[8] It then mentions the *nakṣatras* and days which are auspicious for storing the grains in the granary.[9] It again mentions two *mantras* which are to be written and kept in the granary to augment prosperity.[10] The *Agnipurāṇa* also advises that *mantras* written on a leaf should be placed amidst the heap of grains.[11] The *Vaijayantī* mentions sacks, boxes and baskets in connection with the granary.[12]

---

1 *Vaijayantī*, p. 164, ll. 130-31. Cf. *Deśīnāmamālā*, I, 103; *Vaijayantī*, p. 193, l. 42.
2 *ibid.*, p. 164, ll. 132–35.
3 I, 26, 32, 74; II, 56; III, 11; V, 23; VI, 15; VII, 94.
4 II, 1.
5 *Vaijayantī*, p. 164, l. 129.
6 *Deśīnāmamālā*, III, 10.
7 *Vaijayantī*, p. 161, l.51.
8 v. 237.
9 vv. 241-42. Cf. *Agnipurāṇa*, CXXI, 51.
10 p. 60.
11 CXXI, 52-54.
12 p. 164, ll. 127-28.

BIBLIOGRAPHY

A. *Texts in Indian Languages and Translation.*

Abidhānacintāmaṇi of Hemacandra in the *Abidhānasaṅgraha*, Vol. II. N. S. P. Bombay, Śaka 1818.

Abidhānarājendra of Vijayarājendra Ed. Muni Dīpavijaya. 7 Vols. Ratlam, 1913-25.

Abhidhānaratnamālā of Halāyudha (*Halāyudhakośa*). Ed. Jayaśaṅkara Jośī. Varanasi, Śaka 1879.

Ādipurāṇa of Jinasena I in *Mahāpurāṇa*. Syādvāda-Granthamālā. Indore, Vikrama 1973-5.

Agni Purāṇa. A. S. S. Poona, 1900. Tr. M.N. Dutt. Calcutta, 1903.

Aitareya Brāhmaṇa. Ed. T. Aufrecht. Bonn, 1879. Tr. A. B. Keith. Cambridge, 1920.

Amarakoṣa with Kṣīrasvāmin's commentary. Ed. K. G. Oak. Poona, 1913.

Apabhraṃśa-Kāvyatrayī of Jinadattasūri. Ed. L. B. Gandhi. Baroda, 1927.

Āpastamba Dharmasūtra. Ed. G. Bühler. Bombay, 1892, 1894.

Aparājitap cch [illegible] of Bhuvanadeva. Ed. P. A. Mankad. Baroda, 1950.

Aparārka's commentary on *Yājñavalkyasmṛti*. A. S. S. 2 Vols. Poona, 1903, 1904.

Arthaśāstra of Kauṭilya. Ed. R. Shamasastry. Mysore, 1919. Ed. T. Ganapati Sastri. Trivandrum, 1924-25. Tr. R. Shamasastry. Mysore, 1929.

Āryamañjuśrīmūlakalpa. Ed. T. Ganapati Sastri. Trivandrum, 1920.

Aṣṭāṅgahṛdaya of Vāgbhaṭa. Ed. A. M. Kunte. Bombay, 1880.

Aucityavicāracarcā of Kṣemendra. Ed. Dhuṇḍhirājaśāstrin. Banaras, 1933.

Bauddha Gān O' Dohā. Ed. H. P. Sastri. Calcutta, B. S. 1323.

Bhaṭṭadīpikā on *Pūrvamīmāṃsādarśana* by Khaṇḍadeva. Ed. Madhava Sastri and L. Srinivasacarya. Mysore 1911.

Bhaṭṭasvāmin's commentary on *Arthaśāstra*. *J.B.O.R.S.*, XII.

Bhaṭṭotpala's commentary on *Bṛhatsaṃhitā* of Varāhamihira. Ed. Sudhakara Dwivedi. Banaras, 1895, 1897.

Bhavisayattakahā of Dhanapāla. Ed. C. D. Dalal and P. D. Gune. Baroda, 1923.

Bījagaṇita of Bhāskarācārya. Ed. Achyutananda Jha. Banaras, 1949.

Bodhisattvāvadānakalpalatā of Kṣemendra. B. I. 2 Vols. Calcutta, 1888ff.

Bṛhannāradīya Purāṇa. Ed. P. H. Sastri. Calcutta, 1891.

Bṛhatkathākośa of Hariṣeṇa. Ed. A. N. Upadhye. Bombay, 1943.

Bṛhatkathāmañjarī of Kṣemendra. Ed. Sivadatta and Parab. N.S.P. Bombay, 1931.

Bṛhatkathāślokasaṅgraha of Budhasvāmin. Ed. with Fr. translation. F. Lacôte. 28 Vols. Paris, 1908-1929.

Bṛhat-Parāśara in *Dharmaśāstra-saṅgraha*. Ed. Jīvananda Vidyāsāgara Bhattacharya. Calcutta, 1876.

Caryāgītikoṣa. Ed. P. C. Bagchi and S. B. Sastri. Santiniketan, 1956.

Caturbhāṇi (comprising *Padmaprābhṛtaka* of Śūdraka, *Dhūrtaviṭasaṃvāda* of Īśvaradatta, *Ubhayābhisārikā* of Vararuci and *Pādatāḍitaka* of Śyāmilaka). Ed. Ramkrishna Kavi and S. K. Ramanatha Sastri. Patna, 1922.

Caturvargacintāmaṇi of Hemādri. Ed. Bharatachandra Siromani. B.I. Calcutta, 1873-1911.

Daśakumāracarita of Daṇḍin. Ed. M. R. Kale. Bombay, 1917. Tr. W. Ryder. Chicago, 1927.

Daśavaikālikasūtra. Devchand Lāl-bhāī Jaina-pustakoddhāra Series No. 47. Bombay, 1918.

Dāyabhāga of Jīmūtavāhana (with the commentary of Kṛṣṇa Tarkālaṅkāra). Calcutta, 1829. Tr. H. T. Colebrooke. Calcutta, 1910.

Deśīnāmamālā of Hemacandra. Ed. R. Pischel. 2nd edition by P. V. Ramanujaswami. Vizianagaram, 1938.

Deśopadeśa of Kṣemendra. Ed. M. Kaul. Poona, 1923.

Dharmasindhusāra of Kāśīnāthopādhyāya. Ed. Y. G. Dikshita. Poona, 1911.

Dhūrtākhyāna of Haribhadra Sūri. Ed. A. N. Upadhye and Jina Vijaya Muni. Bombay, 1944.

Dhūrtaviṭasaṃvāda. See *Caturbhāṇi*.

Dohākośa of Sarahapāda. Ed. R. Sāmkṛtyāyana. Patna, 1958.

Dvyāśrayakāvya of Hemacandra. Ed. A. V. Kathvate. 2 Vols. Bombay, 1915, 1921.

Gaṇitasārasaṅgraha of Mahāvīrācārya. Ed. M. Rangacarya. Madras, 1912.

Garuḍa Purāṇa. Tr. M. N. Dutt. Calcutta, 1908.

Gautama Dharmasūtra. Ed. A. F. Stenzler. London, 1876.

Gṛhastharatnākara of Caṇḍeśvara. Calcutta, 1928.

Harṣacarita of Bāṇa. Ed. J. Vidyāsāgara. Calcutta, 1892.

Hindī Kāvya Dhārā. Ed. R. Sāṃkṛtyāyana. Allahabad, 1945.

Jagaḍucarita of Sarvānanda. G. Bühler: Indian Studies No. 1.

Jambūdvīpaprajñapti. Devchand Lāl-bhāī Jaina-pustakoddhāra Series Nos. 52, 54. Bombay, 1920.

Jātakas. Ed. V. Fausboll. London, 1877-97. Tr. E. B. Cowell. Cambridge, 1895-1913.

Jñāneśvarī. Ed. R. V. Madganvakar. Bombay, 1907.

Kalāvilāsa of Kṣemendra in Kāvyamālā I. 34ff. N. S. P. Bombay.

Kāmasūtra of Vātsyāyana. Ed. Durga Prasad. Bombay, 1900. Tr. H. Kern. *J.R.A.S.*, 1870-75.

Karpūramañjarī of Rājaśekhara. Ed. Rāmakumāra Ācārya. Banaras, 1955.

Kathākoṣa. Tr. C. H. Tawney. London, 1895.

Kathākośaprakaraṇa of Jineśvara Sūri. Ed. Jina Vijaya Muni. Bombay, 1949.

Kathāsaritsāgara of Somadeva. Ed. Durga Prasad and

Parab. N. S. P. Bombay, 1930. Tr. C. H. Tawney (*Ocean of Stories*). Calcutta, 1880-87. Reprinted with notes and essays etc. by N. M. Penzer. 10 vols. London, 1924-28.

Kātyāyana-Smṛti-Sāroddhāra. Ed. P. V. Kane. Bombay, 1933.

Kavikaṇṭhābharaṇa of Kṣemendra Ed. Dhuṇḍhirājaśāstrin. Banaras, 1933.

Kavīndravacanasamuccaya. Ed. F. W. Thomas. Calcutta, 1912.

Kāvyamīmāṃsā of Rājaśekhara. Ed. C. D. Dalal and R. A. Sastry. Rev. by K. S. Ramaswami Sastri Siromani. Baroda, 1934.

Kṛṣi-Parāśara. Ed. G. P. Majumdar and S. C. Banerji. B. I. Calcutta, 1960.

Kṛtyakalpataru of Lakṣmīdhara. Ed. K. V. R. Aiyangar. Baroda.
Brahmacāri, 1948.
Dāna, 1941.
Gṛhastha, 1944.
Rājadharma, 1943.
Vyavahāra, 1953.

Kullūka's commentary on the *Manusmṛti*. See *Manusmṛti*

Kumārasambhava of Kālidāsa. Bombay, 1927. Tr. R. T. H. Griffith. London, 1879.

Kuṭṭanīmata of Dāmodara. Ed. M. Kaul. Calcutta, 1944. Tr. E. Powys Mathers. London, 1927.

Kuvalayamālākathā. See *Apabhraṃśa-kāvya-trayī*.

Laṭakamelaka of Śaṅkhadhara. Ed. Durga Prasad and Parab. N. S. P. Bombay, 1923.

Lekhapaddhati. Ed. C. D. Dalal and G. K. Shrigondekar. Baroda, 1925.

Līlāvatī of Bhāskarācārya (Colebrooke's translation of the *Līlāvatī*). Ed. H. C. Banerji. Calcutta, 1893.

Lokaprakāśa of Kṣemendra. Ed. J. D. Zadoo. Srinagar, 1947. Fr. Tr. J. Bloch. Paris, 1914.

Mahābhārata. Ed. with the commentary of Nīlakaṇṭha by R. Kinjawadekar. Poona, 1929-33. Also Critical edition. Poona, 1927 (in progress).

Mānasollāsa of king Someśvara. Ed. G. K. Shrigondekar. 2 Vols. Baroda, 1925, 1930.

Manusmṛti with the *Manubhāṣya* of Medhātithi. Ed. G. Jha. Calcutta, 1932-39. Tr. G. Jha. Calcutta, 1922-29. Ed. with the commentary of Kullūka (*Manvarthamuktāvalī*). Ed. N. R. Acharya. Bombay, 1946.

Medhātithi's commentary on Manu. See *Manusmṛti*.

Medinīkoṣa of Medinīkara. Calcutta, 1884.

Mīmāṃsāsūtra of Jaimini with Śabarasvāmin's commentary. Ed. M. Vidyaratna. Calcutta, 1873. Tr. G. Jha. Allahabad, 1910. Tr. of *Śabarabhāṣya* by G. Jha. Baroda, 1933-36.

Mitākṣarā (commentary by Vijñāneśvara) on *Yājñavalkyasmṛti*. Ed. J. R. Gharpure. Bombay, 1914. Tr. J. R. Gharpure. Bombay, 1936ff.

Moharājaparājaya of Yaśaḥpāla. Ed. Muni Chaturvijaya. Baroda, 1918.

Mṛcchakaṭika of Śūdraka. Ed. R. D. Karmarkar. Poona, 1950.

Naiṣadhīyacarita of Śrī-Harṣa. N. S. P. Bombay, 1933. Tr. K. K. Handiqui. Lahore, 1934.

Nāmamālikā of Bhoja. Ed. E. K. Kulkarni and V. D. Gokhale. Poona, 1955.

Nāradasmṛti. Ed. J. Jolly. Calcutta, 1885. Tr. J. Jolly. Oxford, 1889.

Narmamālā of Kṣemendra. Ed. M. Kaul. Poona, 1923.

Nāyādhammakahā. Agamodayasamiti Mehesana Bombay, 1919.

Nyāyamālāvistara. A. S. S. 1892.

Padmānandamahākāvya of Abhayacandra Sūri. Ed. H. R. Kapadia. Baroda, 1932.

Parāśaramādhavīya. Ed. M. Chandrakanta Tarkalankara. Calcutta, 1890-99.

Prabandhacintāmaṇi of Merutuṅga. Ed. Jinavijaya Muni. Santiniketana, 1933. Tr. C. H. Tawney. Calcutta, 1901.

Prākṛit Vyākaraṇa of Hemacandra (along with the *Kumārapālacarita*). Ed. P. L. Vaidya. Bombay, 1936.

Rājanītiratnākara of Caṇḍeśvara. Ed. K. P. Jayaswal. Patna, 1936.

Rājataraṅgiṇī of Kalhaṇa. Ed. M. A. Stein. Bombay, 1892. Tr. M. A. Stein. Westminster, 1900.

Rāmacarita of Sandhyākara Nandī. Ed. R. C. Majumdar, R. G. Basak and N. G. Banerji. Rajshahi, 1939.

Ratirahasya of Kokkoka. Ed. Sadananda Sastrin Ghildiyal. Lahore, 1923.

Saduktikarṇāmṛta of Śrīdharadāsa. Ed. R. Sharma. Lahore, 1933.

Samarāiccakahā of Haribhadra Sūri. Bombay, 1938. Chs. I-II. Ed. M. C. Modi. Ahmedabad, 1935. Ch. VI. Ed. M. C. Modi. Ahmedabad, 1936.

Samarāṅgaṇasūtradhāra of Bhoja. Ed. T. Ganapati Sastri. Baroda, 1925.

Samayamātṛkā of Kṣemendra. Ed. Durga Prasad and K. P. Parab. Bombay, 1925. Tr. E. Powys Mathers. London, 1927.

Sandeśarāsaka of Abdula Rahamāna. Ed. H. Bhayani. Bombay, 1945.

Sāṅkhyatattvakaumudī of Vācaspatimiśra. Ed. G. Jha. Calcutta, 1896.

Sarasvatīvilāsa of Pratāparudra. Mysore, 1927.

Śārṅgadharapaddhati. Ed. P. Peterson. Vol I. Bombay, 1888.

Śatakatrayādisubhāṣitasaṅgraha. Ed. D. D. Kosambi. Bombay, 1949.

Śatapatha Brāhmaṇa. Ed. A. Weber. London, 1885. Tr. J. Eggeling. Oxford, 1882-1900.

Smṛticandrikā of Devaṇṇabhaṭa (Bibliotheca Sanskrita No. 45). Ed. L. Srinivasacharya. 6 Vols. Mysore, 1914-21. Ed. J. R. Gharpure. Bombay, 1918.

Subhāṣitaratnakoṣa of Vidyākara. Ed. D. D. Kosambi and V. V. Gokhale. Harvard, 1957.

Śukranīti. Ed. G. Oppert. Madras, 1882. Tr. B. K. Sarkar. Allahabad, 1914.

Sūktimuktāvali of Jalhaṇa. Ed. E. Krishnamacharya. Baroda, 1938.

Suvṛttatilaka of Kṣemendra. Ed. Dhuṇḍhirājaśāstrin. Banaras, 1933.

Tilakamañjarīkathā of Dhanapāla. N. S. P. Bombay, 1903.

Trikāṇḍaśeṣa of Puruṣottama. Ed. C. A. Seelakkhandha. Bombay, 1916.

Triṣaṣṭiśalākāpuruṣacarita of Hemacandra. Prasarakasabha, Bhavnagar. 6 Vols. 1905-9. Tr. H. M. Johnson. 4 Vols. Baroda, 1931, 1937, 1949, 1954.

Udayasundarīkathā of Soḍḍhala. Ed. C. D. Dalal and E. Krishnamacharya. Baroda, 1920.

Uktivyaktiprakaraṇa of Dāmodara Paṇḍita. Ed. Jina Vijaya Muni. Bombay, 1953.

Upamitibhavaprapañcākathā of Siddharṣi. Ed. P. Peterson. Calcutta, 1899.

Vaijayantī of Yādavaprakāśa. Ed. G. Oppert. Madras, 1893.

Vāmana Purāṇa. Calcutta, 1885.

Vastupālacarita of Jinaharṣagaṇī. Jamnagara Bhaskarodaya Press.

Viddhaśālabhañjikā of Rājaśekhara. Ed. J. B. Chaudhuri. Calcutta, 1943.

Vikramāṅkadevacarita of Bilhaṇa. Ed. G. Bühler. Bombay, 1875.

Vīramitrodaya of Mitramiśra. Chowkhamba Edn. Banaras. Ed. J. Vidyasagar. Calcutta, 1875. *Vyavahāraprakāśa*. Calcutta, 1875.

Viṣṇu Dharmasūtra. Ed. J. Jolly. Calcutta, 1881. Tr. J. Jolly. Oxford, 1880.

Viśvarūpa's commentary (*Bālakrīḍā*) on *Yājñavalkyasmṛti*. T. Ganapati Sastri. Trivandrum, 1922-24.

Vivādaratnākara of Caṇḍeśvara. Ed. J. Vidyasagara. Calcutta, 1887.

Vyavahāramayūkha of Bhaṭṭa Nīlakaṇṭha. Ed. P. V. Kane. Bombay, 1926.

Vyavahāranirṇaya of Varadarāja. Ed. K. V. R. Aiyangar and A. N. K. Aiyangar. Adyar, 1942.

Vyavahāraprakāśa. See *Vīramitrodaya*.

Yājñavalkyasmṛti. Ed. T. Ganapati Sastri. Trivandrum, 1922-24.

Yuktikalpataru of Bhoja. Ed. Isvara Candra Sastri. Calcutta, 1917.

B. *Foreign Accounts.*

Beal, S.—*Life of Hiuen Tsang by the Shaman Hwui-li*. London, 1911.

Beveridge, A. S.—*Bābur-Nāma* (*Memoirs of Babur*). 2 Vols. London, 1921.

Briggs, J.—*Tarīkh-i-Firishta of Muhammad Qāsim Firishta*. 4 Vols. London, 1827-29.

Chavannes, E.—*Mémoire Compose á l' epoque de la grande dynastie T'ang sur les Religieux Eminents qui allerent chercher ά' loi dans les pays d' Occident, par I-tsing* Paris, 1894.

De, B.—*Tabaqāt-i-Akbarī of Nizām-ud-dīn Ahmad*. 3 Vols. Calcutta, 1913-40.

Defremery, C. and Sanguinetti, B. R.—*Voyages d' Ibn Batoutah*. 4 Vols. Paris, 1853-1914.

Elliot, H. M. and Dowson, J.—*History of India as told by its own Historians*. 8 Vols. London, 1866-77. Vol. II.

Reprinted with Introduction by M. Habib, Commentary by S. H. Hodivala, and Supplement by K. A. Nizami. Aligarh, 1952.

Ferrand, G.—*Relations des Voyages et Textes Géographiques Arabes, Persans et Turks–Relatifs a l' Extrême-Orient du VIIIe au XVIIIe siècles.* 2 Vols. Paris, 1913-14.

Ferrand, G.—*Voyage du Marchand Arabe Sulaymān en Inde et en Chine.* Paris, 1922.

Gibb, H. A. R.—*Ibn Battuta. Travels in Asia and Africa.* London, 1929.

Hirth, F. and Rockhill, W. W.—*Chau Ju-kua.* St. Petersburg, 1911.

Legge, J. H.—*Record of the Buddhist kingdoms, being an account of the Chinese monk Fahien's Travels.* Oxford, 1896.

Major, R. H.—*India in the Fifteenth Century.* Hakluyt Society Series I, No. 22. London, 1857.

McCrindle, J. W.—*Ancient India as described in Classical Literature.* Westminster, 1901.

McCrindle, J. W.—*Ancient India as described by Ptolemy.* Calcutta, 1825.

McCrindle, J. W.—*Christian Topography by Cosmas.* London, 1897.

Minorsky, V.—*Hudūd al-'Ālam.* London, 1937.

Pigeud, Theodore G. Th.—*Java in the 14th century* (*The Nāgara Kĕrtāgama*) by Rakawi Prapañca of Majapahit, 3 Vols. The Hague, 1960.

Reverty, H. G.—*Tabaqāt-i-Nāsirī of Minhāj-ud-dīn b. Sirāj-ud-dīn.* Calcutta, 1873-97.

Renaudot, E.—*Ancient accounts of India and China by two Mohammeden travellers.* London, 1733.

Sachau, E. C.—*Alberuni's India.* 2 Vols. London, 1888.

Schoff, W. H.—*The Periplus of the Erythraean Sea.* London, 1912.

Takakusu, J. A.—*Record of the Buddhist Religion as practised in India and the Malaya Archipelago by I-Tsing.* Oxford, 1896.

Watters, T. Ed. Rhys Davids, T. W. and Bushell, I. W.—*On Yuan Chwang's travels in India.* 2 Vols. London, 1904-5.

Yule, H.—*The Book of Ser Marco Polo.* 2 Vols. London, 1875. Also Tr. Ricci, A. Ed. Ross, D. 1931.

Yule, H. and Cordier, H.—*Cathay and the Way Thither.* 4 Vols. London, 1915-16.

C. Inscriptions and Coins.

Bhattacharya, P. N.—*Kāmarūpaśāsanāvalī.* Rangpur, 1338 B.S.

Bhandarkar, D. R.—*Carmichael Lectures on Ancient Indian Numismatics.* Calcutta, 1921.

Bhandarkar, D. R.—*List of Inscriptions of Northern India.* Appendix to *E.I.*, XIX-XXIII

Bidyabinod, B. B.—*Supplementary Catalogue of the Coins in the Indian Museum, Calcutta.* Non-Muhammadan Series. Vol. I. Calcutta, 1923.

Brown, C. J.—*Coins of India.* Calcutta, 1922.

Cunningham, A.—*Ancient Coinage of Kashmir.* London, 1843.

Cunningham, A.—*Coins of Mediaeval India from the seventh century down to the Muhammadan conquest.* London, 1894.

Durgaprasad, Śivadatta and Parab, K. P.—*Prācīnalekhamālā.* 3 Vols. Kāvyamālā nos. 34, 64, 80. Bombay, 1892, 1897, 1903.

Elliot, W.—*Coins of Southern India.* London, 1896.

Fleet, J. F.—*Gupta Inscriptions. C.I.I.*, Vol.III. Calcutta, 1888.

Gadre, A. S.—*Important Inscriptions from the Baroda State.* Vol. I. Baroda, 1943.

Hiralal—*Descriptive Lists of Inscriptios in the C.P. and Berar.* Nagpur, 1932.

Hultzsch, E.—*South Indian Inscriptions.* 3 Vols. *Archaeological Survey of India.* New Imperial Series, Vols. 9, 10 and 29. Madras, 1890-1929.

Majumdar, N. G.—*Inscriptions of Bengal.* Vol. III. Rajshahi, 1929.

Mirashi, V. V.—*Inscriptions of the Kalachuri-Chedi Era. C.I.I.*, Vol. IV. Ootacamund, 1955.

Nahar, P. C.—*Jaina Inscriptions (Jaina-lekha-saṅgraha).* 3 Vols. Calcutta, 1918-1929.

Peterson, P.—*A Collection of Prakrit and Sanskrit inscriptions.* Bhavnagar Archaeological Department. Bhavnagar, 1905.

Rapson, E. J.—*Catalogue of the Coins of the Andhra Dynasty, the Western Kṣatrapas, the Traikūṭaka Dynasty and the Bodhi Dynasty.* London, 1908.

Sircar, D. C.—*Select Inscriptions bearing on Indian History and Civilization.* Vol. I. Calcutta, 1942.

Smith, V. A.—*Catalogue of the Coins in the Indian Museum, Calcutta, including the cabinet of the Asiatic Society of Bengal.* Vol. I. Oxford, 1906.

Vogel, J. Ph.—*Antiquities of the Chamba State.* Calcutta, 1911.

D. Secondary Sources.

Agrawal, V. S.—*Harṣacarita : eka Sāṃskṛtika Adhyayana.* Patna, 1953.

Agrawal, V. S.—*Kādambarī : eka Sāmskṛtika Adhyayana.* Banaras, 1957.

Aiyangar, K. V. R.—*Aspects of Ancient Indian Economic Thought.* Benares, 1934.

Altekar, A. S.—*Rāshṭrakūṭas and their times.* Poona, 1934.

Altekar, A. S.—*State and Government in Ancient India.* Delhi, 1958.

Arnold, T.—*The Caliphate.* Oxford, 1924.

Badger, G. P.—*A History of the Immams and Sayyids of Oman.* London, 1871.

Bagchi, P. C.—*India and China.* Calcutta, 1944.

Bandyopādhyāya, N. C.—*Kauṭilya, or an Exposition of his Social Ideas and Political Theory.* Vol. I. Calcutta, 1927.

J. N. Banerjea Volume. Calcutta, 1960.

Barnett, L. D.—*Antiquities of India.* London, 1913.

Barua, B. K.—*A Cultural History of Assam (early period).* Vol. I. Nowgong, 1951.

Barua, K. L.—*History of Assam,* Vol. I. Shillong, 1933.

Basham, A. L.—*History and Doctrines of the Ājīvikas.* London, 1951.

Basham, A. L.—*The Wonder that was India*. London, 1954.
Bose, N. S.—*History of the Candellas*. Calcutta, 1956.
Bose, P.—*The Hindu Colony of Cambodia*. Adyar, 1927.
Bose, P.—*The Indian Colony of Champā*. Adyar, 1926.
Chakravarti, N. P.—*India and Central Asia*. Calcutta, 1927.
Chatterji, B. R.—*Indian Cultural Influence in Combodia*. Calcutta, 1928.
Chatterji, B. R.—*India and Java*. Calcutta, 1933.
Chi, Tsui—*A Short history of Chinese Civilization*. London. 1942.
Choudhury, P. C.—*The History of the Civilization of the People of Assam to the twelfth century A.D.* Gauhati, 1959.
Coedés, G.—*Histoire Ancienne des États Hindoisés d' Extrême-Orient*. Hanoi, 1944.
Codrington, K. De B.—*An Introduction to the Study of Mediaeval Indian Sculpture*. London, 1929.
Commissariat, M. S.—*History of Gujarat*. London, 1926.
Dange, S. A.—*India from Primitive Communism to Slavery*. Bombay, 1949.
Das, S. K.—*Economic History of Ancient India*. Calcutta, 1925.
Dasgupta, T. C.—*Aspects of Bengali Society*. Calcutta, 1935.
De, N. L.—*Geographical Dictionary of Ancient and Medieval India*. London, 1927.
Duyvendak, J. J. L.—*China's Discovery of Africa*. London, 1949.
Forbes, A. K.—*Rās Mālā*. Ed. H. G. Rawlinson. London, 1878.
Gait, E.—*History of Assam*. Calcutta, 1926.
Ganguly, D. C.—*History of the Paramāra Dynasty*. Dacca, 1933.
Ghoshal, U. N.—*The Agrarian System in Ancient India*. Calcutta, 1930.
Ghoshal, U. N.—*The Beginnings of Indian Historiography and other Essays*. Calcutta, 1944.
Ghoshal, U. N.—*Contributions to the History of the Hindu Revenue System*. Calcutta, 1929.
Ghoshal, U. N.—*A History of Indian Political Ideas*. Oxford, 1959.
Ghoshal, U. N.—*Studies in Indian History and Culture*. Calcutta, 1957.
Gode, P. K.—*Studies in Indian Literary History*. Vol. III. Bombay, 1953.
Gupta, K. M.—*The Land System in South India between c.* 800 *A.D. and* 1200 *A.D.* Lahore, 1933.
Habib, B.—*Sultan Mahmud of Ghaznin*. Aligarh, 1927.
Habibullah, A. B. M.—*The Foundation of Muslim Rule in India*. Lohore, 1945.
Haig, W.—*The Cambridge History of India*. Vol. III. Cambridge, 1928.
Hasan, H.—*A History of Persian Navigation*. London, 1928.
Hazra, R. C.—*Studies in the Upapurāṇas*. Vol. I. Calcutta, 1958.
Hirth, F.—*China and the Roman Orient*. Leipsic. 1885.
Hodivala, S. H.—*Studies in Indo-Muslim History*. Bombay, 1939. Supplement, Vol. II. Bombay, 1957.

Hourani, G. F.—*Arab Seafaring in the Indian Ocean in Ancient and Early Medieval Times.* Princeton, 1951.

Jolly, J.—*Hindu Law and Custom.* Tr. B.K. Ghosh. Calcutta, 1928.

Kane, P. V.—*History of Dharmaśāstra.* Vols. II-IV. Poona, 1941, 1946, 1953.

Kosambi, D. D.—*An Introduction to the Study of Indian history.* Bombay, 1956.

Latourette, K. S.—*The Chinese: Their History and Culture.* New York, 1946.

Levi, S.—*Le Nepal.* 3 Vols. Paris, 1905.

Maitland, F. W.—*The Constitutional History of England.* Cambridge, 1931.

Maity, S. K.—*Economic Life of Northern India in the Gupta period: cir. A.D.* 300-550. Calcutta, 1957.

Majumdar, A. K.—*Chaulukyas of Gujarat.* Bombay, 1956.

Majumdar, B. K.—*The Military System in Ancient India.* Calcutta, 1960.

Majumdar, R. C.—*Ancient Indian Colonies in the Far East.* Vol. I: *Champa.* Lahore, 1927. Vol. II: *Suvarṇadvīpa* Parts 1 and 2. Dacca, 1937, 1938.

Majumdar, R. C.—*Corporate Life in Ancient India.* Calcutta, 1922.

Majumdar, R. C.—*Hindu Colonies in the Far East.* Calcutta, 1944.

Majumdar, R. C.—*The History of Bengal.* Vol. I. Dacca, 1943.

Majumdar, R. C. and Pusalker, A.D.—*The History and Culture of the Indian People.* Vol. IV: *The Age of Imperial Kanauj.* Bombay, 1955. Vol. V: *The Struggle for Empire.* Bombay, 1957. Vol. VI: *The Delhi Sultanate.* Bombay, 1960.

Majumdar, R. C., Raychaudhuri, H. C. and Datta, K.—*An Advanced History of India.* London, 1958.

Majumdar, S. N.—*Cunningham's Anceint Geography of India.* Calcutta, 1924.

Marshall, Sir J. H.—*A Guide to Sanchi.* Calcutta, 1918.

Mazumdar, B. P.—*Socio-Economic History of Northern India* (1030-1194 A.D.). Calcutta, 1960.

Mitra, S. K.—*The Early Rulers of Khajuraho.* Calcutta, 1958.

Mohan, K. (Miss)—*Kashmir under the Loharas* (A.D. 1003-1171). Thesis for Ph.D. University of London, 1958.

Mookerji, R. K.—*A History of Indian Shipping and Maritime Activity.* London, 1912.

Moti Chandra—*Sārthavāha.* Patna, 1953.

Muir, W.—*Caliphate—its Rise, Decline and Fall.* Revised by T. H. Weir, Edinburgh, 1915.

Mukherji, P. K.—*Indian Literature in China and the Far East.* Calcutta, 1931.

Munshi, K. M.—*The Glory that was Gūrjaradeśa.* Bombay, 1955.

Nadavī, Saiyada Sulemāna—*Araba aur Bhārata ke Sambandha.* Tr. by Rāmacandra Varmmā. Allahabad, 1930.

Nainar, S. M. H.—*Arab Geographers' knowledge of South India.* Madras, 1942.

Nazim, M.—*The Life and Times of Sultan Mahmud of Ghazna.* Cambridge, 1931.

Nath, Pran—*A Study in the Economic Condition of Ancient India.* London, 1924.

Niyogi, R. (Miss)—*The History of the Gāhaḍavāla Dynasty.* Calcutta, 1959.

Ojha, G. H.—*Madhyakālīna Bhāratīya Saṃskṛti.* Allahabad, 1951,

Pirenne, H.—*Economic and Social History of Mediaeval Europe.* London, 1936.

Poole, A. Lane—*Obligations of Society in the XII and XIII centuries.* Oxford, 1946.

Prasad, Beni—*State in Ancient India.* Allahabad, 1923.

Prasad, Beni—*Theory of Government in Ancient India.* Allahabad, 1927.

Prasad, Ishwari—*History of Medieval India.* Allahabad, 1925.

Puri, B. N.—*The History of the Gurjara-Pratihāras.* Bombay, 1957.

Poujade, J.—*La Route des Indes et ses Navires.* Paris, 1946.

Raffles, T. S.—*The History of Java.* London, 1830.

Rapson, E. J.—*Ancient India.* Cambridge, 1916.

Ray, H. C.—*Dynastic History of Northern India.* 2 Vols. Calcutta, 1931, 1936.

Ray, P.—*History of Chemistry in Ancient and Medieval India.* Calcutta, 1956.

Sarkar, B. K.—*The Positive Background of Hindu Sociology.* Book I. Allahabad, 1914.

Sarkar, H. B.—*Indian Influences on the Literature of Java and Bali.* Calcutta, 1934.

Sastri, K. A. N.—*The Colas.* 2 Vols. Madras, 1935, 1937.

Sastri, K. A.N.—*Foreign Notices of South India.* Madras, 1939.

Śastri, K. A. N.—*Śrī Vijaya.* Madras, 1949.

Sen, B.C.—*Some Historical Aspects of the Inscriptions of Bengal.* Calcutta, 1942.

Sharma, D.—*Early Chauhān Dynasties.* Delhi, 1959.

Singh, R. C. P.—*Kingship in Northern India* (cir. 600 A.D.—1200 A.D.). Thesis for Ph.D. University of London, 1957.

Sircar, D. C.—*Studies in the Geography of Ancient and Medieval India.* Delhi, 1960.

Smith, V. A.—*Early History of India.* Oxford, 1924.

Subba Rao, N. S.—*Economic and Political Conditions in Ancient India.* Mysore, 1911.

Thomas, E.—*The Chronicles of the Pathan kings of Delhi.* London, 1871.

Titus, M. T.—*Indian Islam.* London, 1930.

Tripathi, R. S.—*History of Kanauj.* Banaras, 1937.

Vaidya, C. V.—*History of Mediaeval Hindu India.* 3 Vols. Poona, 1921-26.

Wales, H. G. Q.—*The Making of Greater India.* London, 1951.

Wilson, H. H.—*The Persian Gulf.* Oxford 1928.

Yadav, B. N. S.—*Some Aspects of Society in Northern India in the 12th century A.D.* Thesis for D. Phil. University of Allahabad, 1956.

Yazdani, G.—*The Early History of the Deccan.* 2 Vols. London, 1960.

E. Journals, Periodicals and Reports.

Annual Report *of the Archaeological Survey of Western India.*

Annual Report *of the Rajputana Museum, Ajmer.*

Archaeological Survey of India, Reports *by A. Cunningham.*

Arts and Letters.

Bijdragen tot de taal-, land- en Volkenkunde van Nederlandsch-Indië, uitgegeven door het Koninklijk Instituut voor de Taal-, land en Volkenkunde van Nederlandsch Indië.

Bulletin de l' École Francaise d' Extrême Orient, Hanoi.

Chinese Literature. Foreign Language Press, Peking.

Hindustānī.

Epigraphia Indica.

Indian Antiquary.

Indian Archaeology.

Indian Culture.

Indian Historical Quarterly.

Islamic Culture.

Journal Asiatique.

Journal of Indian History.

Journal of the American Oriental Society.

Journal of the Andhra Historical Research Society.

Journal of the Asiatic Society of Bengal.

Journal of the Bihar and Orissa Research Society.

Journal of the Bombay Branch of the Royal Asiatic Society.

Journal of the Department of Letters, University of Calcutta.

Journal of Economic and Social History of the Orient.

Journal of the Indian Society of Oriental Art.

Journal of the Malaya Branch of the Royal Asiatic Society.

Journal of the Numismatic Society of India.

Journal of the Oriental Institute, M.S. University of Baroda.

Journal of the Royal Asiatic Society of Great Britain and Ireland.

Journal of the Royal Geographical Society of London.

Journal of the U.P. Historical Society.

Memoirs of the Asiatic Society of Bengal.

Nāgarī Pracāriṇī Patrikā.

Numismatic Chronicle.

Proceedings and Transactions of the All-India Oriental Conference.

Proceedings of the Asiatic Society of Bengal.

Proceedings of the Indian History Congress.

Sino-Indian Studies.

Tijdschrift voor Indische Taal-, Land-, en Volkenkundu.

T'oung Pao.

University of Allahabad Studies.

Uttara Bhāratī.

F. Dictionaries, Catalogues, Etc.

Bombay Gazetteer.

Dalal, C. D. and Gandhi, L. B.—*A Descriptive Catalogue of MSS in the Jain Bhandars at Jesalmere.* Baroda, 1923.

Encyclopaedia Britanica.

Monier-Williams, M.—*A Sanskrit-English Dictionary.* Oxford, 1899.

'Rasāla', Ramāśaṅkara Śukla—*Bhāṣā-śabda-koṣa.* Allahabad, 1937.

Sheth, Hargovind Das T.—*Pāiā Sadda Mahaṇṇavo.* Calcutta, 1928.

Varmā, Rāmacamdra—*Saṃkṣipta Hindī Śabda Sāgara.* Banaras, V. S. 2008.

INDEX